The American Evasion of Philosophy

The Wisconsin Project on American Writers
A series edited by Frank Lentricchia

The American Evasion of Philosophy

A Genealogy of Pragmatism

Cornel West

The University of Wisconsin Press

The University of Wisconsin Press
1930 Monroe Street
Madison, Wisconsin 53711

3 Henrietta Street
London WC2E 8LU, England

www.wisc.edu\wisconsinpress

8   10   12   13   11   9

Library of Congress Cataloging-in-Publication Data
West, Cornel.
The American evasion of philosophy.
(The Wisconsin project on American writers)
Includes bibliographical references and index.
1. Pragmatism—History. 2. Philosophy, American—
History. I. Title. II. Series.
B944.P72W47   1989   144'.3'0973   88-40446
ISBN 0-299-11960-2
ISBN 0-299-11964-5 (pbk.)

To
my beloved brother
CLIFTON L. WEST III
who sticks closer than a brother

If one must philosophize, then one must philosophize; and if one must not philosophize, then one must philosophize; in any case, therefore, one must philosophize. For if one must, then, given that Philosophy exists, we are in every way obliged to philosophize. And if one must not, in this case too we are obliged to inquire how it is possible for there to be no philosophy; and in inquiring we philosophize, for inquiry is the cause of Philosophy.

— *Aristotle*

Pragmatists keep trying to find ways of making anti-philosophical points in nonphilosophical language.

— *Richard Rorty*

CONTENTS

ACKNOWLEDGMENTS

This book was made possible – as are all my writings – by my loving family and friends: my inimitable parents, Clifton L. West, Jr., and Irene Bias West; my steadfast brother, Clifton L. West III; my supportive sisters, Cynthia West Cole and Cheryl West; my close confidant, James Melvin Washington, Professor of Church History at Union Theological Seminary in New York City; and my wonderful son, Clifton Louis West. I benefited greatly from critical readings of the manuscript by Richard Rorty, Frank Lentricchia, and Stanley Aronowitz. I also am grateful to Allen Fitchen for his patience and support. And lastly, without the presence and inspiration of my lovely companion, this book might have never been completed.

The American Evasion of Philosophy

INTRODUCTION

A small-scale intellectual renascence is occurring under the broad banner of pragmatism. The controversial works of Richard Rorty—aided by the differing views of fellow pragmatists such as Hilary Putnam, Ian Hacking, and Richard Bernstein—have unsettled academic philosophy. Literary critics of the pragmatist persuasion like Frank Lentricchia and Stanley Fish have upset traditional humanists. Creative interpreters of John Dewey—like Sheldon Wolin, Michael Walzer, and Benjamin Barber—who have updated radical democratic thinking now challenge liberal political theory. And pragmatist thinkers such as Jeffrey Stout are reshaping prevailing conceptions of religious thought.

Three basic issues underlie this recent renascence. First, there is a widespread disenchantment with the traditional image of philosophy as a transcendental mode of inquiry, a tribunal of reason which grounds claims about Truth, Goodness, and Beauty. The professional discipline of philosophy is presently caught in an interregnum; mindful of the dead ends of analytical modes of philosophizing, it is yet unwilling to move into the frightening wilderness of pragmatism and historicism with their concomitant concerns in social theory, cultural criticism, and historiography. This situation has left the discipline with an excess of academic rigor yet bereft of substantive intellectual vigor and uncertain of a legitimate subject matter. The unwillingness of many philosophers to tread in the wilderness results from adherence to professional boundaries and academic self-understandings. To put it crudely, most philosophers are neither trained to converse with literary critics, historians, and social theorists nor ready to give up the secure self-image of academicians engaged in "serious" philosophical research.

Second, the disenchantment with transcendental conceptions of philosophy has led to a preoccupation with the relation of knowledge and power, cognition and control, discourse and politics. No longer are humanistic scholars content with a historicizing of science, morality, and art that shuns the ways in which sciences, moralities, and the arts are inextricably linked to structures of domination and subordination. This preoccupation with the materiality of language – such as the ways in which styles of rationality and scientificity or identities and subjectivities are socially constructed and historically constituted – has focused cultural investigations on the production, distribution, and circulations of forms of powers, be they rhetorical, economic, or military powers.

Third, this focus on powers has returned humanistic studies to the primal stuff of human history, that is, structured and circumscribed human agency in all its various manifestations. Gone is the once fashionable post-structuralist claim to eliminate the subject. Yet also gone is the old humanist view that elevates the human agency of elite cultural creators and that ignores social structural constraints, constraints that reinforce and reproduce hierarchies based on class, race, gender, and sexual orientation.

It is no accident that American pragmatism once again rises to the surface of North Atlantic intellectual life at the present moment. For its major themes of evading epistemology-centered philosophy, accenting human powers, and transforming antiquated modes of social hierarchies in light of religious and/or ethical ideals make it relevant and attractive. The distinctive appeal of American pragmatism in our postmodern moment is its unashamedly moral emphasis and its unequivocally ameliorative impulse. In this world-weary period of pervasive cynicisms, nihilisms, terrorisms, and possible extermination, there is a longing for norms and values that can make a difference, a yearning for principled resistance and struggle that can change our desperate plight.

The irony of the contemporary intellectual scene in North America is that after an obsession with European theories and philosophies, we are discovering some of what is needed in the American heritage. This intellectual turn to our heritage ought to be neither a simplistic pro-Americanism in the life of the mind nor a naive parochialism that shuns international outlooks. But this turn is a symptom of just how blinded we often are to certain riches in the American intellectual and political past. Needless to say, we approach this past better equipped owing to European products such as Marxism, structuralism, and poststructuralism. But we also acknowledge the shortcomings of these products, that is, their ultimate inability to come to terms with the specificity of our contemporary predicament. The turn to the American heritage – and especially American pragmatism – is neither a panacea for our ills nor a solution to our problems. Rather, it should be an attempt to reinvigorate our moribund academic life, our lethargic political life, our decadent cultural life, and our chaotic personal lives for the flowering of many-sided personalities and the flourishing of more democracy and freedom.

My basic aim in this book is to chart the emergence, development, decline, and resurgence of American pragmatism. I understand American pragmatism as a specific historical and cultural product of American civilization, a particular set of social practices that articulate certain American desires, values, and responses and that are elaborated in institutional apparatuses principally controlled by a significant slice of the American middle class.

American pragmatism emerges with profound insights and myopic blindnesses, enabling strengths and debilitating weaknesses, all resulting from distinctive features of American civilization: its revolutionary beginning combined with a slave-based economy; its elastic liberal rule of law combined with an entrenched business-dominated status quo; its hybrid culture in combination with a collective self-definition as homogeneously Anglo-American; its obsession with mobility, contingency, and pecuniary liquidity combined with a deep moralistic impulse; and its impatience with theories and philosophies alongside ingenious technological innovation, political strategies of compromise, and personal devices for comfort and convenience. This "hotel civilization" (to use Henry James's apt phrase), with its fusion of the uncertainty of the capitalist market with the quest for security of the home, yielded an indigenous mode of thought that subordinates knowledge to power, tradition to invention, instruction to provocation, community to personality, and immediate problems to utopian possibilities.

American pragmatism is a diverse and heterogeneous tradition. But its common denominator consists of a future-oriented instrumentalism that tries to deploy thought as a weapon to enable more effective action. Its basic impulse is a plebeian radicalism that fuels an antipatrician rebelliousness for the moral aim of enriching individuals and expanding democracy. This rebelliousness, rooted in the anticolonial heritage of the country, is severely restricted by an ethnocentrism and a patriotism cognizant of the exclusion of peoples of color, certain immigrants, and women yet fearful of the subversive demands these excluded peoples might make and enact.

The fundamental argument of this book is that the evasion of epistemology-centered philosophy—from Emerson to Rorty—results in a conception of philosophy as a form of cultural criticism in which the meaning of America is put forward by intellectuals in response to distinct social and cultural crises. In this sense, American pragmatism is less a philosophical tradition putting forward solutions to perennial problems in the Western philosophical conversation initiated by Plato and more a continuous cultural commentary or set of interpretations that attempt to explain America to itself at a particular historical moment.

The pragmatists' preoccupation with power, provocation, and personality—in contrast, say, to grounding knowledge, regulating instruction, and promoting tradition—signifies an intellectual calling to administer to a confused populace caught in the whirlwinds of societal crisis, the cross fires of ideological polemics, and the storms of class, racial, and gender conflicts. This deep intellectual vocation, quite different from our sense of the emasculation of the academic profession, impels the major American pragmatists to be organic intellectuals of some sort; that is, participants in the life of the mind who revel in ideas and relate ideas to action by means of creating, constituting, or consolidating constituencies for moral aims and political purposes. It is no accident that the major figures of American pragmatism use the language of crisis – hence the centrality of critical consciousness in their work – and exude urgency as they search for strategies and tactics to facilitate their exercise of intellectual and moral leadership for their constituency. And on a deeper level, these figures grapple with the problem of evil, producing ever-changing yet definite ideological constructions of an American theodicy.

This book does not purport to be a comprehensive account of American pragmatism. Rather, it is a highly selective interpretation of American pragmatism in light of the present state (or my reading) of American society and culture. For instance, the omission of George Herbert Mead or C. I. Lewis is not a negative comment on their significant intellectual contributions to American pragmatism. Similarly, my focus on John Dewey at the expense of Charles Peirce and William James does not reflect my deep respect for the latter two. Rather, it expresses my sense that the thoroughgoing historical consciousness and emphasis on social and political matters found in Dewey speaks more to my purposes than the preoccupations with logic in Peirce and the obsessions with individuality in James. I consider Peirce and James as profound pioneering figures standing, in part, on the shoulders of Emerson. Yet I believe that it is with Dewey that American pragmatism achieves intellectual maturity, historical scope, and political engagement. In this sense, my genealogy of American pragmatism is an explicitly political interpretation without, I hope, being pejoratively ideological.

My emphasis on the political and moral side of American pragmatism permits me to make a case for the familiar, but rarely argued, claim that Emerson is the appropriate starting point for the pragmatist tradition. Furthermore, by including treatments of a historian (Du Bois), theologian (Niebuhr), sociologist (C. Wright Mills), and literary critic (Trilling), I try to show the way in which Emersonian sensibilities and pragmatist progeny cut across the modern disciplinary division of knowledge.

In regard to method, this work is a social history of ideas. It conceives of the intellectual sphere of history as distinct, unique, and personal sets of cultural practices intimately connected with concomitant developments in the larger society and culture. On the one hand, this book benefits from the ground-breaking research of social historians who delve into the institutional constraints on and agency of exploited and oppressed peoples, yet the book focuses principally on how the complex formulations and arguments of American pragmatists shape and are shaped by the social structures that exploit and oppress. On the other hand, this text learns from — without endorsing — the grand tradition of idealist historiography in that it tries to get inside the formulations and arguments of American pragmatists so that the social roles and functions of ideas do not exhaust their existence or curb intellectual curiosity. This fusion of the intrinsic interest (or hedonistic effect) and the instrumental interest (or political use) of American pragmatism is the goal of this social history of ideas.

This book also attempts to address the crisis of the American left. It does this primarily by providing an interpretation of a progressive tradition that can inspire and instruct contemporary efforts to remake and reform American society and culture. My own conception of prophetic pragmatism — a phrase which I hope is not oxymoronic to the reader after elucidation and illustration — serves as the culmination of the American pragmatist tradition; that is, it is a perspective and project that speaks to the major impediments to a wider role for pragmatism in American thought.

I began this work as an exercise in critical self-inventory, as a historical, social, and existential situating of my own work as an intellectual, activist, and human being. I wanted to make clear to myself my own contradictions and tensions, faults and foibles as one shaped by, in part, the tradition of American pragmatism. My first book, *Prophesy Deliverance! An Afro-American Revolutionary Christianity* (1982), attempted to lay bare the oppositional potential of prophetic Christianity — especially as filtered through the best of the black church tradition. *Prophetic Fragments* (1988) followed in the same vein. My critical acceptance of certain elements of Marxist analysis linked me to the worldwide Christian anti-imperialist and anticapitalist movement often referred to as liberation theology. Yet my promotion of American pragmatism as both a persuasive philosophical perspective and an indigenous source of left politics in America perplexed many people. So just as my earlier texts emerged out of my own political praxis in and my identity with prophetic Christianity, this book consists of my attempt to come to terms with my philosophic allegiances in light of my participation in the U.S. democratic socialist movement (Democratic Socialists of America), my particular role in the American academy (Princeton University), and my existence on the margins of the black church (as a lay preacher).

This book is principally motivated by my own disenchantment with intellectual life in America and my own demoralization regarding the political and cultural state of the country. For example, I am disturbed by the transformation of highly intelligent liberal intellectuals into tendentious neoconservatives owing to crude ethnic identity-based allegiances and vulgar neonationalist sentiments. I am disappointed with the professional incorporation of former New Left activists who now often thrive on a self-serving careerism while espousing rhetorics of oppositional politics of little seriousness and integrity. More important, I am depressed about the concrete nihilism in working-class and underclass American communities — the pervasive drug addiction, suicides, alcoholism, male violence against women, white violence against black, yellow, and brown people, and the black criminality against others, especially other black people. I have written this text convinced that a thorough reexamination of American pragmatism, stripping it of its myths, caricatures, and stereotypes and viewing it as a component of a new and novel form of indigenous American oppositional thought and action, may be a first step toward fundamental change and transformation in America and the world. Like Raymond Williams' *Culture and Society* and Fredric Jameson's *Marxism and Form*, this book is, among other things, a political act.

I write as one who intends to deepen and enrich American pragmatism while bringing trenchant critique to bear on it. I consider myself deeply shaped by American civilization, but not fully a part of it. I am convinced that the best of the American pragmatist tradition is the best America has to offer itself and the world, yet I am willing to concede that this best may not be good enough given the depths of the international and domestic crises we now face. But though this slim and slight possibility may make my efforts no more than an impotent moral gesture, nonetheless, in the heat of battle, we have no other choice but to fight.

1

The Emersonian Prehistory of American Pragmatism

Mr. Emerson's authority to the imagination consists, not in his culture, not in his science, but all simply in himself, in the form of his natural personality. There are scores of men of more advanced ideas than Mr. Emerson, of subtler apprehension, of broader knowledge, of deeper culture . . . Mr. Emerson was never the least of a pedagogue, addressing your scientific intelligence, but an every way unconscious prophet, appealing exclusively to the regenerate heart of mankind, and announcing the speedy fulfillment of the hope with which it had always been pregnant. He was an American John the Baptist, proclaiming tidings of great joy to the American Israel; but, like John the Baptist, he could so little foretell the form in which the predicted good was to appear, that when you went to him he was always uncertain whether you were he who should come, or another.

—Henry James, Sr.

The long shadow cast by Ralph Waldo Emerson over American pragmatism has been often overlooked and rarely examined. Yet Emerson not only prefigures the dominant themes of American pragmatism but, more important, enacts an intellectual style of cultural criticism that permits and encourages American pragmatists to swerve from mainstream European philosophy.[1] Like Friedrich Nietzsche—and deeply adored by him—Emerson is a singular and unique figure on the North Atlantic intellectual landscape who defies disciplinary classification.

Emerson lacks the patience and persistence to be a great poet. He does not have the deep sense of alienation and marginality to be a profound prophet. And he does not possess the talent for logical precision and sustained argumentation to be a rigorous philosopher.[2] Yet Emerson is more than a mediocre man of letters or a meteoric man of lectures. Rather he is a cultural critic who devised and deployed a vast array of rhetorical strategies in order to exert intellectual and moral leadership over a significant segment of the educated classes of his day. The rhetorical strategies, principally aimed at explaining America to itself,[3] weave novel notions of power, provocation, and personality into a potent and emerging American ideology of voluntaristic invulnerability and utopian possibility.

Like his contemporary (and major twentieth-century competitor) Karl Marx, Emerson is a dyed-in-the-wool romantic thinker who takes seriously the embodiment of ideals within the real, the actualization of principles in the practical — in short, some kind of inseparable link between thought and action, theory and practice.[4] Similar to Marx, Emerson focuses on the pressing concerns unleashed by the American, French, and Industrial revolutions: *the scope of human powers and the contingency of human societies.* These concerns are addressed by highlighting the willful self (or selves) up against and overcoming antecedent circumstances, or to put it in the language of social science, the relation between purposeful subjects and prevailing structures, conscious human agents and social constraints.

What distinguishes Marx and Emerson from most of their contemporaries is their stress on the dynamic character of selves and structures, the malleability of tradition and the transformative potential in human history.[5] And what separates Marx from Emerson is that the former's stress on dynamism leads toward a projection of fundamental social transformation through unavoidable class conflict, whereas Emerson's dynamic perspective results in a prescription for courageous self-reliance by means of nonconformity and inconsistency. For Marx, the major foes are class exploitation and people's lack of control of their lives; for Emerson, the principal enemies are personal stagnation and the absence of creative innovation in people's lives. Both Marx and Emerson herald self-realization and promote democracy (different versions thereof). Yet Marx's preoccupation with power, class, and social freedom leaves a tradition of historical materialist analyses, socialist ideologies, and communist parties, whereas Emerson's fascination with power, provocation, and personality bequeaths a legacy of cultural critiques, pragmatic ideologies, and reform efforts. Just as actually existing communist civilization has traduced Marx's dream of human freedom, so has present-day American civilization vulgarized Emerson's hope for personal emancipation. Yet just as Marx would be most proud of the revolutionary socialist tradition (e.g., Rosa Luxemburg, Antonio Gramsci) that sits on the margins of communist civilization, so Emerson would be most appreciative of the American pragmatist tradition (e.g., William James, John Dewey) that rests nearer to the center in American civilization. For despite an oppositional stance toward and cultural critique of American society, both Emerson and major American pragmatists fit comfortably in American civilization. The Emersonian prehistory of American pragmatism provides an initial clue as to why this is so.

Emerson on Power (and Tradition)

Most readings of Emerson accent his flight from history, his rejection of the past, his refusal of authority.[6] Emerson's obsession with the internal struggles of the "imperial" self seems to rest upon a denial of time, a usurpation of superegos, and an abundance of open space. His rapacious individualism and relentless expansionism of the self appear to be motivated by a moral faith in the possibility that goodness and greatness will emerge in the future owing to human creative powers.

Unfortunately, these influential—and often insightful—readings of Emerson hide the degree to which Emerson's perspective is infused with historical consciousness; they also conceal his seminal reflections on power. These interpretive blindnesses result, in part, from situating Emerson in the age of the American literary renaissance (along with Hawthorne, Melville, Thoreau, and Whitman) rather than relating him to the European explosions (both intellectual and social) that produced Karl Marx, John Stuart Mill, Thomas Carlyle, and Friedrich Nietzsche. We can no longer afford or justify confining Emerson to the American terrain. He belongs to that highbrow cast of North Atlantic cultural critics who set the agenda and the terms for understanding the modern world. We must not overlook the parochialism implicit in his call for American cosmopolitanism, but we can no longer view his call through present-day parochial lenses.[7]

This means principally that Emerson is neither simply a self-willed escapee from the American genteel tradition, nor a purveyor of "secular incarnation" in an imperial self, nor an American Vico who perennially remakes himself, nor the grand ideological synthesizer of American nature, the American self, and American destiny.[8] Indeed, these readings yield rich insights into Emerson. Yet they do not go far enough; that is, they do not examine the role and function of Emerson as an organic intellectual primarily preoccupied with the crisis of a moribund religious tradition, a nascent industrial order, and, most important, a postcolonial and imperialist nation unsure of itself and unsettled about its future. Not only does he create a vocation and constituency for himself—new discursive and institutional space in America for the organic intellectual—he also formulates a conception of power that enables himself and others to respond to the crises of his day. And since his response has been a, if not the, major resource for subsequent Americans facing other crises, Emerson's viewpoints must be both historically situated and historically deciphered.

A good place to begin is with Emerson's reflections on power. First, his view of power is multileveled; that is, it encompasses and distinguishes the powers of the nation, the economy, the person, tradition, and language. Second, he celebrates the possession, use, and expansion of certain kinds of power, especially transgressive acts of the literate populace that promote moral aims and personal fulfillment. Third, Emerson's perspective on power accentuates in an unprecedented manner the fluid, protean, and dynamic elements in human relations and transactions with nature. In this regard, Emerson's complex and perceptive reflections on power are guided by a profound historical consciousness.

Let us start with portions of the last section of Emerson's renowned "National Intellectual Declaration of Independence" (as Oliver Wendell Holmes dubbed it), *The American Scholar* (1837):

> If there is any period one would desire to be born in, —is it not the Age of Revolution; when the old and the new stand side by side, and admit of being compared; when the energies of all men are searched by fear and by hope; when the historic glories of the old can be compensated by the rich possibilities of the new era? This time, like all times, is a very good one, if we but know what to do with it.
>
> The literature of the poor, the feelings of the child, the philosophy of the street, the meaning of household life, are the topics of the time. It is a great stride. It is a sign—is it not?—of new vigor, when the extremities are made active, when currents of warm life run into the hands and the feet. I ask not for the great, the remote, the romantic; what is doing in Italy or Arabia; what is Greek art, or Provençal minstrelsy; I embrace the common, I explore and sit at the feet of the familiar, the low. Give me insight into to-day and you may have the antique and future worlds.
>
> Another sign of our times . . . is the new importance given to the single person. Everything that tends to insulate the individual—to surround him with barriers of natural respect, so that each man shall feel the world as his, and man shall treat with man as a sovereign state with a sovereign state—tends to true union as well as greatness . . . The scholar is that man who must take up into himself all the ability of the time, all the contributions of the past, all the hopes of the future. He must be an university of knowledges. If there be one lesson more than another, which should pierce his ear, it is: The world is nothing, the man is all; in yourself is the law of all nature, and you know not yet how a globule of sap ascends; in yourself slumbers the whole of Reason; it is for you to know all, it is for you to dare all. Mr. President and Gentlemen, this confidence in the unsearched might of man belongs, by all motives, by all prophecy, by all preparation, to the American Scholar.[9]

A distinctive feature of Emerson's reflections on power is that he associates a mythic self with the very content and character of America. His individualism pertains not simply to discrete individuals but, more important, to a normative and exhortative conception of the individual *as* America.[10] His ideological projection of the first new nation is in terms of a mythic self. In the passage above, this mythic self is cast as a heroic American Scholar, one who has appropriated God-like power and might and has acquired the confidence to use this power and might for "the conversion of the world."[11]

For Emerson, the powers of the nation are inseparable from the powers of rhetoric to construct "the nation" as a distinct object of discourse. For too long the identity of the country lagged behind its independence from Britain. This lag reinforced a cultural dependence, intellectual parasitism, and national inferiority complex vis-à-vis older European countries. Emerson exalts the powers of new rhetoric — the eloquent and creative weaving of myth, symbol, and narrative — in order to promote the powers of the new nation. He envisages culture as the domain wherein rhetorical powers principally deployed by intellectuals constitute "the nation" as a worthy discursive concern and consolidate "the nation" as a geographical and political entity.

> Men such as they are, very naturally seek money or power; and power because it is as good as money, — the "spoils," so call, "of office." And why not? For they aspire to the highest, and this, in their sleep-walking, they dream is highest. Wake them, and they shall quit the false good, and leap to the true, and leave governments to clerks and desks. This revolution is to be wrought by the gradual domestication of the idea of Culture. The main enterprise of the world for splendor, for extent, is the upbringing of a man.

> Is it not the chief disgrace in the world, not to be an unit; — not to be reckoned one character; — not to yield that peculiar fruit which each man was created to bear, but to be reckoned in the gross, in the hundred, or the thousand, of the party, the section, to which we belong; and our opinion predicted geographically, as the North, or the South? Not so, brothers and friends, — please God, ours shall not be so. We will walk on our own feet; we will work with our own hands; we will speak our own minds. The study of letters shall be no longer a name for pity, for doubt, and for sensual indulgence. The dread of man and the love of man shall be a wall of defence and a wreath of joy around all. A nation of men will for the first time exist, because each believes himself inspired by the Divine Soul which also inspires all men.[12]

Emerson's own rhetorical strategies function in a complex manner. On the one hand, his mythic conception of the exceptional individual as America provides resources for devastating critiques of the "actually existing" America. We find such criticisms scattered throughout his corpus. In a lecture at Waterville College in Maine (later Colby College) on August 11, 1841, he concluded that "we are a puny and feeble folk."[13] Just prior to his second trip to England, Emerson wrote to his friend and compatriot

Margaret Fuller (then in Italy) on June 4, 1847, that the famine in Ireland "only affects potatoes, the sterility in America continues in the men."[14] In late October 1850 he noted, "My own quarrel with America, of course, was that the geography is sublime, but the men are not." The country was infected with pervasive "selfishness, fraud and conspiracy."[15] This perception was primarily in reaction to the agitation for vigorous reinforcement of the Fugitive Slave Law, the law that "has forced us all into politics."[16] In response to his early hero Daniel Webster's March 7, 1850, speech defending Henry Clay's compromise bill (including reinforcement of the Fugitive Slave Law of 1793), Emerson wrote that Webster represented "the American people just as they are, with their vast material interests, materialized intellect and low morals."[17] And in his essay "Politics" published in his *Essays, Second Series* (1844), he refused to privilege uncritically the uniqueness of the American polity.

> In this country, we are very vain of our political institutions, which are singular in this, that they sprung, within the memory of living men, from the character and condition of the people, which they still express with sufficient fidelity, – and we ostentatiously prefer them to any other in history. They are not better, but only fitter for us. We may be wise in asserting the advantage in modern times of the democratic form, but to other states of society, in which religion consecrated the monarchical, that and not this was expedient. Democracy is better for us, because the religious sentiment of the present time accords better with it. Born democrats, we are nowise qualified to judge of monarchy, which, to our fathers living in the monarchical idea, was also relatively right. But our institutions, though in coincidence with the spirit of the age, have not any exemption from the practical defects which have discredited other forms. Every actual State is corrupt. Good men must not obey the laws too well. What satire on government can equal the severity of censure conveyed in the word *politic*, which now for ages has signified *cunning*, intimating that the State is a trick?[18]

Yet, on the other hand, Emerson's mythic conception of the exceptional individual as America supports an ideology of U.S. exceptionalism that posits the invulnerability and unassailability of the American way of life.

> American idea, Emancipation, appears in our freedom of intellection, in our reforms, & in our bad politics, has, of course, its sinister side, which is most felt by the drilled & scholastic. But, if followed, leads to heavenly places.[19]

Despite America's "sinister side," exceptional individuals qua America can overcome all obstacles, solve all problems, go beyond all limitations. This simple Emersonian theodicy – optimistic, moralistic, and activistic – rests upon three fundamental premises. First, it assumes that the basic nature of things, the fundamental way the world is, is congenial to and supportive of the moral aims and progress of the chosen or exceptional people, i.e., Americans. The famous first paragraphs of *Nature* (1836), his first published book-essay, proclaims this Emersonian faith.

> Our age is retrospective. It builds the sepulchres of the fathers. It writes biographies, histories, and criticism. The foregoing generations beheld God and nature face to face; we, through their eyes. Why should not we also enjoy an original relation to the universe? Why should not we have a poetry and philosophy of insight and not of tradition, and a religion by revelation to us, and not the history of theirs? Embosomed for a season in nature, whose floods of life stream around and through us, and invite us by the powers they supply, to action proportioned to nature, why should we grope among the dry bones of the past, or put the living generation into masquerade out of its faded wardrobe? The sun shines to-day also. There is more wool and flax in the fields. There are new lands, new men, new thoughts. Let us demand our own works and laws and worship.
>
> Undoubtedly we have no questions to ask which are unanswerable. We must trust the perfection of the creation so far, as to believe that whatever curiosity the order of things has awakened in our minds, the order of things can satisfy. Every man's condition is a solution in hieroglyphic to those inquiries he would put. He acts it as life, before he apprehends it as truth.[20]

The second Emersonian premise is that the basic nature of things, the fundamental way the world is, is itself incomplete and in flux, always the result of and a beckon to the experimental makings, workings, and doings of human beings. Language, tradition, society, nature, and the self are shot through with contingency, change, and challenge. This perception is captured most vividly in "Circles" published in his *Essays, First Series* (1841).

> Every action admits of being outdone. Our life is an apprenticeship to the truth, that round every circle another can be drawn; that there is no end in nature, but every end is a beginning; that there is always another dawn rise on mid-noon, and under every deep a lower deep opens.
>
> This fact, as far as it symbolizes the moral fact of the Unattainable, the flying Perfect, around which the hands of man can never meet, at once the inspirer and the condemner of every success, may conveniently serve us to connect many illustrations of human power in every department.
>
> There are no fixtures in nature. The universe is fluid and volatile. Permanence is but a word of degrees. Our globe seen by God is a transparent law, not a mass of facts. The law dissolves the fact and holds it fluid.
>
> In nature every moment is new; the past is always swallowed and forgotten; the coming only is sacred. Nothing is secure but life, transition,

the energizing spirit. No love can be bound by oath or covenant to secure it against a higher love. No truth so sublime but it may be trivial tomorrow in the light of new thoughts. People wish to be settled; only as far as they are unsettled is there any hope for them.[21]

The third premise of Emerson's theodicy is that the experimental makings, workings, and doings of human beings have been neither adequately understood nor fully unleashed in the modern world. Furthermore, a more adequate understanding and fuller unleashing will occur when all obstacles, problems, and limitations are dwarfed by the march of giants, the actualizing of the potential of genius of individuals willing to rely on and trust themselves. For Emerson, the modern world needs self-sustaining and self-overcoming individuals who would flex their intellectual, social, political, and economic muscles in order to gain wisdom, i.e., "to see the miraculous in the common," and to build "the Kingdom of man over nature."[22] This panegyric to human power, vision, newness, and conquest is most clearly and forcefully put forward in the last paragraphs of *Nature* (1836):

> At present, man applies to nature but half his force . . . His relation to nature, his power over it, is through the understanding; as by manure; the economic use of fire, wind, water, and the mariner's needle; steam, coal, chemical agriculture; the repairs of the human body by the dentist and the surgeon. This is such a resumption of power, as if a banished King should buy his territories inch by inch, instead of vaulting at once into his throne. Meantime, in the thick darkness, there are not wanting gleams of a better light,—occasional examples of the action of man upon nature with his entire force,—with reason as well as understanding. Such examples are; the traditions of miracles in the earliest antiquity of all nations; the history of Jesus Christ; the achievements of a principle, as in religious and political revolutions, and in the abolition of the Slave-trade; the miracles of enthusiasm, as those reported of Swedenborg, Hohenlohe, and the Shakers; many obscure and yet contested facts, now arranged under the name of Animal Magnetism; prayer; eloquence; self-healing; and the wisdom of children. These are examples of Reason's momentary grasp of the sceptre; the exertions of a power which exists not in time or space, but an instantaneous in-streaming causing power. The difference between the actual and the ideal force of man is happily figured by the schoolmen, in saying, that the knowledge of man is an evening knowledge, *vespertina cognitio*, but that of God is a morning knowledge, *matutina cognitio*.

> The problem of restoring to the world original and eternal beauty, is solved by the redemption of the soul. The ruin or the blank, that we see when we look at nature, is in our own eye . . . The reason why the world lacks unity, and lies broken and in heaps, is, because man is disunited with himself.

> So shall we come to look at the world with new eyes. It shall answer the endless inquiry of the intellect,—What is truth? And of the affections,—

what is good? By yielding itself passive to the educated Will. Then shall come to pass what my poet said: "Nature is not fixed but fluid. Spirit alters, moulds, makes it. The immobility or bruteness of nature, is the absence of spirit; to pure spirit, it is fluid, it is volatile, it is obedient. Every spirit builds itself a house; and beyond its house a world; and beyond its world, a heaven. Know then, that the world exists for you. For you is the phenomenon perfect. What we are, that only can we see. All that Adam had, all that Caesar could, you have and can do. Adam called his house, Heaven and Earth; Caesar called his house, Rome; you perhaps call yours, a cobbler's trade; a hundred acres of ploughed land; or a scholar's garret. Yet line for line and point for point, your dominion is as great as theirs, though without fine names. Build, therefore, your own world."[23]

Emerson's theodicy essentially asserts three things: that "the only sin is limitation,"[24] i.e., constraints on power; that sin is overcomable; and that it is beautiful and good that sin should exist to be overcome.[25] Emerson's articulation of this theodicy led Sydney Ahlstrom to suggest "that Emerson is in fact the theologian of something we may almost term 'the American religion'" and Harold Bloom to conclude that Emerson's "truest achievement was to invent the American religion."[26]

This American religion that extols human power, vision, newness, and conquest domesticates and dilutes the devastating critiques of American civilization put forward by Emerson himself. This is so because Emerson's notion of power—the onward transitions and upward crossings achieved by human willpower—celebrates moral transgression at the expense of social revolution. Emerson is not a social revolutionary because "he believes he is already on the right track and moving towards an excellent destiny."[27] Moral transgression essentially consists for Emerson in the exercise of personal conscience against custom, law, and tradition. It rests upon a deep distrust of the masses, a profound disenchantment with the dirty affairs of politics and fervent defense of individual liberties. In this oft-quoted passage from "Politics," Emerson stakes out the vague ideological perimeters—to the left of liberalism yet scornful of socialism or progressive populism—within which most of his pragmatic legatees will reside:

> Of the two great parties, which, at this hour, almost share the nation between them, I should say, that, one has the best cause, and the other contains the best men. The philosopher, the poet, or the religious man will, of course, wish to cast his vote with the democrat, for free-trade, for wide suffrage, for the abolition of legal cruelties in the penal code, and for facilitating in every manner the access of the young and the poor to the sources of wealth and power. But he can rarely accept the persons whom the so-called popular party propose to him as representatives of these liberalities. They have not at heart the ends which give to the name of democracy what hope and virtue are in it. The spirit of our

American radicalism is destructive and aimless; it is not loving; it has no ulterior and divine ends; but is destructive only out of hatred and selfishness. On the other side, the conservative party, comes of the most moderate, able, and cultivated part of the population, is timid; and merely defensive of property. It vindicates no right, it aspires to no real good, it brands no crime, it proposes no generous policy, it does not build nor write, nor cherish the arts, nor foster religion, nor establish schools, nor encourage science, nor emancipate the slave, nor befriend the poor, or the Indian or the immigrant. From neither party, when in power, has the world any benefit to expect in science, art, or humanity, at all commensurate with the resources of the nation.[28]

Similarly, Emerson's understanding of vision – in fact, much of his obsession with seeing and sight – promotes separateness over against solidarity, detachment over against association, and individual intuition over against collective action. In this most famous of passages from *Nature* (1836), we see how Emerson masterfully dissociates vision from politics, sociality, and materiality of any sort:

Crossing a bare common, in snow puddles, at twilight, under a clouded sky, without having in my thoughts any occurrence of special good fortune, I have enjoyed a perfect exhilaration. I am glad to the brink of fear. In the woods too, a man casts off his years, as the snake his slough, and at what period soever of life, is always a child. In the woods, is perpetual youth. Within these plantations of God, a decorum and sanctity reign, a perennial festival is dressed, and the guest sees not how he should tire of them in a thousand years. In the woods, we return to reason and faith. There I feel that nothing can befall me in life, – no disgrace, no calamity (leaving me my eyes), which nature cannot repair. Standing on the bare ground, – my head bathed by the blithe air, and uplifted into infinite space, – all mean egotism vanishes. I become a transparent eyeball; I am nothing; I see all: the currents of the Universal Being circulate through me; I am part or particle of God. The name of the nearest friend sounds then foreign and accidental: to be brothers, to be acquaintances, – master or servant, is then a trouble and a disturbance. I am the lover of uncontained and immortal beauty. In the wilderness, I find something more dear and connate than in streets and villages. In the tranquil landscape, and especially in the distant line of the horizon, man beholds somewhat as beautiful as his own nature.[29]

Yet this disassociation, though seductive, is deceptive, first because it implies viewing the world *sub specie aeternitatis*, yet Emerson's own dynamic "epistemology of moods" (to use Stanley Cavell's apt phrase) precludes such a viewpoint.[30] Like Hegel, Emerson acknowledges and accents the way in which what we see is mediated by what we see with and see through. Even his "transparent eyeball" is but one horizon among others, *his* horizon which discloses a beauty *to him*. In his great essay "Experience" in *Essays, Second Series* (1844), he affirms this perceptual contextualism.

It is very unhappy, but too late to be helped, the discovery we have made, that we exist. That discovery is called the Fall of Man. Ever afterwards, we suspect our instruments. We have learned that we do not see directly, but mediately, and that we have no means of correcting these colored and distorting lenses which we are, or of computing the amount of their errors. Perhaps these subject lenses have a creative power; perhaps there are no objects.

Thus inevitably does the universe wear our color, and every object fall successively into the subject itself. The subject exists, the subject enlarges; all things sooner or later fall into place. As I am, so I see: use what language we will, we can never see anything but what we are.

I know better than to claim any completeness for my picture, I am a fragment, and this is a fragment of me.[31]

Second, Emerson's disassociation of vision from politics, sociality, and materiality is deceptive in that his dynamic "epistemology of moods" has a teleological dimension; that is, an end and aim of seeing is to "see earliest, to see as though no one ever had seen before us."[32] This telos is not simply a strategy to deny time, reject history, and usurp authority. More important, it is symptomatic of a deep desire to conceive of time, history, and authority as commensurate with and parallel to the vast open spaces of untouched woods, virgin lands, and haunting wilderness. Emerson's notion of vision wipes the temporal slate clean not in order to stop or transcend time but in order to be at the beginning of new time, just as his exhilarating walk through the woods and wilderness locates him on the edge of new space that is on the frontier. This Emersonian quest for placement at the start of new time and space is closely linked to his mythic conception of the exceptional individual as America. As we saw earlier, this mythic individual possesses divine-like power, all-encompassing vision, and a penchant for newness in order to convert the world. Yet this conversion cannot but take the form of conquest because through an Emersonian lens there are only new selves to make, new histories to project, new authorities and traditions to undermine, and new lands and wildernesses upon which heroic energies of exceptional individuals, e.g., singular America, are to be expended. Conversion, for Emerson, is a trope for moral regeneration, which is itself a process motored by struggle, exertion of conflicting wills (within and among selves), and violence. As Michael Lopez perceptively notes,

For Emerson, war *was* "the Father of all things." The world was "a battleground, every principle . . . A war-note." (It is difficult to comprehend Emerson's championing of the creative powers of war if one does not understand this basic aspect of his metaphysic.) In man's "lapsed estate" the crises which try his edge can appear as "the natural history of calamity" rather than that natural history of growth by which the universe proceeds and metamorphoses itself. War was within "the highest right" because it mimicked nature's tendency to "break up the old adhesions" and allow "the atoms of society to take a new order." Similarly, the incessant battle the soul waged within itself required the daily setting aside of its "dead circumstances." The task of self-conquest involved a simultaneous destruction of the self. The history of the expansion of the self is concurrently the history of its defeat.[33]

Conversion of the world and moral regeneration for individuals are related to conquest and violence not solely because Emerson devalues those peoples associated with virgin lands, cheap labor, and the wilderness—e.g., Indians, Negroes, women—but also because for Emerson land, labor, and the wilderness signify unlimited possibilities and unprecedented opportunities for moral development. As he wrote in his journals in May–June 1851:

> The absence of moral feeling in the white man is the very calamity I deplore. The captivity of a thousand Negroes is nothing to me.[34]

In this way, Emerson's "American religion" renders his moral objections and cultural criticisms of America virtually impotent and politically ineffective. More pointedly, his theodicy converges with, though it is in no way identical with, what Richard Slotkin has recently analyzed as the ideological content of the myth of the frontier.[35] This myth bifurcates both American geography and American cultural discourse into two realms: metropolis/civilization associated with scarcity, density, competition, and culture; and wilderness/savagery signifying cheap, abundant resources, usurpation of authority and tradition, and need for colonization. The ever-advancing line of demarcation between these realms is the frontier.

The distinctive features of the myth of the frontier are twofold: first, the association of progress in America with emigration outward from the metropolis; second, a faith that the frontier experience had the capacity to transform on the moral, financial, and cultural levels those who emigrated. Not only does this myth—the oldest and most central in American history—justify opposition to the Old World aristocracy of Europe and subjugation of the New World "savages" of America, i.e., Indians, Negroes, and to some extent white women; it also rationalizes the distinctive pattern of U.S. capitalist development. Imperial conquest and enslavement of New World "savages," along with the resulting cheap land, labor, and surplus capital, serve as the "invisible" basis for American fascination with power, vision, and newness. This internal imperialism, which serves as an antidote for intense class, racial, ethnic, and religious antagonisms within the metropolis, both enables and constrains the utopian value of migration and mobility in America.

Thus Emerson's idea of power fits well with Slotkin's analysis of the myth of the frontier. In his most explicit statement on power, he writes in "Self-Reliance":

Life only avails, not the having lived. Power ceases in the instant of re-
pose; it resides in the moment of transition from a past to a new state, in
the shooting of the gulf, in the darting to an aim. This one fact the world
hates, that the soul *becomes*; for that forever degrades the past, turns all
riches to poverty, all reputation to a shame, confounds the Saint with the
rogue, shoves Jesus and Judas equally aside. Why, then, do we prate
of self-reliance? Inasmuch as the soul is present, there will be power not
confident but agent. To talk of reliance is a poor external way of speaking.
Speak rather of that which relies, because it works and is.[36]

Of course, Emerson's nonconformist conception of self-reliance ("and so
the reliance on Property, including the reliance on governments which
protect it, is the want of self-reliance")[37] resists mere ideological support
of capitalist development. Yet his viewpoint also provides little substantive opposition to it. Emerson scholars have often remarked about his
"omnivorous consciousness," the fact that he "fed" on books yet still starved
owing to a "digestion of vacancy,"[38] and much has been made of his
recorded 1840 dream of "eating" the world.[39] Hence, a simplistic link between digestion, appropriation, and imperial conquest can be made.

Yet I find the keys to both Emerson's critique of and minimal resistance
to U.S. capitalist society in two often overlooked aspects of his life and
writings: his guilt and shame about his inaction and impotence, and his
peculiar sense of praise and thankfulness.[40] There is no doubt that Emerson
believed himself to have failed to respond actively and decisively to the
major events of his day, from the Cherokee Indians affair of 1835, to the
revival of the Fugitive Slave Law (1850), to the Mexican War (1846), to
the Civil War (1861–65). Although he seems to have never been struck
by "ennui" (or lack of will), he is visibly fearful of inaction, impotence,
and powerlessness. In fact, he views this anxiety as characteristic of his age.

> A new disease has fallen on the life of man . . . our torment is Unbelief,
> the Uncertainty as to what we ought to do . . . A great perplexity hangs
> like a cloud on the brow of all cultivated persons, a certain imbecility
> in the best spirits, which distinguishes the period.
>
> The genius of the day does not incline to a deed, but to a beholding.
> It is not that men do not wish to act; they pine to be employed, but
> are paralyzed by the uncertainty what they should do.
>
> This *ennui*, for which we Saxons had no name, this word of France has
> got a terrible significance . . . is there less oxygen in the atmosphere?
> What has checked in this age the animal spirits which gave to our fore-
> fathers their bounding pulse?[41]

For example, his infamous invective letter to President Martin Van
Buren (published in the *National Intelligencer*, May 14, 1835) concerning
the tragic "removal" of Cherokee Indians from Georgia left him feeling
frustrated and powerless. Although he had protested, it seemed futile. In

the more renowned case of George Ripley's Brook Farm, Emerson struggled with himself for months (October–December 1840) as to whether he should join the utopian community. Yet, in the end, he refused to join. In choosing to remain "a parasite, with all the parasites on this rotten system of property,"[42] Emerson was open to joining yet knew that to do so would violate his sense of self.

> Yesterday George & Sophia Ripley, Margaret Fuller & Alcott discussed here the new social plans. I wished to be convinced, to be thawed, to be made nobly mad by the kindlings before my eye of a new dawn of human piety. But this scheme was arithmetic & comfort . . . It was not the cave of persecution which is the palace of spiritual power, but only a room in the Astor House hired for the Transcendentalists. I do not wish to remove from my present prison to a prison a little larger. I wish to break all prisons. I have not yet conquered my own house. It irks and repents me. Shall I raise the siege of this hencoop & march baffled away to a pretended siege of Babylon? It seems to me that so to do were to dodge the problem I am set to solve, & to hide my impotency in the thick of a crowd.[43]

He seems to have felt unable to engage honestly in sustained activism with agitators or reformers.

> When a zealot comes to me & represents the importance of this Temperance Reform my hands drop – I have no excuse – I honor him with shame at my own inaction.
>
> I have been writing with some pains Essays on various matters as a sort of apology to my country for my apparent idleness.[44]

Emerson did become quite active in the abolitionist movement (though, unlike Thoreau, at relatively little risk); virtually shunned the women's movement; and became an enthusiastic proponent of the Union during the Civil War. But the internal struggle between his shortcomings as an actor and agent for social change and his vocation as cultural critic for (and of) the educated populace continued to rage.

> One must also take into account Emerson's temperamental dislike of association in any form. As R. M. Gay has pointed out, what Emerson objected to in Brook Farm was not communism but organization. "At the name of a society," he wrote in 1840 – significantly, to Margaret Fuller – "all my repulsions play, all my quills rise and sharpen." Yet action, in the specific environment of time and place, almost inevitably meant for Emerson "movements," participation in the work of what would now be called "pressure groups," while contemplation seemed possible only through a complete withdrawal from the busy life of the community . . . One wonders, too, whether the precarious state of his health was not an important influence leading him to avoid the strenuous career of a reformer.[45]

There are two rather obvious explanations for this predicament. First, Emerson was simply by temperament contemplative and solitary. Institutions, organizations, movements, parties repulsed him, as they did his favorite poet, the Persian Sa'di.[46] And there is much to this view. But it fails to account for Emerson's co-founding of and vigorous participation in the *Dial* and the Hedge Club, his excitement over his membership in the prestigious Athenaeum Club in London, and his hard work as a member of the Board of Overseers of Harvard College. Second, Emerson wanted the best of two worlds—the world of bourgeois prestige, status, and influence and the world of solitude and contemplation. Engagement with zealous agitators and reformers would tip the balance. And there is some evidence for Emerson's opportunism. For instance, in his lecture "Courage" presented in Boston November 8, 1859 (less than a month after John Brown's raid on the federal arsenal at Harper's Ferry, Virginia), he called Brown "that new saint than whom none purer or more brave was ever led by love of men into conflict and death,—the new saint awaiting his martyrdom, and who, if he shall suffer [execution], will make the gallows glorious like the cross."[47] Yet he omitted these harsh and rebellious words when he published the essay in *Society and Solitude* eleven years later as a Harvard overseer and an invited lecturer in Philosophy at Harvard (selected by the new president, Charles W. Eliot, who had been strongly supported by Emerson for the presidency).

Similarly, Emerson's penchant for bourgeois respectability (despite his doctrines to the contrary) seems to have blinded him to the social misery of working people. In his second trip to England—invited by the Mechanics' Institute established by wealthy industrial capitalists to "educate" their workers—Emerson reveled in the mansions of his hosts, yet in three long months he observed little of poor people's condition, lives, or predicament. Closer to home, he seems to have had little sense of the pervasive exploitation at places like Lawrence, or any criticisms of the deplorable plight of the Irish in Boston. In three brief notes about the Irish he writes:

The poor Irishman—a wheelbarrow is his country.

I like to see our young Irish people, who arrived here in their shabby old country rags, after a few months labor drest so well & gaily. When a young Irishman after a summer's labor puts on for the first time his new coat, he puts on much much more. His good & becoming clothes set him on thinking that he must behave like people who are so drest. And silently & steadily his behavior mends.

I see with joy the Irish emigrants landing at Boston, at New York, & say to myself, there they go—to school.[48]

Even this second explanation fails to fully account for Emerson's relative inaction and minimal active opposition to American capitalist society.

The missing key is Emerson's own brand of mysticism that extols receptivity, detachment, praise, and worship. This mysticism did not encourage Emerson to invest too much of himself—his time, energies, or hopes—in the immediate results of human efforts. It allows him to downplay injustice, suffering, and impotence in the world and rest content with inaction or minimal resistance to evil. His mysticism, as Santayana noted,

> allows his will and his conscience to be hypnotized by the spectacle of a necessary evolution, and lulled into cruelty by the pomp and music of a tragic show . . . In that case the evil is not explained, it is forgotten; it is not cured, but condoned. We have surrendered the category of the better and the worse, the deepest foundation of life and reason; we have become mystics on the one subject on which, above all others, we ought to be men.[49]

Some of Emerson's mysticism is motivated by his political cynicism—his disparaging of the masses and the corruption of American political processes. He has little faith in collective political actions. At times, he writes like his admirer Nietzsche on "The Herd"—with an unabashed elitism.

> One has patience with every kind of living thing but not with the dead alive. I, at least, hate to see persons of that lumpish class who are here they know not why, & ask not whereto, but live as the larva of the ant or the bee to be lugged into the sun & then lugged back into the cell & then fed. The end of nature for such, is that they should be fatted. If mankind should pass a vote on the subject, I think they would throw them in sacks into the sea.
>
> The worst of charity, is, that the lives you are asked to preserve are not worth preserving. The calamity is the masses. I do not wish any mass at all, but honest men only, facultied men only, lovely & sweet & accomplished women only; and no shovel-handed Irish, & no Five-Points; or Saint Gileses, or drunken crew, or mob, or stockingers, or 2 millions of paupers receiving relief, miserable factory population, or Lazzaroni, at all.
>
> If the government knew how, I should like to see it check, not multiply, the population. When it reaches the true law of its action, every man that is born will be hailed as essential.
>
> Imbecility & Energy. The key to the age is this thing, & that thing, & that other, as the young orators describe. I will tell you the key to all ages, Imbecility: imbecility in the vast majority of men at all times & in every man, even heroes, in all but certain eminent moments victims of mere gravitation, custom, fear, sense. This gives force to the strong, that the others have no habit of self-reliance or original action.[50]

And, in fact, subsequent American pragmatists after Emerson will be impelled either to revise his mysticism (William James), displace it with a democratic faith in common people (John Dewey), or promote a full-fledged elitism (Walter Lippmann).

Most of Emerson's mysticism rests upon his silent yet discernible sense of being jubilant and celebratory that he is alive. He discloses a sense of being contented and full of joy that he "dwells" in the house of being.[51] This mystical element in Emerson stands in stark contrast to his dominant Heraclitean side. And his mysticism, though often overlooked, functions well precisely because of its startling juxtaposition with this diametrically opposed perspective. This view of Emerson as psalmist lifting paeans of joy, praise, and thanksgiving captures but one dimension of his heterogeneous discourse. Yet, coupled with his political cynicism, it explains why the grand valorizer of human power when confronted with the relative impotence of political power from below becomes humble and even deferential to an inexplicable and mysterious Power with which humans can get in touch.

> Not thanks, not prayer seem quite the highest or truest name for our communication with the infinite, – but glad and conspiring reception, – reception that becomes giving in its turn, as the receiver is only the All-Giver in part and infancy. I cannot, – nor can any man, – speak precisely of things so sublime, but it seems to me the wit of man, his strength, his grace, his tendency, his art, is the grace and the presence of God. It is beyond explanation. When all is said and done, the rapt saint is found the only logician. Not exhortation, not argument becomes our lips, but paeans of joy and praise.[52]

This mysticism enables Emerson to affirm with unmistakable confidence that "I am *Defeated* all the time; yet to Victory I am born."[53] At the end of the line of his fervid moral voluntarism lies a vague yet comforting mysticism that discourages an engaged political activism.

Emerson on Provocation (and the Market)

The primary aim of Emerson's life and discourse is to provoke; the principal means by which he lived, spoke, and wrote is provocation. At the "center" of his project is activity, flux, movement, and energy. It comes as no surprise that when he defines "that in us which changes not"–his conception of "unbounded substance," "ineffable cause," or "being" itself–he claims that we must

> confess that we have arrived as far as we can go. Suffice it for the joy of the universe, that we have not arrived at a wall, but at interminable oceans. Our life seems not present, so much as prospective; not for the affairs on which it is-wasted, but as a hint of this vast-flowing vigor.[54]

Of course, the enshrinement of activity and energy was commonplace in the various forms of North Atlantic romanticisms. Yet what sets Emerson apart from the others is not simply his critical yet sympathetic attitude toward modern technology and market forces, but, more important, a conception of activity that was fundamentally shaped by a national environment in which the market had a more dominant presence than in other places.

For Emerson, the goal of activity is not simply domination, but also provocation; the telos of movement and flux is not solely mastery but also stimulation. Needless to say, the centrality of provocation and stimulation in a discourse is the product of and helps reproduce a market culture — that is, a market culture in which the past is effaced, the social concealed, and the future projected by the arbitrary clashing wills of individuals. Provocation and stimulation constituted rhetorical strategies of sustaining some sense of the self in the midst of the "currency wars, economic unpredictability, and high incidence of rapid financial failures and new starts" of the Jacksonian era in which Emerson emerged.[55] This material insecurity, social instability, historical fluidity, and imaginative liquidity wrought principally by market forces both enabled and constrained Emerson's valorizing of provocation. As Jean-Christophe Agnew notes in his brilliant genealogy of market culture in early modern Britain, "When freed of ritual, religious, or juridical restraints, a money medium can imbue life itself with a pervasive and ongoing sense of risk, a recurrent anticipation of gain and loss that lends to all social intercourse a pointed, transactional quality."[56]

Like the theater shunned by Emerson's Puritan ancestors, with its personal transgression of social boundaries and multiplication of identities, market forces tend to undermine authority, thwart tradition, and throw the burdens once borne by these onto the individual. Once freed from such superegos, the self can be seen to be a rather contingent, arbitrary, and instrumental affair, a mobile, performative, and protean entity perennially in process, always on an adventurous pilgrimage ("Everything good is on the highway").

> With the emergence of a placeless market, the threshold experience threatened to become coextensive with all that a deritualized commodity exchange touched. Life now resembled an infinite series of thresholds, a profusion of potential passages or opportunity costs running alongside experience as a constant reminder of the selves not taken . . . and why not, since the world was at once a market and a stage.[57]

Emerson's response to market forces is neither nostalgic nor celebratory. Unlike his good friend Thomas Carlyle, he refused to yearn for some golden age prior to the modern age; yet he also did not uncritically revel in the present. Instead, his excessively prospective perspective and exorbitantly parochial preoccupation with America enabled him to adopt the major tropes of the market culture and attempt to turn them against certain aspects of this culture.

On the one hand, Emerson — especially during his early and most fecund period — puts forward powerful moral critiques of market culture.

The depression of 1837 not only adversely affected Emerson's personal fortunes but also awakened him from his complacent slumber by the "loud cracks in the social edifice."[58]

> I see a good in such emphatic and universal calamity as the times bring, that they dissatisfy me with society . . . Society has played out its last stake; it is check-mated. Young men have no hope. Adults stand like daylaborers idle in the streets. None calleth us to labor . . . the present generation is bankrupt of principles and hope, as of property . . . I am forced to ask if the ideal might not also be tried. Is it to be taken for granted that it is impracticable? Behold the boasted world has come to nothing . . . Behold . . . here is the Soul erect and Unconquered still.[59]

He characterizes the emerging capitalist economy as "a system of selfishness . . . of distrust, of concealment, of superior keenness, not of giving but of taking advantage."[60] In fact, he goes as far as to claim that "there is nothing more important in the culture of man than to resist the dangers of commerce."[61] As commerce expands, he quips, "out of doors all seems a market."[62] And in his most succinct statement on the nascent capitalist order, he writes:

> This invasion of Nature by Trade with its Money, its Steam, its Railroad, threatens to upset the balance of man and establish a new Universal Monarchy more tyrannical than Babylon or Rome.
>
> Trade is the lord of the world nowadays — & government only a parachute to this balloon.[63]

On the other hand, Emerson projects a conception of the self that can be easily appropriated by market culture for its own perpetuation and reproduction. In fact, the well-known shift from the idealistic criticisms of the market in the early Emerson to the "realistic" apologies for the market in the later Emerson has much to do with his perceptions of the impotence of his criticisms. Again, this perceived impotence sits well with his relative political inaction.

The Emersonian self — much like the protean, mobile, performative self promoted by market forces — literally feeds off other people. It survives by means of ensuring and securing its own excitement and titillation. Nature itself becomes but a catalyst to the self's energies, a "means of arousing his interior activity."[64] Unlike reification in capitalist exchange relations that objectify and thingify persons, the aim of Emersonian provocation is to subjectify and humanize unique individuals. Mutual provocation and reciprocal stimulation are the ideal for Emersonian human relations. In the abstract, this ideal is antihierarchical, egalitarian, and democratic, for it pertains to personal relations. In the concrete, it virtually evaporates because it cannot but relate to marginal persons on the edges of dominant classes, groups, or elites. In this way, Emerson's view of a self that provokes and thrives on being provoked converges yet never fully coincides with the instrumental self engendered by market forces.

Emerson on Personality (and Race)

Emerson is the preeminent proponent of the dignity and worth of human personality. This means neither that all persons are created equal nor that every person can be as great as every other. Emerson's notion of human personality does not derive from a particular political doctrine or rest upon a theological foundation. Rather it is the starting point and ultimate aim of his project.

> In all my lectures, I have taught one doctrine, namely, the infinitude of the private man.[65]

Yet most Emerson scholars have given him too much of the benefit of the doubt regarding just how universally applicable his notion of personality was meant to be. I suggest that his ideal of the human person, though complex and profound, is inseparable from his understanding of race. This is so not simply because, as Philip Nicoloff has shown, Emerson is a typical nineteenth-century North Atlantic "mild racist."[66] Rather this is so also because Emerson understands the person as a specific mythic entity, an emerging American self or a unique variant of the North Atlantic bourgeois subject. This understanding cannot but be shot through with certain xenophobic sensibilities and racist perceptions of the time. Emerson indeed is no garden-variety racist or ranting xenophobe, yet he is a racist in the American grain in that his notion of human personality is, in part, dependent on and derived from his view of the races.

Emerson spent a significant amount of time and energy keeping up with the science of his day. His purpose seems to have been to be assured that the best knowledge available about nature buttressed and supported his idealism. An important part of his reading focused on "whence came the Negro?"[67] After his early stay in the South and his limited abolitionist activism, he writes,

> What arguments, what eloquence can avail against the power of that one word *niggers*? The man of the world annihilates the whole combined force of all the antislavery societies of the world by pronouncing it.[68]

As a youth, Emerson held a rather traditional conception of nature as a "scale of being" in which different persons, principally owing to their distinct racial endowments, fit on a hierarchical chain of faculties and talents. He records his inchoate thoughts about this only two years after he began keeping a journal:

> I believe that nobody now regards the maxim "that all men are born equal," as any thing more than a convenient hypothesis or an extravagant

declamation. For the reverse is true—that all men are born unequal in personal powers and in those essential circumstances, of time, parentage, country, fortune. The least knowledge of the natural history of man adds another important particular to these; namely, what class of men he belongs to—European, Moor, Tartar, African? Because, Nature has plainly assigned different degrees of intellect to these different races, and the barriers between are insurmountable.

This inequality is an indication that some should lead, and some should serve.

If we speak in general of the two classes Man and Beast, we say that they are separated by the distinction of reason and the want of it.

I saw ten, twenty, a hundred large lipped, lowbrowed black men in the streets who, except in the mere matter of language, did not exceed the sagacity of the elephant. Now is it true that these were created superior to this wise animal, and designed to control it? And in comparison with the highest orders of men, the Africans will stand so low as to make the difference which subsists between themselves & the sagacious beasts inconsiderable. It follows from this, that this is a distinction which cannot be much insisted on.

And if not this, what is the preeminence? Is it in the upright form, and countenance raised to heaven—fitted for command. But in this respect also the African fails. The Monkey resembles Man, and the African degenerates to a likeness of the beast. And here likewise I apprehend we shall find as much difference between the head of Plato & the head of the lowest African, as between this last and the highest species of Ape.

If therefore the distinction between the beasts and the Africans is found neither in Reason nor in figure, i.e. neither in mind or body— where then is the ground of that distinction? Is it not rather a mere name & prejudice and are not they an upper order of inferior animals?[69]

Admittedly, these reflections are made in the context of marshaling arguments against slavery, yet they do reveal the state of North Atlantic science and culture on race at the time. Similarly, in light of the central role that genius plays in his thought Emerson writes sarcastically in his journal,

I notice that Words are as much governed by Fashion as dress, both in written & spoken style. A Negro said of another today "that's a *curious genius*."[70]

The implication here is not only that the status of genius eludes the interlocutors but also that the very word on their lips reveals the degree to which a vulgar leveling cultural process is occurring. By 1840, his doubts and questions regarding the inferiority of Africans and the necessity and desirability of their emancipation from slavery are apparent:

Strange history this of *abolition*. The Negro must be very old & belongs, one would say, to the fossil formations. What right has he to be intruding into the late & civil daylight of this dynasty of the Caucasians & Saxons? It is plain that so inferior a race must perish shortly like the poor Indians. Sarah Clarke said, "The Indians perish because there is no place for them." That is the very fact of their inferiority. There is always place for the superior. Yet pity for these was needed, it seems, for the education of this generation in ethics. Our good world cannot learn the beauty of love in narrow circles & at home in the immense Heart, but must be stimulated by somewhat foreign & monstrous, by the simular man of Ethiopia.[71]

In his most enlightened statement of 1844, Emerson's racism is softened and his sympathy and support for Africans are visible.

When at last in a race a new principle appears, an idea, that conserves it. Ideas only save races. If the black man is feeble & not important to the existing races, not on a par with the best race, the black man must serve and be sold and exterminated. But if the black man carries in his bosom an indispensable element of a new & coming civilization, for the sake of that element no wrong nor strength nor circumstance can hurt him, he will survive & play his part. So now it seems to me that the arrival of such men as Toussaint if he is pure blood, or of Douglas if he is pure blood, outweighs all the English and American humanity. The Antislavery of the whole world is but dust in the balance, a poor squeamishness & nervousness; the might & right is here. Here is the Anti-slave. Here is Man; & if you have man, black or white is an insignificance. Why at night all men are black . . . I say to you, you must save yourself, black or white, man or woman. Other help is none. I esteem the occasion of this jubilee to be that proud discovery that the black race can begin to contend with the white; that in the great anthem of the world which we call history, a piece of many parts & vast compass, after playing a long time a very low & subdued accompaniment they perceive the time arrived when they can strike in with force & effect & take a master's part in the music. The civilization of the world has arrived at that pitch that their moral quality is becoming indispensable, & the genius of this race is to be honoured for itself.[72]

In later allusions to black people, Emerson falls back into his earlier mode, viewing blacks as synonymous with "lowest man" who is "destined for museums like the dodo." In one of his notebooks, he writes:

The duty to our fellow man the slave
We are to assert his right in all companies
     An amiable joyous race who for ages have not been permitted to unfold their natural powers we are to befriend
     I think it cannot be maintained by any candid person that the African race have ever occupied or do promise ever to occupy any very high place in the human family. Their present condition is the strongest proof that they cannot. The Irish cannot; the American Indian cannot; the Chinese cannot. Before the energy of the Caucasian race all the other races have quailed and done obeisance.[73]

Apparently alluding to the racist arguments of the radical Theodore Parker (as in his *The Rights of Man in America*) for the abolition of slavery, Emerson acutely dissects and seems to affirm such views.

> *The Sad Side of the Negro Question.* The abolitionist (theoretical) wishes to abolish Slavery, but because he wishes to abolish the black man. He considers that it is violence, brute force, which, counter to intellectual rule, holds property in man; but he thinks the negro himself the very representative & exponent of that brute base force; that it is the negro in the white man which holds slaves. He attacks Legree, MacDuffie, & slaveholders north & south generally, but because they are the foremost negroes of the world, & fight the negro fight. When they are extinguished, & law, intellectual law prevails, it will then appear quickly enough that the brute instinct rallies and centres in the black man. He is created on a lower plane than the white, & eats men & kidnaps & tortures, if he can. The Negro is imitative, secondary, in short, reactionary merely in his successes, & there is no origination with him in mental & moral spheres.[74]

Despite Emerson's heralded shift from a "scale-of-being" view to an evolutionary perspective prompted by his reading of Robert Chambers' *Vestiges of Creation* in 1845, his belief in the doctrine of discernible racial differences and his ambivalence about the theory of the polygenetic origins of the races (though he was opposed to its use by anti-abolitionists like his good friend Louis Agassiz of Harvard) still rooted him in racist soil. Needless to say, such a perspective severely circumscribed his perception of the capacities and potentialities of non-Europeans (as well as white women).[75]

Yet the major significance of race in Emerson's reflections on human personality has to do with its relation to notions of circumstance, fate, limits—and, ultimately, history. Emerson's slow acknowledgment that there are immutable constraints on the human powers of individuals resulted primarily from his conclusions regarding the relation of persons to their racial origins and endowments. As a trope in his discourse, race signifies the circumstantial, the conditioned, the fateful—that which limits the will of individuals, even exceptional ones. In short, Emerson's sobering encounter with history—a natural history, of course—is principally mediated and motivated by his attempt to make sense of the relation of human personality to race. He writes in his journal in 1845 that he is attracted to two conceptions of "man's" history:

> One is the scientific or skeptical, and derives his origin from the gradual composition, subsidence and refining,—from the Negro, from the ape, progressive from the animalcule savages of the waterdrop, from *volvox globator*, up to the wise man of the nineteenth century.
>
> The other is the believer's, the poet's, the faithful history, always testified by the mystic and the devout, the history of the fall, of a descent

from a superior and pure race, attested in actual history by the grand remains of elder ages.[76]

In both contending conceptions, race plays a major role. This is seen most clearly in the most overlooked text in Emerson's corpus, *English Traits* (1856).[77] On the one hand, history like nature is a continuous ascent from savagery to civilization motored by provocation, challenge, and conquest. This progress required that there be different races of man with some brutish, others mediocre, and still others refined. From the Negro or Indian to the Saxons, this growth and development, he claimed, is visible and undeniable; on the other hand, after a period of ebullient ascent in which the power, vision, and newness of "racial genius," i.e., especially poets, are displayed, descent sets in. The creative energies of those "racial" pioneers recede after provocation wanes, stagnation surfaces, and retrospection predominates. As Philip Nicoloff perceptively notes,

> The motives behind Emerson's affection for such a doctrine of necessitated ascent and decline are rather obvious. It was the sort of sweeping historical generality he loved. It was a view filled with poetic richness: the veneration of great sires; the semi-religious notion of an Olympian sphere of intellect in which some few men in all ages might share. More importantly, it served Emerson's unswerving but sometimes anxious confidence in America's destiny. All of America's rawness and youthful innocence, even her penchant for preposterous boasting, could thus be interpreted in her favor. America was young, Europe was old, and historical necessity would take care of the rest. The jibes of European critics could be ignored. Even the immorality of America's exuberant extermination of Indians and Mexicans could be treated with philosophical patience.[78]

Therefore Emerson's first noteworthy attempt to come to terms with history, circumstances, or fate occurs not in *The Conduct of Life* (1860) in which his classic "Fate" appears, but rather in *English Traits* (1856). In a most perplexing chapter entitled "Race," he tries to "historically" situate and condition the "genius" (power) he had earlier enshrined.

> How came such men as King Alfred, and Roger Bacon, William of Wykeham, Walter Raleigh, Philip Sidney, Isaac Newton, William Shakespeare, George Chapman, Francis Bacon, George Herbert, Henry Vane, to exist here? What made these delicate natures? Was it the air? Was it the sea? Was it the parentage? For it is certain that these men are samples of their contemporaries. The hearing ear is always found close to the speaking tongue, and no genius can long or often utter any thing which is not invited and gladly entertained by men around him.
>
> It is race, is it not? That puts the hundred millions of India under the dominion of a remote island in the north of Europe. Race avails much, if that be true which is alleged, that all Celts love unity of power, and Saxons the representative principle. Race is a controlling influence in the Jew, who for two millenniums, under every climate, has preserved

the same character and employments. Race in the Negro is of appalling importance.[79]

This situating and conditioning of "genius" are complemented by "counter-acting forces to race," though "race works immortally to keep its own."[80] For Emerson, to grapple with the constraints on human power, vision, and newness is to understand first and foremost the role of race in history.

Even in his canonical essay "Fate," Emerson is explicit about the centrality of race in limiting the capacities and potentialities of individual consciousness and will.

> In science, we have to consider two things: power and circumstance . . . Once we thought, positive power was all, now we learn, that negative power, or circumstance, is half. Nature is the tyrannous circumstance, the thick skull, the sheathed snake, the ponderous, rock-like jaw; necessitated activity; violent direction; the conditions of a tool, like the locomotive, strong enough on its track, but which can do nothing but mischief off of it; or skates, which are wings on the ice, but fetters on the ground.
>
> The book of Nature is the book of Fate . . . The face of the planet cools and dries, the races meliorate, and man is born. But when a race has lived its term, it comes no more again.

> We know in history what weight belongs to race. We see the English, French, and Germans planting themselves on every shore and market of America and Australia, and monopolizing the commerce of these countries. We like the nervous and victorious habit of our own branch of the family. We follow the step of the Jew, of the Indian, of the Negro. We see how much will has been expended to extinguish the Jew, in vain. Look at the unpalatable conclusions of Knox, in his "Fragments of Races," —a rash and unsatisfactory writer, but charged with pungent and unforgettable truths. "Nature respects race, and not hybrids." "Every race has its own *habitat*." "Detach a colony from the race, and it deteriorates to the crab."

> Famine, typhus, frost, war, suicide, and effete races, must be reckoned calculable parts of the system of the world.

> The force with which we resist these torrents of tendency looks so ridiculously inadequate, that it amounts to little more than a criticism or a protest made by a minority of one, under compulsion of millions.

> We cannot trifle with this reality, this cropping-out in our planted gardens of the core of the world. No picture of life can have any veracity that does not admit the odious facts. A man's power is hooped in by a necessity. Thus we trace Fate, in matter, mind, and morals, — in race, in retardations of strata, and in thought and character as well.[81]

When Emerson moves toward the lord of fate, the limits of limitation, the specific examples he cites are "the instinctive and heroic races" who are "proud believers in Destiny"[82] — more pointedly, an imperial Saxon race, which nature cannot bear to lose, and, after cooping it up for a thousand years in yonder England, gives a hundred Englands, a hundred Mexicos. All the bloods it shall absorb and domineer: and more than Mexicos,—the secrets of water and steam, the spasms of electricity, the ductility of metals, the chariot of the air, the ruddered balloon, are awaiting you . . .

Very odious, I confess, are the lessons of fate . . .

Fate involves the melioration. No statement of the Universe can have any soundness, which does not admit its ascending effort. The direction of the whole, and of the parts, is toward benefit, and in proportion to the health. Behind every individual closes organization: before him, opens liberty,—the Better, the Best. The first and worst races are dead. The second and imperfect races are dying out, or remain for the maturing of higher. In the latest race, in man, every generosity, every new perception, the love and praise he extorts from his fellows, are certificates of advance out of fate into freedom.[83]

I am suggesting neither that Emerson is an exemplary North Atlantic racist nor that his peculiar form of racism simply rationalizes Euro-American domination and extermination of Native Americans and Mexicans. In fact, his rejection of John Knox's theory of racial physiological incompatibility (hence rigid racial boundaries) and approval of racial "mixing" make Emerson a rather liberal "racist." Furthermore, Emerson's moral support for Indians and Mexican sovereignty is well known, though his organic conception of history renders this "against-the-grain" support rather impotent and innocuous. Regarding the annexation of Texas, he writes,

It is very certain that the strong British race, which has now overrun so much of this continent, must also overrun that tract, and Mexico and Oregon also, and it will in the course of ages be of small import by what particular occasions and methods it was done. It is a secular question.[84]

In English Traits, Emerson views the "animal vigor" of the English and their inheritance (mainly from the Normans) of an "excess of virility" as that which sustains their exercise of power and supports their capacity to provoke and be provoked by new challenges. A telling sign of decline and decay, of eclipse and ebb, is the disappearance of such vigor and virility, will and provocation.

What I am suggesting is that Emerson's conception of the worth and dignity of human personality is racially circumscribed; that race is central to his understanding of the historical circumstances which shape human personality; and that this understanding can easily serve as a defense of Anglo-Saxon imperialist domination of non-European lands and peoples. In this way, Emerson's reflections on race are neither extraneous nor superfluous in his thought. Rather they are the pillar for his later turn toward history, circumstance, fate, and limitation. As Philip Nicoloff aptly concludes,

We must insist . . . that the "transparent eyeball" was progressively spend-
ing less and less time bathing itself in the blithe currents of universal
being and more time scanning the iron pages of geological and biological
history. More and more Emerson was inclined to explain the human
past, present, and future in terms of some long-range destiny implicit
in racial seed and the fated cycle of circumstance. The dominant concern
was no longer with the possibility of private ecstasy, but rather with
the endless pageant of racial man advancing irresistibly out of his "dread
origin" in "the abyss" towards a ripeness of vision which, once held, could
only ebb away into over-fineness and loss of power. The ability to swim
well or ill with the flow of things seemed more and more to lie altogether
outside the area of human volition. Nature called whom she would and
in her own time.[85]

As Emerson probed the conditioned character of human will and
personality, he did not move toward a tragic vision. Rather he deepened
his mysticism, increased his faith in the nature of things, and adjusted
himself (though never fully) to the expanding world dominance of the
"imperial Saxon race." He knew this domination would not last forever,
but given the golden promise of America in his day, it made little sense
for him to speculate on the decline of North Atlantic civilization. So his
later message was clear: the worth of human personality is grand, the
will of great individuals is mighty, and the cycle of fate (symbolized by
ascending and descending races) is almighty – yet it presently tilts toward
the West.

Emerson as Organic Intellectual

Emerson's dominant themes of individuality, idealism, voluntarism, optimism, amelioration, and experimentation prefigure those of American
pragmatism. His complex articulation of a distinct Americanism grounded
on specific interpretations of power, provocation, and personality – that
is, both the content of this ideology and the way in which he presented
it – deeply shaped the emergence and development of American pragmatism. Furthermore, the way in which Emerson formed a constituency constitutes a model for American pragmatists to this day.

In the previous sections I intimated that Emerson's notion of power
was inextricably bound with tradition, provocation with the market, and
personality with racial domination. Here I shall focus on these crucial
connections and affiliations between ideas and institutions, discourses and
infrastructures, intellectual practices and modes of social structuration.
In fact, I suggest that it was Emerson's own sensitivity and attentiveness
to these links that, in part, permitted him to swerve from the predominant epistemological concerns of European philosophers; that is, Emerson
conceived of his project as a form of power, a kind of provocation, and

of himself as an indomitable person whose very presence, i.e., activity, changed the world. Unlike European philosophical giants like René Descartes, John Locke, David Hume, Immanuel Kant, and G. W. F. Hegel, Emerson viewed knowledge not as a set of representations to be justified, grounded, or privileged but rather as instrumental effects of human will as it is guided by human interests, which are in turn produced by transactions with other humans and nature. He had little patience with modern philosophy, for like Pascal, Kierkegaard, and Nietzsche he rejected the epistemology-centered problematic of modern philosophy.[86] He did not rest content with the language of static substances which undergird accidental qualities, disembodied ideas that represent stationary objects, or universal mental schemes possessed by all rational subjects—a language riveted with categories derived from ossified sources. Rather Emerson preferred the language of tentative strategies, contingent functions, enabling tactics, and useful devices—mindful of the profound Wittgensteinian insight that these descriptions apply to language itself. Its character is "to flow and not to freeze."

> All language is vehicular and transitive, and is good, as ferries and horses are, for conveyance, not as farms and houses are, for homestead.[87]

Furthermore, Emerson's alternative to modern philosophy was neither to replace it with a new philosophical problematic nor to deny it by means of a strict and severe skepticism. Rather he *evades* modern philosophy; that is, he ingeniously and skillfully refuses: (1) its quest for certainty and its hope for professional, i.e., scientific, respectability; (2) its search for foundations. This distinctly American refusal is the crucible from which emerge the sensibilities and sentiments of future American pragmatists.

Instead, Emerson pursues a mode of cultural criticism which indulges in a quest for power, a perennial experimental search sustained by provocation and a hope for the enhancement and expansion of the self (viz., America). This pursuit locates Emerson at the "bloody crossroads" between weaving webs of meaning and feeling and criticizing structures of domination and exploitation ("Cut these sentences and they bleed" and "Let us answer a book of ink with a book of flesh and blood)".[88] Thus, he must create a new vocation in the open space and inaugurate (rhetorically) a new history of human freedom beyond the tyrannies (of tropes and troops) in the past. Emerson evades modern philosophy not because it is wrong, unjustified, or uninteresting, but rather because it is antiquated, anachronistic, and outdated *relative to his chosen tasks*. Like the recent European past of unfreedom, Descartes's veil of ideas is a prison, Hume's skepticism a halfway house, and Kant's dualism too debilitating. He resonates a bit with Hegel but shuns the German obsession with method which results in "committing oneself to more machinery than one had any business for."[89] Since this obsession has more to do with reproducing professional culture than with loving wisdom—(not surprisingly) the only culture capable of unifying the elites of a divided German nation until 1871— Emerson's individualism leads him to abhor it. He will not swim in a regulated pool nor allow others to imitate his stroke.

> I have been writing & speaking what were once called novelties, for twenty-five or thirty years, & have not now one disciple. Why? Not that what I said was not true; not that it has not found intelligent receivers but because it did not go from any wish in me to bring men to me, but to themselves. I delight in driving them from me. What could I do, if they came to me? They would interrupt & encumber me. This is my boast that I have no school & no follower. I should account it a measure of the impurity of insight, if it did not create independence.[90]

To evade modern philosophy means to strip the profession of philosophy of its pretense, disclose its affiliations with structures of powers (both rhetorical and political) rooted in the past, and enact intellectual practices, i.e., produce texts of various sorts and styles, that invigorate and unsettle one's culture and society. As we saw earlier, for Emerson this results in neither social revolution nor cultural upheaval but rather moral transgression based on personal integrity and individual conscience. The aim of Emersonian cultural criticism—and subsequently, most of American pragmatic thought—is to expand powers and proliferate provocations for the moral development of human personalities.

> *American Politics.* I have the belief that of all things the work of America is to make the advanced intelligence of mankind in the sufficiency of morals practical; that, since there is on every side a breaking up of the faith in the old traditions of religion &, of necessity, a return to the omnipotence of the moral sentiment, that in America this conviction is to be embodied in the laws, in the jurisprudence, international law, in political economy.[91]

The unconscious underside of this Emersonian aim is the setting aside of tradition and the enshrining of the market by which the Saxon race exercises imperial domination over nature and those peoples associated therewith, e.g., Indians, Mexicans, blacks, women. Emerson's evasion of modern philosophy is one of the ways in which he sets tradition aside; it also is one of the means by which he exercises his own intellectual self-reliance. He refuses to be captive to or caught up in the problematic and vocabulary of those who came before. This Emersonian refusal—both mythic and generative of new myths—sits at the core of his rhetorical strategies and the tools he deploys to create himself as an organic intellectual and to constitute a constituency over which he exercises ideological and moral leadership.

The three major historical coordinates of Emerson's career are the cultural metamorphosis of Victorian New England, the economic repercussions of a nascent industrial capitalist order, and the identity crisis of the first new nation. The cultural metamorphosis consisted of an overcoming of the "agonized conscience" of a moribund Puritanical tradition and of a creating of spontaneous self-manufactured myths to replace the cold rationalism of a stilted Unitarianism. The economic repercussions of rapid primitive capital accumulation—requiring "virgin" lands and exploiting new black, brown, red, yellow, and white labor—included panics and depressions, booms and selective prosperity. And the national identity crisis focused on the most powerful bonds of unity among citizens, namely, the realities of imperial expansion, the ideals of the democratic heritage, and the quest for individual fulfillment.

This historical context shaped Emerson's influential problematic and vocabulary. From his New England origins, he extracts a lasting concern with individual conscience linked to a conception of life as a fundamentally moral process. The emerging market operations encouraged and supported his preoccupation with contingency, flux, unpredictability, and variability. And a postcolonial yet imperialist America's need for collective self-definition prompted his own civil religion of self-reliance and self-trust. The major national events of Emerson's life were the election of Andrew Jackson (1828), the panic of 1837, the Mexican-American War (1846–48), the Civil War (1861–65), the Radical Reconstruction (1865–77), and, most important, the wholesale removal of Indians from their homelands and the making of an American industrial working class. His political response to some of these events is that of moral critique grounded in individual conscience and, at times, personal action. His silence on other events—especially the Radical Reconstruction—is in itself significant, given the direction of his thought in later years. Yet, ironically, his complex rhetoric of power (usurping tradition), provocation (both fearful of and fascinated by the market), and human personality (circumscribed by race, history, and circumstance) provides the very ingredients for varying American ideologies that legitimate and rationalize the dominant theme running through these events—the imperial expansion of the American nation principally in the interests of Saxon male elites.

The major personal events of Emerson's life—the death of his first wife, Ellen Tucker (1831), his resignation of his Unitarian church pastorate (1832), his first trip to Europe (1833), the substantial inheritance from Ellen's will that he won in a contested case before the Massachusetts Supreme Court (1834), the start of a new career of public lecturing (1834), his second marriage to Lydia Stevenson (1835), the death of his brother, Charles, and publication of Nature (1836), the death of his son, Waldo (1842), his public support of antislavery militant John Brown (1859), his Harvard visiting lectureship (1870), the destruction of his house by fire (1872)—fanned and fueled his deep belief in moral transgression against any limits and constraints, be it the death of a loved one, the authority of the church, or the burdens of a European past, college tradition, and old form of human enslavement. The great Emersonian refusal of "being fathered"—of being curtailed by any set of antecedent conditions or restrained circumstances—supports the expansionist sensibilities of post-colonial America, just as the grand Emersonian moralism questions the legitimacy of the conquestorial ambitions of imperial America.

This intricate interplay of rhetorically supporting American expansionism yet morally contesting its consequences for human victims is a key to Emerson's success as a public figure. This double consciousness and dual allegiance to the conqueror and the conquered, powerful and powerless, were highly attractive to a nation obsessed with underdogs yet (believed to be) destined to be the top dog of the world. Emerson's moral criticisms indeed are genuine, yet, as we saw earlier, they are politically impotent. In fact, their principal function is to expiate the "bad conscience" of moralists who acknowledge the "inevitability" of American expansionism yet who cannot accept the amoral self-image such acknowledgment seems to imply. Needless to say, the later Emerson more easily reconciles himself to such "inevitabilism" owing to his conceptions of race, history, and circumstances. Yet even the later Emerson remains a moralist with a strong doctrine of fate.

Emerson's rhetorical strategies were directed at those mildly oppositional elements of the educated portion of the petite bourgeoisie—that is, those "cultured" Saxon gentlemen (and few white women) wedded to elitist notions of individual achievement yet guided by self-images of democratic allegiance. It is no surprise that he castigates the vulgarity and crudity of the Jacksonians yet resonates with some of their democratic ideas.[92] Emerson detaches democratic ideas from Jacksonian activists, in part because he perceives them to be *parvenu* petit bourgeois reformers on the make with their own forms of greed, corruption, manipulation, and selfishness. Furthermore, he views their obsession with material prosperity and social status as symptomatic of a profound absence of moral conscience, as best exemplified in their pernicious policies of Indian removal and anti-abolitionism.[93] Emerson's hostility to the Jacksonians is also due to the fact that they were his rivals for both ideological control over the democratic national heritage and political control over the new constituency of middle-class reformers. Jackson offered them nitty-gritty activism, concrete benefits, and political involvement; Emerson, contemplative reflection, personal integrity, and individual conscience. Yet both share common rhetorics of power, expansion, and limitlessness.

Therefore the primary social base of Emerson's project consists of the mildly oppositional intelligentsia alienated from conservative moneyed interests, and "enlightened" businessmen who long for "culture" as well as profits, e.g., E. B. Phillips, president of the Michigan Southern Railroad.[94] Emerson explicitly shuns the lower class owing to their cultural narrowness and their potential for revolution.

> If the wishes of the lowest class that suffer in these long streets should execute themselves, who can doubt that the city would topple in ruins.
>
> We have had in different parts of the country mobs and moblike legislation, and even moblike judicature, which have betrayed an almost godless state of society . . . There is reading, and public lecturing too, in this country, that I could recommend as medicine to any gentleman who finds the love of life too strong in him.[95]

This social location of Emerson's constituency imposes severe restrictions on the political possibilities of his project. On the one hand, the group of people with which he is aligned is dependent on the very moneyed class he is criticizing. Therefore they can bark only so loud. On the other hand, the very interests of his own group are circumscribed by their attitude toward the "mob," or working-class majority of the populace, so that any meaningful links with social movements or political organizations from below are foreclosed. Hence, one may discern Emersonian themes of self-reliance and self-sufficiency in the radical egalitarianism of Thomas Skidmore, yet one can never envision Emerson supporting Skidmore's workingmen's association.[96]

Emerson's ability to exercise moral and intellectual leadership over a small yet crucial fraction of the educated middle classes and enlightened business elites of his day principally rests upon his articulation of a refined perspective that highlights individual conscience along with political impotence, moral transgression devoid of fundamental social transformation, power without empowering the lower classes, provocation and stimulation bereft of regulated markets, and human personality disjoined from communal action. Emerson is neither a liberal nor a conservative and certainly not a socialist or even civic republican. Rather he is a petit bourgeois libertarian, with at times anarchist tendencies and limited yet genuine democratic sentiments. It is no accident that the most sustained institutional commitment of Emerson's life is a pedagogical one: to his lifelong friend Bronson Alcott's "progressive" school in Boston. In fact, he and Alcott often discussed setting up a special innovative and open college with limited enrollment and courses in Concord.[97] For Emerson, politics is not simply the clash of powers and pleasures but also another terrain on which the moral development of individuals should take place. Needless to say, his disappointment with and distrust of governments ran deep. This further reinforced his sense of political impotence.

The organic intellectual activity of Emerson serves as a useful prehistory of American pragmatism not only because he prefigures the major themes (power, provocation, personality) and crucial motifs (optimism, moralism, individualism) but also because Emerson creates a style of cultural criticism which evades modern philosophy, deploys a set of rhetorical strategies that attempt to both legitimize and criticize America, and situates his project within and among the refined and reformist elements of the middle class—the emerging and evolving class envisioned as the historical agent of the American religion.

2

The Historic Emergence
of American Pragmatism

Pragmatism could be characterized as the doctrine that all problems are
at bottom problems of conduct, that all judgments are, implicitly, judgments of value, and that, as there can be ultimately no valid distinction
of theoretical and practical, so there can be no final separation of questions of truth of any kind from questions of the justifiable ends of action.

C. I. Lewis

American pragmatism can be understood as what happens to the Emersonian evasion of epistemology-centered philosophy when forced to justify
itself within the professional perimeters of academic philosophy. The first
articulators of American pragmatism – members of the Metaphysical Club
in Cambridge, Massachusetts – were learned professionals principally interested in demystifying science and, a few, in modernizing religion.[1] Unlike
Emerson, they were preoccupied with method, yet their understanding
of method was quite Emersonian. Much like Emerson, they were intent
on viewing science as continuous with religion – both shot through with
moral purpose.

American pragmatism also can be seen as a variety of creative interpretations of the Emersonian notions of power, provocation, and personality
in the context of academic culture, capitalist industrialization, and national
consolidation in America. The crucial shifts accelerating after the Civil
War – from agrarian to urban industrialization, from vocational education
to professional training, and from entrepreneurial capitalism to monopoly

capitalism—created new circumstances and challenges for Emersonian discourse. The two great "founding" figures of American pragmatism—Charles Sanders Peirce and William James—provide the most penetrating revisions of the Emersonian evasion of modern philosophy and the most provocative affirmations of the Emersonian theodicy. Both figures acknowledged an inescapable influence of Emerson.[2]

Peirce on Scientific Method, Community, and Christian Love

Charles Sanders Peirce is the most profound philosophical thinker produced in America. Like our greatest literary artist, Herman Melville, Peirce was largely ignored in his own time. Yet a kind of Peircean renaissance has been under way for some time. At present his genius is widely accepted among professional philosophers. Despite superb treatments of Peirce's thought, he remains, in many ways, an enigmatic figure.[3] This is so not only because his corpus is so enormous with astonishing scope, but also because his viewpoints often remain underdeveloped.

There is no doubt that Peirce is at his best in dealing with highly technical issues of semiotics, mathematical logic, rational technique, and scientific method. I suggest that though these issues are of great intrinsic interest to semioticians, logicians, and philosophers of science, they are, in Peirce's perspective, inseparable from his more speculative views about ethics, politics, and religion. Furthermore, Peirce's original conceptions of pragmatism—and later pragmaticism—are indebted to Emersonian sensibilities of philosophy as cultural criticism with moral purpose. Peirce is first and foremost a logician, with metaphysical proclivities, endeavoring to augment the human power to respond to provocation by new problems, for the purpose of fulfilling the potentialities of human personalities. In this sense, he revises and reinforces the Emersonian evasion and theodicy in American thought.

There are three fundamental claims in Peirce's pragmatism, first, that the most reasonable way of arriving at warranted and valid beliefs is by means of scientific method; second, that scientific method is a self-correcting social and communal process promoted by smoothly functioning habits, i.e., beliefs, upset by uncertain expectations, i.e., doubts, and whose sole end is "the settlement of opinion";[4] and third, that this scientific quest for truth is inextricably linked, though in no ways reducible, to the ultimate good of furthering "the development of concrete reasonableness," i.e., evolutionary love.[5]

It is apparent that Peirce is deeply wedded to the relatively new authority in the modern world, that is, science and its method. But, in good Emersonian fashion, he refuses to defer uncritically to this authority. Instead, he demystifies the scientific method into a human affair, into a set of distinct social practices by which knowledge is produced. This role of pragmatism as cultural demystifying activity (focused on the supreme modern authority, science) permits Peirce to defend religion, not devalue or dismiss it. In fact, Peirce's conception of scientific method as a value-laden and normative social activity not only conjoins science and ethics but also posits (and invokes) a religious telos.

Like Emerson, Peirce evades epistemology-centered philosophy by refusing a search for foundations and quest for certainty. In stark contrast to Emerson, Peirce engages in a detailed critical examination of this modern Cartesian search and quest.[6] He wants to know why and how modern philosophy got off track—and René Descartes ("The Spirit of Cartesianism") emerges as the culprit. Cartesian attempts to provide acceptable grounds for knowledge claims rest upon four fatal errors about the nature of knowledge and philosophical method.

First, Cartesians hold that philosophy must begin with universal doubt. Peirce views such doubt as but a fiction inapplicable to itself (since doubt about itself is not doubt but self-consciousness, the very starting point for Cartesianism); inappropriate to that of which we know nothing (since doubt about nothing cannot account for why we doubted in the first place); and impossible to adopt since doubt presupposes something to doubt, i.e., past beliefs.

Second, Cartesians argue that the ultimate test for certainty is to be found in individual consciousness. Peirce rejects this discarding of past authorities and testimonies, especially certain forms of human collective experience. For Peirce, the Cartesian primacy of self-consciousness leads toward a full-fledged subjectivism, an imprisonment in the veil of ideas with no reliable bridge between ideas and things, consciousness and reality, subject and object.

Third, Cartesians leave inexplicable those facts that people most want to know. By using God as a *deus ex machina* to account for the self and world, Cartesianism supplies little knowledge about either. Fourth, the Cartesian philosophical method of inference overlooks the relatedness of ideas to other ideas, propositions to other propositions. Indubitable foundations and absolute certainty are beyond human attainment, but warranted claims and reasonable conclusions result from a "multitude and variety" of forms and styles of argumentation that "form an integral unbroken part of the great body of truth." Peirce's image here is not that of "a chain which is no stronger than its weakest link, but a cable whose fibers may be ever so slender, provided they are sufficiently numerous and intimately connected."[7]

Peirce's dissection and rejection of the four major Cartesian errors constitute the profound pragmatic revision of the Emersonian evasion of modern philosophy. He summarizes this pragmatic swerve away from the epistemology-centered problematic of Cartesianism—including its

British empiricist, Scottish common-sensical realist, and German idealist versions—in the following way.

> 1. We have no power of introspection, but all knowledge of the internal world is derived by hypothetical reasoning from our knowledge of external facts.
> 2. We have no power of intuition, but every cognition is determined logically by previous cognitions.
> 3. We have no power of thinking without signs.
> 4. We have no conception of the absolutely incognizable.[8]

These conclusions map out the new terrain on which American pragmatism will reside. By highlighting the centrality of contingent and revisable social practices in acquiring knowledge, Peirce undermines the pillars of modern philosophy—indubitable immediate awareness, noninferential or intrinsically credible beliefs, nonlinguistic representations, and inaccessible (and unthinkable) things-in-themselves. As W. B. Gallie states: "It would be difficult to find, in the whole history of philosophy, a battery of criticisms more devastating and complete than those . . . from the second of Peirce's papers of 1868."[9]

This grand breakthrough is to be understood as not only Peirce's seminal effort to come to terms with modern philosophy, but also a distinctly American response to a European discourse that overlooked and ignored transactional relations between the self and nature, communal relations between the self and other selves, and especially the radical *contingency* and *revisability* of both relations. Just as Emerson writes in a society more permeated by the commodity form than any other, so Peirce writes in a culture more pervaded by the workings of science and technology (under the aegis of capital) than any other. And just as Emerson deploys the rhetoric of a market society against this society in defense of human personality, so Peirce uses the rhetoric of the natural sciences against the rugged individualism of his day for the sake of individuality in community.

In his significant yet often overlooked 1893 essay "Evolutionary Love," Peirce explicitly writes that the distinctive feature of the nineteenth century is that it is

> "the economical century." For "political economy has more direct relations with all the branches of its activity than has any other science." Well, political economy has its formula of redemption, too. It is this: Intelligence in the service of greed ensures the justest prices, the fairest contracts, and the most enlightened conduct of all the dealings between men, and leads to the *summum bonum*, food in plenty and perfect comfort. Food for whom? Why, for the greedy master of intelligence . . . The great attention paid to economical questions during our century has induced an exaggeration of the beneficial effects of greed and of the unfortunate results of sentiment, until there has resulted a philosophy

which comes unwittingly to this, that greed is the great agent in the elevation of the human race . . . and in the evolution of the universe.[10]

In direct and conscious opposition to Hobbesian egoists, Smithian individualists, Benthamite utilitarians, and Social Darwinists, Peirce castigates the notion of human selfishness as the great agent for natural or social evolution. Instead he promotes a conception of Christianity in which creative love is the motor of natural and social evolution.

> The gospel of Christ says that progress comes from every individual merging his individuality in sympathy with his neighbors. On the other side, the conviction of the nineteenth century is that progress takes place by virtue of every individual's striving for himself with all his might and trampling his neighbor under foot whenever he gets a chance to do so. This may accurately be called the Gospel of Greed.[11]

On the surface, it would appear that Peirce's emphasis on scientific method and community is at odds with Emerson's abhorrence of method and enshrinement of the individual. And indeed Peirce's penchant for rigor and exactness in logical reasoning is alien to the poetic sensibilities of Emerson. Yet it is crucial to point out that Peirce carefully and cautiously *restricts* the application of the scientific method – with its tentative claims and provisional conclusions – to the scientific community involved in rational inquiry. The authority of the scientific method does not hold sway in ethics and religion. In this sense science is neither a guide to conduct nor an instrument for a practical end.

> If a proposition is to be applied to action, it has to be embraced, or believed without reservation. There is no room for doubt, which can only paralyze action. But the scientific spirit requires a man to be at all times ready to dump his whole cartload of beliefs, the moment experience is against them. The desire to learn forbids him to be perfectly cocksure that he knows already. Besides positive science can only rest on experience; and experience can never result in absolute certainty, exactitude, necessity, or universality. But it is precisely with the universal and necessary, that is, with Law, that science can concern itself. Thus the real character of science is destroyed as soon as it is made an adjunct to conduct.

> A useless inquiry, provided it is a systematic one, is pretty much the same thing as a scientific inquiry. Or at any rate if a scientific inquiry becomes by any mischance useful, that aspect of it has to be kept sedulously out of sight during the investigation, or its hopes of success are fatally cursed.[12]

Like Emerson, Peirce falls back on moral sentiment and instinctive action as the alternative to a "scientific" ethics. His rather vague and arcane moral viewpoint surprisingly gives reason no significant role in conduct. Yet in stark contrast to Emerson, his understanding of sentiment and instinct is rooted in the older traditions and testimonies of the Christian church. Dogma is inescapable in the "vital" moral and political actions of people.

> Thus, pure theoretical knowledge, or science, has nothing directly to say concerning practical matters, and nothing even applicable at all to vital crises. Theory is applicable to minor practical affairs; but matters of vital importance must be left to sentiment, that is, to instinct.

> Uncompromising radical though I be upon some questions, inhabiting all my life an atmosphere of science, and not reckoned as particularly credulous, I must confess that the conservative sentimentalism I have defined recommends itself to my mind as eminently sane and wholesome. Commendable as it undoubtedly is to reason out matters of detail, yet to allow mere reasonings and reason's self-conceit to over-awe the normal and manly sentimentalism which ought to lie at the cornerstone of all our conduct seems to me to be foolish and despicable.

> Reasoning is of three kinds—the first is necessary, but it only professes to give us information concerning the matter of our own hypotheses and distinctly declares that, if we want to know anything else, we must go elsewhere. The second depends upon probabilities. The only cases in which it pretends to be of value is where we have, like an insurance company, an endless multitude of insignificant risks. Wherever a vital interest is at stake, it clearly says, "Don't ask me." The third kind of reasoning tries what *il lume naturale*, which lit the footsteps of Galileo, can do. It is really an appeal to instinct. Thus reason, for all the frills it customarily wears, in vital crises, comes down upon its marrow-bones to beg the succour of instinct.[13]

How do we account for Peirce's valorizing of change, revision, open-ness, and newness in science and his defense of dogma, custom, habit, and tradition in ethics and religion? On the one hand, Peirce is a fearless intellectual pioneer, deeply devoted to the life of the mind and forever traversing the boundaries of methodological reflections on science. As an active scientist well acquainted with the actual practices of the scien-tific community and fascinated with the powers unleashed by scientific inquiry, Peirce revels in the contingency and revisability promoted by the scientific method.

On the other hand, Peirce is highly sensitive to the eclipse of *Gemein-schaft* owing to urban industrialization and professional specialization under an ever-expanding monopoly capitalism. As a Boston Brahmin and Harvard graduate (son of a Harvard professor), yet still an outsider to the academy, Peirce is acutely affected by the feelings of loneliness and homelessness of modern existence. Emerson's individualistic revolt against the moribund tradition of the church has lost its cultural shock and appeal. Instead, one either embraces or ignores the church. The nascent indus-trial order of the 1830s has developed into the class-ridden, conflict-prone society of the late nineteenth century. And the identity crisis of the young postcolonial and imperialist nation of Emerson's day has evolved into a postpuberty stage of romantic nationalism, chauvinistic nativism, and aspirations for a world empire. Given this context, his personal temperament, and his burning intellectual vocation, Peirce embraces the Episcopal church, castigates the individualism, professionalism, and Americanism of his day, and thoroughly devotes himself to the life of the mind and the ideas of community and love.[14] On the church, he writes:

> Many a scientific man and student of philosophy recognizes that it is the Christian church which has made him a man among men. To it he owes consolations, enjoyments, escapes from great perils and whatever rectitude of heart and purpose may be his. To the monks of the medieval church he owes the preservation of ancient literature; and without the revival of learning he can hardly see how the revival of science would have been possible. To them he owes the framework of his intellectual system, and if he speaks English, a most important part of his daily speech. The law of love which, however little it be obeyed, he holds to be the soul of civilization, came to Europe through Christianity. Besides, religion is a great, perhaps the greatest, factor of that social life which extends beyond one's own circle of personal friends. That life is everything for elevated, and humane, and democratic civilization; and if one renounces the church, in what other way can one as satisfactorily exercise the faculty of fraternizing with all one's neighbors? . . .
>
> The raison d'être of a church is to confer upon men a life broader than their narrow personalities.[15]

Regarding rapacious individualism and sordid Americanism, Peirce notes:

> To pursue "topics of vital importance" as the first and best can lead only to one or other of two terminations—either on the one hand what is called, I hope not justly, Americanism, the worship of business, the life in which the fertilizing stream of genial sentiment dries up or shrinks to a rill of comic tit-bits, or else on the other hand, to monasticism, sleepwalking in this world with no eye nor heart except for the other. Take for the lantern of your footsteps the cold light of reason and regard your business, your duty, as the highest thing, and you can only rest in one of those goals or the other. But suppose you embrace, on the contrary, a conservative sentimentalism, modestly rate your own reasoning powers at the very mediocre price they would fetch if put up at auction, and then what do you come to? Why, *then*, the very first command that is laid upon you, your quite highest business and duty, becomes, as everybody knows, to recognize a higher business than your business; *not* merely an avocation after the daily task of your vocation is performed, but a generalized conception of duty which completes your personality by melting it into the neighboring parts of the universal cosmos. If this sounds unintelligible, just take for comparison the first good mother of a family that meets your eye, and ask whether she is

not a sentimentalist, whether you would wish her to be otherwise, and lastly whether you can find a better formula in which to outline the universal features of her portrait than that I have just given.

To sum it up, all sensible talk about vitally important topics must be commonplace, all reasoning about them unsound, and all study of them narrow and sordid.[16]

And on the vulgar professionalism of his time, just prior to giving a set of visiting lectures at Harvard (the same year, 1869–70, Emerson gave his lectures!), Peirce says,

I repeat that I know nothing about the Harvard of today, but one of the things which I hope to learn during my stay in Cambridge is the answer to this question, whether the Commonwealth of Massachusetts has set up this university to the end that such young men as can come here may receive a fine education and may thus be able to earn handsome incomes, and have a canvas-back and a bottle of Clos de Vougeot for dinner . . .[17]

Peirce's double consciousness of experimental inquiry and common human sentiments and his dual allegiance to scientific method and Christian faith serve as the soil upon which the seeds of American pragmatism sprout. Peirce found himself split between the two cultures of science and religion throughout his life in late Victorian New England, Baltimore (Johns Hopkins University teaching position, 1879–84), and Milford, Pennsylvania (where he lived in isolation). The historic emergence of American pragmatism principally results from Peirce's profound evasion of "the spirit of Cartesianism" owing to his obsession with the procedures of the scientific community, his loyalty to a Christian doctrine of love, and the lure of community in the midst of anomic *Gesellschaften* of urban, industrial capitalist America. This Peircean evasion consists, in part, of a creative revision of Emersonian themes of contingency and revisability and an Emersonian theodicy that promotes human progress, betterment, and moral development.

The famous pragmatic maxim—that the basic aim is to reach "a clearness of thought of higher grade than the 'distinctness' of the logicians"[18]— first appears in his seminal essay of 1878 "How to Make Our Ideas Clear," within the context of a discussion adjudicating between the Catholic and Protestant doctrines of transubstantiation:

It is foolish for Catholics and Protestants to fancy themselves in disagreement about the elements of the sacrament, if they agree in regard to all their sensible effects, here and hereafter.

It appears, then, that the rule for attaining the third grade of clearness of apprehension is as follows: Consider what effects, that might conceivably have practical bearings, we conceive the object of our conception to have. Then, our conception of these effects is the whole conception of the object.[19]

In an often overlooked lengthy footnote (added in 1893) to this pragmatic maxim, Peirce attempts to link the idea of pragmatism to the Christian gospel and to an Emersonian evolutionary optimism about collectivities, not individuals, in human history.

> Before we undertake to apply this rule, let us reflect a little upon what it implies. It has been said to be a sceptical and materialistic principle. But it is only an application of the sole principle of logic which was recommended by Jesus; "Ye may know them by their fruits," and it is very intimately allied with the ideas of the gospel. We must certainly guard ourselves against understanding this rule in too individualistic a sense. To say that man accomplishes nothing but that to which his endeavors are directed would be a cruel condemnation of the great bulk of mankind, who never have leisure to labor for anything but the necessities of life for themselves and their families. But, without directly striving for it, far less comprehending it, they perform all that civilization requires, and bring forth another generation to advance history another step. Their fruit is, therefore, collective; it is the achievement of the whole people. What is it, then, that the whole people is about, what is this civilization that is the outcome of history, but is never completed? We cannot expect to attain a complete conception of it; but we can see that it is a gradual process, that it involves a realization of ideas in man's consciousness and in his works, and that it takes place by virtue of man's capacity for learning, and by experience continually pouring upon him ideas he has not yet acquired. We may say that it is the process whereby man, with all his miserable littlenesses, becomes gradually more and more imbued with the spirit of God, in which nature and history are rife . . . We are all putting our shoulders to the wheel for an end that none of us can catch more than a glimpse at—that which the generations are working out. But we can see that the development of embodied ideas is what it will consist in.[20]

For Peirce, pragmatism is not a philosophical *Weltanschauung* or a new metaphysics of truth and reality. Rather it is a method of rendering ideas clear and distinct and ascertaining the meaning of words and concepts. The pragmatic method, which locates this meaning in the consideration of "what practical consequences might conceivably result by necessity from the truth of an intellectual conception," is but the application of the experimental method of the natural sciences to traditional philosophical problems.[21] In addition to being a monumental revolt against Cartesianism, his pragmatism is influenced by three intellectual predecessors: Immanuel Kant, Duns Scotus, and Charles Darwin.

His lifelong struggle with Kant is well known. What is less noted is that Peirce sees Kant as a "scientific man beneath the skin,"[22] as one who came to philosophy from physics. What attracted Peirce to Kant was neither the transcendental idealism of the *Critique of Pure Reason* nor the notion of autonomy in the *Critique of Practical Reason*; rather it was Kant's methodological and critical reflections, especially the idea of modeling philosophical thinking on the methods of natural scientists.

From Duns Scotus, Peirce acquired philosophical ammunition against modern nominalism and idealism. Scotian realism encouraged Peirce not only to postulate a real world upon which scientists work but also to hold to the existence of universals and general principles operative in nature. Despite his stress on the contingency and revisability of scientific claims and theories, Peirce preserves the permanency and independence of what those claims and theories are about. In his most succinct description of the scientific method ("The Fixation of Belief" [1877]) he writes,

> To satisfy our doubts, therefore, it is necessary that a method should be found by which our beliefs may be caused by nothing human, but by some external permanency—by something upon which our thinking has no effect . . . such is the method of science. Its fundamental hypothesis, restated in more familiar language, is this: there are real things, whose characters are entirely independent of our opinions about them; those realities affect our senses according to regular laws, and, though our sensations are as different as our relations to the objects, yet, by taking advantage of the laws of perception, we can ascertain by reasoning how things really are; and any man, if he have sufficient experience and reason enough about it, will be led to the one true conclusion.[23]

At this point it seems appropriate to view Peirce's pragmatism as a kind of "Kantianism without things-in-themselves" (a description he once used). Yet he also appears to admit that the status of reality must be presupposed by scientific method rather than derived from it. This does not endorse a Berkeleyan doctrine that objects do not exist until they are perceived or a Kantian view that these objects exist as constituted by human conceptions yet are not real. Rather Peirce's pragmatism links the notion of what is real to what the scientific community agrees on *in the long run*. Penultimately, we must accept the best available yet revisable theories of reality; ultimately, convergence and agreement among scientists will disclose reality. Of course, such ultimate agreement never comes; it is simply a regulative ideal and a hope that sustains rational adjudication and motivates scientific inquiry in the present. In reply to a critic on this matter, Peirce writes:

> Dr. Carus holds that from my social theory of reality, namely, that the real is the idea in which the community ultimately settles down, the existence of something inevitable is to be inferred. I confess I never anticipated that anybody would urge that. I thought just the reverse might be objected, namely, that all absoluteness was removed from reality by that theory . . . I admitted the obvious justice, as it seemed to me, of that objection. We cannot be quite sure that the community ever will settle down to an unalterable conclusion upon any given question. Even if they do so for the most part, we have no reason to think the unanimity

will be quite complete, nor can we rationally presume any overwhelming *consensus* of opinion will be reached upon every question. All that we are entitled to assume is in the form of a *hope* that such conclusion may be substantially reached concerning the particular questions with which our inquiries are busied.[24]

This pragmatic "leap of faith" in the procedures and conclusions of the scientific community itself assumes a peculiar form of scholastic realism—namely, that general truths, though contingent, revisable, and independent of human opinions, are objectively real. This assumption permits Peirce to escape subtle forms of relativism and nominalism, yet it also forces him to "embrace the doctrine of absolute chance." This doctrine—dubbed tychism by Peirce—precludes inevitabilism, necessitarianism, and determinism; it accents growth, variety, diversity, and spontaneity in the universe. It also provides a possibility in an infinite future for convergence and agreement among inquirers.

Darwin's *Origin of Species* exercised a great influence on Peirce. He cast his own conclusions of scientific method, reality, and community in an evolutionary framework. Prompted by his friend and fellow member of the Metaphysical Club Chauncey Wright's wholesale enthusiasm for Darwin and his disdain for evolution infused with moral ends, Peirce was impelled to criticize Darwin and defend moral evolutionary teleology. Peirce's need to defend the theoretical coherence and logical consistency of his pragmatism and its compatibility with Christianity led him to put forward his own speculative evolutionary perspective, that is, agapism. This viewpoint holds, in stark contrast to Darwin, that what motors evolution is not mechanical necessity, i.e., variation and natural selection, but rather an amalgam of this necessity, chance, and, most important, love. The very laws of nature themselves are regulated by a supreme law of the universe; chance is a crucial factor in the universe but even it begets order and harmony promoted by evolutionary love.[25]

Peirce's objections to Darwin are both scientific and moral. He holds not only that sheer mechanical necessity could not account for the emergence and development of the universe, but also that Darwinism projects the "gospel of greed" into the subject matter of natural scientists.

> The *Origin of Species* of Darwin merely extends politico-economical views of progress to the entire realm of animal and vegetable life. The vast majority of our contemporary naturalists hold the opinion that the true cause of those exquisite and marvelous adaptations of nature for which, when I was a boy, men used to extol the divine wisdom, is that creatures are so crowded together that those of them that happen to have the slightest advantage force those less pushing into situations unfavorable to multiplication or even kill them before they reach the age of reproduction. Among animals, the mere mechanical individualism is vastly reenforced as a power making for good by the animal's ruthless greed. As

Darwin puts it on his title-page, it is the struggle for existence; and he should have added for his motto: every individual for himself, and the devil take the hindmost! Jesus, in his Sermon on the Mount, expressed a different opinion.[26]

Peirce admits that this form of moral criticism of Darwin "will probably shock my scientific brethren," yet he cannot deny his "passionate predilection" for "the agapistic theory of evolution" that speaks for "the normal judgement of the Sensible Heart."[27] As we saw earlier, Peirce conceives of such judgments as requisite for social life, including the social practices of scientists.

It may seem strange that I should put forward three sentiments, namely interest in an indefinite community, recognition of the possibility of this interest being made supreme, and hope in the unlimited continuance of intellectual activity, as indispensable requirements of logic. Yet, when we consider that logic depends on a mere struggle to escape doubt, which, as it terminates in action, must begin in emotion, and that, furthermore, the only cause of our planting ourselves on reason is that other methods of escaping doubt fail on account of the social impulse, why should we wonder to find social sentiment presupposed in reasoning? As for the other two sentiments which I find necessary, they are so only as supports and accessories of that. It interests me to notice that these three sentiments seem to be pretty much the same as that famous trio of Charity, Faith, and Hope, which, in the estimation of St. Paul, are the finest and greatest of spiritual gifts. Neither Old nor New Testament is a textbook of the logic of science, but the latter is certainly the highest existing authority in regard to the dispositions of heart which a man ought to have.[28]

This passage beautifully weaves together Peirce's basic notions of scientific method, community, and love. Emersonian preoccupations with the dynamism of human power and the perennial progress generated by provocation are situated within the new authority in American culture, namely, the scientific community and its concomitant institutions such as the academy and professions. Emerson's enshrinement of the moral development of individuals is transformed under industrial capitalist conditions by Peirce into a concern with this personal development within communities, especially within traditional Christian churches. And the Emersonian theodicy of overcoming all limitations by means of sheer human will buttressed by the congeniality of reality to such efforts is restated and reaffirmed in the combined and cumbersome rhetorics of scientific procedure, evolutionary biology, German idealism, scholastic realism, and Christianity. Peirce's pragmatism revises and reforms the Emersonian evasion of modern philosophy in the languages of and in dialogue with academic philosophers. In this sense, Peirce is not only the greatest of American professional philosophical thinkers but also the first who

makes a distinctively American intervention into the professional conversation, an intervention that contains strong Emersonian residues and
"bacilli." The only literary reference of Peirce to Emerson in his enormous
corpus is:

> The old sphinx bit her thick lip—
>   Said, "Who taught thee me to name?
> I am thy spirit, yore-fellow,
>   Of thine eye I am eyebeam."
> "Thou art the unanswered question;
>   Couldst see thy proper eye,
> Always it asketh, asketh;
>   And each answer is a lie."[29]

And a proposed book (in 1890) which "if ever written . . . will be one
of the births of time," Peirce entitles "A Guess at the Riddle," with a vignette
of the sphinx below the title.[30] Emerson's "lie-against-time" in order to
occupy or control space and expand human powers still haunted Peirce's
pragmatic revision of it.

James on Individuality, Reconciliation, and Heroic Energies

William James is the most famous of American philosophical figures. With
the exception of Emerson, no one but James deserves to be considered
the preeminent American man of letters. Ironically, he was more a product
of and participant in American academic life than any of the other major
personages in the American pragmatic tradition. This partly accounts for
his adversarial disposition toward professionalism of any sort.

James is the exemplary Emersonian embodiment of intellectual power,
provocation, and personality. He is first and foremost a moralist obsessed
with heroic energies and reconciliatory strategies available to individuals.
Unlike Peirce, James moves the focus of Emersonian theodicy away from
the community and back to the individual person. James's efforts to
popularize pragmatism enact the very heroic energies and reconciliatory
strategies his moral meliorism promotes. And given his more sparkling
personality and vibrant style, James maybe even more than Emerson
thrives on excitement and engagement, revels in provocation and stimulation. In this sense, James actually "out-Emersons" Emerson.

James is not a traditional philosopher by either temperament or
training. Rather he is a cultural critic trained in medicine, fascinated with
the arts, imbued with a scientific conscience, and attracted to religion.
This unique combination of skills, talent, and interests leads him onto
philosophical terrain where he leaps—quickly and often unsatisfactorily
but as it suits his fancy—from one major issue to another. He is neither

afraid to traverse disciplinary boundaries nor hesitant to pronounce premature panaceas for centuries-old problems. In short, he is an authentic
American intellectual frontiersman, not so much staking land in a wilderness but rather, like Mark Twain's Huckleberry Finn, expanding the moral
possibilities of individuals on a raft that floats near land and society yet
never really banks for long. In an important sense, experience is a river—a
set of actions and reactions connected with ethical purpose.[31] Yet, in
contrast to Emerson, James is not a detached contemplative man of the
spirit, but rather an attached restless patrician of the street. If Emerson
signifies Man Thinking, and Peirce, Man Inquiring, then James discloses
Man Willing.

Like Peirce, James promotes an Emersonian evasion of epistemology-
centered philosophy. But, unlike Peirce, his end-around moves are
motivated not primarily by scientific method but rather by the aspira-
tion to adhere to a certain kind of vision and the preference for a specific
way of life. Whereas Peirce applies Emersonian themes of contingency
and revisability to the scientific method, James extends them to our
personal and moral lives. This extension principally consists of populariz-
ing the personal and moral implications of the pragmatic perspective
initiated by Peirce. The basic aim of this popularization is to mediate
between the old and the new—religion and science, Gemeinschaft and
Gesellschaft, country and city, vocation and profession—in order to lessen
the shock of the new for the educated middle class. Similar to Emerson,
James constituted a constituency and created a public role for himself
which, in turn, opened new cultural space for a significant segment of
middle-class professionals and intellectuals. Of course, James was supported
by the authority and salary of a Harvard professorship (though he hardly
needed the money), whereas Emerson had no such support.

I do not want to imply that James was a shallow or derivative thinker.
To the contrary, his Principles of Psychology (1890) is a profound work,
one of the few great books produced by an American intellectual. Furthermore, James wrote some of the most subtle and significant essays in American letters. Rather what I am suggesting is that the major role of William
James as a figure in the American pragmatist tradition is that of Emersonian
individualist, moralist, meliorist, popularizer, and intellectual hero to crucial
fractions of the refined and reformist middle class.

The first public mention of "pragmatism" occurs in James's lecture
entitled "Philosophical Conceptions and Practical Results" delivered at
the University of California at Berkeley in 1898. In this historic presentation, James credits Peirce with both the term and the ideas associated
with it. James is both honest and modest. Peirce indeed is the originator
of pragmatism, yet James's seminal analyses of emotions and streams of
consciousness in his Principles of Psychology contribute greatly to pragmatic
thought. As Paul Conkin cleverly notes, if psychology lost its soul with

Kant, it lost its mind with James[32] — without falling into the trap of a vulgar behaviorism. Instead, James's dynamic functionalism and transactional instrumentalism call into question the Cartesian dualisms of mind and matter, subject and object, immediate awareness and external world. In this way, James's *Principles of Psychology* prefigures crucial pragmatic viewpoints.

At the start, Peirce acutely and accurately discerns the difference between his pragmatism and that of James. First, James is rooted in the British tradition of empiricism, a tradition never highly attractive to Peirce. Hence, James locates the meaning of a concept in terms of sensation, not conduct (or conceived action). More important, James construes the meaning of a concept in terms of particular experiences, whereas Peirce does so in terms of general ideas (or intellectual purport).[33] Owing to this difference and subsequent misuses of the term, Peirce notes,

> the writer, finding his bantling "pragmatism" so promoted, feels that it is time to kiss his child goodby and relinquish it to its higher destiny; while to serve the precise purpose of expressing the original definition, he begs to announce the birth of the word "pragmaticism," which is ugly enough to be safe from kidnappers.[34]

The differences between Peirce and James are significant, but they ought not to obscure the common ground shared by the two thinkers. Both shun the Cartesian problematic; both turn away from foundations, certainties, and bases and toward effects, consequences, and practices; and both view pragmatism as a method for clear thinking, not a new philosophy. For Peirce, "practical bearings" means the purpose of action, such as to promote "the growth of concrete reasonableness," whereas for James, it means specific sensations that enable particular actions. In addition, for Peirce, *agathon* (the idea of the good) lies in convergence and coalescence, corporateness and oneness; for James, in diversity and individuality, concreteness and plurality.

Peirce and James were the first major figures to emerge on the American intellectual scene thoroughly conversant with the best offered by the European philosophical traditions. Yet James took it upon himself to translate and transform his conversation with these traditions into a language intelligible to educated middle-class Americans. Hence, his lectures or essays sound not like books but rather like juicy intellectual gossip that beckons the audience and readers to eavesdrop on what is being said. James wants us to "taste the milk in the cocoanut" and be nourished. The aim of thought is neither mere action nor further thought; rather it is to be more fully alive, more attuned to the possibilities of mystery, morality, and melioration.

For James, as for Emerson, abundant life is always found on the highway. Yet for him, such life can be sustained only in the middle lane. Openness, flexibility, and improvisation characterize his intellectual attitude and personal temperament, but he always ends by residing in the golden mean, between two extremes. On the one hand, James affirms a pungent Emersonian individualism, with "an almost physical horror of club senti- ment and of the stifling atmosphere of all officialdom," a deep hatred of the "*non possumus* of any constituted authority."[35] On the other hand, James encourages individuals to be critically reconciled with past authorities when the only alternative is to undermine these authorities. Again, similar to Emerson, he promotes moral transgression based on personal integrity and individual conscience rather than social revolution by means of collec- tive action.

James's favorite rhetorical strategy in support of his fervent indi- vidualism and comforting "middle-of-the-roadism" is the juxtaposition of exorbitant polar positions. His most famous example is put forward in *Pragmatism* (1907):

The Tender-Minded	The Tough-Minded
Rationalistic (going by "principle")	Empiricist (going by "facts")
Intellectualistic	Sensationalistic
Idealistic	Materialistic
Optimistic	Pessimistic
Religious	Irreligious
Free-Willist	Fatalistic
Monistic	Pluralistic
Dogmatical	Sceptical[36]

James attempts primarily to dissolve the distinctions by combining the best of each, rejecting the rest, and affirming a protean pluralism that occupies middle space. The end is, in the name of openness and revisability, to unsettle and undo our excessive claims and thereby preclude wholesale undermining or undergirding of the status quo. The role of pragmatism is that of "a happy harmonizer" and "a mediator and reconciler . . . that 'unstiffens' our theories. She has in fact no prejudices whatever, no obstruc- tive dogmas, no rigid canons of what shall count as proof. She is completely genial. She will entertain any hypothesis, she will consider any evidence."[37]

James's "mediating" conception of pragmatism rests upon three basic assumptions: first, that reconciliation is possible between the two extremes; second, that this reconciliation can be arrived at in an amiable manner; and third, that this amiable reconciliation will be better than either extreme. Of course, these assumptions chime well with the Emersonian theodicy of optimism, moralism, and voluntarism. Emerson and James simply fail to entertain the possibility that overcoming a limitation or reconciling extremes may result in an outcome that is worse than its ante- cedent conditions; they cannot imagine wholesale regression owing to human will and action.

James is much more attuned to the depths of evil in the world than Emerson. Hence he speaks much less of divine providence and much more of human promise, much less of the good as victorious and more of good people winning particular battles. In fact, James's more sober perspective leads him to highlight the heroic energies of people precisely because they are up against so much. James's recognition of evil leads not to Emersonian mysticism but rather to a more pronounced voluntarism. Entrenched evil is a precondition for voluntarism—a host upon which heroism is parasitic.

James's emphasis on heroism is his way of revising Emerson's notion of power. Like Emerson, he focuses mainly on the energies of individuals. Yet James is even more anthropocentric than Emerson; man truly is the measure of all things for him. This romantic veneration of the creative powers and combative energies of human beings leads him to view the strenuous life as the only life worth living. In his essay (delivered to the YMCA in 1895) "Is Life Worth Living?" he notes:

> It is, indeed, a remarkable fact that sufferings and hardships do not, as a rule, abate the love of life; they seem, on the contrary, usually to give it a keener zest. The sovereign source of melancholy is repletion. Need and struggle are what excite and inspire us; our hour of triumph is what brings the void . . . The history of our own race is one long commentary on the cheerfulness that comes with fighting ills.[38]

And in "What Makes a Life Significant" (in lectures on psychology to Cambridge teachers in 1892): "The thing of deepest—or, at any rate, of comparatively deepest—significance in life does seem to be its character of *progress,* or that strange union of reality with ideal novelty which it continues from one moment to another to present."[39] His most vehement defense of heroism is found in two masterful and famous essays, "The Energies of Man" (presidential address before the American Philosophical Association in 1906, later published as "The Powers of Man") and "The Moral Equivalent of War" (1910). These essays reveal the degree to which James promotes notions of martial spirit and masculine virility in order to reinvigorate and regenerate individuals for moral purpose. These notions indeed on the surface resemble the progressivist and imperialistic rhetorics of heroism put forward by Theodore Roosevelt and Brooks Adams, yet also diverge from them. Notwithstanding his peculiar admiration of Rudyard Kipling, a staunch proponent of imperialism, James promotes a moral heroism, martial in form, that gets at the hearts and souls of people, rather than political heroism, militarist in content, that stakes out land and colonizes people.

> We must make new energies and hardihoods [that] continue the manliness to which the military mind so faithfully clings . . .
> The war-party is assuredly right in affirming and reaffirming that the martial virtues, although originally gained by the race through war, are absolute and permanent human goods. Patriotic pride and ambition in their military form are, after all, only specifications of more universal and enduring competitive passion. They are its first form, but that is

no reason for supposing them to be its last form . . . who can be sure that *other aspects of one's country* may not with time and education and suggestion enough, come to be regarded with similarly effective feelings of pride and shame? . . .

The martial type of character can be bred without war . . . The only thing needed hereforward is to inflame the civic temper as past history has inflamed the military temper.[40]

James uses the dominant imperialist militaristic language of his time but turns it back against American imperialism and militarism. As vice-president of the Anti-Imperialist League and a member of the upper classes, James opposes American intervention abroad and understands the need for heroism among the anxiety-ridden "weaklings" and neurasthenic "molly-coddles" of the well-to-do. Yet James also rejects the myth of the rustic commoner in which the heroic is to be "only in the dirty boots and sweaty shirt of someone in the fields."[41] True to the interests of his audience and aim of his discourse, James exclaims, "It is with us really under every disguise," if we would but see and deepen it. Jamesian rhetoric of moral heroism intends to energize people to become exceptional doers under adverse circumstances, to galvanize zestful fighters against excruciating odds.

Like Emerson's, James's preoccupation with power ("A Pragmatist Turns toward Action and Power")[42] shuns the collective and corporate activities of people. In his famous letter to Mrs. Henry Whitman (June 7, 1899) he writes:

I am against bigness and greatness in all their forms, and with the invisible molecular moral forces that work from individual to individual, stealing in through the crannies of the world like so many soft rootlets, or like the capillary oozing of water, and yet rending the hardest monuments of man's pride, if you give them time, the bigger the unit you deal with, the hollower, the more brutal, the more mendacious is the life displayed. So I am against all big organizations as such, national ones first and foremost; against all big successes and big results; and in favor of the eternal forces of truth which always work in the individual and immediately unsuccessful way, under-dogs always, till history comes, after they are long dead, and puts them on the top.[43]

This Emersonian individualism runs deep, very deep in James. It yields a genuine empathy with those undergoing hardship and rather apolitical notions of how to change the world. James is quite aware of the political means of effecting change; he just thinks that such means do not cut deep enough for his moral purposes. In his revealing political comments in "What Makes a Life Significant," James hits hard on the issue of social change and moral regeneration:

—We are suffering today in America from what is called the labor-question; and when you go out into the world, you will each and all of you be caught up in its perplexities. I use the brief term labor-question to cover all sorts of anarchistic discontents and socialistic projects, and the conservative resistances which they provoke. So far as this conflict is unhealthy and regrettable—and I think it is so only to a limited extent —the unhealthiness consists solely in the fact that one-half of our fellow-countrymen remain entirely blind to the internal significance of the lives of the other half . . .

—Society has, with all this, undoubtedly got to pass towards some newer and better equilibrium, and the distribution of wealth has doubtless slowly got to change; such changes have always happened, and will happen to the end of time. But if, after all that I have said, any of you expect that they will make any *genuine vital difference*, on a large scale, to the lives of our descendants, you will have missed the significance of my entire lecture. The solid meaning of life is always the same eternal thing—the marriage, namely, of some unhabitual ideal, however special, with some fidelity, courage, and endurance; with some man's or woman's pains.—And whatever or whenever life may be, there will always be the chance for that marriage to take place.[44]

For James, the moral development of human personalities is related to but far from determined by social circumstances. Like Emerson, he is prohibited by his individualism from taking seriously fundamental social change; instead, he opts for a gradualism supported by moral critique. Notwithstanding his comments regarding a probable socialism (influenced by H. G. Wells's Fabian socialist book *First and Last Things*), James is no radical or revolutionary.[45]

James is a man of neither the left nor the right. He certainly does not "transcend" politics, but, like Emerson, he fits uncomfortably with any political party or movement. He is a libertarian, with circumscribed democratic sentiments, an international outlook, and deep moral sensitivity.[46] This perspective is one of political impotence, yet it buttresses moral integrity and promotes the exercise of individual conscience.

James's position is symptomatic of his class background, family upbringing, and personal temperament. The crises he encountered were personal and existential, not political or economic. His iconoclastic socialist father, Henry James, Sr.—the most interesting and complex of all the James family—cultivated the freedom of his children. This good friend of Emerson was convinced that in his family "every one should paddle his own canoe, especially on the high seas."[47] Therefore, James was preoccupied with the state of his and others' souls, not the social conditions of their lives.

Yet James does believe that he has a particular role and responsibility —especially to his class. As a publicist, he wants to guide them through the cultural and personal crises of turn-of-the-century America. His role is that of mediator; his responsibility, to keep alive the Emersonian evasion and theodicy in new circumstances. In regard to politics, James has nothing profound or even provocative to say. He simply takes his cues from

E. L. Godkin's *Nation* which has the unique distinction "of always being right"[48] and he sides with the mugwumps in mild revolt from the Republican party. The task of the pragmatic publicist is to "blow cold upon the hot excitement, and hot upon the cold motive."[49] This judicial and dispassionate function consists of reconciling passionately held extreme perspectives and mediating between the nostalgic and the utopian. Such a reconciliation appeals to the educated classes in that it permits them to combine reformist sentiments with refined sensibilities. In a description that echoes that of Emerson, James notes,

> Speaking broadly, there are never more than two fundamental parties in a nation: the party of red blood, as it calls itself, and that of pale reflection; the party of animal instinct, jingoism, fun, excitement, bigness; and that of reason, forecast, order gained by growth, and spiritual methods . . . Briefly put, the party of force and that of education . . . the Tories in any country and the mob will always pull together in the red-blood party . . . and liberalism will be between the upper and the nether millstone if it have no magnetic leader . . . The chronic fault of liberalism is its lack of speed and passion.[50]

It is important to note that James's conception of a class here is primarily a cultural one. He pits the enlightenment of the middle class against the greed, conservatism, and vulgar radicalism of the others. His distrust of the masses is undeniable.

> Our socialistic peace-advocates all believe absolutely in this world's values; and instead of the fear of the Lord and the fear of the enemy, the only fear they reckon with is the fear of poverty if one be lazy. This weakness pervades all the scholastic literature with which I am acquainted . . . It suggests, in truth, ubiquitous inferiority.[51]

This cultural reading of American capitalist society enables James to conceive of his publicist role; the reading itself is part and parcel of his mediating function. James is most explicit on this role and function in a presentation targeted precisely at his ideal constituency, "The Social Value of the College-Bred." Delivered at the meeting of the Association of American Alumnae at Radcliffe College on November 7, 1907, and published in *McClure's Magazine* in February 1908, this lecture articulates the cultural politics often concealed by his moral individualism.

> The sense of human superiority ought, then to be considered our line, as boring subway is the engineer's line and the surgeon's is appendicitis . . . The best claim we can make for the higher education is . . . it should enable us to *know a good man when we see him* . . .
> In this very simple way does the value of our educated class define itself: we more than others should be able to divine the worthier and better leaders . . . in our democracy, while everything else is so shifting, we alumni and alumnae of the colleges are the only permanent presence

that corresponds to the aristocracy in older countries. We have continuous traditions, as they have; our motto, too, is *noblesse oblige*; and,
unlike them, we stand for ideal interests solely, for we have no corporate
selfishness and wield no powers of corruption. We ought to have our
own class-consciousness. "Les intellectuels!" . . .
    If democracy is to be saved it must catch the higher, healthier tune.
If we are to impress it with our preferences, we ourselves must use the
proper tune, which we, in turn, must have caught from our own teachers.
It all reverts in the end to the action of innumerable imitative individuals
upon each other and to the question of whose tune has the highest
spreading power. As a class, we college graduates should look to it that
ours has spreading power. It ought to have the highest spreading power.[52]

This is a crucial and peculiar passage in James's corpus. It is crucial in
that as a popularizer and publicist of American pragmatism he explicitly
specifies its historical agent—the educated classes—and its ideological aim:
to cultivate moral criticism for the preservation of highbrow culture, the
election of refined political leaders, and the moderate extension of
democracy. This passage is peculiar because we find James elevating elitism,
tradition, collective consciousness, and social power—the very notions
he deplores elsewhere. Furthermore, he uncritically privileges his class—
no selfishness? no corruption?—in a rather deceptive and deficient manner.
Like Emerson, though unlike Peirce, James endeavors to articulate and
elaborate a distinctive American ideology that weaves the themes of individuality, reconciliation, and heroic energies in order to facilitate his exercise of intellectual and moral leadership over a significant element of the
middle class, that is, the professional and reformist elements of this class.
    This ideology indeed cuts against the grain of turn-of-the-century
America—it is critical of the "predatory lusts" of the robber barons, the
"bitch goddess, success," of the tycoons, and the cultural parochialism
of the working class.[53] It promotes basic transformation at the level of
the individual; for society, it supports slow gradual change. It encourages
incessant transgression at the level of the individual; for society, it heralds
reconciliation and mediation. Last, it extols the heroic energies of willful
action at the level of the individual; for society, it fosters judicious and
dispassionate judgments of limits and constraints.[54] In this way, the social
base of James's pragmatism is the professional and reformist elements of
the middle class, a class expanding rapidly and destined to move into
the higher echelons of political power. Similarly, the cultural bias—distance
from the working class, women, and people of color—of James's pragmatism is toward the ambivalent democratic commitments and insecure highbrow elitist allegiances of this class.
    This social base and cultural bias are seen most clearly in James's anti-
imperialist activities (1898–1903). The bases of James's opposition to U.S.
imperialism in the Caribbean and Asia are moral and patriotic, although

James empathizes with the victims and supports their right to self-determination. Like Emerson's abolitionism, James's anti-imperialism is based on a concern with what imperialism reveals about his own class and white fellow citizens. As we saw earlier, James approves of the martial spirit and militaristic temper, yet he rejects the use of this spirit and temper for purposes of conquest and colonization. Such misuse—exemplified in Theodore Roosevelt's famous pro-imperialist speech "The Strenuous Life" (April 11, 1899)—stems from jingoistic rhetorics of moral abstractions, manifest destiny, and "barbaric patriotism."[55] In reply to this speech, James writes,

> Although in middle life . . . and in a situation of responsibility concrete enough, he is still mentally in the *Sturm und Drang* period of early adolescence, treats human affairs, when he makes speeches about them, from the sole point of view of the organic excitement and difficulty they may bring, gushes over war as the ideal condition of human society, for the manly strenuousness which it involves, and treats peace as a condition of blubberlike and swollen ignobility, fit only for huckstering weaklings, dwelling in gray twilight and heedless of the higher life. Not a word of the cause—one foe is as good as another . . . He swamps everything together in one flood of abstract bellicose emotion.[56]

James observes that his fellow Americans suffer from what he notes in his well-known piece "On a Certain Blindness in Human Beings" as an inability to adopt a sympathetic and sensible point of view toward those who seem distant, alien, and even unintelligible.[57] The pro-imperialists have dehumanized and objectified the Filipinos, thereby rendering their humanity and, especially, their individuality invisible. The chauvinistic crusade to save the world, legitimated by missionary efforts to civilize and uplift inferior peoples and races, was a sham and a shame.

> It is obvious that for our rulers at Washington the Filipinos have not existed as psychological quantities at all . . . we have treated [them] as if they were a painted picture, an amount of mere matter in our ways. They are too remote from us ever to be realized as they exist in their inwardness.[58]

> We are to be missionaries of civilization, and to bear the white man's burden, painful as it often is . . . the individual lives are nothing. Our duty and our destiny call, and civilization must go on! Could there be a more damning indictment of that whole bloated idol termed "modern civilization" than this amounts to? Civilization is, then, the big, hollow, resounding, corrupting, sophisticating, confusing torrent of mere brutal momentum and irrationality that brings forth fruits like this![59]

Although three years later James would be advocating the candidacy of the jingoistic and racist Roosevelt for the presidency of Harvard—partly because "his heart is in the right place"—his moral critique of American imperialism is vehement and vociferous. The very civilization that the educated classes are to preserve is being destroyed by their need for stimulation, provocation, and satisfaction. The dullness and banality of American middle-class life generated a need for excitement, an excitement channeled in a jingoistic manner. Rooseveltian chauvinists attract the same educated class and appeal to the same psychological states as James. In this way, his struggle against anti-imperialism is required if he is to exercise any significant intellectual and moral leadership over the reformist and professional elements of the middle class. Needless to say, on this issue he loses hands down—and quickly moves on to a more tame terrain.

Ironically, some of James's characterization of Roosevelt's obsession with "excitement and difficulty" holds for James himself. Furthermore, James's very conception of truth is cast in terms of stimulation, provocation, and satisfaction. We noted earlier that the mediating role of pragmatism is such that "every sane and sound tendency in life can be brought in under it."[60] This power to subsume aspects of other contending positions permits pragmatism to domesticate and dilute for its own purposes. One form of this demystifying and compromising activity is to apply Emersonian notions of contingency and revisability to truth. Yet because James lacks Peirce's communal eschatology, it is not clear whether any "truth" is left after James gets through with it.

This is so because James accepts neither a coherence theory of truth nor a traditional correspondence theory of truth. That is, ideas become true not simply owing to how they cohere with other "true" ideas or solely because they copy or correspond to objective reality. James is ultimately a realist about truth in that he holds that "with some such reality any statement, in order to be counted true, must agree."[61] But his focus is on how "new" truths become so and on the role of human active cognitive powers in this process. This double question is understood in terms of the degree to which the new upsets the old, the extent to which discontinuity disrupts continuity. Just as his cultural mission is one of reconciliation, so James's conception of truth attempts to unite the novel and the familiar with a minimum of friction and a maximum of openness to the future.

> New truth is always a go-between, a smoother-over of transitions. It marries an old opinion to new fact so as ever to show a minimum of jolt, a maximum of continuity. We hold a theory true just in proportion to its success in solving this "problem of maxima and minima." But success in solving this problem is eminently a matter of approximation . . . to a certain degree therefore, everything here is plastic.[62]

James rightly calls attention to human values such as elegance, simplicity, and expediency, which help determine which theories we deem true. But the most important value is that of continuity. James's sense of tradition—the presence of the past in things present—is both conservative and prospective. He links pragmatism to the new, yet roots it in the familiar and customary. The successful innovator

> preserves the older stock of truths with a minimum of modification, stretching them just enough to make them admit the novelty, but conceiving that in ways as familiar as the case leaves possible. An *outrée* explanation, violating all our preconceptions, would never pass for a true account of a novelty. We should scratch round industriously till we found something less eccentric. The most violent revolutions in an individual's beliefs leave most of his old order standing.[63]

Like Peirce's, James's attempt to incorporate contingency and revision into a theory of truth is radical; yet in its gradualism his theory applies a Burkean notion of tradition to the production of knowledge and truth. Of course, new knowledge and truths must build on the old, but James's preoccupation with continuity minimizes disruption and precludes subversion.

For James, the universe is incomplete, the world is still "in the making" owing to the impact of human powers on the universe and the world. Therefore, inquiry into truth about this universe and world produces contingent and revisable claims that are convincing. And what we find convincing is assimilable to certain crucial claims we found convincing in the past.

> True ideas are those that we can assimilate, validate, corroborate and verify . . .
>   Truth *happens* to an idea, it *becomes* true, is *made* true by events. Its verity *is* in fact an event, a process: the process namely of its verifying itself, its veri-fication. Its validity is the process of its valid-ation.[64]

James's insight is that the process is human-all-too-human ("the trace of the human serpent is thus over everything").[65] This means not only that truth claims are fallible but also that they have *value* as truth claims primarily because they provoke human powers. For James, Truth is not a value-free notion independent of human interests, needs, or wants, but rather a value-laden one shot through with specific interests, needs, or wants.

> The possession of truth, so far from being here an end in itself, is only a preliminary means toward other vital satisfactions . . . true is the name for whatever idea starts the verification-process, useful is the name for its completed function in experience. True ideas would never have been singled out as such, would never have acquired a class-name, least of all a name suggesting value, unless they had been useful from the outset in this way.[66]

James's pragmatic theory of truth affirms the basic Emersonian notion that powers are to be augmented by means of provocation for the purpose of the moral development of human personalities. Furthermore, his conception of truth—a human "truth" for us—is partly shaped by the cultural predicament of his reformist and professional middle-class constituency caught between the old and the new, the familiar and the novel. Philosophically speaking, his viewpoint is radical; its cultural cues are conservative; and it is put to the service of enhancing individuals.

> A new opinion counts as "true" just in proportion as it gratifies the individual's desire to assimilate the novel in his experience to his beliefs in stock. It must both lean on old truth and grasp new fact; and its success (as I said a moment ago) in doing this, is a matter for the individual's appreciation. When old truth grows, then, by new truth's addition, it is for subjective reasons. We are in the process and obey the reasons . . . That new idea is truest which performs most felicitously its function of satisfying our double urgency.

> Pragmatism gets her general notion of truth as something essentially bound up with the way in which one moment in our experience may lead us towards other moments which it will be worth while to have been led to. Primarily, and on the common-sense level, the truth of a state of mind means this function of *a leading that is worth while*.[67]

James's claim that whatever the verification process leads to will be worthwhile is but a statement of his Emersonian faith that powers which feed on provocation enhance personalities. For James, the problem is not the deleterious ends this process may lead to, but rather "our powers . . . [and] . . . our means of unlocking them or getting at them."[68]

For James, truth itself is, in part, an instrument—prompted by provocation, promoted by melioristic faith, and deployed by strenuous heroic persons against obstacles in order to further the moral development of individuals. In this sense, James's conception of truth is inseparable from— though in no way reducible to or identical with—the cultural situation of his class and his own personal struggle against neurasthenia and "the easy-going mood." Thus, truth is a species of the good.[69] In fact, James's own defense of religion—though it is religion of an unorthodox and idiosyncratic type as displayed in *The Varieties of Religious Experience* (1902)—rests not on his pandering to middle-class pieties but rather on his view that religion generates human heroic energies and facilitates personal struggle in the world.

> The capacity of the strenuous mood lies so deep down among our natural human possibilities that even if there were no metaphysical or traditional grounds for believing in a God, men would postulate one simply as a pretext for living hard, and getting out of the game of existence its keenest possibilities of zest. Our attitude towards concrete evils is entirely different in a world where we believe there are none but finite demanders, from what it is in one where we joyously face tragedy for an infinite demander's sake. Every sort of energy and endurance, of courage and capacity for handling life's evils, is set free in those who have religious faith. For this reason the strenuous type of character will on the battlefield of human history always outwear the easy-going type, and religion will drive irreligion to the wall.[70]

Santayana indeed is insightful when he writes that James "did not really believe; he merely believed in the right of believing that you might be right if you believed"[71] – but Santayana is not right. James did believe – in a finite god, for example – though his authentic faith was an Emersonian apotheosis of human will and struggle.

My social reading of James's pragmatic theory of truth avoids the common misunderstandings of it. This theory is not a recapitulation of subjectivism or positivism (or their flip side, skepticism), for it rejects all forms of epistemological foundationalism yet preserves a realist ontology. It is not a crude appeal to action in that new ideas made true must fit with previous ideas. This fit is related to but in no way reducible to action.

James's theory of truth is not simply an explanation of how we arrive at truth; it also provides an account of what truth is. This account locates truth at the end of a verifying process, though it remains contingent and revisable. To be in time means to be in pursuit of new and basic truths; any truth is subject to change though the best available truths are warranted and acceptable. Last, James's notion of truth is neither antitheoretical nor anti-intellectual – it simply rejects the positions of theoreticism and intellectualism. Its stress on the distinctively concrete, particular, and effective – as opposed to the abstract, general, and vague – includes ideas, concepts, and theories. It simply devalues the inert, prolix, arcane, and unclear in both theory and practice.[72]

James's pragmatic theory of truth, though far less rigorously worked out than that of Peirce, is a serious American intervention into the international philosophical conversation. The major impact of this theory is to shift talk about truth to talk about knowledge, and talk about knowledge to talk about the achievements of human powers and practices. Therefore James retains a correspondence theory of truth, yet it is rather innocuous in that rational acceptability is the test for truth claims we accept. In short, James demotes truth without eliminating it; he temporalizes knowledge and links it to human satisfaction and success. At times, it seems he is confusing truth with justification or ontological claims with epistemic ones. This seems so principally because truth and ontology have so little work to do in James's pragmatism; that is, they principally are explained in terms of justification and epistemology, but not explained away. At other times, James's popular terms like the "cash-values" of an idea or the "expediency" of a concept suggest a vulgar practicalism or narrow utilitarianism. This is so simply because James accents the active and dynamic character of truth-achieving against the abstract and passive versions of rationalism of his day. As we noted earlier, James is a bourgeois individualist, but he is no bourgeois philistine; he rejects the possessive individualism of America at the turn of the century.

With James, American pragmatism sees the light of day. Grounded in the Emersonian evasion and theodicy, and initiated by the genius of Charles Peirce, American pragmatism finds its popularizer and proselytizer in William James. And in many ways, James embodies the tensions of pragmatism in its early stages: a professional scornful of professionalism, a mediator fascinated with the extreme and the eccentric, a moralist skeptical of politics, a trained doctor mindful of the limited scope of science, an individualist and patriot critical of American egoism and jingoism — and last, a pragmatist, proud of the honorific status "philosopher" in an age of academic titles, yet convinced that philosophy is a "virulent disease" allied "with a feverish personal ambition," an Emersonian ambition to "settle the universe's hash" yet not "ruffle its majesty."[73] What George Santayana writes of James could be said of Emerson, though less of Peirce:

> There is a sense in which James was not a philosopher at all. He once said to me: "What a curse philosophy would be if we couldn't forget all about it!" In other words, philosophy was not to him what it has been to so many, a consolation and sanctuary in a life which would have been unsatisfying without it. It would be incongruous, therefore, to expect of him that he should build a philosophy like an edifice to go and live in for good. Philosophy to him was rather like a maze in which he happened to find himself wandering, and what he was looking for was the way out.[74]

The Coming-of-Age
of American Pragmatism:
John Dewey

The endeavor to democratize the idea of God goes hand in hand with
pragmatism, and both arise out of the spirit of "This, Here, and Soon."

— *Johan Huizinga*

American pragmatism reaches its highest level of sophisticated articulation
and engaged elaboration in the works and life of John Dewey. To put
it crudely, if Emerson is the American Vico, and James and Peirce our
John Stuart Mill and Immanuel Kant, then Dewey is the American Hegel
and Marx! On the surface, these farfetched comparisons reveal the poverty
of the American philosophical tradition, the paucity of intellectual world-
historical figures in the American grain. But on a deeper level, these comparisons disclose a distinctive feature of American pragmatism: its diversity circumscribed by the Emersonian evasion of epistemology-centered
philosophy and the Emersonian theodicy of the self and America.

John Dewey is the greatest of the American pragmatists because he
infuses an inherited Emersonian preoccupation with power, provocation,
and personality — permeated by voluntaristic, amelioristic, and activistic
themes — with the great discovery of nineteenth-century Europe: a mode of
historical consciousness that highlights the conditioned and circumstantial
character of human existence in terms of changing societies, cultures, and

communities. Dewey is the first American pragmatist who revises Emersonian motifs of contingency and revisability in the light of modern historical consciousness.[1]

For Emerson, history is a spatialized form of temporality awaiting occupation by a self that creates itself; hence, history is heroic autobiography. For James, history is an undifferentiated background against which heroic individuals fight and struggle. Similar to Emerson's, James's conception of the cosmos and nature celebrates plurality and mystery, yet in both of their views, history roughly amounts to temporal frontiers to be confronted and conquered by willful persons. For Peirce, history is an evolutionary process in need of human direction and communal guidance. He introduces a crucial social element that offsets the Emersonian and Jamesian individualisms. Yet this social element stresses the communal at the expense of the societal; that is, it takes seriously intermediate human associations and collectivities, but fails to consider the larger social structures, political systems, and economic institutions.

The grand breakthrough of Dewey is not only that he considers these larger structures, systems, and institutions, but also that he puts them at the center of his pragmatic thought without surrendering his allegiance to Emersonian and Jamesian concerns with individuality and personality. Like Hegel, Dewey views modern historical consciousness—awareness of the radical contingency and variability of human societies, cultures, and communities—as the watershed event in contemporary thought. To cross this Rubicon is to enter a new intellectual terrain—to shun old philosophic forms of dualism, absolutism, and transcendentalism and to put forward new social theoretic understandings of knowledge, power, wealth, and culture. Just as Marx conceives the *Aufhebung* of philosophy to be a social theory of society and history and of revolution and emancipation, so Dewey holds pragmatism to be a historical theory of critical intelligence and scientific inquiry and of reform and amelioration.

The privileged moral tropes in both Marx and Dewey are individuality, social freedom, and democracy. Yet Marx's vision and project are more ambitious than those of Dewey. This is so, in part, because as a more profound social theorist than Dewey, Marx sees and understands more clearly why and how early industrial capitalist conditions preclude individuality, social freedom, and democratic participation for the majority of the European and American populace. Furthermore, Marx theorizes from the vantage point of and in solidarity with the industrial working class of nineteenth-century Europe—an exploited, unfranchised, and downtrodden people—whereas Dewey writes from the vantage point of and in leadership over that rising professional fraction of the working class *and* managerial class that is in sympathy with and has some influence among an exploited yet franchised industrial working class in the United States.

True to the American pragmatic grain, Dewey rejects the metaphysical residues in Marx: the Hegelian-inspired penchant toward totalizing history, universalizing collectivities, and simplifying emancipation. These residues tend to overlook the vast complexities of history, the sheer heterogeneity of collectivities, and the various complications of emancipation. Therefore, for Dewey, Marxist perspectives (given his rather frail yet still noteworthy grasp of them)[2] tend toward premature totalities, and homogeneities that ignore uniqueness, difference, and diversity. Yet, like any other viewpoint, Marxisms have to be put to the tests of critical scrutiny, experimental consequences, and moral valuation. In the twenties (after his visit to Russia), Dewey celebrates the Soviet experiment in education, but by the mid-twenties he castigates Stalinism in quite harsh terms.[3] For Dewey, the march of freedom in history is embodied in the best of American democracy, and the march of America in history is to be viewed critically in light of the best of American democracy. He puts pragmatism on the international historical stage, yet he still views history through an American lens. In this way, Dewey—like Hegel and Marx—historicizes philosophy; and, like Emerson, James, and Peirce, Americanizes history.

In short, Dewey tries to take history seriously as he creatively revises the Emersonian evasion of modern philosophy, carefully affirms the Emersonian theodicy, and critically enriches the American pragmatic tradition. John Dewey is not only the giant of this tradition and *the* towering force in American philosophy; he is also the sifting funnel through which much of the best and some but little of the worst of American culture flow. As Horace Kallen noted in 1939, "As I see it, it will be Dewey, not Ford, not Edison, not Roosevelt, who, when the last word has been said and the last vote has been counted, will figure as the pregnant symbol of what is best in the America of today and most hopeful for the Americanism of tomorrow."[4]

Dewey on Historical Consciousness, Critical Intelligence, and Creative Democracy

John Dewey is the culmination of the tradition of American pragmatism. After him, to be a pragmatist is to be a social critic, literary critic, or a poet—in short, a participant in cultural criticism and cultural creation. This does not mean that Dewey provides panaceas for philosophical problems or solutions to societal crises. Rather, Dewey helps us see the complex and mediated ways in which philosophical problems are linked to societal crises. More important, Dewey enables us to view clashing conceptions of philosophy as struggles over cultural ways of life, as attempts to define the role and function of intellectual authorities in culture and society. For Dewey, to take modern historical consciousness seriously in philosophy is first and foremost to engage in metaphilosophical reflection, to reform and reconstruct philosophy as a mode of intellectual activity. To reform and reconstruct philosophy is both to demystify and to defend the most reliable mode of inquiry in modern culture, namely, critical intelligence best manifest in the community of scientists. And to demystify and defend critical intelligence is to render it more and more serviceable for the enhancement of human individuality, that is, the promotion of human beings who better control their conditions and thereby more fully create themselves (i.e., advance creative democracy).

Dewey's fundamental concerns with the metaphilosophical implications of modern historical consciousness, the cultural ramifications of demystifying and defending critical intelligence, and the political consequences of expanding creative democracy are put forward in his poignant and poetic panegyric to Ralph Waldo Emerson. In this unusual Dewey essay, his typical bland sentences become lively sparks of expression; his glib formulations, vivacious evocations; his flat logical constructions, dancing, staccato metaphors and tropes. Like James and Peirce, Dewey could not avoid or candidly jettison Emerson. Like James—though unlike Peirce—Dewey implicitly acknowledges and explicitly celebrates his own debts to Emerson. In fact, his brief essay on Emerson is, surprisingly, far more insightful and revealing than the more renowned sharp treatments by William James, George Santayana, Robert Frost, and Maurice Maeterlinck (with whom Dewey fully agrees in regarding Emerson as "the sage of ordinary days").[5]

Dewey begins the Emerson essay on a metaphilosophical note.

> It is said that Emerson is not a philosopher. I find this denegation false or true according as it is said in blame or praise—according to the reasons proffered. When the critic writes of lack of method, of the absence of continuity, of coherent logic, and, with the old story of the string of pearls loosely strung, puts Emerson away as a writer of maxims and proverbs, a recorder of brilliant insights and abrupt aphorisms, the critic, to my mind, but writes down his own incapacity to follow a logic that is very finely wrought.[6]

The problem with "the critic"—or those who quickly dismiss Emerson as mere stylist and recorder—is that they look for a method separate from the lives and practices of human beings. They need a set of propositions or algorithms "separately propounded" from people's intuitions and judgments. Dewey then unequivocally—and maybe exorbitantly—states:

> I am not acquainted with any writer, no matter how assured his position in treatises upon the history of philosophy, whose movement of thought is more compact and unified, nor one who combines more adequately diversity of intellectual attack with concentration of form and effect.[7]

Of course, Plato, Montaigne, Pascal, and Nietzsche immediately come to mind as competitors here (to say the least!). But Dewey's aim is not really to "rank" Emerson as the greatest X or Y, but rather to force philosophers to take Emerson seriously as a challenge to their narrow conceptions of philosophy, conceptions that encourage them to devalue and debunk the Emersons of *modern* philosophical discourse. Dewey is claiming not that Emerson is first and foremost a philosopher but rather that Emerson's evasion of philosophy has deep metaphilosophical implications.

> Perhaps those are nearer right, however, who deny that Emerson is a philosopher, because he is more than a philosopher. He would work, he says, by art, not by metaphysics, finding truth "in the sonnet and the play." "I am," to quote him again, "in all my theories, ethics and politics, a poet"; and we may, I think, safely take his word for it that he meant to be a maker rather than a reflector. His own preference was to be ranked with the seers rather than with the reasoners of the race, for he says, "I think that philosophy is still rude and elementary; it will one day be taught by poets."[8]

Dewey understands Emerson's evasion of modern philosophy as neither a simple replacement of philosophy by poetry nor a sophomoric rekindling of the Platonic quarrel between poetry and philosophy. Instead, this evasion is to be understood as a situating of philosophical reflection *and* poetic creation in the midst of quotidian human struggles for meaning, status, power, wealth, and selfhood. The abstract dualisms, philosophic absolutisms, autonomous discourses, professional divisions, and academic differentiations are veiled efforts to escape from these struggles—efforts doomed to failure. The Emersonian evasion not only resituates these escapes within the contingent and revisable dynamics of power, provocation, and personality; it also views poetry and philosophy neither as identical nor as antagonistic but as different metaphor-deploying activities to achieve—by means of agon and struggle—specific aims. And what poetry and philosophy have in common is that both exemplify the heights of human intelligence at work, the best of conscious and reflective human activity.

> The spirit of Emerson rises to protest against exaggerating his ultimate value by trying to place him upon a plane of art higher than a philosophic platform. Literary critics admit his philosophy and deny his literature. And if philosophers extol his keen, calm art and speak with some depreciation of his metaphysic, it also is perhaps because Emerson knew something deeper than our conventional definitions . . . Looked at in the open, our fences between literature and metaphysics appear petty—signs of an attempt to affix the legalities and formalities of property to the things of the spirit . . .
>
> And for Emerson of all others, there is a one-sidedness and exaggeration, which he would have been the first to scorn, in exalting overmuch his creative substance at the expense of his reflective procedure. He says in effect somewhere that the individual man is only a method, a plan of arrangement. The saying is amply descriptive of Emerson. His idealism

is the faith of the thinker in his thought raised to its *n*th power . . . There
are times, indeed, when one is inclined to regard Emerson's whole work
as a hymn to intelligence, a paean to the all-creating, all-disturbing power
of thought.[9]

Dewey is well aware of the various characterizations of Emerson (and
pragmatism) as anti-intellectual, irrational, and vitalistic: and neither
Emerson nor the pragmatists make a fetish of reason. But they also do
not reject the intellect per se. Rather they view it as a distinctive function of and inseparable from the doings, sufferings, and strivings of everyday people. Dewey prefers "the word *intelligence* to *reason* because of the
long anti-empirical history back of the latter word."[10] And he praises
Emerson for his transactional concept of intelligence, a conception which
views mind as both a form of experience and a facilitator in experience.
For Dewey, Emerson goes beyond the paltry ideas of experience in Locke,
Berkeley, and Hume in that he views experience in terms of relations and
interactions. There is an immediacy in this notion of experience, an
immediacy that has little to do with vivacious mentalistic episodes or
indubitable modes of awareness. Rather it is associated with the present,
novelty, use, and projected futures.

> And so, with an expiatory offering to the Manes of Emerson, one may
> proceed to characterize his thought, his method, yea, even his system.
> I find it in the fact that he takes the distinctions and classifications which
> to most philosophers are true in and of and because of their systems,
> and makes them true of life, of the common experience of the everyday
> man . . . The idealism which is a thing of the academic intellect to the
> professor, a hope to the generous youth, an inspiration to the genial
> projector, is to Emerson a narrowly accurate description of the facts of
> the most real world in which all earn their living.
>
> Such reference to the immediate life is the text by which he tries
> every philosopher . . . I fancy he reads the so-called eclecticism of Emer-
> son wrongly who does not see that it is reduction of all the philosophers
> of the race, even the prophets like Plato and Proclus whom Emerson holds
> most dear, to the test of trial by the service rendered the present and
> immediate experience. As for those who condemn Emerson for superficial
> pedantry because of the strings of names he is wont to flash like beads
> before our eyes, they but voice their own pedantry, not seeing, in their
> literalness, that all such things are with Emerson symbols of various uses
> administered to the common soul.[11]

This passage reveals Dewey's own creative misreading of Emerson, even
though it does highlight the experiential dimension of Emerson. More tellingly, the defensive and even apologetic tone shows just how desperate and
determined Dewey is to convince his audience that a figure like Emerson is
not alien to his own pragmatic perspective and project. We noted earlier
Emerson's ambivalence toward the common folk and their experiences;

we also saw the contemplative and mystical aspects of Emerson, reminiscent more of Plato's Seventh Letter and Plotinus than of Dewey and
the pragmatists. Yet Dewey presses on—with his strong insights and obvious
blindnesses—to picture Emerson as not only a proponent of critical
intelligence but also a poet of the ever-changing present. Dewey candidly
acknowledges—though only implicitly—that Emerson's Heraclitean flux
is far from modern historical consciousness. Yet the Emersonian themes
of contingency and revisability are healthy swerves from the ossified concepts and petrified systems of so many European philosophers and Emerson's own American contemporaries.

> The Idea is no longer either an academic toy nor even a gleam of poetry,
> but a literal report of the experience of the hour as that is enriched and
> reinforced for the individual through the tale of history, the appliance
> of silence, the gossip of conversation and the exchange of commerce . . .
>   Emerson's philosophy has this in common with that of the tran-
> scendentalists; he prefers to borrow from them rather than from others
> certain pigments and delineations. But he finds truth in the highway,
> in the untaught endeavor, the unexpected idea, and this removes him
> from their remotenesses. His ideas are not fixed upon any Reality that
> is beyond or behind or in any way apart, and hence they do not have
> to be bent. They are versions of the Here and the Now, and flow freely.
> The reputed transcendental worth of an overweening Beyond and Away,
> Emerson, jealous for spiritual democracy, finds to be the possession of
> the unquestionable Present. When Emerson, speaking of the chronology
> of history, designated the There and Then as "wild, savage, and pre-
> posterous," he also drew the line which marks him off from transcenden-
> talism—which is the idealism of a Class.[12]

The last sentence of this passage inaugurates Dewey's misleading yet
master stroke in his essay: the designation of Emerson as "the philosopher
of democracy."[13] Dewey rightly construes Emerson's conception of history
in spatial terms, but he wrongly views this conception as somehow transcending Emerson's class. In fact, class is not the issue here, but rather
the power and pervasiveness of the frontier myth that permeates all classes
in America—especially in Emerson's day. His "pioneer" consciousness is
neither the sole possession of the common man nor a perspective opposed
by alienated middle-class intellectuals like the transcendentalists. Rather
the Emersonian spatialized image of history fit well with the internal
imperialism taking place despite Emerson's moral protests. Dewey's attempt
to read Emerson in his own image remains incisive and revealing, but
it fails at the point where Emerson emerges as somehow transcending his
class and becomes an exemplary radical plebeian democrat in solidarity
with peoples struggling against imperialisms. Emerson is indeed a kind
of spiritual democrat (circumscribed by his "mild" racism); but he surely
is no full-fledged democrat like Dewey himself. Yet Dewey strains to see

his own "creative democracy" in Emerson's refusal to privilege authority.[14] In this way, he not only authorizes his own project by deploying Emerson as authority, but also uses Emerson as a means of provoking his own self-creation—thereby valorizing a father figure in order to father himself. This Emersonian manner of reading Emerson reveals as much about Dewey's pragmatism as does the obvious continuity of similar themes from Emerson, through Peirce and James, to Dewey.

> Against creed and system, convention and institution, Emerson stands for restoring to the common man that which in the name of religion, of philosophy, of art, and of morality, has been embezzled from the common store and appropriated to sectarian and class use. Beyond any one we know of, Emerson has comprehended and declared how such malversation makes truth decline from its simplicity, and in becoming partial and owned, become a puzzle of and trick for theologian, metaphysician and litterateur—a puzzle of an imposed law, of an unwished for and refused goodness, of a romantic ideal gleaming only from afar, and a trick of manipular skill, of specializing performance.
>
> For such reasons, the coming century may well make evident what is just now dawning that Emerson is not only a philosopher, but that he is the Philosopher of Democracy . . . thinking of Emerson as the one citizen of the world fit to have his name uttered in the same breath with that of Plato, one may without presumption believe that even if Emerson has no system, none the less he is the prophet and herald of any system which democracy may henceforth construct and hold by, and that when democracy has articulated itself, it will have no difficulty in finding itself already proposed in Emerson.[15]

This exorbitant enshrinement of Emerson is an apt description of Dewey—one of the best we have. For Dewey, Emerson signifies what Dewey himself actually tried to do. Dewey views Emerson as the founder and inventor of the American religion—of the Emersonian evasion, theodicy, and refusal—yet he delineates his own project as the authentic content and substance of it. In this way, Dewey implicitly rejects Henry James, Sr.'s, view of Emerson as John the Baptist, with an American messiah yet to come. Instead, Dewey plays Joshua to Emerson's Moses, with Peirce a groundbreaking yet forgotten Aaron and James a brilliant and iconoclastic Eleazar.

Following Emerson, Dewey envisions the emerging reformist and professional elements of the middle class as the preferable historical agent of the American religion. Yet mere Emersonian breaks with ecclesiastical authorities and independent lecturing tours would not suffice in the Gilded Age and thereafter. Instead, Dewey participates in and exercises moral and intellectual leadership over the rising university culture and teaching profession. As an organic intellectual of the urbanized, professional, and reformist elements of the middle class, Dewey had far more immediate impact on society than Emerson, Peirce, or James.

The changing circumstances of the country during Dewey's lifetime partly account for this impact. Dewey was born on October 20, 1859, the day after the abolitionist John Brown was taken to jail for his famous raid on the federal arsenal at Harper's Ferry, Virginia; Dewey died during the Korean War—at seven o'clock on June 1, 1952.[16] During his long life span, America was transformed from a divided, rural, entrepreneurial capitalist country into a consolidated, urban, industrial, multinational capitalist world power. At his death, the United States was the most wealthy and mighty nation in the world. He was born and raised in Burlington, Vermont, a small yet growing town (second largest lumber depot in the United States) with a suffering Irish and French-Canadian working class (over 40 percent of the populace in 1870) and a Yankee bourgeoisie. His father, Archibald, was the first urban entrepreneur in a family of four generations on the farm. Clever, humorous, yet unambitious, Dewey's father was a patriot who reached his stride in life only after he volunteered for the Union army in 1861. Stationed in Virginia, Archibald served with valor. After three years, his wife, Lucina—twenty years younger than Archibald and a descendant of famous Vermont statesmen (her father a state legislator, and her grandfather a U.S. congressman)—brought Dewey and his two brothers to Virginia. They returned to Vermont in 1867. Owing to his mother's religious piety as well as that of his minister, Lewis Ormond Brastow, Dewey was bred a liberal, evangelical Congregationalist.[17] He would not break with the church until he was nearly thirty years old; the reformist energies encouraged by the church would never leave him.

At the age of fifteen Dewey entered the University of Vermont—a solid and small college of eight faculty and less than a hundred students. He graduated in a class of eighteen with a mediocre record and limited exposure to the new intellectual developments: T. H. Huxley, Auguste Comte, and Herbert Spencer. After a two-year high school teaching stint in Oil City, Pennsylvania, and a year near Burlington, Dewey embarked upon a professional career in philosophy. Encouraged by William T. Harris, the renowned St. Louis Hegelian who edited the *Journal of Speculative Philosophy* in which Dewey had published his first article, and supported by a loan from his aunt, Dewey enrolled in the first American secular institution of graduate studies, Johns Hopkins University in Baltimore in 1882.

Ironically, Dewey gravitated not toward Charles Sanders Peirce, then a visiting lecturer at Hopkins, but rather to the neo-Hegelian George Sylvester Morris and the experimentalist psychologist G. Stanley Hall. Both Vermonters, evangelicals in early life who attended Union Theological Seminary and German universities, Morris and Hall competed for Dewey's loyalty and outlook. Dewey's early exposure to German philosophy, principally owing to his undergraduate teacher, Henry A. P. Torrey, inclined him toward Morris. Hall, who was a disciple of Wilhelm Wundt's physiological psychology and gained the first U.S. doctorate in psychology under William James at Harvard, attracted Dewey with his scientific approach. Yet Morris won him over with a right Hegelian defense of theism and idealism. Moreover, the works of an American Protestant theologian, Newman Smith, held out the possibility of synthesizing Hall's scientific empiricism and Morris's Hegelian idealism by means of an evolutionary biology shot through with moral teleological and theistic conclusions.[18] After finishing his dissertation in 1884 on Kant's psychology (now lost), Dewey was invited by Morris to join him at the University of Michigan in Ann Arbor. Here Dewey was to teach courses primarily in psychology and a few in the history of philosophy and ethics. In his first major book, *Psychology* (1887), Dewey's Hegelianism was heavy-handed and unconvincing to the leading psychologists of the day—especially to G. Stanley Hall and William James.[19] Yet the book showed great skills and gave him international exposure. It was written as a textbook for classroom instruction and served this end quite well.

Dewey left for the University of Minnesota in 1888 but returned to Michigan upon the untimely death of his mentor, Morris. This return signaled not only a greater freedom in teaching but a shift in focus— from psychology to ethics. This shift was prompted by two new critical influences: the works of the neo-Hegelian liberal T. H. Green and Dewey's marriage to Alice Chipman. In an important essay, "The Ethics of Democracy" (1888), Dewey used Green's original conception of society, defense of self-realization, and support for democracy as the primary resource against Sir Henry Maine's influential attack on democracy in his *Popular Government* (1886). Green enabled Dewey to make explicit the moral teleology required by his psychology—and to support his growing democratic political convictions.

This increased sense of political engagement was largely due to Alice Chipman, Dewey's philosophy student at Michigan and wife. Raised by her maternal grandparents upon the early death of her parents, Alice acquired a strong social conscience and fervent political activism. Her grandfather, Frederick Riggs, was an adopted member of the Chippewa tribe ("learned their language so that an Indian could not tell by his voice that he was a white man")[20] and worked with them in their efforts to get justice from white people. Alice was a month older than Dewey, having studied music at a Baptist seminary and taught in Michigan schools before enrolling at the university. She and Dewey lived in the same boarding house. She took three advanced courses with Dewey, and must have impressed the young aloof bachelor. They were married two years later in July 1886.

Not only did Alice encourage Dewey's social activism by her example, but her deep belief "that a religious attitude was indigenous in natural experience and that theology and ecclesiastical institutions had benumbed rather than promoted it"[21] had great impact on Dewey. For example, in his various addresses to the student Christian association and in his energetic work in Ann Arbor's First Congregational Church, Dewey had stressed that the church was "the highest product of the interest of man in man."[22] Yet a few years after his marriage, he held that the role of the church was to universalize itself and pass out of existence. By 1894, Dewey had stopped attending church and refused to send his three children to Sunday school—much to the chagrin of his pietistic mother who was then living with him. In short, Alice opened Dewey's eyes to the social misery in industrial capitalist America. And there indeed was much to see and do.

Between 1860 and 1900 the population of the United States leapt from roughly 31 million to nearly 76 million.[23] Immigrants—mainly from southern and eastern Europe—accounted for some 14 million in this rapid growth. This population explosion resulted primarily from the tremendous economic boom in late-nineteenth-century America. In the same forty-year period, investments in manufacturing plants jumped from a billion dollars to $12 billion; the annual value of manufacturing products from $1.9 billion to over $11 billion; and the number of workers employed in U.S. factories from 1.3 million to 5.5 million. With an apparently inexhaustible supply of raw materials, a friendly and receptive national government, a great domestic market guarded against foreign competition by tariffs and connected by rail and water transportation, remarkable technological innovation and effective subordination of cheap labor, America became the first manufacturing nation of the world.

The distinctive features of this economic growth were large-scale organizations (especially monopolies, trusts, pools, and holding companies in production) motivated by unregulated and unrestrained competition for unprecedented profits; the development of a downtrodden and despised industrial working class of different ethnic origins and religious loyalties; and intense, often bloody strife between profit-making industrialists and profit-producing laborers. In short, America underwent boomtown industrial class formation with the rise of the large-scale industrial and financial capitalists and the eclipse of the old southern planters and northeastern merchants; the managerial and professional sectors of the middle class replaced the commercial and yeoman groupings of the past petite bourgeoisie; and the industrial proletariat edged out the artisans and journeymen. Rural America certainly did not disappear, but it no longer was where the central action occurred. In 1860 agriculture represented 50 percent of the total national wealth, in 1900 only 20 percent; farmers received 30 percent of the national income in 1860, only 18 percent in 1910. And the South, still on the margins of much of this growth, lingered in colonial subjugation as white supremacy reigned supreme over helpless though far from hopeless Afro-Americans.[24]

The social misery upon which Dewey opened his eyes in the late nineteenth century was principally that of economic deprivation, cultural dislocation, and personal disorientation. Although real wages increased in this period of falling prices and consequent decline in the cost of living, panics, depressions, and economic turndowns often punctuated the wage increases. Roughly 10 million Americans out of 76 million lived in abject poverty. The average workday was ten hours, for a six-day week, with an absolutely appalling accident rate. For example, one in every 26 railroad laborers was injured, one in every 399 killed annually. Unskilled and semi-skilled laborers were crowded into squalid slums where families huddled in one-room apartments with inadequate sanitary facilities. Epidemics killed thousands. And with little public monies and little concern with the common good, most cities lacked funds to dispose of their sewage and garbage, to ensure the purity of their water supply, and to fight deadly fires. In short, industrial capitalist America was a "distended" society – a society without a core, a society unhinged, a nation in a pathological state.[25]

Dewey's response to this situation took three major forms. First, he contemplated and almost executed a plan to "sell critical intelligence" to the literate masses by means of radical journalism. Second, he became associated with WASP-run humanitarian efforts to assimilate and acculturate immigrants into the American mainstream. Third, he decided to exercise leadership over the expanding teaching profession by means of practical example and writing.

Dewey's first response was shaped by his own growing disenchantment with American life. Politically awakened by Alice and intellectually influenced by T. H. Green, Dewey was ideologically guided by his friend and classmate Henry Carter Adams. Adams studied political economy at Hopkins and was awarded the university's first Ph.D. in 1876. After studying for a year in Germany, Adams returned an unorthodox socialist intent on building on aspects of American liberalism. In an 1881 essay in the *New Englander* entitled "Democracy," Adams argued for a cooperative commonwealth of workers' control that would "realize socialistic aims by individualistic means." He went on to call for the abandonment of the wage system and the establishment of industries upon a cooperative basis. These radical sentiments made it extremely difficult for Adams to obtain a job in the academy. For instance, his public support for the Knights of Labor led to his dismissal from Cornell University – a dismissal led by the trustee Russell Sage. Adams finally did get a permanent position at Michigan but only after President James B. Angell severely questioned his political views including his "unwise" support of the Knights.

Adams' guidance can be seen in Dewey's 1888 essay "The Ethics of Democracy" when he states, "There is no need to beat about the bush in saying that democracy is not in reality what it is in name until it is industrial, as well as civil and political . . . ; a democracy of wealth is a necessity."[26] Yet Dewey is much more cautious than Adams; that is, he is unwilling to risk his professional career for his political beliefs.

This is seen most clearly in Dewey's first major effort to intervene into politics: the journalistic *Thought News* affair with the iconoclastic Franklin Ford. Stimulated by Ernest Renan's notion of socializing intelligence and distributing scientific results as put forward in *The Future of Science* (1880),[27] Dewey and Ford decided to plunge into the world of journalism. What was needed was a newspaper that would provide the enlightenment requisite for intelligent social action. It would not be directed at any one class nor would it raise "the war cry of a false socialism," but rather, as Dewey stated, it would "show that philosophy has some use . . . Instead of trying to change the newspaper business by introducing philosophy into it, the idea is to transform philosophy somewhat by introducing a little newspaper business into it."[28]

Dewey's prospective editorship of *Thought News* excited and stimulated him. He concluded that he lived in a world-historical period in which one must struggle to fulfill the promise of the "modern Zeitgeist." It was during this time that Dewey's two books on ethics appeared[29] — responsive to Ford's Renanian viewpoint, William James's *Principles of Psychology* (1890), and the social psychology (and socialist sentiments) of his new colleague George Herbert Mead. These texts reveal a new departure for Dewey: the practical character of reflective intelligence looms large. William James, who had been thoroughly disappointed in Dewey's earlier *Psychology*, was one of the few to see this.[30]

Yet preparation for the appearance of *Thought News* consumed Dewey's time. His scholarly production sagged; his writing became more hard-hitting, bold, and hortatory. He had to muster the courage to go through with a project that would surely have deleterious consequences for his professional career. As he confided to a former student, "These things would sound more or less crazy to a professor of philosophy in good and regular standing, but I intend henceforth to act on my conviction regardless."[31]

In his two major publications at this time, neither of which is scholarly, Dewey's passionate rhetoric and activistic fervor echo that of the young left Hegelian Marx. In his commencement address entitled "Poetry and Philosophy" delivered at Smith College, Dewey proclaimed,

> In the last few centuries the onward movement of life, of experience, has been so rapid, its diversifications of regions and methods so wide, that it has outrun the slower step of reflective thought. Philosophy has not as yet caught the rhythmic swing of this onward movement, and written it down in a score of black and white which all may read . . . But this movement, which has so escaped the surer yet heavier tread of critical thought, has in manifold ways danced itself into the poetic measures of our century . . .
> . . . the same movement of the spirit, bringing man and man, man and nature into wider and closer unity, which has found expression

by anticipation in poetry, must find expression by retrospection in philosophy.[32]

And in his contribution to the *Inlander*, a Michigan student magazine, entitled "The Scholastic and the Speculator," Dewey castigated the ivory-tower scholar frightened by the dirty world of politics and afraid of the consequences of active engagement. Aware of what his colleagues thought of his journalistic endeavor and political involvement, Dewey used harsh language to debunk his profession as a remake of medieval scholasticism.

> The monastic cell has become a professional lecture hall; an endless mass of "authorities" have taken the place of Aristotle. *Jahresberichte*, monographs, journals without end occupy the void left by the commentators upon Aristotle. If the older Scholastic spent his laborious time in erasing the writing from old manuscripts in order to indite thereon something of his own, the new scholastic has also his palimpsest. He criticizes the criticisms with which some other Scholastic has criticized other criticisms, and the writing upon writings goes on till the substructure of reality is long obscured.[33]

What was needed was not academic complacency but active engagement with the events and affairs of the world. In short, Dewey wanted a worldly philosophy and a more philosophical world, i.e., a world guided by intelligence. His rhetorical figure of the speculator – a market metaphor more pronounced than James's "cash-values" – was that of a philosopher who refuses to hoard his fund of knowledge and who takes risks owing to his political action in the world.

> Intelligence must throw its fund out again into the stress of life; it must venture its savings against the pressure of facts . . .
>   . . . all the great philosophers have had something of this ruthless adventure of thought, this reckless throwing of the accumulated store of truth . . . Action upon truth marks the merchant of thought, who, though he both saves and spends, yet neither embezzles nor gambles.[34]

As the deadline for the first issue neared, Dewey and Ford – along with Ford's brother, Corydon, and the young Robert Park (later to be a leading U.S. sociologist at the University of Chicago) – put out a circular announcing the newspaper. To Dewey's surprise, Ford published another announcement a few weeks later lauding "a new idea in journalism and education" that would, "by applying the historical method to the reporting of everyday life," bridge "the chasm between education and real life, between theory and practice."[35] This manifesto-like statement caught Dewey off guard; and the response of the daily press gave him cold feet. A lead editorial in the *Detroit Tribune* lashed out at the putdown of ordinary newspapers. Dewey was lampooned as the new Benjamin Franklin, with *Thought News* the "kite" with which "he proposes to bring philosophy down to life and make it, like the lightning, turn the wheels of society." It later suggested that the first "mystery within the social organism" Dewey and company should try to solve was the interest of Michigan male students in Ypsilanti factory girls. In an article headlined "He's Planned No Revolution," Dewey recanted, backpedaled, and disassociated himself from *Thought News*. No issue of the newspaper ever appeared.

In his autobiography two years later, Corydon Ford put the matter this way regarding Dewey:

> Clogged of the dead institution, he could not move; his salary meant that he was to keep quiet as to the overturning concepts. He must either forego his bribe and become the tramp upon the highway that he might have voice; or he could remain to take the sop of convention and upstew the old ideas with the new as the made-dish of apart theory.[36]

Needless to say, this characterization of Dewey is unfair. Ford did break trust by failing to inform Dewey of his announcement, though, in all candor, Ford's statement was not that far removed from Dewey's initial intention. What becomes most clear—and is quite understandable—is Dewey's refusal to risk his career (especially with an eccentric chap like Ford) or to be marginalized or even banished by the professional elements of the middle class. Instead, he would work with those reformers of his class serious about social change while preserving his own professional status and prowess.

Dewey's second response to the deplorable state of industrial capitalist America took the form of securing a prestigious position in an urban environment, then joining forces with middle-class progressives and radicals forming links with the downtrodden. He moved in 1894 to John D. Rockefeller's University of Chicago (a move engineered by his friend and former colleague James H. Tufts), where his work in Jane Addams' Hull House became a focus of his activity. From then on, Dewey practiced professional caution and political reticence. He remained deeply engaged in civic affairs, but shunned controversy. As George Dykhuizen notes, Dewey failed to

> touch upon any of the explosive issues of the day in any published article while at Chicago. Nothing among Dewey's writings at this time is analogous to Thorstein Veblen's *The Theory of the Leisure Class*, Charles Zueblin's *American Municipal Progress*, or to articles by Albion Small, Edward W. Bemis and W. I. Thomas which discuss vital and controversial issues. The closest Dewey came to a published statement about a social issue was his remark that the school is "the primary and most effective instrument of social progress and reform."[37]

I am suggesting neither that opportunism motivated Dewey's behavior in Chicago, nor that he lacked the courage of other colleagues. Rather I am claiming that his highfalutin left-Hegelian rhetoric of a few years earlier had simmered back down into professional research and respectable civic activism. This was so not only because he was slowly but surely shedding his neo-Hegelianism—as his famous 1896 essay "The Reflex Arc Concept in Psychology" reveals—but also because his left sentiments devolved into public progressive sentiments. At Hull House, Dewey had the opportunity to meet a number of socialists, communists, and anarchists, and he preferred bourgeois progressives like Jane Addams and Henry George. He remained committed yet directed his energies into middle-class channels, especially education.

Dewey's third response to industrial capitalist America, now that he was living in the exemplary city of a changing country, was to invest and involve himself in the new emerging structure of loyalty in the middle class: professionalism. Dewey was quite critical of various aspects of the rising professionalism; yet he remained its proponent and promoter. He was convinced that the only way in which America could acquire a core and cohesion was by producing and cultivating critical intelligence by experts. As head of the Department of Pedagogy (and Philosophy), he could focus on education, especially of children. As a professor, he could focus on his colleagues, i.e., occupational autonomy. The professional middle class was growing by leaps and bounds—with teachers increasing more than fourfold between 1890 and 1910 and then more than doubling again in the next decade.[38]

Dewey's shift to pedagogical practices was not a retreat from politics. Rather it proceeded from an acknowledgment of just how entrenched economic power was in America—seen quite clearly in the Pullman strike of 1894—and how circumscribed progressive action actually was. Moreover, Chicago's school system was a national scandal as revealed by Joseph Mayer Rice's muckraking pieces in the *Forum* (1892, 1893). After working with and supporting the renowned Colonel Francis Parker's Cook County Normal School, including sending his kids there, Dewey emerged as the leading progressive pedagogue in the city. His laboratory school, known as the "Dewey School," opened in January 1896.

The aim of the school was not only to serve as a model of how meaningful and enriching education could take place, but also to make a practical intervention into the national debate on education. This practical intervention was, for Dewey, a form of political activism in that the struggle over knowledge and over the means of its disposal was a struggle about power, about the conditions under which cultural capital (skills, knowledge, values) was produced, distributed, and consumed. In sharp contrast to curriculum-centered conservatives and child-centered romantics, Dewey advocated an interactive model of functionalistic education that combined autonomy with intelligent and flexible guidance, relevance with rigor and wonder. Of course, Dewey's functionalistic education, a critical education for democratizing society, could easily be mistaken for a functional education, a fitting education that simply adjusts one to the labor market possibilities.

Unfortunately, Dewey himself failed to articulate a plan for social reform to which his progressive schools could specifically contribute. He was aware that schools by themselves could not bear the weight of a full-fledged reform of society; yet he also knew that the schools themselves were ideologically contested terrain, always worth fighting for and over. And in 1904 Dewey's school came to an end after a series of mergers and the subtle dismissal of Dewey's wife from its principalship by University of Chicago president William Rainey Harper. Dewey immediately resigned from the university. Luckily, Columbia University moved quickly and financed a new chair in philosophy for him. And the luck was American pragmatism's too, for it was in New York City, and maybe it had to be there, that Dewey emerged as a world-historical figure. At Columbia, Dewey put forward his mature formulations of the impact of historical consciousness on philosophy, the social function of critical intelligence, and the content and character of creative democracy. Dewey got his start in Michigan and excelled in Chicago, but in New York he became a giant.

The coming-of-age of American pragmatism occurs just as the United States emerges as a world power. There is no direct causal relation between these two phenomena, yet it also is no mere accident. Dewey's mature formulations of pragmatism were certainly encouraged by the entrée of America on the international stage of history. This entrée required not only "the end of American innocence," i.e., an end to America's naive optimism and uncritical penchant for romantic simplicity, or a "revolt against formalism," i.e., an engagement with a dynamic reality in a functional and contextual manner.[39] It also forced American intellectuals to develop *a particular kind* of international and historical consciousness, a consciousness open to other streams of thought yet rooted in the American experience and capable of nourishing, sustaining, and guiding America through its coming crises and challenges. The genius of Dewey is that he infuses a cosmopolitan and historical outlook into American pragmatism, remains open to Baconian, Enlightenment, and Hegelian sensibilities yet faithful to the Emersonian evasion and theodicy. In this sense, if Emerson is the inventor of the American religion, Dewey is its Luther — that is, he must seriously think through the implications of the notions of power, provocation, and personality, the themes of voluntarism, optimism, individualism, and meliorism in relation to the plethora of intervening intellectual breakthroughs and in light of the prevailing conditions in order to give direction as well as vitality to the American religion. We saw earlier how Dewey attempts to dress himself in Emersonian garb by dressing Emerson in Deweyan garb.

Dewey fights this battle — that is, develops and deepens American pragmatism with its Emersonian prehistory — on three basic fronts. As a professional philosopher, for reasons of conscience and status, he must address fellow professional philosophers — hence his preoccupation with metaphilosophy. As a cultural critic, he has to come to terms with the major authority in the culture, and so we get his focus on scientific inquiry. And as a social critic, he must reflect upon the meaning and application of the dominant values in the national political tradition—hence his profound concern with democracy and individuality. Dewey's fight to keep alive the best of the American religion is not simply incisive and instructive; it also is awesome and inspiring. For too long it has lain dormant in the American unconscious, venerated by parochial epigoni, depreciated by myopic specialists, yet seriously interrogated by few. He deserves better. In fact, I believe a renascence of Dewey is soon to come. I simply hope it is accompanied by a deeper sense of historical consciousness, a subtle and nuanced grasp of critical intelligence, and a profound commitment to the expansion of creative democracy.

On the philosophical front, Dewey articulates a conception of philosophy that gives professional expression to the Emersonian evasion of epistemology-centered philosophy. In fact, the dominant theme of his metaphilosophy is that philosophy is neither a form of knowledge nor a means to acquire knowledge. Rather philosophy is a mode of cultural critical action that focuses on the ways and means by which human beings have, do, and can overcome obstacles, dispose of predicaments, and settle problematic situations. He states this succinctly in his "Philosophy and Democracy" address to the Philosophical Union of the University of California (November 29, 1918), the place where James publicly put forward pragmatism in 1898 and Santayana mused about the genteel tradition in 1911.

> There is, I think, another alternative, another way out. Put badly, it is to deny that philosophy is in any sense whatever a form of knowledge. It is to say that we should return to the original and etymological sense of the word, and recognize that philosophy is a form of desire, of effort at action—a love, namely, of wisdom; but with the thorough proviso, not attached to the Platonic use of the word, that wisdom, whatever it is, is not a mode of science or knowledge. A philosophy which was conscious of its own business and province would then perceive that it is an intellectualized wish, an aspiration subjected to rational discriminations and tests, a social hope reduced to a working program of action, a prophecy of the future, but one disciplined by serious thought and knowledge.[40]

For Dewey, philosophy is a mode not of knowledge but of wisdom. And wisdom is conviction about values, a choice to do something, a preference for this rather than that form of living. Wisdom involves discriminating judgments and a desired future. It presupposes some grasp of conditions and consequences, yet it has no special access to them. Rather methods of access must be scrutinized in order to decide which ones are most reliable for the task at hand. In this way, Dewey does not devalue knowledge but only situates it in human experience.

Dewey's first mature reflections on the metaphilosophical implications of American pragmatism are found in his seminal essay "The Need for a Recovery of Philosophy" (1917). This statement is to American pragmatism what the Theses on Feuerbach are to Marxism: the political presentation of a new world-historical perspective that both builds on and goes beyond modern philosophy. The setting is the entrance of the United States into World War I—the event that marks the real end of the nineteenth century for Europe—and the recent realist and idealist credos issued by American professional philosophers. This essay not only affirms the Emersonian evasion in professional terminology; it also constitutes the first of the three classic essays of twentieth-century American philosophy, the other two being W. V. O. Quine's "Two Dogmas of Empiricism" (1951), and Donald Davidson's "On the Very Idea of a Conceptual Scheme" (1974).[41]

Dewey begins the essay bemoaning the fact that the cloistered and conservative character of modern philosophy has produced a cultural situation in which "direct preoccupation with contemporary difficulties is left to literature and politics."[42] This has resulted, he claims, principally from the "professionalizing of philosophy" that fails to consider "what modifications and abandonments of intellectual inheritance are required by the newer industrial, political, and scientific movements."[43] At the outset, Dewey makes it clear that this is more an essay in cultural history about the ahistorical blindnesses of modern philosophy than an academic treatment of problems in modern philosophy.

> This essay may, then, be looked upon as an attempt to forward the emancipation of philosophy from too intimate and exclusive attachment to traditional problems. It is not in intent a criticism of various solutions that have been offered, but raises a question *as to the genuineness, under the present conditions of science and social life, of the problems.*[44]

Like Ludwig Wittgenstein and J. L. Austin decades later and his self-styled descendant Richard Rorty in our own time, Dewey notes,

> It is a commonplace that the chief divisions of modern philosophy, idealism in its different kinds, realisms of various brands, so-called common sense dualism, agnosticism, relativism, phenomenalism, have grown up around the epistemological problem of the general relation of subject and object. Problems not openly epistemological, such as whether the relation of changes in consciousness to physical changes is one of interaction, parallelism, or automatism, have the same origin. What becomes of philosophy, consisting largely as it does of different answers to these questions, in case the assumptions which generate the questions have no empirical standing? Is it not time that philosophers turned from the attempt to determine the comparative merits of various replies to the questions to a consideration of the claims of the questions?[45]

Dewey's aim is to evade the epistemological problematic of modern philosophy and thereby emancipate philosophy from its arid scholasticism and cultural conservatism. Just as Peirce evaded Cartesianism, so Dewey calls into question the most fundamental project of modern philosophy: the bridging of the gulf between subject and object by means of epistemological mechanisms. Unlike Peirce – and similar to James – Dewey embarks on his critique by interrogating the notion of experience deployed by modern philosophers and suggests a deeper and richer conception of experience. His basic claim is that the marginal significance of modern philosophy in North Atlantic cultures results from paltry notions of experience derived from a "spectator theory of knowledge" and the "idea of invidiously real reality." Dewey's goal is to show just how poverty-ridden (and wrong!) these notions of experience are; to reveal the concomitant spectator theory of knowledge as a blinding philosophic fiction; and to blame the idea that philosophy somehow knows Reality more ultimately than other science for the cultural isolation and irrelevance of philosophy. In this way, Dewey's metaphilosophy is a kind of counterepistemology; that is, a creative revision of Emerson's evasion of epistemology-centered modern philosophy.

For Dewey, modern philosophy has five paradigmatic notions of experience: first, as a knowledge affair; second, as a psychical thing shot through with "subjectivity"; third, as registering what has taken place, with an exclusive focus on the past; fourth, as an aggregation of simple particulars; and last, as antithetical to thought. For Dewey, these five governing conceptions of experience constitute the pillars upon which rests the subject-object epistemological problematic of modern philosophy.

His own transactional conception of experience, buttressed by Darwinian biology and historical consciousness as well as rooted in Emersonian sensibilities, rejects each of these paltry ideas of experience. His three definitions of experience in the essay lay bare his rejection and threefold debt.

> Experience is primarily a process of undergoing: a process of standing something; of suffering and passion, of affection, in the literal sense of these words. The organism has to endure, to undergo, the consequence of its own actions.
>
> Experience, in other words, is a matter of *simultaneous* doings and sufferings. Our undergoings are experiments in varying the course of events; our active tryings are trials and tests of ourselves . . . Nothing can eliminate all risk, all adventure.
>
> The obstacles which confront us are stimuli to variation, to novel response, and hence are occasions for progress.

> If biological development be accepted, the subject of experience is at least an animal, continuous with other organic forms in a process of more complex organization. An animal in turn is at least continuous with chemico-physical processes which, in living things, are so organized as really to constitute the activities of life with all their defining traits. And experience is not identical with brain action; it is the entire organic

agent-patient in all its interaction with the environment, natural and social. The brain is primarily an organ of a certain kind of behavior, not of knowing the world. And to repeat what has already been said, experiencing *is* just certain modes of interaction, of correlation, of natural objects among which the organism happens, so to say, to be one. It follows with equal force that experience means primarily not knowledge, but ways of doing and suffering. Knowing must be described by discovering what particular mode—qualitatively unique—of doing and suffering it is.[46]

Dewey's metaphilosophy is essentially an act of intellectual regicide; he wants to behead modern philosophy by dethroning epistemology. For too long, modern philosophy has deferred to the authority of "knowledge" in the name of science, without questioning this authority and demystifying science, i.e., bringing it down to earth, as it were. Therefore, the diversity, complexity, and plurality of experience have been "assimilated to a nonempirical concept of knowledge."[47] This impoverished empiricism "has said Lord, Lord, Experience, Experience, but in practice it has served ideas *forced into* experience, not *gathered from* it."[48]

As I noted earlier, Dewey is demoting knowing without devaluing it. In fact, one can more fully appreciate the value of knowledge when it is viewed as an indispensable functional activity within the larger context of experience. Neglect of context leads toward gross distortion and truncation in epistemology-centered philosophy.[49]

Like Peirce, Dewey rejects the subjectivist turn of Descartes. This turn undergirds the second narrow view of experience. Dewey refuses to get caught in the veil of ideas, to be imprisoned behind the bars of immediate awareness or within the confines of self-consciousness. Instead, he begins with intersubjectivity—the multiform interactions of human organisms with nature and with each other. The problem is not whether there is epistemic justification for the status or existence of an external world outside the veil of ideas, but rather how one goes about dealing and coping—less or more intelligently—with one's environment. The alternative is not between indubitable knowledge and full-fledged skepticism, but rather between critical intelligence and uncritical reflection, with genuine doubt and effective problem solving making the difference. For Dewey, the modern philosophic obsession with epistemic skepticism presupposes a subjectivist starting point; such skepticism is an inextricable parasite upon the epistemological problematic of modern philosophy. Dewey champions doubt—it is the very motor for provocation—yet he sidesteps modern skepticism. As he states in his masterful Gifford Lectures, *The Quest for Certainty* (1929):

> It is always in place to be doubtful and skeptical about particular items of supposed knowledge when evidence to the contrary presents itself. There is no knowledge self-guaranteed to be infallible, since all knowledge is the product of special acts of inquiry. Agnosticism as confession of

ignorance about special matters, in the absence of adequate evidence, is not only in place under such circumstances, but is an act of intellectual honesty. But such skepticism and agnosticism are particular and depend upon special conditions; they are not wholesale; they do not issue from a generalized impeachment of the adequacy of the origins of knowing to perform their office. Theories which assume that the knowing subject, that mind or consciousness, have an inherent capacity to disclose reality, a capacity operating apart from any overt interactions of the organism with surrounding conditions, are invitations to general philosophical doubt.[50]

Against the third conception of experience as retrospective, Dewey lauds anticipation and projection as distinctive features of human doings and undergoings. Cartesians and their empiricist, transcendentalist, and realist descendants tend to focus on knowing as recollection, a summoning of the past by means of memory. Following his Emersonian sentiments, Dewey highlights the future, the forward-looking character of human experience. This stress follows from pragmatism's shift away from first principles, self-evident truths, and epistemic foundations to effects, fruits, consequences. The contingency of the self, community, and world as well as the revisability of theories, knowledges, and moralities leads Dewey to quip, "What should experience be but a future implicated in a present!"[51] In this sense, experience is experimental.[52]

Therefore, Dewey rejects the obsession of modern philosophy with what has been or is "given."[53] Prefiguring much of Wilfred Sellars' classic attack "The Myth of the Given" nearly forty years later,[54] Dewey stresses the active, selective, and instrumental character of human experience. In his Gifford Lectures, he chides modern philosophy by cleverly noting:

> The history of the theory of knowledge or epistemology would have been very different if instead of the word "data" or "givens," it had happened to start with calling the qualities in question "takens." Not that the data are not existential and qualities of the ultimately "given"—that is, the total subject-matter which is had in non-cognitive experiences. But *as* data they are *selected* from this total original subject-matter which gives the impetus to knowing; they are discriminated for a purpose:—that, namely, of affording signs or evidence to define and locate a problem, and thus give a clew to its resolution.[55]

Like James, Dewey intends not to push empiricism aside but rather to deepen its understanding of experience. This deepening includes taking seriously the role of the future. We earlier saw Peirce struggling to come to terms with the status of the future in his perspective: in addition to the Emersonian theodicy, i.e., faith claims, he musters only an inadequate notion of continuity derived from modern logic. James and Dewey simply fall back on the Emersonian theodicy that accents the practical and moral character of reality—a reality always open to change and not excessively antagonistic to human aspirations. In one of his few historical reflections on the origins and traits of pragmatism entitled "The Development of American Pragmatism" (1922), Dewey states,

> Pragmatism, thus, presents itself as an extension of historical empiricism, but with this fundamental difference, that it does not insist upon antecedent phenomena but upon consequent phenomena; not upon the precedents but upon the possibilities of action. And this change in point of view is almost revolutionary in its consequences. An empiricism which is content with repeating facts already past has no place for possibility and for liberty . . .
>
> Pragmatism thus has a metaphysical implication. The doctrine of the value of consequences leads us to take the future into consideration. And this taking into consideration of the future takes us to the conception of a universe whose evolution is not finished, of a universe which is still, in James' term "in the making," "in the process of becoming," of a universe up to a certain point still plastic.
>
> Consequently reason, or thought, in its more general sense, has a real, though limited, function, a creative constructive function . . . Under these conditions the world will be different from what it would have been if thought had not intervened. This consideration confirms the human and moral importance of thought and of its reflective operation in experience.[56]

Dewey's prospective instrumentalist viewpoint here is deeply indebted to Emerson, yet his pervasive historical consciousness leads him to take with more seriousness than Emerson the role of the past in the present and its use for the future.

> Imaginative recovery of the bygone is indispensable to successful invasion of the future, but its status is that of an instrument . . . the movement of the agent-patient to meet the future is partial and passionate; yet detached and impartial study of the past is the only alternative to luck in assuring success to passion.[57]

The fourth conception of experience as particularistic principally results from imposing a rather artificial and abstract epistemic notion of experience upon the fluidity, plurality, and diversity of experience. Of course, we have no unmediated access to the fundamental nature of the world, but it certainly is more complex and mysterious than is claimed by the empiricists' particularism (or the rationalists' monism). Influenced by James—and sounding much like the great metaphysician of experience Alfred North Whitehead—Dewey holds that connections, continuities, and relations are neither alien to experience (as Hume thought) nor supplemented by nonempirical sources (as Kant believed). Rather they permeate experience. In fact, their interaction, diversity, and changeability constitute "irreducible traits found in any and every subject of scientific inquiry."[58]

The last notion of experience Dewey examines pits experience against thought. He associates this contrast with the philosophic device of the modern subject, a device that undergirds the fictive spectator theory of knowledge. This modern philosophical view holds

> that experience centers in, or gathers about, or proceeds from a center or subject which is outside the course of natural existence, and set over against it — it being of no importance, for present purposes, whether this antithetical subject is termed soul, or spirit, or mind, or ego, or consciousness, or just knower or knowing subject . . .
>
> The essential thing is that the bearer was conceived as outside of the world; so that experience consisted in the bearer's being affected through a type of operations not found anywhere in the world, while knowledge consists in surveying the world, looking at it, getting the view of a spectator.[59]

Dewey's account of this subject-object relation primarily mediated by epistemic mechanisms is more historical and concrete than that of Martin Heidegger and more materialist than that of Jacques Derrida. On the one hand, modern philosophers modeled their epistemological problematic upon an immaterial and supernatural soul or spirit (be it a transcendent God or immanent within humans) that knows and thereby exercises power over a material and natural world. With the marginalizing of religious dogma among modern philosophers, principally due to the influence of science, the only replacement for the immaterial, supernatural soul or spirit was a Cartesian nonextended substance, Kantian transcendental subject, or Hegelian *Weltgeist*. On the other hand, this problematic results in large part from the elevating of an intellectual form of knowledge, that of the eternal, universal, invariable, and the devaluing of another, practical kind of knowledge, that of the temporal, particular, and variable. This elevation is a cultural and ideological translation "into a rational form the doctrine of escape from the vicissitudes of existence by means of measures which do not demand an active coping with conditions."[60] For Dewey, this translation — quite attractive to those with much to lose from change by human action — simply "substituted deliverance through reason" for "deliverance by means of rites and cults."[61] Even if activity is valorized, as with the Greeks, it is distinguished from action (making and doing), especially for those subordinated and subjugated.

For Dewey, philosophy emerged out of the human stock of religious, poetic, and dramatic practices — it, like them, told seductive lies-against-time. Modern philosophy simply tells its lies-against-time by elaborate and technical epistemological means. Emerson's evasion of modern philosophy constitutes a refusal to tell such European lies-against-time and thereby locates America (the self) at the beginning of time, i.e., history, and before open space, i.e., Indian and Mexican lands. Dewey's creative revision of Emerson's evasion historicizes all philosophic lies-against-time, yet he historicizes in an Emersonian manner. That is, he views America as the best exemplar in time. He wants to emancipate, recover, and reconstruct philosophy, in part so that this can remain so and all reap the benefits of this shining example.

The epistemological problematic of modern philosophy now, in Dewey's view, stands in the way of American and world progress. Like religion, for him, it misdirects human powers and misleads human energies. Similar to the opiates of old, this problematic lingers on owing to cultural lethargy, academic entrenchment, and existential quests for certainty. To go beyond the epistemological problematic is to be a twentieth-century pioneer "wandering in a wilderness" (his self-description in his only auto-biographical account)[62] ready to reflect critically upon and realize new possibilities for a better future. Almost in exasperation, Dewey throws up his hands at his fellow professional philosophers and proclaims,

> When dominating religious ideas were built up about the idea that the self is a stranger and pilgrim in this world; when morals, falling in line, found true good only in inner states of a self inaccessible to anything but its own private introspection; when political theory assumed the finality of disconnected and mutually exclusive personalities, the notion that the bearer of experience is antithetical to the world instead of being in and of it was congenial. It at least had the warrant of other beliefs and aspirations. But the doctrine of biological continuity or organic evolution has destroyed the scientific basis of the conception. Morally, men are now concerned with the amelioration of the conditions of the common lot in this world. Social sciences recognize that associated life is not a matter of physical juxtaposition, but of genuine intercourse—of community of experience in a non-metaphorical sense of community. Why should we longer try to patch up and refine and stretch the old solutions till they seem to cover the change of thought and practice? Why not recognize that the trouble is with the problem?[63]

Dewey echoes these metaphilosophical sentiments in his 1919 lectures at the Imperial University in Tokyo, Japan, published as *Reconstruction in Philosophy* (1920).

> Modern philosophic thought has been so preoccupied with these puzzles of epistemology . . . that many students are at a loss to know what would be left for philosophy if there were removed both the metaphysical task of distinguishing between the noumenal and phenomenal worlds and the epistemological task of telling how a separate subject can know an independent object. But would not the elimination of these traditional problems permit philosophy to devote itself to a more fruitful and more needed task? Would it not encourage philosophy to face the great social and moral defects and troubles from which humanity suffers, to concentrate its attention upon clearing up the causes and exact nature of these evils and upon developing a clear idea of better social possibilities . . . ?[64]

Dewey's rejection of the epistemological problematic of modern philosophy leads him to cast aside all metaphysical inquiries into the "really Real."

For him, such inquiries promote the conception of philosophy as a form of knowledge with access to a more deep and fundamental Reality than that of the sciences and arts. This conception views philosophy as an autonomous discipline over and above other disciplines, a tribunal of reason with access to deep reality before which other disciplines (with only partial glimpses of reality) must be judged. Dewey associates this metaphysical pretension with the epistemological puzzles of modern philosophy. Therefore the "spectator theory of knowledge" and "the idea of invidiously real reality"—both linked to paltry notions of experience—go hand in hand. He acknowledges that to reject these fundamental pillars of modern philosophy "seems to many to be the suicide of philosophy,"[65] yet the uniqueness of pragmatism is precisely to make this denial without embracing skepticism or positivism.

> It is often said that pragmatism, unless it is content to be a contribution to mere methodology, must develop a theory of Reality. But the chief characteristic trait of the pragmatic notion of reality is precisely that no theory of Reality in general, *überhaupt*, is possible or needed . . . it finds that "reality" is a *denotative* term, a word used to designate indifferently everything that happens . . .
>
> The only way in which the term reality can ever become more than a blanket denotative term is through recourse to specific events in all their diversity and thatness. Speaking summarily, I find that the retention by philosophy of the notion of a Reality feudally superior to the events of everyday occurrence is the chief source of the increasing isolation of philosophy from common sense and science.[66]

Dewey is often accused of going from the more plausible claim that there is no "Reality in general" to the objectionable claim that no general theory of reality is possible.[67] And those intent on simply incorporating Dewey into the tradition of modern philosophy point out Dewey's own descriptive metaphysical project in his classic work *Experience and Nature* (1925). If these critics are right, my claim that Dewey evades and emancipates modern philosophy is exorbitant. And, I believe, these critics are partially right in that Dewey is ambiguous—especially as he reaches retirement at Columbia—about this evasion and emancipation. On the one hand, his commitment to historical consciousness, evolutionary biology, and Emersonian sentiments of contingency, revisability, and amelioration leads him to affirm evasion and emancipation. Needless to say, this affirmation entails not a negation or rejection of philosophy per se but rather a modest view of philosophy as social and cultural criticism. On the other hand, Dewey's attraction to the naturalistic Aristotelian model in the Greek philosophical tradition—a model made more challenging and attractive by his influential Columbia colleague F. J. E. Woodbridge—and his allegiance to his professional identity and status leave him uneasy with his modest view of philosophy.[68] Dewey continually struggles with questions such as: What are the detailed philosophical implications of a limited conception of philosophy as social and cultural criticism? Does not this conception itself require a tentative and provisional basis—a basis which a descriptive metaphysics might provide? But does not an emancipation of philosophy result in a setting aside of such philosophic talk about "basis"? Yet, if this is so, what is an academic philosopher to teach and write— how to preserve one's sense of profession—when the whole enterprise rests upon the conception of philosophy one rejects?

These queries are both serious philosophic ones and intensely personal and professional ones. Of course, they never arose for Emerson since he enacted a poetic evasion of modern philosophy. Despite Peirce's theoretical originality and personal eccentricity, he remained deeply wedded to the philosophic tradition, especially to certain medieval strains. And James, though always concerned with the honorific title of "philosopher" (partly owing to his having neither a B.A. nor a Ph.D.), would simply not have given a damn about these questions. For him, philosophy was not first and foremost socially engaged; rather, it mediated essential rifts in the self. Moreover, James abhorred the demands and pressures of professionalism. He taught what caught his fancy at Harvard. Yet Emerson, Peirce, James, and Dewey still remain in the American grain, with pragmatism a useful rubric with which to group and understand them.

Dewey's dilemma is best depicted in Richard Rorty's highly perceptive essay "Dewey's Metaphysics."[69] Rorty begins by noting that near the end of his life, Dewey hoped to write a new edition of *Experience and Nature*, changing the title as well as the subject matter to "Nature and Culture." In a letter to his friend and collaborator Arthur Bentley, Dewey writes:

> I was dumb not to have seen the need for such a shift when the old text was written. I was still hopeful that the philosophic word "experience" could be redeemed by being returned to its idiomatic usages—which was a piece of historical folly, the hope I mean.[70]

This admission is more perplexing than Rorty admits, for several reasons. First, Dewey initially announced the need for a shift in philosophy in the name of a deep and richer notion of "experience." We saw this earlier. Second, "nature" in the original title is as much a source of Dewey's metaphysical motivations as "experience." To jettison the latter notion does not necessarily preclude a Deweyan "naturalistic metaphysics." And last, *Experience and Nature*, though Dewey's principal work on and in metaphysics, is not the only Deweyan text in which metaphysical inquiry rears its head. For instance, his classic William James Lectures, *Art as Experience* (1934), are shot through with an organic idealism unbecoming a card-carrying pragmatist.[71] Ought he to have renamed and rewrote this book as "Art as Culture"? In short, the notion of experience is simply too fundamental and omnipresent in Dewey's work for us to put much weight on a quip to Bentley in later life.

In fairness to Rorty, he does admit that Dewey remains ambiguous about the role of metaphysics in his metaphilosophy.

> For better or worse, he *wanted* to write a metaphysical system. Throughout his life, he wavered between a therapeutical stance toward philosophy and another, quite different stance—one in which philosophy was to become "scientific" and "empirical" and to do something serious, systematic, important, and constructive. Dewey sometimes described philosophy as the criticism of culture, but he was never quite content to think of himself as a kibitzer or a therapist or an intellectual historian. He wanted to have things both ways.[72]

And as a self-styled descendant of Dewey, Rorty laments Dewey's seduction by metaphysics as manifest in *Experience and Nature*.

> Dewey's mistake—and it was a trivial and unimportant mistake, even though I have devoted most of this essay to it—was the notion that criticism of culture had to take the form of a redescription of "nature" or "experience" or both. Had Dewey written the book called *Nature and Culture*, which was to replace *Experience and Nature*, he might have felt able to forget the Aristotelian and Kantian models and simply have been Hegelian all the way, as he was in much of his other (and best) work.[73]

In other words, Rorty wishes Dewey to be a more consistent historicist pragmatist. And I agree. Yet from a pragmatic point of view, the criticism of culture can take many forms, including redescriptions of nature and experience. The redescriptions ought not to be viewed as metaphysical inquiries into "the generic traits manifested by existences of all kinds without regard to their differentiation into physical and mental," but rather as metaphorical versions of what one thinks the way the world is in light of the best available theories. I find nothing wrong with this kind of intellectual activity as long as one acknowledges the needs and interests it satisfies. In Dewey's case it seems to permit him to scratch a metaphysical itch—an itch, I might add, that serves as the principal cultural motivation for various scientific and artistic forms of redescriptions and revisions of the world. It also appears to minimize Dewey's professional anxieties, especially given the fact that few people other than professional philosophers would ever bother reading and grappling with the issues raised in a densely written 437-page tome like *Experience and Nature*. I say this not to devalue Dewey's achievement, but rather to situate historically and evaluate pragmatically the reasons why Dewey chooses to write in this way. For many pragmatists do not and ought not to choose to do so. And the kind of choices pragmatists do make regarding *the content and style* of their work depends greatly on their historical situation, personal aims, and sociocultural location. Dewey himself realizes this when he notes,

> If the ruling and the oppressed elements in a population, if those who wish to maintain the *status quo* and those concerned to make changes,

had, when they became articulate, the same philosophy, one might well be skeptical of its intellectual integrity.[74]

Women have as yet made little contribution to philosophy. But when women who are not mere students of other persons' philosophy set out to write it, we cannot conceive that it will be the same in viewpoint or tenor as that composed from the standpoint of the different masculine experience of things.[75]

Dewey's metaphilosophy, despite his own ambiguity about it, accentuates the role of critical intelligence in human experience. Critical intelligence, for him, is simply the operation of the scientific attitude in problematic situations. This attitude often—though by no means always (as in art)—results in deploying the scientific method to resolve problems. This distinction between scientific attitude and scientific method is crucial for Dewey; those who overlook it view him as a vulgar positivist, one who makes a fetish of scientific method. But this is simply not so. Dewey indeed distinguishes dogmatic thinking from critical thinking, yet the latter is not simply the monopoly of scientific method.

Here is where ordinary thinking and thinking that is scrupulous diverge from each other. The natural man is impatient with doubt and suspense: he impatiently hurries to be shut of it. A disciplined mind takes delight in the problematic, and cherishes it until a way out is found that approves itself upon examination. The questionable becomes an active questioning, a search; desire for the emotion of certitude gives peace to quest for the objects by which the obscure and unsettled may be developed into the stable and clear. The scientific attitude may almost be defined as that which is capable of enjoying the doubtful; scientific method is, in one aspect, a technique for making a productive use of doubt by converting it into operations of definite inquiry.[76]

The aims of critical intelligence are to overcome obstacles, resolve problems, and project realizable possibilities in pressing predicaments. A scientific attitude is indispensable for achieving these aims; the scientific method is usually the best means by which they are achieved. The first important point here is that critical intelligence is available to all peoples; it is neither the birthright of the highbrow nor the property of the professional. Rather it is "a human undertaking, not an esthetic appreciation carried on by a refined class or a capitalistic possession of a few learned specialists, whether men of science or of philosophy."[77]

The second crucial point is that though critical intelligence deploys the scientific method, the results of science do not constitute the disclosure of the real. Dewey is no epistemological realist or ontological positivist, but rather a pragmatist with great faith in the power of critical intelligence. The cultural implication here is that Dewey's acceptance of the authority of science is itself instrumental—science is simply the best tool we conscious

organisms have to cope with our environment. The metaphysical implication is that although science has no monopoly on what is true and real,
its predictive and explanatory powers help us deal more effectively with
the world than anything else available to us.

Although the popular opinion of Dewey is that he was a scientistic
thinker, he actually held that science provides one kind of description
(or set of descriptions) of the world among other kinds of equally acceptable descriptions, e.g., those of art. He promotes science when it best
enables us to achieve specific aims and satisfy certain interests. Science
in no way provides us with the fundamental nature of reality. Nor are
the descriptions of science appropriate in every context. Dewey is quite
emphatic about this:

> There is something both ridiculous and disconcerting in the way in which
> men have let themselves be imposed upon; so as to infer that scientific
> ways of thinking of objects give the inner reality of things, and that they
> put a mark of spuriousness upon all other ways of thinking them, and
> of perceiving and enjoying them. It is ludicrous because these scientific
> conceptions, like other instruments, are hand-made by man in pursuit
> of realization of a certain interest.
>
> Thus the recognition that intelligence is a method operating within the
> world places physical knowledge in respect to other kinds of knowing
> . . . there is no kind of inquiry which has a monopoly of the honorable
> title of knowledge. The engineer, the artist, the historian, the man of
> affairs attain knowledge in the degree they employ methods that enable
> them to solve the problems which develop in the subject-matter they
> are concerned with. As philosophy framed upon the pattern of experi-
> mental inquiry does away with all wholesale skepticism, so it eliminates
> all invidious monopolies of the idea of science. By their fruits we shall
> know them.[78]

Dewey is not claiming that all epistemic claims have the same status; that
an unregulated relativism reigns in pragmatic counterepistemologies; that
science is a mere fictive discourse spreading false consciousness; or that
the common man's natural explanations are as warranted as those of the
trained physicist. Rather Dewey is saying that there are a variety of knowledges, each rigorously regulated by procedures that take seriously the role
of hypothesis, evidence, and inference; that this epistemic pluralism gives
no procedure privileged access to Truth and Reality; that science, though
it posits unobservable entities, is the most reliable procedure regarding
control of phenomena; and that commonsense reasoning is continuous
with scientific method. Dewey's biblical conclusion, echoing Emerson and
Peirce, is neither an anti-intellectual praise of action nor an elevation of
praxis over theory, but rather an affirmation of the inseparability of
thought and action and an acknowledgment of the role of consequences
in reflective deliberation.[79] In other words, Dewey's pragmatism yields

an epistemic pluralism that does not consist of some metaphysical unity of theory and praxis or an antitheoreticist vitalism. Instead, he promotes a critical intelligence that defers to no authority other than the enrichment of human experience and the alleviation of the human plight.

Dewey's conception of truth reflects an Emersonian refusal to posit any authority other than human efforts and creation. Therefore he rejects Reality as the ultimate court of appeal in adjudicating between conflicting theories – and subsequently any correspondence theory of truth or realist ontology. He also rules out logical consistency and theoretical coherence as definitive criteria for acceptable theories about the world – and so coherence theories of truth or idealist ontologies are shunned. This does not mean that Dewey holds that there are no real objects or that consistency and coherence are unimportant in accepting true theories. Instead, I am suggesting that the predominant element in Dewey's view of truth is social practice, the human procedures of critical intelligence that yield warranted assertions. For Dewey, the only alternative for pragmatists is to settle for truth-as-warranted-assertibility; ideas are neither copies of the world nor representations linked principally to one another, but rather ingredients for rules and for plans of action.

The crucial question according to Dewey is whether ideas are reliable, worthy of acting upon given the ways by which we accept them. These all-important "ways" consist of social practices, rational procedures created by, aspired to, and approximated by human beings. The only truths we historical creatures have access to are those cautiously filtered through these error-prone yet self-correcting procedures concocted and enacted by ourselves. In fact, Dewey goes as far as to claim in his masterful *Logic: The Theory of Inquiry* (1938) not only that we accept these procedures on principally instrumental grounds, but also that logical forms themselves emerge owing to and within the operations and aims of inquiry.[80] Dewey essentially accepts Peirce's notion of truth as "the opinion which is fated to be ultimately agreed to by all who investigate";[81] that is, he distinguishes ontological truth from epistemic validity yet puts the weight on the latter. As Bertrand Russell points out in a perceptive, provocative, yet wrong-headed attack on Dewey's treatment, "Truth is not an important concept in Dr. Dewey's logic."[82]

Like James's, Dewey's idea of truth has simply little to do; all the work is loaded on warranted assertibility. Hilary Putnam has persuasively argued that truth is not an epistemic notion and if so regarded leads to intractable problems.[83] For example, to put it crudely, if warranted assertible claims at t_1 are no longer so at t_2 then Truth has changed in an unacceptable and unconvincing way. This implies not that Dewey regards truth as mere contingent generalized wishful thinking – as Russell suggests and James at his worst intimates – but rather that Dewey simply should not view truth as warranted assertibility. Instead, he should say that the latter is all we're going to come up with when we make our tentative and revisable truth claims. On this view, truth is not reducible to warranted assertibility, yet to analyze the meaning and nature of truth in terms of correspondence with Reality or coherence with other sentences actually entails falling back on warranted assertibility in practice. To hold onto such analyses of truth soothes the agonized consciences of realists and idealists—with no payoff, no work being done. In short, there is no significant difference between the nature of truth and the test of truth, but the two are never identical. I suspect that talking of truth in terms of correspondence and coherence is a deep-seated rhetoric in North Atlantic cultures that does little harm when taken in a commonsensical manner, yet is grossly misleading when burdened with philosophic freight. In fact, if such rhetoric facilitates and motivates more careful inquiry, thus producing more and better-warranted assertible claims, it may be pragmatically justified as long as it remains philosophically innocuous.

The pragmatic conception of truth can be viewed as a kind of Americanization of the notion of truth, an Emersonian effort at democratization and plebeianization of the idea of truth that renders it "various and flexible," "rich and endless" in resources, and it is hoped "friendly" in its conclusions. More pointedly, pragmatism conceives of truth as a species of the good; the procedures that produce warranted assertions are themselves value-laden and exemplary of human beings working in solidarity for the common good. In this way, Dewey's metaphilosophy and his accentuation of the role of critical intelligence are inseparable from his promotion of creative democracy.

Earlier we saw Dewey's deep commitment to democracy, influenced especially by T. H. Green, Henry Carter Adams, and his wife, Alice. I am suggesting that his profound revision of the Emersonian evasion of epistemology-centered philosophy is, in large part, motivated by his efforts to keep alive and vital the Emersonian theodicy under new circumstances and challenges. I am not claiming that Dewey had no intrinsic interest in the metaphysical and epistemological problems he attempts to dissolve. Rather I am suggesting that Dewey is first and foremost an Emersonian evangelist of democracy who views the expansion of critical intelligence as requisite for the more full development of human individuality and personality. His metaphilosophy is essentially an intellectual ax—a weapon of his pioneering activity—"to help get rid of the useless lumber that blocks our highways of thought, and strive to make straight and open the paths that lead to the future"; it is to ensure that his fellow Americans and world citizens do *not* "believe that the wilderness is after all itself the promised land."[84] In this way, Dewey's technical treatments and sweeping critiques of the philosophic tradition constitute an Emersonian prophetic condemnation of "an ingenious dialectic exercised in professorial corners by a few who have retained ancient premises while rejecting their application to the conduct of life."[85] Philosophy, after its evasion and emancipation in the name of critical intelligence and creative democracy, "ceases to be a device for dealing with the problems of philosophers and becomes a method, cultivated by philosophers, for dealing with the problems of men."[86] For Dewey, the task at hand is to call his fellow Americans and world citizens back to the American religion, an updated and revised Emersonian theodicy for a new world power with great economic might and colonial possessions, yet a persistent provincial mentality.

> We thus tend to combine a loose and ineffective optimism with assent to the doctrine of take who take can: a deification of power. All peoples at all times have been narrowly realistic in practice and have then employed idealization to cover up in sentiment and theory their brutalities. But never, perhaps, has the tendency been so dangerous and so tempting as with ourselves. Faith in the power of intelligence to imagine a future which is the projection of the desirable in the present, and to invent the instrumentalities of its realization, is our salvation. And it is a faith which must be nurtured and made articulate: surely a sufficiently large task for our philosophy.[87]

Ironically, Dewey himself often fails to examine seriously the degree to which the Emersonian theodicy, including his subtle version of it, contributes to this "loose and ineffective optimism" and "deification of power." He does not entertain the possibility that his own evangelical zeal for creative democracy falls prey to this optimism and deification of power. I am not claiming that it does this in a crude or vulgar fashion; but I do hold that Dewey does not fully escape the clutches of such optimism and enshrinement of power.

> When we have used our thought to its utmost and have thrown into the moving unbalanced balance of things our puny strength, we know that though the universe slay us still we may trust, for our lot is one with whatever is good in existence. We know that such thought and effort is the condition of the coming into existence of the better. As far as we are concerned it is the only condition, for it alone is in our power.[88]

Needless to say, Dewey's democratic faith is neither a religious commitment in the dogmatic sense nor an unreasonable conviction in the moral sense. Yet it is tainted by the very provincial mentality he scorns; that is, he simply cannot shed a rather narrow cultural and communal model for his creative democracy. This model rests upon, as C. Wright Mills notes, "a relatively homogeneous community which does not harbor any chasms of structure and power not thoroughly ameliorative by discussion."[89] The point here is not that Dewey possesses a deep nostalgia for a lost golden age of harmonious *Gemeinschaften*, but rather that he believes that social conflict can be resolved and societal problems overcome by a widely held consensus more characteristic of artisanal towns or farming communities than of industrial cities or urban capitalist societies.

This focus does permit Dewey to see more clearly than most—especially his Marxist and liberal contemporaries—the cultural dimension of the crisis of American civilization; yet it also distorts his view regarding the role of critical intelligence in dislodging and democratizing the entrenched economic and political powers that be. Thus, Dewey's central concern is to extend the experimental method in the natural sciences to the social, political, cultural, and economic spheres rather than to discern the social forces and historical agents capable of acting on and actualizing (i.e., approximating) his creative democracy. His relative confinement to the professional and reformist elements of the middle class makes such discernment unlikely. And his distrust of resolute ideological positioning, as in political parties and social movements from below, leads him to elevate the dissemination of critical intelligence at the expense of the organization of collective insurgency. As C. Wright Mills notes, this insight partly explains

> why Dewey has been rather liberally mugwumpish in politics, and why "action" is *not* linked with a sizable organization, a movement, a party with a chance at power. The concept of action in Dewey obviously does not cover the kinds of action occurring within and between struggling, organized political parties . . . Politically, pragmatism is less expediency than it is a kind of perennial mugwump confronted with rationalized social structures.[90]

The point is not simply that Dewey adopts a gradualist view of social change and remains a reformer rather than a revolutionary. Rather it is the *kind* of gradualism he promotes and the *form* of reformism he propagates; that is, his gradualism is principally pedagogical in content, and his reformism is primarily dialogical in character. He shuns confrontational politics and agitational social struggle. The major means by which creative democracy is furthered is education and discussion.

Yet it is misleading to characterize Dewey as a liberal in the tradition of Jeremy Bentham and John Stuart Mill. He indeed is influenced by this tradition as are all progressive political thinkers, but, in the end, he swerves from it. Unfortunately, he failed to grapple seriously with the Marxist tradition, not just Marx himself but Karl Kautsky, Rosa Luxemburg, Georg Lukács, Anton Pannekoek, Karl Korsch, C. L. R. James, and others. In fact, Max Eastman notes that Dewey admitted to him that he never read Marx. Moreover, Dewey himself confessed in 1930—at the age of seventy-one—that he did not know enough about Marx to discuss his philosophy. This seems not to have deterred him from listing *Capital* as the most influential book in the past twenty-five to fifty years.[91] To many Dewey appears to be a left-wing Jeffersonian, an egalitarian more radical than liberalism and more individualistic than Marxism.[92] And this is a plausible though not persuasive viewpoint. In a reply to Jim Cork, Dewey himself states, "I can be classed as a democratic socialist. If I were permitted to define 'socialism' and 'socialist' I would so classify myself today."[93] Yet even this admission warrants suspicion. It seems Dewey adopts this label more by default than by choice. Thus we are not surprised when he admits that no "existing brand of socialism has worked out an adequate answer to the question of *how* industry and finance can progressively be conducted in the widest possible human interest and not for the benefit of one class . . . I think that the issue is not as yet sufficiently definite to permit of any answer save that it has to be worked out experimentally. Probably my experimentalism goes deeper than any other 'ism.' "[94] I suggest that this "experimentalism" takes the form of creative democracy—a form of personal and social life that includes liberal, Jeffersonian, and socialist dimensions yet is ultimately guided by Emersonian cultural sensibilities.

Dewey is in search of a culture of democracy, of ways of life guided by experimental method, infused with the love of individuality and community, and rooted in the Emersonian theodicy. He did not articulate this vision in an elaborate fashion; and he never found an adequate label for it. His list of candidates ranges from the "new individualism," to "renascent liberalism," to "the great community."[95] These candidates are inadequate primarily because they fail to capture the most crucial aspect of Dewey's vision: the need for an Emersonian *culture* of radical democracy in which self-creation and communal participation flourish in all their diversity and plurality. For Dewey, the aim of political and social life is the cultural enrichment and moral development of self-begetting individuals and self-regulating communities by means of the release of human powers provoked by novel circumstances and new challenges. He thought that the crisis of American civilization was first and foremost a cultural crisis of distraught individuals, abject subjects, and ruptured communities alienated from their own powers, capacities, and potentialities. In the conclusion to his defense of "the new individualism" in *Individualism: Old and New*, he first invokes Emerson's democratization of genius and proceeds, by means of a central capitalist metaphor—the fence—to link this expansion of power to the energizing of people's everyday life in industrial America.

"It is in vain," said Emerson, "that we look for genius to reiterate its miracles in the old arts; it is its instinct to find beauty and holiness in new and necessary facts, in the field and in the roadside, in the shop and mill." To gain an integrated individuality, each of us needs to cultivate his own garden. But there is no fence about this garden: it is no sharply marked-off enclosure. Our garden is the world, in the angle at which it touches our own manner of being. By accepting the corporate and industrial world in which we live, and by thus fulfilling the precondition for interaction with it, we, who are also parts of the moving present, create ourselves as we create an unknown future.[96]

In his formulation of a "renascent liberalism," Dewey echoes the best of Marx, calling for "the social control of economic forces" as "the means of free individual development," the way to "release human energy for the pursuit of higher values."[97] This echo prompted Sidney Hook—the leading student of Dewey—to predict that this text, *Liberalism and Social Action*, "may well be to the twentieth century what Marx and Engels' *Communist Manifesto* was to the nineteenth."[98] And there is some warrant for the comparison, though not for the prediction. Contrary to Hook, I am suggesting that Dewey is closer to the concerns of a left culturalist like William Morris than to those of a socialist theorist like Karl Marx, though his work resonates with the democratic sentiments of both. But Dewey's ideal is neither the mythic medieval society of Morris nor the mythic Greek polis of Marx but rather a future Emersonian culture. He believes a "renascent liberalism," radical in outlook and pedagogical in strategy, can contribute to the making of such a culture.

> The greatest educational power, the greatest force in shaping the disposi-
> tions and attitudes of individuals, is the social medium in which they
> live. The medium that now lies closest to us is that of unified action
> for the inclusive end of a socialized economy. The attainment of a state
> of society in which a basis of material security will *release the powers of
> individuals for cultural expression* [italics mine] is not the work of a day.
> But by concentrating upon the task of securing a socialized economy
> as the ground and medium for the release of the impulses and capacities
> men agree to call ideal, the now scattered and often conflicting activities
> of liberals can be brought to effective unity.[99]

In his major work in political philosophy, *The Public and Its Problems* (1927), Dewey calls for an Emersonian culture of radical democracy in the form of "the great community." Responding, in part, to Walter Lippmann's stinging attack on substantive democracy and his "pragmatic" defense of bureaucratic elitism in *Public Opinion* (1922) and *The Phantom Public* (1925), Dewey claims that the major task of radical democrats is to constitute a public sphere out of the various amorphous and unarticulated publics generated by "the great society" of industrial capitalist processes.

> It is not that there is no public, no large body of persons having a
> common interest in the consequences of social transactions. There is
> too much public, a public too diffused and scattered and too intricate
> in composition. And there are too many publics, for conjoint actions
> which have indirect, serious and enduring consequences are multitudi-
> nous beyond comparison, and each one of them crosses the others and
> generates its own group of persons especially affected with little to hold
> these different publics together in an integrated whole.[100]

The major obstacles to creating a public sphere—a discursive and dialogical social space wherein the various "publics" can find common ground—are the proliferation of popular cultural diversions from political concern such as sports, movies, radio, cars; the bureaucratization of politics; the geographical mobility of persons; and most important, the cultural lag in ideas, ideals, and symbols that prohibits genuine communication. Again, Dewey views the crisis as a cultural problem to be addressed by education and discussion, especially the application of the experimental method of the sciences to affairs of society. The rugged—or, as Dewey notes, ragged—individualism and smothering conformity of American culture are out of step with the advances of science and technology. To use Santayana's imagery, the colonial mansion still sits next to the skyscraper. Dewey attributes much of this to the very frontier experience he valorizes in other ways. This frontier experience inculcates in Americans "the fear of whatever threatens the security and order of a precariously attained civilization."[101] American provincialism stays alive and well owing not to lack of exposure to change, but rather to a "frontier fear" of rapid change that threatens an already tenuous stability. In this way, Dewey observes—far more acutely than Frederick Jackson Turner—that the frontier experience contributes to conformity and scorns tolerance, openness, and curiosity.

> We have been so taught to respect the beliefs of our neighbors that few will respect the beliefs of a neighbor when they depart from forms which have become associated with aspiration for a decent neighborly life. This is the illiberalism which is deeply-rooted in our liberalism.[102]

In this sense, American culture is highly underdeveloped—anti-intellectual, escapist, repressive, hedonistic, intolerant, xenophobic—while the American economy is impressively developed, though the wealth is maldistributed. Dewey acknowledges the latter point—"The oligarchy which now dominates is that of an economic class" or "Our institutions, democratic in form, tend to favor in substance a privileged plutocracy"[103]—yet his focus is on the cultural problem. And this problem is the creation of an Emersonian culture of radical democracy.

> No government by experts in which the masses do not have the chance to inform the experts as to their needs can be anything but an oligarchy managed in the interests of the few. And the enlightenment must proceed in ways which force the administrative specialists to take account of the needs. The world has suffered more from leaders and authorities than from the masses.
>
> The essential need, in other words, is the improvement of the methods and conditions of debate, discussion and persuasion. That is *the* problem of the public. We have asserted that this improvement depends essentially upon freeing and perfecting the processes of inquiry and of dissemination of their conclusions.[104]

Similar to the concerns of Jürgen Habermas in our own time, Dewey's preoccupation with communication proceeds out of a deep commitment to rational dialogue in an irrational culture. Dewey's notion of communication, however, does not simply undergird a regulative ideal that forecloses relativistic conclusions, but, more important, serves as *the* vehicle to create and constitute actual communities for the amelioration of existing circumstances. For Dewey, the move from "our Babel"[105] to "the great community" is a matter of cultural politics, in which communication resting upon shared values and promoting diversity must play a combative role.

On the surface, it appears that Dewey has not really moved too far from his *Thought News* project with Franklin Ford of forty-three years earlier or the democratic sentiments he shared with T. H. Green, Henry Carter Adams, and his first wife, Alice (who died in 1927). But, on a deeper level, we can see that this is not so. First, Dewey is now more intent on making the experimental method accessible than on making the facts available. Second, he is more aware—though, in many ways, still not sufficiently aware—of the dynamics of power in capitalist America (especially given the Depression) than he was before. Third, his project is no longer a matter of simply making philosophy relevant by means of journalistic intervention in the popular marketplace of ideas, but rather of making society democratic by pitting popular cultural transformation against a dominating economic oligarchy.

The major problem with Dewey's project is that his cultural transformation envisions a future Emersonian and democratic way of life that has the flavor of small-scale, homogeneous communities. This is not necessarily a nostalgia for rural America, especially given Dewey's no-turning-back attitude toward "the great society" and "the machine age." Moreover, much of present-day America remains ethnically and racially homogeneous, with its "chocolate cities and vanilla suburbs" (to use George Clinton's lyrics). Dewey's project is problematic not because he yearns for a bygone cultural golden age but rather because his emphasis on culture leads him to promote principally pedagogical and dialogical means of social change. Despite, and maybe because of, his widespread involvement in political organizations, groups, and even third parties, Dewey never did get over his Emersonian distrust of them. Hence, he falls back on "communication" as the major way in which "the great community" comes into existence. This communication signifies not only intellectual exchange and academic discussion, but also "close and direct intercourse and attachment."[106] The emergence of "the great community" assures the cultural revitalization and moral regeneration of local communities. Dewey's cultural project calls for changes that fundamentally affect the personal and institutional relations in society. He does not go into details, but he has a pregnant though vague idea of what his ideal would look like.

We have but touched lightly and in passing upon the conditions which must be fulfilled if the Great Society is to become a Great Community; a society in which the ever-expanding and intricately ramifying consequences of associated activities shall be known in the full sense of that word, so that an organized, articulate Public comes into being. The highest and most difficult kind of inquiry and a subtle, delicate, vivid and responsive act of communication must take possession of the physical machinery of transmission and circulation and breathe life into it. When the machine age has thus perfected its machinery it will be a means of life and not its despotic master. Democracy will come into its own, for democracy is a name for a life of free and enriching communion. It had its seer in Walt Whitman. It will have its consummation when free social inquiry is indissolubly wedded to the art of full and moving communication.[107]

Contrary to popular opinion, Dewey's project never really got off the ground. Like Emerson's moralism, Dewey's culturalism was relatively impotent. Why? Principally because his favored historical agents—the professional and reformist elements of the middle class—were seduced by two strong waves of thought and action: managerial ideologies of corporate liberalism and bureaucratic control, and Marxist ideologies of class struggle and party organization. Both engendered utopian energies and group loyalties and could point to concrete victories. The first not only seized the imagination of his professional constituency, but also penetrated the very practices of his own occupational space, the university; the second attracted a number of his students, including talented ones such as Max Eastman and Sidney Hook. It is important to remember that Dewey's pragmatism is quite different from the practicalism of corporate liberalism. It is significant that Dewey's project of creative democracy differed greatly from Franklin D. Roosevelt's liberal program. Dewey opposed Roosevelt's strategies to patch up the crisis-ridden capitalist system, strategies that left significant power in the hands of the privileged plutocracy.[108] To put it bluntly, Dewey tried to create a third party and ended up voting for Norman Thomas on the Socialist party ticket in 1932, 1936, and 1940. In the midst of the war and a debilitated American left, he voted for FDR in 1944. In short, he was not a supportive ideologue for the most exemplary corporate liberalism in American history.

In regard to Marxism, Dewey remained a stranger, a novice, an extreme critic. Despite his courageous, diligent, and fair investigations concerning the "trial" of Leon Trotsky and his son, Dewey harbored deep prejudices against Marxism without the benefit of a serious study of its founder or its intellectual tradition.[109] I suspect that Dewey never came to terms with Marxism for three basic reasons. First, as a young left Hegelian himself for a short time, Dewey's worldly reflections were shaped by British and American writers such as T. H. Green, Henry Carter Adams,

Edward Bellamy, Henry George, Jane Addams, and his Chicago colleague Thorstein Veblen. In fact, in 1928 Dewey still described Henry George as "one of the world's great social philosophers."[110] Here surely his earlier youthful enthusiasm blurred his judgment and bloated his rhetoric.

The second reason Dewey ignored Marxism was that it was anathema to the professional and academic circles he traveled in. Just as he had kept his distance from political controversy at Chicago, Dewey held Marxism at arm's length for career purposes. Even giving Marxism the dignity of close intellectual scrutiny could provoke the wrath of conservative trustees or university administrators.

Last, and most important, Dewey understood in later life that the major battle in the twentieth century was that between the United States and the Soviet Union, between Americanism and communism, between the legacy of Emerson and that of Marx. His role in mediating these battles in Russia (1928), Japan (1919), China (1920), Turkey (1924), South Africa (1934), and Mexico (1926, 1937) bears this out.[111] In the Soviet Union, Dewey saw not simply a new society being created but a new civilization emerging. In his article "Leningrad Gives the Clue" he writes, "The outstanding fact in Russia is a revolution, involving a release of human powers on such an unprecedented scale that it is of incalculable significance not only for that country, but for the world."[112] And in his piece "A New World in the Making" Dewey states: "The final significance of what is taking place in Russia is not to be grasped in political or economic terms, but is found in change, of incalculable importance, in the mental and moral disposition of a people, an educational transformation."[113] At a crucial moment in this article, Dewey compares the United States with the Soviet Union with respect to creativity, ebullience, and pioneering spirit, and finds his own country lacking.

> We all know a certain legend appropriate to the lips and pen of the European visitor to America: here is a land inhabited by a strangely young folk, with the buoyancy, energy, naïveté and immaturity of youth and inexperience. That is the way Moscow impressed me, and very much more so than my own country. There, indeed, was a life full of hope, of confidence, almost hyperactive, naïve at times and on some subjects incredibly so, having the courage that achieves much because it springs from that ignorance of youth that is not held back by fears born from too many memories.[114]

In other words, Dewey describes postrevolutionary Russia in Emersonian terms.

Dewey was wise enough to realize that even after Russia underwent vast regimentation and repression under Stalin, its utopian energies and revolutionary rhetoric could not but attract and inspire new generations of colonized peoples around the world yearning to be free. His description of how "socialistic literature, anarchism, Marx and Kropotkin" were running "like wild-fire through reading circles" in China after the student revolt of May 4, 1919, was indeed prescient.[115]

Why then would Dewey not take the time to come to terms with this Marxism that possesses the capacity to sweep the globe? It is important to distinguish between Marxism as distinct political movements and Marxism as a diverse intellectual tradition. Dewey kept tabs on the former both as a foe of his Emersonian culture of radical democracy and as a source of insights to be incorporated into his project. Dewey largely discarded the latter as a monistic footnote to Hegel, a mere string of dogmatic platitudes and political slogans. As I noted earlier, Dewey considered Marx's magnum opus *Capital* as the most influential book of the half century preceding 1930. I am suggesting he did this not because he believed Marx had laid bare the iron laws of capitalism but rather because the book had such impact through political movements in the world. In short, Dewey's evangelical zeal for his version of Emersonian democracy deterred him from reading the classics of Marxism, just as Christians rarely read the Koran and Protestants pay little attention to Catholic catechisms. It seems to have never occurred to Dewey that the dominant communist movements may have traduced Marxism just as major "pragmatic" activists truncated his own views.

Notwithstanding his relative neglect of Marxism, Dewey's one effort to write about and against it is still noteworthy. In his book *Freedom and Culture* (1939), he attempts to take on foes of creative democracy on cultural grounds; that is, he critically compares the pluralistic and individualistic ways of life in a "democracy" and the monistic and collectivistic ways of life under "totalitarianism." The words in quotes remain abstractions throughout the book—atypical for Dewey. Yet his analyses do point out the significant degree to which Marxist conceptions of society often valorize totality, universal classes, unified movements, and homogeneous groupings at the expense of different social spheres, particular strata within classes, and diverse and heterogeneous ethnic, racial, and gender groups across classes. While Dewey hammers away at his old theme of allying democracy "with the spread of the scientific attitude,"[116] he also makes claims somewhat similar to those currently debated in contemporary post-Marxist circles concerning the explanatory weight of economic, political, cultural, and psychological spheres in history and society. Like Ernesto Laclau and Chantal Mouffe, Stanley Aronowitz and Frank Cunningham, Dewey raises the methodological question:

> Is there any one factor or phase of culture which is dominant, or which tends to produce and regulate others, or are economics, morals, art, science, and so on only so many aspects of the interaction of a number of factors, each of which acts upon and is acted upon by the others?[117]

Dewey quickly replies that his pragmatism rejects any attempts to invoke necessity and discern any single all-embracing causal force. Instead,

"*probability* and *pluralism* are characteristics of the present state of science."
Therefore, "the fundamental postulate of the discussion is that isolation
of any one factor, no matter how strong its workings at a given time,
is fatal to understanding and to intelligent action."[118]

Dewey remains unable to conceive of Marxism as anything but a "uni-
formitarian theory" that "throws out psychological as well as moral considerations" in the name of "objective" forces.[119] He goes as far as to claim
that this is true of "Marx and every Marxist after him."[120] This is blatantly
false—and Dewey adduces no evidence, no close readings of Marx, Engels,
Labriola, Lukács, Korsch, et al. Dewey's critique certainly applies to a
crude version of Marxism, and the implications of his critique could supply
interesting subject matter for dialogue with a sophisticated Marxist. Unfortunately, Dewey—here at his worst—forecloses such dialogue by presenting
the weakest versions of his imagined interlocutor.

Dewey is often accused of either assuming a pluralist-interactionist
view of society that overlooks the larger structural forms of power or promoting an explanatory nihilism that fails to give more weight to one factor
over another and therefore yields no explanations.[121] I think Dewey is
innocent of both charges. In fact, Dewey approaches Marxism in highlighting the economic, though he is actually closer to Charles Beard's Madi-
sonian economic determinism than that of Marx. Dewey is claiming
neither that all factors may have the same weight nor that structural forms
of power should be ignored. Rather he is saying that the weight that factors
do have is determined not a priori but a posteriori, never by dialectical
fiat but by empirical investigation. Of course, such investigation is necessarily theory-laden, but one's assumptions and theoretical entry points
can still be kept tentative, provisional, revisable, and open to reasonable
objections. Hence, there are no genuine theories of History and Society,
only detailed, concrete analyses of particular peoples and specific societies. An analysis is acceptable according to how well it accounts for complex phenomena, not how well it conforms to some general theory. The
debate between Marxists and non-Marxists should proceed likewise.

> The only way to decide would be to investigate, and by investigation
> in the concrete decide just what effects are due, say, to science, and just
> what to the naked, so to say, forces of economic production. To adopt
> and pursue this method would be in effect to abandon the all-compre-
> hensive character of economic determination. It would put us in the
> relativistic and pluralistic position of considering a number of interacting
> factors—of which a very important one is undoubtedly the economic.[122]

Critics of Dewey are on firmer ground when they claim that *Freedom
and Culture* tends to stress individuals more than communities and institutions as the safeguard to democracy. In his 1939 revised statement of his
1930 "What I Believe," Dewey writes:

I should now wish to emphasize more than I formerly did that individuals are finally decisive factors of the nature and movement of associated life.

The cause of this shift of emphasis is the events of the intervening years. The rise of dictatorships and totalitarian states and the decline of democracy have been accompanied with loud proclamation of the idea that only the state, the political organization of society, can give security of individuals . . .

It has been shown in the last few years that democratic *institutions* are no guarantee for the existence of democratic individuals. The alternative is that individuals who prize their own liberties and who prize the liberties of other individuals, individuals who are democratic in thought and action, are the sole final warrant for the existence and endurance of democratic institutions . . .

In rethinking this issue in the light of the rise of totalitarian states, I am led to emphasize the idea that only the voluntary initiative and voluntary co-operation of individuals can produce social institutions that will protect the liberties necessary for achieving development of genuine individuality.[123]

In this revealing passage, Dewey is responding to that with which American pragmatists of his time and those who come later must grapple: the implications of fascism and Stalinism for American civilization. And, to complicate matters, the world-historical process of the decolonization of the third world accelerates while the United States emerges as *the* world power after World War II. Dewey's long and gallant struggle to creatively revise the Emersonian evasion and affirm the Emersonian theodicy exemplifies the coming-of-age of American pragmatism. Historical consciousness—like America in world history—seizes center stage. The Emersonian evasion recedes to the background, of limited interest and little importance to post-Deweyan pragmatists who become social critics, literary critics, or poets; and the Emersonian theodicy becomes more difficult to revise and reaffirm. A deep sense of tragedy and irony creeps into American pragmatism, a sense alien to Emerson, Peirce, James, and Dewey. American pragmatism, like America itself, reaches maturity. But can the post-Deweyan pragmatists keep the legacy alive? Can American pragmatism meet the new challenges of the American century? Or will it lose its footing in this new wilderness?

4

The Dilemma of the Mid-Century Pragmatic Intellectual

> When it is acknowledged that under the disguise of dealing with ultimate reality, philosophy has been occupied with the precious values embedded in social traditions, that it has sprung from a clash of social ends and from a conflict of inherited institutions with incompatible contemporary tendencies, it will be seen that the task of future philosophy is to clarify men's ideas as to the social and moral strifes of their own day. Its aim is to become as far as is humanly possible an organ for dealing with these conflicts.
>
> — *John Dewey*

The legacy of American pragmatism for mid-century intellectuals was the project of promoting an Emersonian culture of creative democracy by means of critical intelligence and social action. The major proponents of this project and legacy were no longer white Yankees but rather two second-generation Jewish Americans, Sidney Hook and Lionel Trilling; a second-generation American of German extraction, Reinhold Niebuhr; an Irish Southwesterner, C. Wright Mills; and a fifth-generation American of African descent, W. E. B. Du Bois. Unlike Emerson, Peirce, James, and Dewey, they neither were born and bred in the world of the northeastern highbrow culture and bourgeois society nor took for granted its privileges and opportunities. American pragmatism had gone native in new and diverse ways.

The major dilemma facing these pragmatic intellectuals was the limited social and discursive space for an Emersonian culture of creative democracy.

To them, it seemed as if the end of the intellectual and political frontier for American pragmatism had come. They were suspicious of the bureaucratization of politics, the corporate liberalism that regulated the social engineers at the helm of American capitalist society. They could not hold for long with the seductive yet antiseptic Marxisms of the day. They were unsettled by and distrustful of the artistic modernisms produced in a devastated and declining Europe. They objected to the philistinism of the emerging popular culture of consumption in American society. And they were amazed at the persistence and pervasiveness of virulent racism and vulgar religion in the country. In short, meretricious Stalinism, pernicious fascism, obstinate imperialism, and myopic Americanism were formidable foes that left American pragmatism with little room to maneuver.

Sidney Hook—close friend, student, and loyal critic of Dewey—first moved toward Marxism yet soon became disillusioned with its deformation in the Soviet Union. He then became a leading cold warrior trying to carve out social democratic space on the edges of corporate liberalism as a philosophy professor and social activist. C. Wright Mills abandoned philosophy after obtaining his M.A. degree in the discipline and turned to social theory only to find it dominated by Parsonian theory supporting the corporate liberal establishment. He declared war on Talcott Parsons' sociology, turned his guns on it, and found himself isolated in and disgusted with a conformist and complacent academy.

W. E. B. Du Bois also gave up philosophy after studying under William James at Harvard, turning to the study of history and society. An organic intellectual of the first order, he edited the periodical of the leading U.S. civil rights organization, moved later toward Marxism, suffered intense marginality, and ultimately expatriated to Ghana. Reinhold Niebuhr was deeply influenced by a Jamesian pragmatism which permitted him to preserve and promote his socialism and later his cold war liberalism. Even more than Hook, given the postwar revival of religion, Niebuhr rode the coattails of corporate liberalism to fame and fanfare—though to little pecuniary fortune. Last, Lionel Trilling, who arguably does not belong with this motley crew of distinguished pragmatists, found in James and Dewey precisely what he saw best exemplified by Matthew Arnold: an intense yet flexible moral imagination critically engaged with life. After a brief encounter with Marxism, Trilling guided his liberal anticommunist readers through the melioristic literary terrain of moral realism and the terrifying jungles of literary modernism. Unlike the other figures, Trilling ended world-weary, overwhelmed by fate and circumstances and in search of personal serenity and small-scale tranquillity. In other words, Trilling discarded the Emersonian theodicy.

The central problem for these thinkers is the waning powers of willful persons against stubborn circumstances. Pervasive in their writings are a sense of the tragic, a need for irony, a recognition of limits and constraints, and a stress on paradox, ambiguity, and difficulty. I suggest that this central problem, along with these pervasive traits, is symptomatic of the eclipse of radical utopian desires among most of the intelligentsia and much of the populace in America. The aftermath of World War II, especially the economic boom and the introspective turn of the country, witnessed not the rebirth of Emersonian optimism but rather an Augustinian pessimism regarding the human lot coupled with a fervent privatism and careerism in an expanding economy. The symbols of the war—the concentration camp and the mushroom cloud—left indelible stamps on the minds of Americans, reminding them that they lived in a cruel, dangerous, and precarious world. The basic issues facing intellectuals in the pragmatist grain were how to promote and sustain human agency in a tragic world; how to distinguish between utopian and melioristic energies without succumbing to a glib optimism or a paralyzing pessimism; and, most important, how to keep alive the intellectual and political possibility of an Emersonian culture of creative democracy in a world of shrinking options. The fate of American pragmatism depended, in part, on how these thinkers reaffirmed, revised, or rejected the Emersonian theodicy in light of the brutal realities and urgent problems of the mid-twentieth century.

Sidney Hook: The Deweyan Political Intellectual

Sidney Hook is the postwar heir to John Dewey's mantle as the leading socially engaged pragmatist philosopher. He is in many ways an intriguing figure whose intricate trajectory has left a long trail of intellectual carnage. Hook is a Deweyan sharpshooter who begins his career with Dewey as his first target.

Born to Jewish parents in New York City in 1902, Hook was raised in working-class slums.[1] Like so many energetic and talented Jewish youths, he attended the College of the City of New York, where he came under the influence of Morris Raphael Cohen, a naturalist philosopher with a Harvard Ph.D. earned under Royce and James and the editor of the first collection of essays by Charles Peirce.[2] After matriculating to the graduate school of Columbia University, Hook was attracted to F. J. E. Woodbridge and John Dewey. This dual attraction is significant in that Hook has always considered himself as much a naturalist as a pragmatist. For him, the two positions are inseparable though not identical. This is why he is extremely uncomfortable with the idea of a theistic pragmatist such as James or Niebuhr and consistently opposed to God-talk per se.

Hook's first public criticisms of Dewey were generated by his own attraction to Woodbridge's modified naturalistic Aristotelian metaphysics. In his dissertation, *The Metaphysics of Pragmatism* (1927)—with an introduction by Dewey—Hook mildly accuses Dewey of presupposing a "metaphysics of the instrument" (be it tools or the activity of thought itself) that remains unarticulated in pragmatic philosophy. Hook claims that "unless pragmatism is to experience the same fate which has befallen the positivism of Comte and the phenomenalism of Mach—philosophies proudly and avowedly anti-metaphysical—it must analyze the implications of what it means to have a method and examine the generic traits of existence which make that method a fruitful one in revealing them."[3] The major aim of Hook's dissertation is not to disagree fundamentally with Dewey's pragmatism—distinguished sharply from James's "mystical and nominalistic pragmatism"[4]—but rather to show the degree to which it is similar to Woodbridge's Aristotelian naturalism. In a rare act in professional philosophy, Hook begins his naturalistic defense of the primacy of circumstance for human action by interpreting a frontispiece to William Blake's prophetic poem *Europe*. Entitled *The Ancient of Days* and supposedly suggested by lines 224–31 of book 7 of Milton's *Paradise Lost*, it shows God creating the perimeters of the world. Hook writes:

> Whatever else of frenzied fancy this picture may symbolize, it illustrates a profound metaphysical meaning. For it may be given to a primal divinity to *create* subject matter with the very instruments which can only be intelligibly used or applied *within* that subject matter and which logically presuppose it. But man in his workaday practices—if not in his holiday wisdom—must content himself with guiding instruments which mark out and define distinctions in a universe of existence or discourse whose confines, if not irrevocably given, are at least tentatively assumed.[5]

Hook's point is not simply that creativity presupposes preexistent material (like Plato's *ananke* and *chora* in the *Timaeus*), but also that circumstances and conditions circumscribe the highest forms of transformative agency. On the one hand, Hook wants to shun all epistemological idealist tendencies in pragmatism. Hence, even a proponent of human creativity like Blake must presuppose antecedent conditions. On the other hand, Hook wants to affirm the Aristotelian naturalism of Woodbridge as continuous with Dewey's pragmatism at its best: "I cannot but believe that the fundamental positions of scientific pragmatism are in consonance with the doctrines so persuasively set forth in Professor Woodbridge's *Realm of Mind*."[6] Most important, Hook wants to affirm the "mainspring of pragmatism's great vitality"—that is, its "passionate moral interest in the creative power and possibilities of human thinking"—while accenting the circumstantial and the conditioned. Thus a "metaphysics of the instrument" is a kind of metaphysics of nature; namely, human freedom depends on a natural order, but this order does not determine itself or dictate to this freedom. The major culprits of Hook's pragmatic naturalism are fatalism, determinism, and inevitabilism as well as unconditioned voluntarism and acontextual creationism (in the philosophic sense of the word). He does not claim that Dewey falls prey to any of these, but Dewey's emphasis tends at times to slight the circumstantial in order to stress human creative powers. In other words, Dewey's Emersonian theodicy requires a slightly deeper grounding in nature and history; Hook wants to take with extreme seriousness Marx's insight that people act and create but not under circumstances of their own choosing.

While writing his dissertation, Hook was reading voraciously in Marx and the Marxist tradition (including translating Lenin).[7] And after studying in Berlin, Munich, and the Marx-Engels Institute in Moscow—as well as becoming the first Marxist philosophy professor in the United States at New York University—Hook wrote the two best American philosophic treatments of Marx we have, *Towards the Understanding of Karl Marx: A Revolutionary Interpretation* (1933) and *From Hegel to Marx* (1936). In the first book, Hook paints a highly plausible and, at times, persuasive picture of Marx as a left Deweyan. Conversant with Georg Lukács's *History and Class Consciousness* (1923), and *Marxism and Philosophy* (1925) by Karl Korsch with whom he studied in Berlin, Hook put forward a clear and novel interpretation of Marx's writing unheard of at the time—and hardly heard of since. In the second book, Hook simply walks one through the central developments and various figures of German idealist philosophy, showing the philosophic significance of Marx's historical materialist breakthrough. Both texts are classics in Marxist scholarship.

Hook's basic aim in both books is to introduce the Marxist tradition to the American intelligentsia. This introduction is necessary not simply because knowledge of Marxism is in itself an asset, but, more pointedly, because this knowledge is required for those who take seriously critical intelligence and creative democracy. Hook's probe into Marxist theory and analysis is grounded in his commitment to Dewey's project of creating an Emersonian culture of radical democracy. For Hook, Dewey's gallant efforts to infuse American pragmatism with historical consciousness must be extended to include the Marxist stress on historical specificity, class struggle, and even violent revolution. Moreover, Dewey's rejection of violent social change is reasonable in that it recognizes the tremendous cost in human lives and energy. Yet his hope for nonviolent change reeks of an optimism that turns its face from realities of history and present-day society.

> When has any ruling class permitted itself to be bowed out of power without putting up the most desperate kind of resistance? . . . It should also be borne in mind that in virtue of their past training, ideology, and class status, the ruling class necessarily regards the defense of its property interests as the defense of civilization against barbarism, the preservation of the refinements of its culture as the preservation of all culture against the vandalism of the rabble. Out of this subjective sincerity there often arises . . . a desire to go down fighting for what they consider honor and the good life.
>
> That the workers will have to resort to force to achieve the socialist

revolution, is for Marx, then, as likely as anything can be in history
. . . To be sure, there is always the *abstract possibility* that power may
be won peacefully. But history is not determined by abstract possibilities.[8]

In direct response to Dewey's argument concerning the cost of such
violent force, Hook reverts to the imperfect world of limited options in
which we live and the heavy costs being paid by those suffering in the
present situation.

> The Marxist replies that he is willing to judge any project by its cost.
> But to judge anything *only* by its cost is to condemn everything ever
> undertaken and carried to completion in this imperfect world . . . both
> logic and morality demand, however, that before we reject a proposal
> because of its cost, we consider the cost of rejecting it for any of the
> available alternatives. The Marxist contention is that the costs of social
> revolution are far less than the costs of chronic evils of poverty, unem-
> ployment, moral degradation, and war, which are immanent in capi-
> talism; that the ultimate issue and choice is between imperialistic war
> which promises nothing but the destruction of all culture, yes, of the
> human race itself, and an international revolution which promises a new
> era in world history.[9]

And in his superb book *John Dewey: An Intellectual Portrait* (1939), Hook
reaffirms this hope for powerful change yet rejects—based on the evidence—
Dewey's unwarranted optimism.

> Will the overlords of American industrial and financial life accept a demo-
> cratically arrived-at decision? Or will they attempt to abet a "proslavery"
> rebellion? No matter how one answers these questions, since we cannot
> be sure one way or the other and since so much depends upon it, it
> is a necessary part of political wisdom to be prepared for every even-
> tuality. In the light of recent events in Europe, even in the light of Ameri-
> can history, there does not seem to be much ground for optimism.[10]

What is significant here is not simply Hook's revolutionary rhetoric
deployed to further Dewey's project but also Hook's use of the notions
of "imperfection," "limited alternatives," and "history" to burst Dewey's
optimistic bubble. In short, Hook attempts to promote Dewey's Emersonian culture of creative democracy by radically historicizing Dewey's
Emersonian theodicy.

Yet Hook's own efforts are redirected as the deformation of Marxism
proceeds under Stalin and as Hitler extends his domination over Europe.
Slowly but surely Hook's focus shifts from denouncing a deficient capitalist
democracy to defending an "imperfect" one against the threats of Stalinism
and fascism. It is no accident that in Hook's major book *The Hero in History*
(1943), in which he breaks from his earlier Marxism, he falls back on the
Emersonian preoccupation with the creative powers of unique individuals
in history, on the issues of genius, fate and circumstance, and democracy.

In this sense, Hook's meditations on "event-making" men, e.g., Lenin, in history cover the same territory as Perry Miller's canonical essay "Emersonian Genius and the American Democracy" (1953). As Hook notes, his purpose is to provide a satisfactory account of the historical relation "between the part men played and the conditioning scene which provided the materials."[11]

The major revelation in this text is not Hook's long tenth chapter "The Russian Revolution: A Test Case" in which he concludes that without Lenin there would have been no Russian Revolution and goes on to speculate unconvincingly that without the revolution, a Soviet constitutional republic would have emerged that would have prevented the rise of fascism et al.[12] Rather what is crucial about Hook's book is the use of notions of "imperfection," "limitation," and "history" to argue against his own earlier belief in the possibility of revolutionary change. If Dewey's response to Hook's earlier critique was "OK, violence is necessary for change, but all we realistically have at our disposal is critical intelligence and reformist strategies," then Hook's 1943 response to his earlier critique was "Yes, violence is necessary for change, but such violence may undermine the incomplete democracy in place, especially given the threat by totalitarian regimes abroad and within." In other words, Hook was still historicizing the Emersonian theodicy but now with the result of highlighting the difficulty of creating an Emersonian culture of radical democracy.

In effect, Hook arrives where Dewey was; he accepts Dewey's position, but with one crucial addition: Hook has a profound sense of betrayal and disappointment. At forty-one, he is forced to fundamentally give up the Marxism that guided and sustained him for over two decades. Four years later, he stated:

> For the last twenty years I have presented an interpretation of Marx which has run counter to customary views and conceptions of his fundamental doctrines . . . It would appear that if I were justified in my interpretation of Marx's meaning, I would be perhaps the only true Marxist left in the world. This is too much for my sense of humor, so I have decided to abandon the term as a descriptive epithet of my position.[13]

Unsurprisingly, much—though not all—of Hook's intellectual energy is geared toward those still stuck, as it were, in Marxism rather than toward the American industrial and financial overlords. Like Dewey, he finds himself forced into the corporate liberal camp, uneasy with their top-down social engineering but grateful for their patriotic welcome. And he is deeply ashamed of his Marxist past, not only his enthusiastic support of the Communist party presidential candidate of 1932 (William Z. Foster) but also his ground-breaking book of 1933. Needless to say, he has little patience for those Marxists still attracted to the only noteworthy left organizations remaining in the country, the Stalinist Communist party and the

Trotskyist Socialist Workers party. As the most learned Marxologist in the country, Hook embarks on a kind of moral crusade, fueled by patriotic intentions and bitter memories, against the Marxist left. Yet in 1947, Hook still divided the world not in terms of capitalist West and communist East, as in the usual cold war rhetoric, but rather in terms of democratic socialism and Soviet totalitarianism with America yet to choose.

> The crisis of twentieth century man is the crisis of twentieth century society. It is expressed most fundamentally in the conflict between western democratic socialism as typified in the pattern slowly emerging in England today, and byzantine totalitarianism as typified in Soviet Russia. American culture will slowly make its way toward one or the other.[14]

But only two years later, in a move surely accelerated by the Wallace campaign of 1948, Hook falls in line with the cold war rhetoric of "the elementary truth that what divides the world today is . . . the issue of political freedom versus despotism."[15] The "logic" of this rhetoric is as follows. The Soviet Union is the greatest threat to peace and freedom in the world; the United States, as the leader of the "free" world, should contain the expansion of the Soviet empire; this containment is the top priority of U.S. foreign policy; and this policy precludes any further democratization (e.g., in the economic sphere) of American society. Hook affirms all but the last of these claims. As a cold war social democrat, he still calls for more social control of the economy; and as an old civil rights activist (though an opponent of affirmative action), he knows that black America still gets a bum deal.[16]

Hook's most mature and memorable statement of his post-Deweyan pragmatism is his "Pragmatism and the Tragic Sense of Life" (1960). In this essay, Hook explicitly historicizes the Emersonian theodicy in the direction of limitations, constraints, and circumstance. He does not eliminate or discourage human will and agency, but rather circumscribes them owing to a paucity of options and alternatives. In other words, Hook declares himself less a pioneer seizing unprecedented opportunities and more a latecomer preserving the best in the present. He remains a meliorist, yet he looks more to the past than to the future—or, to put it another way, when he looks to the future what he sees is but a repetition of the past.

In this important essay, Hook tries to remain true to the fundamental pragmatist themes of an open universe, the role of human powers in shaping the present, and the need for critical intelligence for guiding action for a better future. Yet he also defines pragmatism as a "temper of mind towards the vital options which men confront," a temper of mind that acknowledges the "inescapable limitations" of human powers and "the reality of piecemeal losses."[17] He invokes William James—once thought by Hook too "mystical"—as insistent on the centrality of "ineluctable woes and losses" to the pragmatic view.

This aspect of the philosophy of pragmatism has been almost completely ignored by its critics. It seems to me, however, to be central in pragmatism, and to provide an illuminating perspective from which to survey the problems and predicaments of men. It is grounded in a recognition of the tragic sense of life.[18]

Hook goes on to contest narrow pragmatic conceptions of philosophy that reduce it to mere moralizing and social reform. Instead, he defends Dewey's broader view of philosophy as a "sustained reflective pursuit of wisdom."[19] He then associates this pragmatic quest for wisdom with a recognition of the tragic sense of life. Hook admits that this association appears puzzling given common perceptions of pragmatism's link with optimism, possibilities, and upbeat outlooks:

The juxtaposition of the expressions "pragmatism" and "the tragic sense of life" may appear bewildering to those who understand "pragmatism" as a narrow theory of meaning and "the tragic sense of life" as the hysterical lament that man is not immortal—the theme song of Unamuno's book of that title. To speak of pragmatism and the tragic sense of life is somewhat like speaking of "the Buddhism of John Dewey" or "the Dewey nobody knows."
    I am not aware that Dewey ever used the phrase "the tragic sense of life," but I know that growing up in the shadow of the civil war he felt what I shall describe by it and that it is implied by his account of moral experience.[20]

In this passage, Hook moves much too quickly. First, many reasonable people grew up in "the shadow of the civil war"—just as many today did during the Holocaust—without acquiring a tragic sense of life. The key is not simply the circumstances under which one lives, but how one interprets those circumstances. Second, the tragic sense of life may be implied in Dewey's project, but the crucial issue is how one uses this tragic sense and for what purposes. Historical consciousness requires an encounter with intractable constraints, choices between conflicting goods and limited options. This encounter can generate a tragic sense that promotes utopian energies, as we saw in his early writings, or that keeps social desires within reformist confines, as in the later Hook and Dewey. Needless to say, a tragic sense also can endorse the futility of human will and agency, a view rejected by both Hook and Dewey.

Hook considers the tragic to be a moral phenomenon, a predicament that involves human conflictual choice. The natural phenomena of sickness, old age, and death may appear pitiful but are not, for Hook, in and of themselves tragic. The tragic consists of moral choices that must be made in the face of irreconcilable values, and especially conflicting obligations.

The most dramatic of all moral conflicts is not between good and good, or between good and right, but between right and right . . . On the international scene it is expressed in the conflict of incompatible national claims, each with *some* measure of justification, as in the Israeli-Arab impasse . . .

Irony is compounded with tragedy in the fact that many of the rights we presently enjoy we owe to our ancestors, who in the process of winning them for us deprived others of their rights. In some regions of the world the very ground on which people stand was expropriated by force and fraud from others by their ancestors. Yet as a rule it would be a new injustice to seek to redress the original injustice by depriving those of their possessions who hold present title to them. Every just demand for reparations against an aggressor country is an unjust demand on the descendants of its citizens, who as infants were not responsible for the deeds of aggression. That is why history is the arena of the profoundest moral conflicts in which some legitimate right has always been sacrificed, sometimes on the altars of the god of war.[21]

Hook's injection of a notion of irony here is instructive. It functions essentially as an impetus to acknowledge difficulty and complexity, to sympathize with the victims on the underside of history while defusing any utopian energies or subversive desires on the part of oneself *and* the victims. Note that the "us" to which he refers are "the winners" deemed so by the bloody process of history. The real losers are the "them"—the Indians in the Americas, aboriginal peoples of Australia, Palestinians in Israel, and indigenous black people in South Africa. To put it crudely, irony serves as a way of morally condemning Thrasymachus' doctrine of might makes right yet politically accepting the historical verdict of the "winners"—i.e., "us."

Ironically, Hook's attempt to infuse American pragmatism with a deeper and richer form of historical consciousness than that of Dewey falls back on James's view of pragmatism as mediating and reconciling extreme positions. Within the historical arena, absent in James, this mediating and reconciling is tilted toward the victors rather than the victims of history, the first category including past victims who are present-day victors. This bias looms large in Hook's comparison of pragmatism with Hegelian historicism and Christian love.

> There are three generic approaches to the tragic conflicts of life. The first approach is that of history. The second is that of love. The third is that of creative intelligence in quest for ways of mediation which I call here the pragmatic.[22]

Hook rejects the Hegelian historicist approach because it "attempts to console man with a dialectical proof that his agony and defeat are not really evils but necessary elements in the goodness of the whole."[23] This "tapestry" theodicy rides roughshod over genuine tragedy, refusing to acknowledge how terrible history is. Hook also casts aside the agapic approach that overlooks the conflicts between the various love commitments people have. And the love ethic yields no means of adjudicating between these conflicts.

For Hook, the appeal to divine love is empty since God loves everybody equally; this leads to the objectionable conclusion, for Hook, that "God loves Stalin no less than Stalin's victims."[24]

Hook claims that the pragmatic approach neither vulgarizes nor spiritualizes tragedy. It is more serious and heroic than the other approaches because its method of critical intelligence provides a guide for human beings who can both create tragic history and benefit from this creation. The key to this guide is a dominant trope in cold war rhetoric – the lesser evil.

> Every mediation entails some sacrifice. The quest for the unique good of the situation, for what is to be done here and now, may point to what is better than anything else available, but what it points to is also a lesser evil. It is a lesser evil whether found in a compromise or in moderating the demand of a just claim or in learning to live peacefully with one's differences on the same general principle which tells us that a divorce is better for all parties concerned than a murder.[25]

What is troubling here is not so much the trope of "the lesser evil" itself but the use to which it is put. This use – to mediate and compromise within a given context – is itself value-laden, ideologically charged, and socially loaded. Again, as we saw with the early Hook, the choice of a "lesser evil" from the vantage point of victims may be fundamental social change or revolution. This trope, much like the notion of the tragic, becomes the possession of cold war liberal reformists (or conservative Tories) when a shift occurs in the vantage point from which one assesses alternatives. As Hook showed in his early works, the point is not really who has a tragic sense (i.e., who is wise, sophisticated, and refined) and who does not (i.e., who is unwise, crude, and naive), but rather what conception of it does one have and to what uses is it put in light of one's interests and purposes.

This issue becomes even more complicated when the rhetoric of critical intelligence not only rests upon brute force but also conceals its complicity with brute force, as happens in the case of the later Hook who claims that the proper task of all critical intellectuals is to promote the war-making capacities of the United States to offset the menace of the Soviet Union. Hook hits this issue head on.

> The intelligent use of force to *prevent* or crush the use of force, where a healthy democratic process, equitable laws and traditions and customs of freedom make it possible to vent differences in a rational and orderly way, is therefore justifiable even if on prudential grounds one may forego such action. This means that tolerance always has limits – it cannot tolerate what is itself actively intolerant.[26]

Again Hook's "realistic," no-nonsense perspective makes pragmatism more a handmaiden to cold war corporate liberalism than an amelioristic releasing of human powers for genuine individuality. Ironically, it pictures the latter view of pragmatism itself as mere idealistic moralizing. Hook describes monopoly capitalist America as enjoying "a healthy democratic process with equitable laws" – notwithstanding (in 1960 when this was written) institutionalized terrorism undergirding a one-party, whites-only political system in the South and corporate domination of the system elsewhere in the country. The issue of whose vantage point one adopts is crucial here. His preoccupation with the limits of critical intelligence and tolerance seems premature, dictated and motivated by tendentious cold war ideology. Hook's views display a preservative, defensive, and retrospective sensibility rather than an exploratory, expansive, prospective temper.

In his conclusion, Hook adopts a Deweyan rhetoric, fused with Emersonian tropes of human creativity and possibility but purged of any utopian, optimistic, and subversive Emersonian elements.

> As I understand the pragmatic perspective on life, it is an attempt to make it possible for men to live in a world of inescapable tragedy – a tragedy that flows from the conflict of moral ideals – without lamentation, defiance or make-believe. According to this perspective, even in the best of human worlds there will be tragedy – tragedy perhaps without bloodshed, but certainly not without tears . . .
>
> Pragmatism . . . sees in men something which is at once, to use the Sophoclean phrase, more wonderful and more terrible than anything else in the universe, viz., the power to make themselves and the world around them better or worse. In this way, pragmatic meliorism avoids . . . romantic pessimism . . . and grandiose optimism.
>
> Pragmatism, as I interpret it, is the theory and practice of enlarging human freedom in a precarious and tragic world by the arts of intelligent social control. It may be a lost cause. I do not know of a better one, and it may not be lost if we can summon the courage and intelligence to support our faith in freedom – and enjoy the blessings of a little luck.[27]

Unlike Emerson, Peirce, James, and Dewey, Hook conveys the sense of being cramped and constrained, a feeling of being hemmed in. He affirms the voluntaristic and moralistic aspects of the Emersonian theodicy, yet he refuses to accept the Emersonian idea that the world is somehow congenial to human – especially American – aspirations. Hook believes neither nature nor history is biased in favor of human progress. In direct reference to Emerson, Hook writes:

> Even those unconventionally religious men like Emerson and Whitman who accept the world, and believe that man can find security in cheerful affirmation of the natural conditions of his being, must recognize that Nature is no respecter of human purposes or human existence, that Nature can run amok – that the sufferings produced by the mindless intrusions of fire, ice, flood and wind in human affairs often dwarf those resulting from human cruelty. Jehova or Nature are bound by no rules of man.[28]

Hook does not criticize the anthropocentrism of American pragmatism, a criticism most notably put forward by George Santayana. Yet he does not view nature—or history as temporalized nature—in terms of open space for human occupation, domination, or communion. Rather nature (and history) is a terror that human will can and will never tame. Instead, human beings tragically fight against reversible yet ultimately fateful circumstances.

Unfortunately, Hook's voluminous, scattered writings and long, winding career have received limited attention and scrutiny. This is so, in part, because his cantankerous style and aggressive exchanges—especially during the wave of utopian and subversive activities in the sixties—win him few disciples and followers. More important, his rapacious anticommunism and strong cold war views have concealed the degree to which he was the first original Marxist philosopher in America. Given Dewey's project of an Emersonian culture of radical democracy, it is no accident that the pragmatist tradition produced such a thinker. But the ideological trajectory of Sidney Hook—from Deweyan Marxist through anti-Stalinist democratic socialist to cold war social democrat—portrays American pragmatism in deep crisis.

C. Wright Mills: The Neo-Deweyan Radical Social Critic

C. Wright Mills understood the crisis of American pragmatism better than anyone else in postwar America. For him, this crisis took the form of the incorporation and cooptation of American pragmatism by corporate liberalism in the political sphere; the degeneration of creative democratic aspirations into quests for capitalist profitable production and bourgeois conspicuous consumption in the economic realm; and, most important, the decline of critical intelligence and genuine individuality in American culture. Mills views the near disappearance of the intellectual articulation of and political struggle for an Emersonian culture of radical democracy as a symptom of the pervasive moral decay and intellectual failure of nerve in consumer capitalist America. His aim is not to rejuvenate American pragmatism, but rather to keep alive the best of its vision of a radical democratic and libertarian America.

Born, bred, and educated in Texas, Mills was trained at the graduate level at the University of Wisconsin, where the first major intellectual influence on him was that of the American pragmatists. His own rugged individualism and self-image as an iconoclast fit well with the Emersonian animus against conformity and routine; his enshrinement of moral conscience sat well with the basic ethical impulse of American pragmatism; and Mills's sense of existential outrage at the sheer absurdity of human existence was channeled into a native political radicalism buttressed by American pragmatist promotion of creative democracy.

C. Wright Mills was obsessed with two basic features of postwar America: the decreasing availability of creative human powers in the populace and the stultifying socio-economic circumstances that promoted this decrease. His works can be read as a series of studies of those few persons or groups who still were making history and how this exercise of their powers rendered the rest of the populace nearly powerless. This interplay of Promethean elites and manipulated masses is a central theme in his corpus. His main purpose, moral in motivation and political in character, was to awaken the Promethean energies of the masses by means of critical intelligence and social action; that is, means most readily available to intellectuals whose cultural capital is, supposedly, critical intelligence.

These themes and concerns can be readily detected in Mills's dissertation later published as *Sociology and Pragmatism: The Higher Learning in America* (1964, though finished in 1942). Ostensibly this study "consist[s] in explaining the relations between one type of philosophy, pragmatism, and the American social structure, 'between' philosophy and society; operating as a crude but most tangible link are the educational institutions of higher learning."[29] Yet when one probes deeper the dissertation can be seen as an inquiry into the most sophisticated intellectual articulation of the values and aspirations of the professional and reformist elements of the middle class in industrial America. For Mills, the history of pragmatism is not only inseparable from the history of the academic profession in America, but also inextricably bound up with the rise of a progressive intelligentsia who are dependent on yet critical of capitalist industrialists and financiers and who try to create a world in their own professional and moral image.

In this study, Mills is interested not simply in the coherence and consistency of the pragmatists' formulations or in the social base of their operations; but also, more important, in the intellectual anatomy of the distinctive source of both twentieth-century American liberalism (e.g., progressivism and later the New Deal) and a possible native American radicalism. One of his aims is to show why the latter was smothered by the former principally owing to Dewey's nostalgia for small-town America and his biologically based technological interpretation of reality. I find these claims provocative yet questionable—as is evident from the previous chapter. Yet, for Mills, they serve as the basis of his fundamental critique of Dewey: that Dewey does not take history and society seriously enough to adequately come to terms with political and economic power.

Mills notes Dewey's belief that science and technology are exemplary of the modern exercise of human powers. Mills then writes:

> On the surface it would seem that science and technology were morally neutral, that empirically they should be looked upon as means, which may limit the range of possible ends, but which, nevertheless, do not set them. For some time the scope of technologically possible ends has been very wide, indeed, they range from utter comfort to stark death.

Technological power is then socially neutral and those who would celebrate it must face the question: Power for what? Dewey has celebrated "man's" growth of power through science and technology; he has not clearly answered the question involved in that celebration. To do so would have committed him to face squarely the political and legal problem of the present distribution of power as it exists within this social order. And this Dewey has never done.[30]

Mills is suggesting here that the coming-of-age of American pragmatism in Dewey—upon whom he spends nearly two hundred pages as opposed to eighty-nine for Peirce and sixty-one for James—may professionalize the Emersonian invasion of modern philosophy and update the Emersonian theodicy; yet it fails to push pragmatic historical consciousness into persuasive structural analysis of society. For Mills, to be a sophisticated social critic wedded to the pragmatic ideals of individuality and democracy is to be grounded in the classic tradition of sociology, that is, in the discourses of Karl Marx, Max Weber, Emile Durkheim, Georg Simmel, and others.

Dewey's neglect of Marx and Weber, according to Mills, results in biologizing human conflict and thereby bypassing the fundamental issues of value and power. Echoing Randolph Bourne's earlier challenging argument that Dewey's pragmatism subordinates ends to technique owing to an all-purpose, e.g., biologic, notion of "growth,"[31] Mills holds that the biologism of Dewey prevents him from accenting structural social conflict and struggle.

The biological model of action and reflection serves to minimize the cleavage and power divisions *within* society, or put differently, it serves as a pervasive mode of posing the problem which locates all problems between *man and nature*, instead of between *men and men*.

It, therefore, aids the general attempt at intellectuality, i.e., the attempt to assimilate all value, power, or human problems to a statement of the function of intelligence. The answer to all problems becomes man's use of intelligence to work "his" way out of the difficulties "he" faces. The biological, environment-organism adjustment schematum underlies the cogency of this type of "problemization" and its answer. It jibes with the drive for more education as a solution to social problems: All that is needed is the diffusion of "intelligence."

Through the concept of adaptation, the biological model strengthens the drive toward specificity of problems. And this specificity implements —to put it crudely and briefly here—*a politics of reform of situation.* Adaptation is one step at a time; it faces one situation at a time.[32]

Mills's creative misreading of Dewey in this crucial passage sets the stage for his own more historical and social analytical project. His reading is creative in that in Emersonian fashion, by means of provocation, he is using Dewey to spark his own creative energies. Mills indeed has real insights to offer, such as the inadequacy of Dewey's conception of political and economic power, but the claim that this inadequacy is due exclusively (or primarily) to Dewey's reduction of social practices to biological adaptation is unconvincing. In fact, Dewey argues against such a reduction.[33] Mills here misrepresents Dewey, yet this creates new discursive space for Mills himself and provides impetus to his own *Aufhebung* of American pragmatism.

Whether Mills is literally a pragmatist or not is beside the point. He certainly considers himself a critical proponent of Dewey's efforts to promote an Emersonian culture of radical democracy by means of critical intelligence and social action. This is why his critique of Dewey is an immanent one; that is, he faults Dewey by appealing to Dewey's own standards, principles, and bias. In fact, his critique of Dewey *is* his critique of liberalism: that it has little understanding of the realities of social, economic, and political power in modern society. Yet Mills heralds the *ideals* of liberty, democracy, and equality.

> Liberalism, as a set of ideals, is still viable, and even compelling to Western man. That is one reason why it has become a common denominator of American political rhetoric; but there is another reason. The ideals of liberalism have been divorced from any realities of modern social structure that might serve as the means of their realization. Everybody can easily agree on general ends; it is more difficult to agree on means and the relevance of various means to the ends articulated. The detachment of liberalism from the facts of a going society make it an excellent mask for those who do not, cannot, or will not do what would have to be done to realize its ideals . . . if the moral force of liberalism is still stimulating, its sociological content is weak; it has no theory of society adequate to its moral aims.[34]

For Mills, the crisis of American liberalism is best crystallized in Dewey's dilemma: both exalt the exercise of human power by means of critical intelligence for democratic ends, yet neither can grasp why it is that a majority of the populace are so far removed from control over their lives, i.e., rendered powerless. The problem is not with the ideals of liberalism that flow from the grand "secular tradition of the West," but rather with the class uses of and structural constraints imposed by this liberalism of "one class inside one epoch."[35]

Mills argues that this crisis has produced a sense of "closed frontiers," of no way out for intellectuals and those who look to them for insight and inspiration. The major utopian response was Marxism, yet its deformation in the Soviet Union has dampened socialist hopes. So corporate liberalism with its offer of a lucrative career and comfortable living, and ideologies of the futility of radical collective action, vie for the legacy of American pragmatism.

> Pragmatism was the nerve of progressive American thinking for the first several decades of this century. It took a rather severe beating from the

fashionable left-wing of the thirties and since the latter years of that decade it has obviously been losing out in competition with more religious and tragic views of political and personal life. Many who not long ago read John Dewey with apparent satisfaction have become vitally interested in such analysts of personal tragedy as Sören Kierkegaard. Attempts to reinstate pragmatism's emphasis upon the power of man's intelligence to control his destiny have not been taken to heart by American intellectuals. They are obviously spurred by new worries and after new gods.[36]

The two greatest blinders of the intellectual who today might fight against the main drift are new and fascinating career chances, which often involve opportunities to practice his skill rather freely, and the ideology of liberalism, which tends to expropriate his chance to think straight. The two go together, for the liberal ideology, as now used by intellectuals, acts as a device whereby he can take advantage of the new career chances but retain the illusion that his soul remains his own.[37]

Therefore Mills's attempt to keep alive the Deweyan project of an Emersonian culture of radical democracy by supplying it with a more adequate historical and social analysis of political and economic power in capitalist America must fight on three basic intellectual fronts. First, it must expose corporate liberalism as an elitist ideology that pays lip service to the ideas of democracy and freedom and conceals gross inequality and people's powerlessness and lack of control over their lives. Second, it has to contend with Marxism by critically appropriating its powerful insights regarding class inequality and the power of capital while discarding its rather grand expectations of the working class. Third, Mills must hold at arm's length the pervasive "tragic-sense-of-life" perspectives that either foreclose social action or limit it to piecemeal social engineering.

The major obstacles to Mills's project are not simply mounting arguments against these prevailing viewpoints, but also the difficulty of casting his project as a realizable possibility in mid-century America. Mills's own debts to American prgamatism make him uneasy about simply presenting his project as a mere utopian hope. Rather he struggles to present it as a vital option, an alternative with some chance of being actualized. But, how will it be actualized, who—or what historical agents—will do it? This question haunts Mills throughout his career. Yet he first turns toward the exposé of corporate liberalism.

Mills's famous trilogy—*The New Men of Power* (1948), *White Collar* (1951), and *The Power Elite* (1956)—is essentially an attempt to highlight the dynamics of power, both sources and effects, in corporate liberal America. By boldly going against the grain of his profession—especially the "higher statisticians" who specialize in myopic preference surveys of the populace, and the "grand theorists" who pontificate about a forest concocted from their academic readings and trees constructed from their elite positions[38]—Mills tries to paint a picture of a radically undemocratic and culturally stilted corporate liberal America. Labor leaders appear as a strategic elite who sell the souls, i.e., the autonomy and self-determination, of their proletariat constituency for the pottage of mere higher wages and benefits. The waning old middle class and expanding new middle class are portrayed as hungry for professional status and prestige, fearful of social slippage, and hostile to those below. And the ruling elite—political, economic, and military big shots—live and revel in a cultural form of life that cements them into a group characterized by coordinated actions, unified interests, and a highly limited range of opinions and outlooks.

Despite his radical social analysis of corporate liberal America, Mills resisted the conspiratorial theories of vulgar Marxists and the subtle class analyses of sophisticated ones. This was so primarily because Mills was deeply concerned with the psychological and cultural effects of power on those individuals who wield it. Therefore he puts stress on their schooling, social life, personal networks, and self-images as well as on their "objective class position" in society. Mills was also interested in what the power of these elites was doing to those below. This psychological and cultural emphasis led Mills not only to set aside the notion of "false consciousness" (impeding working-class insurgency) but, even more drastic, to reject as overly economistic the idea of a ruling class.[39]

Mills had little patience with the "tragic-sense-of-life" perspective. He had a deep sensitivity to terrors and sufferings in history, yet he claimed that to present the tragic in the way in which cold war liberals and religious conservatives did simply divested people of the energies to confront and minimize the terrors and sufferings. More pointedly, these perspectives reflected a class position and often a living standard that rendered their authenticity suspect. Echoing Georg Lukács's view of Jean-Paul Sartre's early existentialism as the "grand hotel abyss," Mills cast a suspicious eye and demystifying mind on those "tragic realists" in the comfortable middle class.

> The "tragic view of life," . . . is not "barred" to me. Having examined it carefully, I have rejected it as a political blind alley, as sociologically unreal, and as morally irresponsible. It is a romanticism which in his social and personal loneliness the American adolescent finds very attractive, but it is not a mood that will stand up to even a little reflection. It is a way of saying to oneself: "We're all in this together, the butcher and the general and the ditch digger and the secretary of the treasury and the cook and the president of the United States." But "we" are *not* all in this together—so far as such decisions as are made and can be made are concerned. "We" are *not* all in this together—so far as bearing the consequences of these decisions is concerned. To deny either statement is to deny the facts of power, in particular the fact that different men hold very different portions of such power as is now available. Only if all men everywhere were actors of equal power in an absolute democracy of power could we seriously hold the "tragic view" of responsibility.[40]

Yet Mills's trenchant critiques of corporate liberalism, Marxism, and the cold war tragicians still do not touch the burning issue of how to realize his own neo-Deweyan project of genuine individuality and democracy. Again the interplay of willful agents and constraining circumstances — human creative powers and fate — presents itself. In his first major piece of political journalism, "The Powerless People: The Role of the Intellectual in Society" (1944) in Dwight Macdonald's independent left journal, *Politics*, Mills characterizes this interplay as one between powerful, irresponsible elites and powerless, manipulated masses: the exercise of power by the few results in the fateful predicaments of the many.

> In a world of big organizations the lines between powerful decisions and grass-root democratic controls become blurred. And tenuous, and seemingly irresponsible actions by individuals at the top are more encouraged . . . The sense of tragedy in the intellectual who watches this scene is a personal reaction to the politics and economics of irresponsibility.
>
> Never before have so few men made such fateful decisions for so many people who themselves are so helpless . . . On every hand, the individual is confronted with seemingly remote organizations and he feels dwarfed and helpless . . . in climactic times like the present, dominated by the need for swift action, the individual feels dangerously lost.[41]

The "individual" Mills has in mind is principally the "intellectual" — and, more pointedly, himself. The circumstances of mid-century America make it difficult for intellectuals to speak their mind and to assume personal responsibility for their actions. In political journalism, Hollywood, or the academy, the intellectual is a "hired man" dependent upon employers who wield power over his life. The intellectual, once a free-floating artisan and autonomous craftsman with a self-investment in style and control over his work, has sacrificed critical intelligence for the sake of institutional affiliation and career enhancement.

> Between the intellectual and his potential public stand technical, economic, and social structures which are owned and operated by others. The world of pamphleteering offers to a Tom Paine a direct channel to readers that the world of mass circulations supported by advertising cannot usually afford to provide one who does not say already popular things. The craftsmanship which is central to all intellectual and artistic gratification is thwarted for an increasing number of intellectual workers.[42]

And though the universities "are still the freest of places in which to work,"

> the real restraints are not so much external prohibitions as control of the insurgent by the agreements of academic gentlemen.[43]

Mills's moral outrage at this situation stems from his allegiance to "the ethics and politics of democracy," which rest upon a notion of responsibility "central in the ethics and politics of John Dewey and of the late

German sociologist, Max Weber."⁴⁴ For Mills, Dewey speaks to the democratic implications of responsibility; Weber, to the personal vocational
consequences of this notion. Mills's notion of responsibility resembles the
Enlightenment idea of *Mundigkeit*, best articulated in Immanuel Kant's
What Is Enlightenment? (1784). This idea implies both self-determination
and maturity, rational exercise of human powers and control over one's
destiny; it applies to personal and political affairs. This link between the
personal and the political, between private troubles and public issues, is
a distinctive feature of Mills's project,⁴⁵ a feature that deeply influenced
young activists in the sixties after the repressive, introspective fifties. At
times sounding like a member of the Frankfurt School, yet tellingly distinguished by his moralism and individualism, Mills states the aim of
political strategy to be the actualization of an Emersonian culture of
radical democracy.

> The shaping of the society we shall live in and the manner in which
> we shall live in it are increasingly political. And this society includes
> the realms of intellect and of personal morals. If we demand that these
> realms be geared to our activities which make a public difference, then
> personal morals and political interests become closely related; any philos-
> ophy that is not a personal escape involves taking a political stand. If
> this is true, it places great responsibility upon our political thinking.
> Because of the expanded reach of politics, it is our own personal style
> of life and reflection we are thinking about when we think about politics.
>   The independent artist and intellectual are among the few remaining
> personalities equipped to resist and to fight the stereotyping and con-
> sequent death of genuinely lively things. Fresh perception now involves
> the capacity continually to unmask and to smash the stereotypes of vision
> and intellect with which modern communications swamp us. These
> worlds of mass-art and mass-thought are increasingly geared to the
> demands of politics. That is why it is in politics that intellectual soli-
> darity and effort must be centered. If the thinker does not relate himself
> to the value of truth in political struggle, he cannot responsibly cope
> with the whole of live experience.⁴⁶

This crucial passage reveals two basic themes in Mills's project: the
central role of personal style in political combat, and the elevation of intellectual work as the prime and privileged enactment of this combat. These
themes highlight Mills's own ambiguous relation to American pragmatism:
he affirms the primacy of critical intelligence yet also stresses its limits.
He revels in personal revolts against routine and conformity, yet calls
for group solidarity and action. He promotes radical democracy yet focuses
on intellectual elites as primary historical agents. In other words, Mills's
defense of personal style and intellectual work, though courageous and
noble, reeks of an individualism and elitism, alongside democratic sentiments, more reminiscent of Emerson than of Dewey. Yet, like Dewey, Mills

employs a mythic artisanal model of intellectual autonomy and responsibility characteristic of a nostalgia for preindustrial America.

Mills's preoccupation with style is best seen in his cast of heroes in history: Tom Paine, the Wobblies (IWW syndicalist rebels), and, above all, Thorstein Veblen. What is characteristic of them is that they were, in some sense, failures in life; that is, they gallantly fought against great odds yet their eccentric styles, idiosyncratic manners, and rebellious spirits doomed them to obscurity (as with Paine in death), bankruptcy (as with the IWW in strategies), or marginality (as with Veblen in life). In his highly self-revealing introduction to a 1953 edition of Thorstein Veblen's first and best book, *The Theory of the Leisure Class* (1894), Mills writes:

> It has been fashionable to sentimentalize Veblen as the most alienated of American intellectuals, as the Prince outside even the ghetto. But Veblen's virtue is not alienation; it is failure. Modern intellectuals have made a success of "alienation" but Veblen was a natural-born failure. To be conspicuously "alienated" was a kind of success he would have scorned most. In character and in career, in mind and in everyday life, he was the outsider, and his work the intellectual elaboration of a felt condition . . .
>
> There is no failure in American academia quite so great as Veblen's. He was a masterless, recalcitrant man, and if we must group him somewhere in the American scene, it is with those most recalcitrant Americans, the Wobblies. On the edges of the higher learning, Veblen tried to live like a Wobbly. It was a strange place for such an attempt. The Wobblies were not learned but they were, like Veblen, masterless men, and the only non-middle class movement of revolt in twentieth-century America. With his acute discontent and shyness of program Veblen was a sort of intellectual Wobbly.[47]

Yet, in addition to being such a "failure," Mills considered Veblen to be "the best critic of America that America has produced."[48] Veblen represented the first generation of major intellectuals outside of the WASP Northeast who seized center stage in critically examining American society. Not surprisingly, Mills includes himself (Columbia University professor since 1945) in this rebellious group of American thinkers.

> The figure of the last-generation American faded and the figure of the first-generation American—the Norwegian immigrant's son, the New York Jew teaching English literature in a Midwestern university, the Southerner come North to crash New York—was installed as the genuine, if no longer 100 per cent American, critic.[49]

The Norwegian's son is, of course, Veblen, and the Southerner is Mills, but who the New York Jew is remains obscure. The impact of Selig Perlman on Mills at the University of Wisconsin was immense, but Perlman was a Jewish intellectual who wrote ground-breaking labor history, not literary criticism. And though Lionel Trilling taught briefly at Wisconsin in the mid-thirties, by the fifties Mills had little positive to say of him.[50] What is important here is that Mills believes that the new "professional anti-specialist first-generation American critics," who could still "choose their own ancestors,"[51] had now a monopoly on intellectual style in America; they wrote "works of art"—like Mills's own "sociological poems"—heralding the "all-American values of efficiency, of utility, of pragmatic simplicity."[52] Mills suggests that it is Veblen's sheer style that sustains interest in him; unlike most other social scientists, he wrote books that, "like all works of art, you must 'read' . . . for yourself."[53] You read not for instruction or even for edification but for Emersonian provocation, for stimulation of your own creativity. Prefiguring the culture of creative democracy was a Veblen-like Wobbly with no masters or authorities. In this, Mills was at one with Emerson—he wanted to leave his unique stamp on the world in the form of his personality, even if books remained the major medium in the future.

In a world of bosses and sheriffs, the Wobblies too sought self-determination and self-development with no formal leadership.

> "When that boatload of Wobblies come
> up to Everett, the sheriff says
> don't you come no further.
> Who the hell's yer leader anyhow?
> *Who's yer leader?*
> And them Wobblies yelled right back—
> *We ain't got no leader.*
> *We're all leaders.*
> And they kept right on comin'."

This exchange from an interview with an unknown worker in Sutcliffe, Nevada, in June 1947 serves as the epigraph of Mills's first book, *The New Men of Power: America's Labor Leaders* (1948). In this text, Mills seriously entertains the possibility of an alliance of independent left intellectuals like himself with the labor movement. The Deweyan aim of this alliance is "to democratize the structure of modern society."[54] True to Dewey's vision, Mills conceives of this aim not in merely political and economic terms, but principally in larger cultural terms which embrace the political and economic. There must be a filtering of the Emersonian culture of creative democracy throughout the everyday lives of people, a process and product of human empowerment.

> Power won by election, revolution, or deals at the top will not be enough
> to accomplish this. In the day-by-day process of accumulating strength
> as well as in times of social upset, the power of democratic initiation
> must be allowed and fostered in the rank and file.[55]

Like Dewey's, Mills's project includes liberal, socialist, and Jeffersonian (civic republican) aspects, yet it goes beyond them principally owing to his

Emersonian sensibilities. Yet, similar to Dewey, he strives for the inadequate label of democratic socialism.

> A socialist political program could not be successfully carried through in this society unless training were provided in the more direct democracy of daily life, in the shop and in the unions. Those who are serious about democracy must begin by giving the impulses of man a chance to realize themselves creatively in work. That is the basis for a politics of demo-cratic socialism.[56]

For Mills, the pressing challenge is to constitute a left public sphere in which intellectuals and labor project moral visions, work out policies, and exert pressure against "the main drift" of corporate liberal America. He concludes with realistic assessments of the prevailing situation coupled with an unconditional moral steadfastness to the democratic cause.

> To those who object that the program the left advances can only attract another little group that cannot win, the left intellectuals reply: You may be right; no one knows; we do not believe it. Even if it were so, we would still be for the attempt, we are among those who decided to throw in with "the little groups that cannot win," in fact, the big groups never win; every group loses its insurgency; maybe that is all that is meant by winning. It is a question of where one decides to keep placing one's weight.[57]

It is interesting to note that in this passage the intellectuals, not the workers, reply to the objections and that the position of the ruling groups is viewed as unstable, and in flux. In a few years, Mills concludes that labor is, for the most part, inextricably incorporated into the corporate liberal estab-lishment and that this establishment—led by political, economic, and mili-tary elites—is virtually invincible.

In his next book, *White Collar: The American Middle Classes* (1951), Mills presents an American epic of decline and decay, confinement and confusion. Like Arthur Miller in his classic play *Death of a Salesman* (1949), Mills tells a sociological story of the white-collar person (more often a woman than a man) who

> is more pitiful than tragic, as he is seen collectively, fighting personal inflation, living out in slow misery his yearning for the quick American climb. He is pushed by forces beyond his control, pulled into movements he does not understand; he gets into situations in which his is the most helpless position. The white collar man is the hero as victim, the small creature who is acted upon but who does not act, who works along unnoticed in somebody's office or store, never talking loud, never talking back, never taking a stand.[58]

Gone is the free, independent entrepreneur. Gone is the craftsmanship of work. Gone is the Emersonian individual "with no authoritarian center, but held together by countless, free, shrewd transactions."[59] Gone is the historical agent of the American religion, of the radical democratic visions of Dewey and Mills. Nowhere else in his corpus does Mills's nostalgia for Emerson's America come to the surface so clearly. He is at one with the very Dewey he criticized in his dissertation.

This nostalgia is symptomatic of Mills's attempt to hold onto some sense of hope and agency in the face of the overwhelming hopelessness and neurasthenia he finds in bourgeois America. These existential and cultural issues — inseparable from but irreducible to the socio-economic predicament — illustrate the blindness of the two forms of political consciousness available, liberalism and Marxism, which assume "that men, given the opportunity, will naturally come to political consciousness of interest, of self or of class."[60] This rationalist assumption is unwarranted in light of a seductive culture of consumption which thrives on privatism and escapism and generates a pervasive indifference toward political life.

> Such indifference is the major sign of both the impasse of liberalism and the collapse of socialist hopes. It is also at the heart of the political malaise of our times.[61]

In *White Collar*, Mills concludes that corporate liberal America is a "bureaucratized society of privatized men" that is quite stable and secure. The middle classes, like the commodities they chase, are "up for sale: Whoever seems respectable enough, strong enough, can probably have them."[62]

This brazen condemnation of the middle classes leads Mills to examine those major actors, those history makers in American society who do make a difference. *The Power Elite* (1956), though analytically weaker than the first two books, reaches even gloomier conclusions regarding the possibility of actualizing an Emersonian culture of creative democracy. Mid-century America lacks the requisite moral and cultural resources to actualize Dewey's project.

> A society that is in its higher circles and on its middle levels widely believed to be a network of smart rackets does not produce men with an inner moral sense; a society that is merely expedient does not produce men of conscience. A society that narrows the meaning of "success" to the big money and in its terms condemns failure as the chief vice, raising money to the plane of absolute value, will produce the sharp operator and the shady deal. Blessed are the cynical, for only they have what it takes to succeed.[63]

In this society "no man makes himself."[64] Instead there is the "self-used man" who shapes himself to fit into the social hierarchies of the corporation, government, military, and academy. In short, the Emersonian space in America is, for Mills, virtually nonexistent. Buttressed by the very pragmatism Emerson inspired, mid-century America has simply foreclosed the chance for an Emersonian culture of creative democracy to take root and flourish.

America—a conservative country without any conservative ideology—appears now before the world a naked and arbitrary power, as, in the name of realism, its men of decision enforce their often crackpot definitions upon world reality. The second-rate mind is in command of the ponderously spoken platitude. In the liberal rhetoric, vagueness, and in the conservative mood, irrationality, are raised to principle. Public relations and the official secret, the trivializing campaign and the terrible fact clumsily accomplished, are replacing the reasoned debate of political ideas in the privately incorporated economy, the military ascendancy, and the political vacuum of modern America.[65]

Out of a poignant—though not paralyzing—pessimism, Mills turns to intellectuals as a last hope. He knows they can never actualize his Deweyan ideals, but they can, at least, keep them alive. Similar to Alasdair McIntyre in his influential book *After Virtue* (1981), Mills believes he resides in the new Dark Ages with barbarians in power. But, whereas McIntyre wants to preserve the neo-Aristotelian tradition of the virtues, Mills wants to preserve the Deweyan ideals of an Emersonian culture of creative democracy. Mills envisions a fourth epoch—a "*post-modern* climax" of centralized private economies, bureaucratized politics, commodified cultures, and gargantuan military arsenals—in which "the human mind as a social fact might be deteriorating in quality and cultural level," and certainly where there was an "absence of mind of any sort of public force."[66] Mills understands "mind" here as precisely the Deweyan notion of critical intelligence whose effects have "liberating public relevance."

> And what this [absence of mind] makes possible is the prevalence of the kindergarten chatter, as well as decisions having no rational justifications which the intellect could confront and engage in debate.[67]

For Mills, the only way to preserve any recognizable "mind" in the post-modern era is to keep alive Deweyan ideals. This preserving activity is not exclusively or even primarily political, though it has immense political consequences.

> The intellectual ought to be the moral conscience of his society, at least with reference to the value of truth, for in the defining instance, that *is* his politics . . .
>
> Whatever else the intellectual may be, surely he is among those who ask serious questions, and, if he is a political intellectual, he asks his questions of those with power. If you ask to what the intellectual belongs, you must answer that he belongs first of all to that minority which has carried on the big discourse of the rational mind, the big discourse that has been going on—or off and on—since Western society began some two thousand years ago in the small communities of Athens and Jerusalem. This big discourse is not a vague thing to which to belong—even if as lesser participants—and it is the beginning of any sense of belonging that is worthwhile, and it is the key to the only kind of belonging that

free men in our time might have. But if we would belong to it, we ought to try to live up to what it demands of us. What it demands of us, first of all, is that we maintain our sense of it. And, just now, at this point in human history, that is quite difficult.[68]

This may sound like highbrow humanist rhetoric, but, for Mills, it is a language of intellectual combat in an America in which "mind" no longer has democratic relevance. Mills is here engaged in a deeply felt struggle not only for Deweyan ideals but also for the very existence of the oppositional potential of the secular tradition in the West.

In an interesting sense, Mills ends up grappling with two very Emersonian concerns:

> I must make two points only: one about fate and the making of history; the other about the roles many intellectuals are now enacting.[69]

Mills holds that though humans can—and a few do—make history, the eclipse of critical intelligence and utopian energies has left intellectuals bereft of personal vocation and moral purpose. Bureaucratic encroachments in the academy and lucrative enticements for research have encapsulated and directed intellectual work. Professors often become more administrative academics than independent intellectuals.

> After he is established in a college, it is unlikely that the professor's milieu and resources are the kind that will facilitate, much less create, independence of mind. He is a member of a petty hierarchy, almost completely closed in by its middle-class environment and its segregation of intellectual from social life. In such a hierarchy, mediocrity makes its own rules and sets its own image of success and the path of ascent is as likely to be administrative duty as creative work.[70]

Even less favorable conditions exist for graduate students in the "feudal system" of the academy in which "the student trades his loyalty to one professor for protection against other professors."[71]

As intellectuals find it more and more difficult to constitute and build a public, academics expand their markets. The image of the self-cultivating man declines and that of the specialist flourishes. Mills, of course, sees these trends as worldwide. In the communist East, intellectuals are locked up, whereas Western intellectuals "lock themselves up" by often refusing to put forward palpable critiques of the status quo. Cold war intellectuals rightly defend the liberties of dissent (though often not for all); yet they themselves rarely use these liberties to dissent in a serious manner.

Therefore Mills views the vocation of being an intellectual as the only alternative to an emaciated liberalism, a traduced communism, and an impotent tragic viewpoint. His conception of the intellectual vocation is value-laden; that is, it is shot through with the Deweyan ideals of critical intelligence and creative democracy. In this way, Mills affirmed the

Emersonian theodicy of American pragmatism as all progressive American frontiers seemed to close. He was encouraged by the Cuban revolution—as is set forth in his *Listen, Yankee: The Revolution in Cuba* (1960)—but realized that U.S. policies would more than likely not allow it to "achieve a thoroughly neutralist and genuinely independent orientation in world affairs."[72] Such anti-imperialist ventures, though worthy of support, were exemplary of the new contours of the Fourth Epoch on the horizon—a new historical period in which Mills, who died in 1962, never had the chance to exercise his engaged sense of the intellectual vocation grounded, in large part, in American pragmatism.

> In summary, what we must do is to define the reality of the human condition and to make our definitions public; to confront the new facts of history-making in our time, and their meanings for the problem of political responsibility; to release the human imagination by transcending the mere exhortation of grand principle and opportunist reaction in order to explore all the alternatives now open to the human community.
>
> If this—the politics of truth—is merely a holding action, so be it. If it is also a politics of desperation, so be it. But in this time and in America, it is the only realistic politics of possible consequence that is readily open to intellectuals. It is the guide line and the next step. It is an affirmation of one's self as a moral and intellectual center of responsible decision; the act of a free man who rejects "fate"; for it reveals his resolution to take his *own* fate, at least, into his own hands.[73]

W. E. B. Du Bois: The Jamesian Organic Intellectual

The career of W. E. B. Du Bois serves as a unique response to the crisis of American pragmatism in the twentieth century. Although he was born nine years after John Dewey (and about a hundred miles away) and died one year after Mills, Du Bois already saw the contours of the "Fourth Epoch," a period fundamentally shaped by the decolonization of the third world. As an American intellectual of African descent—the greatest one produced in this country—Du Bois looks at the United States through a different lens from those of Emerson, Peirce, James, Dewey, Hook, and Mills. As one grounded in and nourished by American pragmatism, Du Bois—both by personal choice and by social treatment—allies himself in word and deed with the wretched of the earth. In the United States, this principally takes the form of performing intellectual work within the institutions, organizations, and movements of Afro-Americans or those that focus on their plight.

A New Englander by birth and rearing, Du Bois did not undergo the usual racial discrimination and depreciation during his childhood. He was the only black child in his secondary schools and attended an all-white Congregational church. His family, headed by his mother, was poor, yet not as poor or socially ostracized as the Irish immigrant mill workers in his town. Upon graduation from high school, Du Bois wanted to attend Harvard College, but the poor academic quality of his high school and some white discouragement (though white financial support ultimately allowed him to go) made him settle for Fisk University – the black Yale, as it were. Admitted as a sophomore owing to his excellent record, Du Bois experienced segregation and encountered Afro-American culture for the first time. Unacquainted with the kinetic orality, emotional physicality, and combative spirituality of black music, language, and customs, Du Bois harbored ambiguous attitudes toward this culture. In his graduating class of five in 1888, Du Bois gave a commencement address on his hero, Bismarck, who "had made a nation out of a mass of bickering peoples."[74] As he notes in one of his autobiographies: "I was blithely European and imperialist in outlook; democratic as democracy was conceived in America."[75]

From Fisk, Du Bois matriculated to Harvard College, entering as a junior owing to the "lower standards" at Fisk. Despite having no social life at Harvard, including a rejection from the glee club, Du Bois thrived there intellectually. Emotionally sustained by his involvement in the black community, Du Bois was most impressed at Harvard by William James – and his pragmatism.

> I was in Harvard for education and not for high marks, except as marks would insure my staying . . . above all I wanted to study philosophy! I wanted to get hold of the basis of knowledge, and explore foundations and beginnings. I chose, therefore, Palmer's course in ethics, but he being on Sabbatical for the year, William James replaced him, and I became a devoted follower of James at the time he was developing his pragmatic philosophy.[76]

Du Bois seems to have been attracted to pragmatism owing to its Emersonian evasion of epistemology-centered philosophy, and his sense of pragmatism's relevance to the Afro-American predicament.

> I hoped to pursue philosophy as my life career, with teaching for support . . . My salvation here was the type of teacher I met rather than the content of the courses. William James guided me out of the sterilities of scholastic philosophy to realist pragmatism . . .
>
> I revelled in the keen analysis of William James, Josiah Royce and young George Santayana. But it was James with his pragmatism and Albert Bushnell Hart with his research method, that turned me back from the lovely but sterile land of philosophic speculation, to the social sciences as the field for gathering and interpreting that body of fact which would apply to my program for the Negro . . .
>
> I knew by this time that practically my sole chance of earning a living combined with study was to teach, and after my work with Hart in United States history, I conceived the idea of applying philosophy to an historical interpretation of race relations.[77]

Du Bois never spelled out what he meant by the "sterilities of scholastic philosophy," but given what we know of James's pragmatism, it surely had something to do with sidestepping the Cartesian epistemological puzzles of modern philosophy. Yet, unlike James and more like Dewey, Du Bois took a turn toward history and the social sciences. In 1890, Du Bois received his Harvard cum laude bachelor's degree in philosophy. Du Bois' move toward history and the social sciences, reinforced by James's candid advice (untinged with racial bias) that there is "not much chance for anyone earning a living as a philosopher," resulted in his receiving a fellowship to stay at Harvard for graduate work. Since sociology as a discipline did not yet exist at Harvard, Du Bois studied in the history and political science departments. Moreover, the fact that Du Bois "came to the study of sociology by way of philosophy and history"[78] — that is, primarily James's pragmatism and Hart's documentary approach — put him on the cutting edge of new intellectual developments in late-nineteenth-century America.

Upon the encouragement of his supervisor, Hart, Du Bois spent two years (1892–94) at the University of Berlin. In Germany, Du Bois studied economics, history, and sociology in the seminars of Gustav von Schmoller and Adolf Wagner (both "socialists of the chair"); and he heard Max Weber lecture as a visiting professor. Yet the heroic romantic nationalism of Heinrich von Treitschke, the famous Prussian historian and political theorist, impressed Du Bois most. Though Du Bois had come far from his uncritical praise of Bismarck, he still was attracted to Treitschke's notion that history was made by the powerful wills of great men who unify and guide their own peoples. Needless to say, Du Bois saw this role for himself in regard to black Americans. On his twenty-fifth birthday he dedicated "himself as the Moses of his people."[79]

Du Bois' stay in Europe had a tremendous impact on his view of himself and America. On the one hand, it gave him a way "of looking at the world as a man and not simply from a narrow racial and provincial outlook."[80] On the other hand, it provided him with an outlet for his hostility toward America and insight into its provinciality.

> I found to my gratification that they, with me, did not regard America as the last word in civilization. Indeed, I derived a certain satisfaction in learning that the University of Berlin did not recognize a degree even from Harvard University, no more than Harvard did from Fisk . . . All agreed that Americans could make money and did not care how they made it. And the like. Sometimes their criticism got under even my anti-American skin, but it was refreshing on the whole to hear voiced my own attitude toward so much that America had meant to me.[81]

In June 1894, Du Bois arrived back in "nigger-hating" America.[82] Sailing aboard a ship full of European immigrants, he noted as it arrived in New York harbor:

I know not what multitude of emotions surged in others, but I had to recall that mischievous little French girl whose eyes twinkled as she said: "Oh yes the Statue of Liberty! With its back toward America, and its face toward France!"[83]

Since teaching in white universities was unthinkable, Du Bois accepted a job teaching Greek and Latin at a black parochial school in Xenia, Ohio—Wilberforce University. Having shed his dogmatic religious beliefs under James, Du Bois found it difficult to cope with the deeply pietistic atmosphere at the school. For instance, at one gathering it was announced

that "Professor Du Bois will lead us in prayer." I simply answered "No, he won't," and as a result nearly lost my new job.[84]

Du Bois quite understandably felt constrained at Wilberforce, though he did complete his Harvard dissertation there on the suppression of the African slave trade. In 1896, it was published as the first volume of the Harvard Historical Studies. As Arnold Rampersad has noted, this work, though full of original and ground-breaking research, is essentially "a chapter of the moral history of his country"—ethical motives and national conscience are stressed.[85]

Du Bois stayed at Wilberforce for only two years, thanks to an offer to study the black community in Philadelphia (then the largest black community in the North). This offer was a grand opportunity not just to leave Wilberforce with his new wife but also to test his scientific skills and narrow Enlightenment outlook on race relations.

The Negro problem was in my mind a matter of systematic investigation and intelligent understanding. The world was thinking wrong about race, because it did not know. The ultimate evil was stupidity. The cure for it was knowledge based on scientific investigation.[86]

This outlook guided not only his pioneering study *The Philadelphia Negro* (1899), but also the *Atlanta University Publications* (1896–1914) he directed during his thirteen years as professor of economics at Atlanta University. At the first stage of Du Bois' career, he worked diligently as a social scientist and professor gathering the first empirical data on the social conditions of black Americans. Yet as the institutionalized terrorism escalated in the South with tighter Jim Crow laws and more lynchings, Du Bois' moral idealism along with the scholarly strategy of disclosing the facts and revealing the truth of black oppression became less credible.

Two considerations thereafter broke in upon my work and eventually disrupted it: first, one could not be a calm, cool and detached scientist while Negroes were lynched, murdered and starved; and secondly, there was no such definite demand for scientific work of the sort that I was doing, as I had confidently assumed there would be easily forthcoming. I regarded it as axiomatic that the world wanted to learn the truth and if the truth were sought with even approximate accuracy and painstaking devotion, the world would gladly support the effort.[87]

Du Bois became more and more convinced not only that "most Americans answer all questions regarding the Negro *a priori*,"[88] but also that issues of power, interests, and status played more important roles than he had realized. This recognition led him to put less faith in scientific research as a weapon of social change and to focus more on middlebrow journalism and writing for a general literate public. His American classic, *The Souls of Black Folk* (1903), consisted of eight revised essays already published in leading magazines (mostly *Atlantic Monthly*) and five new pieces. Like Emerson, Du Bois always viewed himself as a poet in the broad nineteenth-century sense; that is, one who creates new visions and vocabularies for the moral enhancement of humanity. This poetic sensibility is manifest in his several poems and five novels. Yet it is seen most clearly in *The Souls of Black Folk*.

Du Bois' classic text can be viewed as being in the Emersonian grain, yet it conveys insights ignored by most of white America. Du Bois attempts to turn the Emersonian theodicy inside out by not simply affirming the capacity of human powers to overcome problems, but, more important, raising the question "How does it feel to be a problem?"[89] in America—a problem America neither admits it has nor is interested in solving. The aim of his text is to convey and enact "the strange experience" of "being a problem:—that is, being an American of African descent."

> The Negro is a sort of seventh son, born with a veil, and gifted with second-sight in this American world—a world which yields him no true self-consciousness, but only lets him see himself through the revelation of the other world. It is a peculiar sensation, this double-consciousness, this sense of always looking at one's self through the eyes of others, of measuring one's soul by the tape of a world that looks on in amused contempt and pity. One ever feels his twoness—an American, a Negro; two souls, two thoughts, two unreconciled strivings; two warring ideals in one dark body, whose dogged strength alone keeps it from being torn asunder.[90]

Du Bois is writing about "the experience of being a problem" at a time in which discernible signs of the awakening third world appear, such as the defeat of Russia by Japan (1904), the Persian revolt (1905), and the Mexican revolution (1911). And as America emerges as a world power, much of the credibility of its rhetoric of freedom and democracy is threatened by the oppression of black Americans.

Emerson had grappled with the "double-consciousness" of being an American, of having a European culture in an un-European environment. Yet, for him, being an American was not a problem but rather a unique occasion to exercise human powers to solve problems. Du Bois' "double-consciousness" views this unique occasion as the *cause* of a problem, a

problem resulting precisely from the exercise of white human powers celebrated by Emerson. In short, Du Bois subverts the Emersonian theodicy
by situating it within an imperialist and ethnocentric rhetorical and
political context.

But, ironically, Du Bois' subversion is aided by his own revision of
the Emersonian theodicy. This revision principally consists of exercising
his own powers in order to overcome the blindnesses, silences, and exclu-
sions of earlier Emersonian theodicies. The aim remains self-creation and
individuality, though with a more colorful diversity; the end is still a culture
in which human powers, provoked by problems, are expanded for the
sake of moral development of human personalities.

> The history of the American Negro is the history of this strife—this
> longing to attain self-conscious manhood, to merge his double self into
> a better and truer self. In this merging he wishes neither of the older
> selves to be lost. He would not Africanize America, for America has
> too much to teach the world and Africa. He would not bleach his Negro
> soul in a flood of white Americanism, for he knows that Negro blood
> has a message for the world. He simply wishes to make it possible for
> a man to be both a Negro and an American, without being cursed and
> spit upon by his fellows, without having the doors of opportunity closed
> roughly in his face.
>
> This, then, is the end of his striving: to be a co-worker in the king-
> dom of culture, to escape both death and isolation, to husband and use
> his best powers and his latent genius.[91]

Following his mentor Hart's racialist view of history in which each
"race" possesses certain gifts and endowments, Du Bois holds that those
of the Negro consist of story and song, sweat and brawn and the spirit.[92]
Du Bois claims that these gifts of black folk have given America its only
indigenous music, the material foundations of its empire, and ethical critiques to remind America of its own moral limits. The music expresses the
protean improvisational character of America itself, always responding to,
adapting, and experimenting with new challenges. Slavery, the foundation
of America's power, exemplifies the tragic and usually overlooked costs concealed by American prosperity. Black ethical critiques, themselves often
based on American-style Protestantism and U.S. political ideals, expose the
hypocrisy of the American rhetoric of freedom and democracy.

As a highly educated Western black intellectual, Du Bois himself often
scorns the "barbarisms" (sometimes confused with Africanisms) shot
through Afro-American culture. In fact, I count eighteen allusions to the
"backwardness" of black folk.[93] He even goes as far as to support a form
of paternalism that leads toward black self-determination.

> I should be the last one to deny the patent weaknesses and shortcomings
> of the Negro people . . . I freely acknowledge that it is possible, and
> sometimes best, that a partially undeveloped people should be ruled by

the best of their stronger and better neighbors for their own good, until
such time as they can start and fight the world's battles alone.[94]

This paternalism fits well with his early doctrine of the talented tenth –
the educated, cultured, and refined like himself leading the benighted,
ignorant, and coarse black masses out of the wilderness into the promised
land. Yet, even in this first stage of his career, Du Bois acknowledges and
accents the creative powers of the black masses in the cultural sphere,
especially in their music.

Du Bois' stress on black music is significant in that here he sees black
agency at work. Like Emerson and other pragmatists, Du Bois posits culture
making as the prime instance of history making. He does this not only
because for Afro-Americans all other spaces were closed, but also because
in every society, no matter how oppressive, human creativity can be dis-
cerned in culture making. In good Emersonian fashion, Du Bois' democratic
mores are grounded in the detection of human creative powers at the
level of everyday life.

Du Bois' departure from Atlanta University and his acceptance
of the editorship of the Crisis, organ of the newly formed National
Association for the Advancement of Colored People, inaugurated a
second stage in his career. In the eyes of some black figures like Walker
Trotter, the NAACP was too interracialist; in the view of those like William
James, it was too militant for the times. Yet Du Bois along with other
black and white activists, including John Dewey, pushed on for social
reform and civil rights by means of public agitation and political pressure.
As director of publications and research, Du Bois was the only black
national officer in the organization. The first issue of the Crisis was
published in November 1910 and consisted of a thousand copies; by 1918
a hundred thousand copies were being printed. He held this position for
twenty-four years.

Like Dewey, Du Bois supported Woodrow Wilson in 1912 and American entrance into World War I. Both figures later regretted these decisions
and became more radical as a consequence. Du Bois' radicalism principally
took the form of an international perspective focused on the decolonization
of Africa. As an organic intellectual directly linked to black social agency –
and possible insurgency – Du Bois was put at the center of ideological and
political debates in America and abroad. He organized the second Pan-
African Congress in February 1919 in Paris in order "to have Africa in
some way voice its complaints to the world during the Peace Congress
at Versailles."[95] Still under the sway of a talented-tenth doctrine, Du Bois
drew up an elitist, neocolonial platform for "semi-civilized peoples" in Africa;
still influenced by a moral idealism with an insufficient grasp of the role
of economic and political power, he had great hopes that the League of
Nations would curb American and European racism. Regarding the Pan-
African Congress, he wrote:

We got, in fact, the ear of the civilized world and if it had been possible
to stay longer and organize more thoroughly and spread the truth—
what might not have been accomplished? . . .
The world-fight for Black rights is on![96]

The Red Summer of 1919 dampened Du Bois' hopes. Southern black
migration into northern industries spurred racial competition between
black and white workers, and the decoration of many black soldiers back
from the war generated white resentment. During that year seventy-seven
blacks were lynched, including a woman and eleven soldiers; there also
were race riots in twenty-six cities.

With the collapse of the League of Nations, and debilitating ideological
strife in the Pan-African movement, Du Bois found himself loyal to a
cause with no organization. The tumultuous rise of Marcus Garvey, the
brouhaha over the Harlem "Renaissance," and white racist entrenchment
forced Du Bois—now in his late fifties—to reexamine his gradualist perspective. More important, the Russian Revolution, initially held at arm's
length by Du Bois, challenged him in a fundamental way. He had considered himself a democratic socialist—a "socialist of the path"—since 1907
and, in fact, joined the Socialist party for a while. In response to left
critiques by socialists such as Claude McKay, A. Phillip Randolph, and
Chauncey Owens in 1921, Du Bois replied:

> The editor of The Crisis considers himself a Socialist but he does not
> believe that German State Socialism or the dictatorship of the proletariat
> are perfect panaceas. He believes with most thinking men that the present
> method of creating, controlling and distributing wealth is desperately
> wrong; that there must come and is coming a social control of wealth;
> but he does not know just what form that control is going to take, and
> he is not prepared to dogmatize with Marx or Lenin.[97]

Du Bois' basic concern is the specific predicament of Afro-Americans
as victims of white capitalist exploitation at the workplace and of white
capitalists and workers in the political system and cultural mores of the
country.

The major impact of the Russian Revolution on Du Bois was to compel
him to take seriously the challenge of Marxism as a mode of intellectual
inquiry. Marxist historical and social analysis forced Du Bois to go beyond
his moralistic democratic socialism, with its primary stress on "light, more
light, clear thought, accurate knowledge, careful distinctions."[98] Marxism
indeed contained a commitment to scientific knowledge, a crucial require-
ment for a social scientist with Du Bois' training; but it also highlighted
the realities of power struggles in which moral suasion played a minor
role, to say the least. In this way, the Russian Revolution for Du Bois
was less a historical event and more an intellectual beckoning to Marxist
thought, a school of thought that made him see that

beyond my conception of ignorance and deliberate illwill as causes of race prejudice, there must be other and stronger and more threatening forces, forming the founding stones of race antagonisms, which we had only begun to attack or perhaps in reality had not attacked at all. Moreover, the attack upon these hidden and partially concealed causes of race hate, must be led by Negroes in a program which was not merely negative in the sense of calling on white folk to desist from certain practices and give up certain beliefs, but direct in the sense that Negroes must proceed constructively in new and comprehensive plans of their own. I think it was the Russian Revolution which first illuminated and made clear this change in my basic thought.[99]

On his first visit to Russia in 1926, Du Bois' utopian energies were rekindled. He considered Russia "the most hopeful land in the modern world."[100] But he still unequivocally rejected the strategies of the Communist party in the United States. Even after acknowledging the realities of power in America, Du Bois insisted that revolution would be a "slow, reasoned development" informed by "the most intelligent body of American thought."[101]

The most significant product of Du Bois' encounter with Marxist thought was his seminal book *Black Reconstruction: An Essay Toward a History of the Part Which Black Folk Played in the Attempt to Reconstruct Democracy In America, 1860–1880* (1935). This text is seminal not simply because it focused on the postemancipation struggle over the control of black and white labor rather than on the obfuscating racist mythologies of the leading Reconstruction historians, John W. Burgess and William A. Dunning, nor because the book represented ground-breaking research, for it relied exclusively on secondary sources. Rather Du Bois' *Black Reconstruction* is a seminal work because it examines the ways in which the struggle for democracy was stifled at a critical period in American history from the vantage point of the victims (including both black and white laborers).

In *Black Reconstruction*, Du Bois is still exploring "the strange experience of being a problem," but this exploration has taken a structural socioeconomic and political form. Unlike any of the other pragmatists, Du Bois provides an account of the means by which industrial America imposed severe constraints upon an emerging or at least potential creative democracy. The economic power of northern capitalists and southern planters, the racist attitudes of white workers and politicians and the struggles of black freed persons conjoined in a complex way to give initial hope for but ultimately defeat creative democracy in America. And the defeat of any effective movements for radical democracy is inseparable from the lack of even formal democracy for most black Americans.

Du Bois' analysis illustrates the blindnesses and silences in American pragmatist reflections on individuality and democracy. Although none of the pragmatists were fervent racists themselves—and most of them took public stands against racist practices—not one viewed racism as contributing greatly to the impediments for both individuality and democracy. More specifically, neither Dewey, Hook, nor Mills grappled in a serious way, in essay or texts, with how racism impeded the development of an Emersonian culture of creative democracy. By "racism" here I mean not merely discrimination and devaluation based on race but, more important, the strategic role black people have played in the development of the capitalist economy, political system, and cultural apparatuses in America. To what degree have the demands of blacks fostered and expanded American democracy? In which way is democracy dependent on these demands, given their spin-off effects in demands made by larger ethnic groups, women, gays, lesbians, and the elderly? Du Bois' *Black Reconstruction* implicitly raises these questions in a serious and urgent manner. In graphic and hyperbolic language he writes:

> America thus stepped forward in the first blossoming of the modern age and added to the art of beauty, gift of the Renaissance, and to freedom of belief, gift of Martin Luther and Leo X, a vision of democratic self-government: the domination of political life by the intelligent decision of free and self-sustaining men. What an idea and what an area for its realization—endless land of richest fertility, natural resources such as earth seldom exhibited before, a population infinite in variety, of universal gift, burned in the fires of poverty and caste, yearning toward the Unknown God; and self-reliant pioneers, unafraid of man or devil. It was the Supreme Adventure, in the last Great Battle of the West, for that human freedom which would release the human spirit from lower lust for mere meat, and set it free to dream and sing.
>
> And then some unjust god leaned, laughing, over the ramparts of heaven and dropped a black man in their midst.
>
> It transformed the world. It turned democracy back to Roman imperialism and fascism; it restored caste and oligarchy; it replaced freedom with slavery and withdrew the name of humanity from the vast majority of human beings.
>
> But not without struggle . . .
>
> Then came this battle called Civil War . . . The slave went free; stood a brief moment in the sun; then moved back again toward slavery. The whole weight of America was thrown to color caste. The colored world went down before England, France, Germany, Russia, Italy and America. A new slavery arose. The upward moving of white labor was betrayed into wars for profit based on color caste. Democracy died save in the hearts of Black folk.[102]

Du Bois provides American pragmatism with what it sorely lacks: an international perspective on the impetus and impediments to individuality and radical democracy, a perspective that highlights the plight of the wretched of the earth, namely, the majority of humanity who own no property or wealth, participate in no democratic arrangements, and whose individualities are crushed by hard labor and harsh living conditions. James possessed the ingredients for such a view, but he did not see social structures, only individuals. Dewey indeed saw social structures and individuals yet primarily through an American lens. Hook too adopts a cosmopolitan viewpoint, but his cold war sentiments give a tunnel vision of the third world as a playground for the two superpowers. Mills comes closer than the others, yet, for him, postmodern historical agency resides almost exclusively in the Western (or Westernized) intelligentsia. Du Bois goes beyond them all in the scope and depth of his vision: creative powers reside among the wretched of the earth even in their subjugation, and the fragile structures of democracy in the world depend, in large part, on how these powers are ultimately exercised.

Convinced "that the whole set of the white world in America, in Europe, and in the world was too determinedly against racial equality, to give power and persuasiveness to our agitation,"[103] Du Bois advocated a program of voluntary segregation based on institution building and a separate cooperative economy. This ideological break from the liberal integrationist reformism of the NAACP led to his resignation in 1934. He returned to Atlanta University as head of the Department of Sociology. There he founded and edited *Phylon* and set up a series of conferences on programs to alleviate the economic condition of black people after the war. Yet, unexpectedly, Du Bois was retired by the trustees of the university. Even more surprising, he was asked to return to the NAACP. But after four years of bickering with the NAACP leadership, especially over his support of Henry Wallace in 1948, Du Bois was dismissed.

With the Pan-African movement rejuvenated in 1945 and the peace movement escalating, Du Bois' preoccupation with decolonization found him more and more drawn into the cold war, not only as interlocutor but also as target. In *Color and Democracy: Colonies and Peace* (1945) he excoriated cold warriors as handmaidens of the American imperial empire. The Marshall Plan was the tool of a new postwar colonialism; the containment strategy, a threat to world peace. In 1950, he ran on the Labor party ticket for U.S. Senate, a sure sign of his closer relations with the Communist party. The following February, Du Bois' peace information center, which had disbanded four months earlier, was indicted by a grand jury in Washington, D.C., for "failure to register as agent for a foreign principal." At the age of eighty-three and after over half a century in pursuit of individuality and democracy in America and abroad, Du Bois was an indicted criminal, handcuffed and facing a maximum sentence of five years in prison.

> I have faced during my life many unpleasant experiences; the growl of a mob; the personal threat of murder; the scowling distaste of an audience. But nothing has cowed me as that day, November 8, 1951, when I took my seat in a Washington courtroom as an indicted criminal.[104]

The widespread vilification of Du Bois as a Russian agent in the press—both white and black—left him virtually alone with leftist friends and some black loyal supporters in McCarthyite America. But support overflowed from overseas. And although the government could not prove "subversion" against him (or his colleagues at the peace center), the stigma stuck for the general populace. He was refused the right to travel abroad and to speak on university campuses (and at local NAACP branches!), his manuscripts were turned down by reputable publishers, and his mail was tampered with.

> It was a bitter experience and I bowed before the storm. But I did not break . . . I found new friends and lived in a wider world than ever before—a world with no color line. I lost my leadership of my race . . . the colored children ceased to hear my name.[105]

Six years later Du Bois' request for a passport was finally granted (owing to a Supreme Court ruling). He traveled abroad for nearly a year to China, France, England, Sweden, Germany, Russia, and Czechoslovakia. In 1961, Kwame Nkrumah invited Du Bois to Ghana to begin work on the Encyclopedia Africana, a project Du Bois had proposed in 1909. Du Bois accepted, but before he left for Ghana he joined the Communist Party, U.S.A. Locked into the narrow options of American political culture, Du Bois ultimately preferred a repressive communism that resisted European and American imperialism to a racist America that promoted the subjugation of peoples of color. A few weeks before he departed for Ghana, Du Bois wrote to a friend:

> I just cannot take any more of this country's treatment. We leave for Ghana October 5th and I set no date for return . . . Chin up, and fight on, but realize that American Negroes can't win.[106]

After two years of working on the encyclopedia, Du Bois became a Ghanaian citizen. In that same year, 1963, he died—the very day that 250,000 people gathered in Washington, D.C., to hear Martin Luther King, Jr., immortalize the black Emersonian quest for the American dream. Like Malcolm X and later even King himself, Du Bois concluded that this dream was more a nightmare for those whose measuring rod is the plight of most black Americans. For him, an Emersonian culture of creative democracy had become a mere chimera: a racist, sexist, and multinational capitalist America had no potential whatsoever to realize the pragmatist ideals of individuality and radical democracy. Yet Du Bois still encouraged struggle. About a month before leaving America, Du Bois attended a banquet for Henry Winston, a leading and courageous black communist released from prison after losing his sight owing to jail neglect. In words that aptly describe his own life and work, Du Bois quoted from Emerson's "Sacrifice":

> Though love repine and reason chafe,
>> There came a voice without reply
> 'Tis Man's perdition to be safe
>> When for the truth he ought to die[107]

And though Du Bois may have lost his own ideological "sight" owing greatly to national neglect and limited political options, there is no doubt that what he did "see" remains a major obstacle for an Emersonian culture of radical democracy in America.

Reinhold Niebuhr: The Jamesian Cultural Critic

Reinhold Niebuhr was the most influential cultural critic in mid-century America. With one foot in evangelical liberal Protestantism and another in American pragmatism, Niebuhr articulated a "Christian pragmatism"[108] that in its socialist and liberal ideological forms seized the imagination of an American intelligentsia bereft of utopian hopes yet still enamored of human creative powers. The distinctive contribution of Niebuhr was to deploy a tragic perspective—stamped with a Christian imprimatur—as an impetus to moral critique of and heroic struggle in corporate liberal America. As with Hook, his critique lost much of its cutting edge as political alternatives shriveled, yet his subtle dialectic of human will and historical limits, individual volition and fateful circumstances, sustained a generation of Americans on the left, center, and right.

Like Emerson, Niebuhr was a sheer dynamo of intellectual energy; his perpetual, restless movement embodied a pioneer spirit in an America in search of new frontiers. He was similar to James in that his ebullient style and sparkling personality were as impressive as his voluminous books and articles. And, as with Dewey, his social activism touched on nearly every issue of importance to middle-class reformist Americans. In short, as writer, activist, and "circuit rider," Niebuhr was *the* Emersonian figure in mid-century America—though less intellectually awesome than Dewey.

Ironically, two prominent features plagued Niebuhr throughout his life: intellectual insecurity and anxiety about his nationality. In a world of professionalism and academic credentials, he had neither a B.A. nor a Ph.D.; and in a patriotic and nativistic America, he labored to shed and shun his German immigrant heritage. Niebuhr's intellectual insecurity made him both envious and suspicious of academic prestige and achievement. His anxiety about his nationality fed his relentless ambitions to leave his mark in the world as an American.

Born in 1892 and raised in the Midwest (Illinois and Missouri), Niebuhr lived in a parochial German-speaking enclave for his first twenty-one years. The son of an energetic and stern German Evangelical pastor and an unschooled yet imaginative mother, Niebuhr matriculated to Elmhurst College and Eden Theological Seminary. Elmhurst (with no accredited

B.A. program) was actually a mediocre boarding school that offered a truncated classical education—Latin and ancient history with no English, sciences, or modern history—to high school pupils. In fact, Niebuhr took his last courses in math and science at fourteen years old at a small high school in Lincoln, Illinois! Eden was a three-year denominational seminary (from which his father had graduated) with five dedicated yet provincial professors. After graduating as valedictorian (in a class of twenty), Niebuhr applied to Union Theological Seminary in New York and Yale Divinity School in New Haven for further intellectual training for the ministry. He was rejected at Union owing to his lack of a recognized B.A. and accepted at Yale Divinity School, then an academic backwater. The sudden death of his beloved father just months before his ordination and departure for Yale deepened his sense of vocation and forced tremendous financial responsibilities on him. For most of his life Niebuhr supported his widowed mother.

At Yale, Niebuhr was thoroughly intimidated and marginalized ("a mongrel among thoroughbreds").[109] This bastion of WASP gentility made him aware of his inferior schooling and ashamed of his midwestern German accent. He arrived as a third-year B.D. student and quickly came under the influence of the thought of William James. This influence resulted from the empiricist leanings of Professor Douglas Clyde Macintosh, a young new addition from Canada of Baptist orientation.

Macintosh was no proponent of pragmatism as his magnum opus, *Theology as an Empirical Science* (1919), makes clear, but he exposed Niebuhr to a new world of epistemological puzzles and perplexities. Niebuhr's struggle with epistemology-centered philosophy can be seen in his thirty-eight-page B.D. thesis entitled "The Validity and Certainty of Religious Knowledge." Niebuhr's rough performance, although betraying his lack of fluency in the English language, still contained two crucial themes: the appeal to human experience as the justification of religious claims, and a Jamesian notion of religion as a provocation for meaningful human struggle and heroic moral action. Niebuhr held that knowing is not an "outward look" but rather an activity instrumental in achieving certain goals and satisfying specific needs:

> We need or think we need, immortality, God, freedom, responsibility, for our soul and therefore we believe them to be true, and in so far as we can verify our needs and values we have a certainty that they are true.
>
> The revolt of men like William James against the determinism of the universe . . . is the revolt of a growing moral consciousness in men, that is becoming increasingly impatient with a universe in which its struggles are without effect and its powers not its own. Man *wants to know* that the battle of life is not a sham battle.[110]

Needless to say, Niebuhr's sophomoric rendering of James's will-to-believe doctrine, itself already a rather vulgar interpretation of pragmatism, is utterly unconvincing. But what is important here is not the persuasiveness of Niebuhr's claims but rather the fact that he invokes James to defend them. In later life, Niebuhr explicitly noted:

> I stand in the William James tradition. He was both an empiricist and a religious man, and his faith was both the consequence and the presupposition of his pragmatism.[111]

Even more important are the distinctive features of the pragmatist perspective Niebuhr shared with James. Arthur Schlesinger, Jr., perceptively observed:

> Niebuhr was a child of the pragmatic revolt . . . He shared with William James a vivid sense of the universe as open and unfinished, always incomplete, always fertile, always effervescent with novelty. Where James called it a "pluralist universe," Niebuhr would call it a "dynamic universe"; but the sense of reality as untamed, streaming, provisional, was vital for both. Similarly both revolted against the notion that this unpredictable universe could be caught and contained in any closed philosophical system. The burden of James's polemic was against the notion that there was any human viewpoint in which the world could appear as an absolutely single fact; the crudity of experience, said James, remained an eternal element of experience. Similarly, Niebuhr: "A perfectly consistent world view is bound to outrage some actual facts in the life of nature and the history of man" . . . Where James would accept the intractability of experience and the incompleteness of perception as the essence of reality, Niebuhr, committed to ultimate explanation, developed the category of "paradox" to deal with the antinomies which had formed the substance of James's "radical empiricism."[112]

In fairness to Niebuhr, Schlesinger is wrong to claim that Niebuhr is "committed to ultimate explanation." Rather by appropriating Kierkegaard's notion of "paradox" Niebuhr forecloses a search for ultimate explanation and therefore settles for energizing myths and galvanizing symbols that will generate human creative powers and guide them toward the enhancement of human personality.

In short, Niebuhr in his own awkward fashion affirms the Emersonian evasion of epistemology-centered philosophy. His early crude appropriation of James led him away from the problems of Cartesian-inspired epistemology and toward the moral life of the individual. After another year at Yale—thus obtaining both his B.D. and M.A. degrees there—Niebuhr decided not to pursue further graduate work. He wrote, "Epistemology bored me . . . and frankly the other side of me came out: I desired relevance rather than scholarship."[113] It was this viewpoint that provoked Paul Tillich's famous critique of Niebuhr:

> The difficulty of writing about Niebuhr's epistemology lies in the fact that there is no such epistemology. Niebuhr does not ask, "How can I

know?"; he starts knowing. And he does not ask afterward, "How could I know?," but leaves the convincing power of his thought without epistemological support.[114]

Tillich was expressing his frustrations—fueled by his German idealist assumptions about what epistemology is—toward the Emersonian evasion enacted by American pragmatists and accepted by Niebuhr.

James's influence on Niebuhr also can be seen in Niebuhr's prize-winning essay "The Paradox of Patriotism." With the outbreak of World War I and the German phobia growing in the country, Niebuhr both appropriated James's notion of a "moral equivalent of war" and articulated a strong patriotism. The ethical duty of the Christian church was to provide "adequate moral substitutes for war" and enable "the heroes of moral struggles to take the places of the heroes of war in our own halls of fame."[115]

Niebuhr left Yale for the pastorate of Bethel Evangelical Church in Detroit, eager to put his Christian Jamesian moral heroism into practice. Ironically, Niebuhr spent more time on lecturing and writing than on preaching and pastoring. Disappointed in the parochial German-speaking church, fed by journalistic ambitions, and forced by financial needs, Niebuhr never focused his energies in the pastorate. Having "cast his lot with the English" language at Yale and become "a violent American patriot" during the First World War, Niebuhr principally lent his skills to the Americanization of his denomination in face of rising anti-German hysteria, exemplified by George Creel's Committee on Public Information.[116] As head of the denomination's War Welfare Commission and as writer of such influential essays as "The Failure of German-Americanism" in the *Atlantic*, Niebuhr threw his weight behind the patriot cause. Yet he still felt too far removed from the cosmopolitan corridors of influence and visibility.

> If I were a doctor people would consult me according to the skill I had and the reputation I could acquire. But being a minister I can appeal only to people who are labeled as I am . . . Perhaps if I belonged to a larger denomination this wouldn't irk me so much. I suffer from an inferiority complex because of the very numerical weakness of my denomination. If I belonged to a large one I might strut about and claim its glory for myself. If I give myself to religion as a profession I must find some interdenominational outlet for my activities. But what?[117]

Niebuhr also yearned to serve in the war. When he visited military chaplains—one of whom was his younger brother, H. Richard—he envied their sense of sacrifice and service.

> As ministers of the Christian religion I have no particular respect for them. Yet I am overcome by a terrible inferiority complex when I deal with them. Such is the power of a uniform . . . The uniform itself is the

symbol of their devotion to the God of battles. It is the uniform and not the cross which impresses me and others. I am impressed even when I know that I ought not be.[118]

The persistent sense of an "inferiority complex" in Niebuhr was not simply a lack of self-confidence. It was also a form of self-critique and self-challenge in the intellectual and moral dimensions of his life. On the one hand, he was unsure of his intellectual abilities and moral fortitude; on the other hand, he would push himself to the brink of nervous breakdown to develop and exercise both. He seized every opportunity to grow, advance, and shine. At his nadir, he defended Rockefeller's "evident sincerity" and "sense of stewardship" when he headed the Rockefeller-funded Interchurch World Movement in 1921. At his best, he fought along with automobile workers against Henry Ford. The latter struggle prompted him to endorse socialism for the first time in 1926. And his chance to go "big time" came with an offer from Union Theological Seminary in 1928, a part-time teaching offer financially underwritten by his good friend Sherman Eddy. Like Dewey, Niebuhr became a giant in New York. But he did so with an explicit Jamesian sense of antiprofessionalism and active political engagement in the world.

This sense of engagement, along with his histrionic style and Midwestern accent, did not sit well with his stodgy senior colleagues. Even more upsetting were Niebuhr's radical political activities. He joined the Socialist party, openly supported Norman Thomas (a 1911 graduate of Union), and worked with left-leaning trade unions. He actually ran for the state senate in 1930 and for Congress in 1932 on the Socialist ticket. He and Dewey worked together in both campaigns. Yet Niebuhr's achievements were not to be in his political activism but in his texts—one good reason why Union kept him.

At the age of forty, Niebuhr wrote his first major book, *Moral Man and Immoral Society* (1932). And it remains today the best Christian defense of an American democratic socialism, even if violent struggle is required to bring such socialism about. Niebuhr's major targets were secular liberals who viewed "critical intelligence" as the major motor of progress and religious liberals who posited "love" as this motor. Among the former, Niebuhr highlighted Dewey; of the latter, he accented Walter Rauschenbusch. Both commit the cardinal sin of liberalism: that of promoting "the illusions and sentimentalities of the age of Reason."[119]

> What is lacking among all these moralists, whether religious or rational, is an understanding of the brutal character of all human collectives, and the power of self-interest and collective egoism in all intergroup relations. Failure to recognize the stubborn resistance of group egoism to all moral and inclusive social objectives inevitably involves them in unrealistic and confused political thought . . . They do not see that the limitations of the human imagination, the easy subservience of reason

to prejudice and passion, and the consequent persistence of irrational egoism, particularly in group behavior, make social conflict an inevitability in human history, probably to its very end.[120]

Needless to say, Niebuhr's accusations against liberals—especially Dewey and Rauschenbusch—are sweeping and often unfair. Yet they serve as fodder for his cannon. In many ways, Niebuhr is engaging in a self-critique, in a wholesale rejection of his own earlier liberalism, both political and religious. For it was he who wrote:

> There doesn't seem to be much malice in the world. There is simply not enough intelligence to conduct the intricate affairs of a complex civilization.[121]

And, despite his stress on power, struggle, egoism, and conflict, Niebuhr remained tied to the love ethic of liberal Christianity. He severely circumscribed its operation, however, and invoked justice as its approximation in interpersonal and collective spheres. More fundamentally, notwithstanding his association of liberalism with the rising bourgeoisie and the illusions of progress, peace, and brotherhood, Niebuhr remains a liberal Christian in that he conceives of religion as an impetus to moral and social transformation. Niebuhr indeed gives up the illusions of liberalism—perfection, kingdom of God on earth, ultimate harmony—but they become mythical ideals that still regulate human action and inspire heroic energies in a harsh and tragic world.

Niebuhr's best critic, his brother H. Richard, captures this when he writes:

> You think of religion as a power—dangerous sometimes, helpful sometimes. That's liberal. For religion itself religion is no power, but that to which religion is directed, God . . . I think the liberal religion is thoroughly bad. It is a first-aid to hypocrisy. It is the exaltation of goodwill, moral idealism. It worships the God whose qualities are "the human qualities raised to the nth degree," and I don't expect as much help from this religion as you do. It is sentimental and romantic. Has it ever struck you that you read religion through the mystics and ascetics? You scarcely think of Paul, Augustine, Luther, Calvin. You're speaking of humanistic religion so far as I can see. You come close to breaking with it at times but you don't quite do it.[122]

And even after Niebuhr turned to the Pauline and Augustinian traditions he remained a liberal Christian. I suggest this is so because Niebuhr's roots in American pragmatism do not permit him to decenter human creative powers. His pragmatism locks him into the dialectical interplay of a willful self and fateful circumstances, human volition and historical constraints. His conception of religion must fit into this interplay, and for Niebuhr the profound insights of the religious worldview beckon human achievement yet recognize the unachievable.

The Emersonian moments in *Moral Man and Immoral Society* bear this out. On the one hand, "all history is a conflict between human character and impersonal fate, and since one may never be certain which of the two is more potent in a given instant, there is something of an overstatement in any philosophy of history which reads the future in terms of the complete triumph of one or the other."[123] Therefore, history is open-ended, with new possibilities and problems, novel challenges and constraints always presenting themselves.

On the other hand, religion is

> a vision prompted by the conscience and insight of individual man, but incapable of fulfillment by collective man . . . The vitality of the vision is the measure of man's rebellion against the fate which binds his collective life to the world of nature from which his soul recoils. The vision can be kept alive only by permitting it to overreach itself. But meanwhile collective man, operating on the historic and mundane scene, must content himself with a more modest goal.[124]

In this passage Niebuhr not only makes the exemplary Emersonian gesture of historicizing "collective man" more than "individual man" but also mediates between the two by means of "rebellion"—a Promethean trope of human creative powers. Hence, Niebuhr can meet the objections of his brother only by giving up his pragmatism and thereby severing his link to Emerson.

Furthermore, Niebuhr's religious liberalism can be seen in his attitude toward modern science. Despite his rhetorical castigations of Dewey's enshrinement of "reason," Niebuhr actually defers to science more than does Dewey. As we saw earlier, Dewey does not endow science with authority over "the way the world is"; rather it provides the best instrumental descriptions for predicting and explaining natural phenomena. For Niebuhr, however, science does have an ontological authority—it simply leaves out issues of meaning and value. Therefore mythic thinking is "pre-scientific" and "primitive" if its myths that give meaning and value are taken literally, and "supra-scientific" and "permanent" if these symbols are taken symbolically, dramatically, and poetically.[125]

This fundamental issue of the referent of Niebuhr's myths has perplexed many critics and followers of Niebuhr. Emil Brunner, a leading neo-orthodox theologian during Niebuhr's day, took up this concern directly with Niebuhr.

> As over against Bultmann's elimination of the "mythical" sayings of biblical eschatology, Reinhold Niebuhr would no doubt stress the point that these symbols are not to be eliminated but are, rather, to be taken seriously as symbols. But what kind of reality lies hidden beneath these symbols? Is it an everlasting life, for which we should hope in the hour of death? Is it the fulfillment of the biblical expectation of the kingdom of God?

> . . . does one not have a right to expect of every thinking Chris-
> tian—and a *fortiori* of every Christian thinker—that he be cognizant of
> what he has to hope for in Christ? To what extent there stands behind
> Niebuhr's "eschatological symbols" a *reality*, and what kind of reality—
> or whether perhaps these eschatological symbols are merely "regulative
> principles" in the Kantian sense—these are questions on which we should
> like to have him make a definite pronouncement.[126]

In the same volume, Niebuhr does not reply to Brunner's queries.
Yet he indirectly touches on the issue when he responds to another con-
tributor to the volume.

> I must add that I am puzzled by Father Weigel's assertion that I believe
> in the Trinity and in the divinity of Christ "symbolically but not literally."
> I do not know how it is possible to believe in anything pertaining to
> God and eternity "literally." But I do not equate "symbolically" with "sub-
> jectively." Father Weigel cannot be expected to follow all the nuances
> of Protestant theology. Therefore he equates my ideas with those of Bult-
> mann. I think on the other hand that Bultmann does not distinguish
> rigorously between pre-scientific myths and permanently valid
> symbols.[127]

This response is pure philosophic mush—tinged with a tone of condescen-
sion. Niebuhr leaves open the question as to whether it is possible to believe
in anything literally, science included. If it is not possible, he then slides
down the slippery Nietzschean slope of wholesale metaphorical constructions of "reality." If it is possible, then in what sense are scientific beliefs
more "literal" than religious ones? He skirts these issues by invoking a
distinction which hangs on a conception of science which is both unarticulated and uninterrogated. I suspect he has simply bitten off more than
he can chew. I also suspect that there is an implicit positivism—a homage
to modern science—lurking beneath his Christian pragmatism; and that
this positivism has less to do with philosophical argumentation than with
the prejudices of his liberal middle-class milieu.

This is best seen when Niebuhr stunned a Catholic interviewer by
saying: "Now I don't think that anybody really believes in the resurrec-
tion of the body . . ."

> *Interviewer*: Do you seriously think that many Christians do not believe
>   in the resurrection of the body?
> *Dr. Niebuhr*: Of course. How can they?[128]

Yes, Niebuhr's religious liberalism ran deep, but his powerful critiques of a
version of it compounded with political liberalism put him squarely in the
socialist camp in the thirties—yet always with Christian underpinnings.

Just as Hook was the leading American Marxist thinker in the thirties,
so Niebuhr was the leading Christian leftist thinker of the decade. Yet
Niebuhr's trajectory is more complex, though they both end up with similar

cold war ideological positions after World War II. Ironically, Niebuhr becomes, for a brief moment, more politically radical as he moves in a more theologically conservative direction. In his *Reflections on the End of an Era* (1934), Niebuhr announced:

> The following reflections are merely tracts for the times . . . The basic conviction which runs through them is that the liberal culture of modernity is quite unable to give guidance and direction to a confused generation which faces the disintegration of a social system and the task of building a new one. In my opinion adequate spiritual guidance can come only through a more radical political orientation and more conservative religious convictions than are comprehended in the culture of our era. The effort to combine political radicalism with a more classical and historical interpretation of religion will strike the modern mind as bizarre and capricious. It will satisfy neither the liberals in politics and religion, nor the political radicals nor the devotees of traditional Christianity.[129]

Niebuhr moved to the left politically because he sensed the impotence of American democratic socialism and closely followed its death in Germany with the rise of Hitler. Always Anglophilic and now married to an Englishwoman, Niebuhr turned to English radical models for hope. He found such a model in Sir Stafford Cripps's Socialist League, a left opposition group that broke with Ramsay MacDonald after his alliance with the Tories. Yet Niebuhr knew that such hope was feeble—the German scenario seemed to prefigure the fate of North Atlantic civilization. Yet he refused to join the communists principally owing to their fervent secularism and atheism.

Niebuhr's attempt, egged on by his brother's Reformation theological critiques, to plumb the depths of the Christian tradition pushed him toward reflections on "the Assurance of Grace" and "the Experience of Grace." This language was essentially a way of sustaining hope and promoting human action in a seemingly hopeless and fateful situation. The capitalist present looked bleak.

> American capitalism is like a once robust man who suffers from premature senility but fails to note his critical situation, partly because he has enough wealth to escape the immediate consequences of his ineffectiveness, partly because the optimistic psychology of a rather recent youthfulness obscures the tragic facts of his present situation and partly because there is no one about strong enough to snatch the vestiges from impotent hands.[130]

And for Niebuhr the communist alternative was not attractive.

> There are indications that communism will substitute a mechanistic collectivism for the mechanistic individualism of a bourgeois civilization. Its collectivism is mechanistic partly because it is, like capitalism, the

product of a mechanical civilization and partly because it is, like liberalism, a fruit of rationalism. In this, as in some other respects, communism is too much the child of capitalism and lives too much by a precise negation of the vices of the latter to bring real peace and happiness to mankind. One of the pathetic aspects of human history is that the instruments of judgment which it uses to destroy particular vices must belong to the same category of the vice to be able to destroy it.[131]

Niebuhr's alternative is a vague mishmash of democratic socialism and prophetic religion held together by a pragmatist stress on human creative powers.

An adequate approach to the social and moral problem must include a political policy which will bring the most effective social check upon conflicting egoistic impulses in society; a moral idealism which will exploit every available resource of altruistic impulse and reason to extend life from selfish to social ends; and a religious world-view which will do justice to the ideals of the spirit which reach beyond the possibilities of historic achievement and thereby challenge every concrete attainment with the vision of the unattained.[132]

This provocative yet unpacked vision marked a turning point in Niebuhr's "Christian pragmatism." From now on, he would focus first and foremost on the development of a Christian mythology that engaged the social but proceeded from the aspirations, responsibility, and anxieties of the self. In short, he decided to take Christian theology seriously—or at least as seriously as a Christian pragmatist can. He remained politically active, founding the Fellowship of Socialist Christians and the journal *Radical Religion*, but he was preoccupied with discerning and preserving Christian identity grounded in the uniqueness of the self. This quest is the main impulse in his major books of this period, *An Interpretation of Christian Ethics* (1935), *Beyond Tragedy* (1937), and his magnum opus, the two-volume *The Nature and Destiny of Man* (1941, 1943); the intellectual expression of this quest and impulse constitutes the most ambitious and influential American theology in the twentieth century.

The starting point of Niebuhr's theological anthropology is precisely the problematic of mid-century American pragmatism: the interplay of the willful self and fateful circumstances, human volition and historical limits. Niebuhr claims that this dynamic and perennial interplay can be attributed to a primordial ontological state of anxiety. Following Søren Kierkegaard's insights in *The Concept of Dread* and responding to the vast devastation of North Atlantic civilization (depressions and World War II), Niebuhr posits a fundamental insecurity at the core of the human condition, an insecurity that engenders the exercise of human creative powers for good or for evil. For Niebuhr, anxiety is neither good nor evil; rather it is the precondition for the evaluation and enactment of good or evil.

> In short, man, being both free and bound, both limited and limitless, is anxious. Anxiety is the inevitable concomitant of the paradox of freedom and finiteness in which man is involved . . .
>
> Man is anxious not only because his life is limited and dependent and yet not so limited that he does not know of his limitations. He is also anxious because he does not know the limits of his possibilities. There are, of course, limits but it is difficult to gauge them from any immediate perspective.[133]

In other words, Niebuhr begins with an Emersonian self eager to exercise its creative powers yet also caught in the radical contingency of things so that these powers may yield development or disaster. Like Dewey, Niebuhr historicizes Emersonian theodicy, but Niebuhr's Reformation theology accents disaster just as much as development. This accent results from the inevitability, though not the necessity, of sin; that is, the pervasive, though not programmed, wrong use of human freedom. This wrong use is an effect of the human refusal to acknowledge one's radical contingency, finiteness, and conditionedness. Following Karen Horney's *The Neurotic Personality of Our Time*, Niebuhr views Alfred Adler's "will to power" and Sigmund Freud's "libido impulse" as the two dominant forms of dealing with anxiety. The first form corresponds to the sin of pride – an aggressive search for security in power, knowledge, self-righteousness, and spiritual purity. The second corresponds to the sin of sensuality – an unrestrained pursuit of hedonistic self-indulgence to escape the responsibility of one's own freedom. The genius of Niebuhr's Christian revision of Emersonian theodicy is that it accounts for both Herman Melville's Ahab and F. Scott Fitzgerald's Gatsby without devaluing human powers or denouncing tragedy.

> Anxiety, as a permanent concomitant of freedom, is thus both the source of creativity and a temptation to sin. It is the condition of the sailor, climbing the mast (to use a simile), with the abyss of the waves beneath him and the "crow's nest" above him. He is anxious about both the end toward which he strives and the abyss of nothingness into which he may fall. The ambition of man to be something is always partly prompted by the fear of meaninglessness which threatens him by reason of the contingent character of his existence. His creativity is therefore always corrupted by some effort to overcome contingency by raising precisely what is contingent to absolute and unlimited dimensions. This effort, though universal, cannot be regarded as normative. It is always destructive. Yet obviously the destructive aspect of anxiety is so intimately involved in the creative aspects that there is no possibility of making a simple separation between them. The two are inextricably bound together by reason of man being anxious both to realize his unlimited possibilities and to overcome and to hide the dependent and contingent character of his existence.[134]

Niebuhr's Christian pragmatist anthropology puts the Emersonian self on a slippery tightrope, walking—even running—between the Scylla of quest for Promethean perfection and the Charybdis of escape into Dionysian abandonment. The inevitable fall signifies human depravity; attempts to get back up and continue the ordeal disclose human dignity. Yet, in a way that is true to his liberal Christianity, grace is not a supernatural rescue from the ordeal but rather a form of empowerment for those on the tightrope—"Grace as Power in, and Mercy towards, Man" manifest as "the Christ in us."

> It is important to emphasize that the two sides of the experience of grace are so related that they do not contradict, but support each other. To understand that the Christ in us is not a possession but a hope, that perfection is not a reality but an intention; that such peace as we know in this life is never purely the peace of achievement but the serenity of being "completely known and all forgiven"; all this does not destroy moral ardour or responsibility. On the contrary it is the only way of preventing premature completions of life, or arresting the new and more terrible pride which may find its roots in the soil of humility, and of saving the Christian life from the intolerable pretension of saints who have forgotten that they are sinners.[135]

Niebuhr presents his Christian pragmatist anthropology as a modern synthesis of the best of the Renaissance and Reformation. Yet it is more an attempt to salvage Emersonian theodicy within a Protestant Christian framework for a distraught and disoriented American middle class numbed by depression and war. Despite its academic ambitions, Niebuhr's project remained a mid-century Emersonian jeremiad condemning liberal illusions, lamenting past blindnesses, and projecting new possibilities for America. His most harsh yet perceptive critic, Professor Robert Calhoun of Yale, noted,

> No cautious weigher of evidence here . . . but a preacher expounding the Word in line with his private revelation . . .
> The real ground of the author's doctrine is not what he has read but what has happened to him as a struggling self [which] . . . must become a permanent part of any reader's thinking.[136]

As socialist options waned after the Nazi-Russian pact in 1939, Niebuhr increasingly moved toward Roosevelt. And the Battle of Britain—his beloved England—was the straw that broke the leftist camel's back. At stake were not simply family interests—given his British wife—but also his image of Britain as the exemplar of North Atlantic civilization. In 1941, he helped found the Union for Democratic Action and the journal *Christianity and Crisis*; the primary aim of both was to gain U.S. support for the Allies' effort in order to save democracy from German barbarism.

A noteworthy aspect of Niebuhr's interventionist activity was his focus on the plight of Jews in Germany. He not only pushed the Roosevelt administration for increased European Jewish immigration to the United States, but also publicly endorsed the Zionist argument for a Jewish homeland in Palestine.[137] This endorsement was understandable given the indescribably evil treatment of Jews under Hitler; yet it sounded a bit strange coming from a progressive deeply committed to secular, democratic values. Even he admitted this tension when he wrote: "Yet the ideal of a political homeland for the Jews is so intriguing that I am almost willing to sacrifice my convictions for the sake of it."[138] The important point here is not so much Niebuhr's Zionist politics as the scope of the application of democratic ideals. Ironically, just as Niebuhr was articulating his powerful defense of democracy in *The Children of Light and the Children of Darkness* (1944), he also was reluctant to extend democracy beyond those in North Atlantic civilization. In a revealing piece in the British journal the *Spectator* of August 16, 1946, he defended his Zionism in the following way:

> There is, I know, not sufficient consideration in America either of Arab rights or of the embarrassment of Britain in dealing with the Arab world. I find it baffling, on the other hand, that the average person here speaks of Arab "opinion" without suggesting that such opinion is limited to a small circle of feudal overlords, that there is no middle-class in this world and that the miserable masses are in such abject poverty that an opinion is an impossible luxury for them. One difficulty with the Arab problem is that the technical and dynamic civilization which the Jews might have helped to introduce and which should have the support of American capital, and which would include river development, soil-conservation and use of native power, would not be acceptable to the Arab chieftains though beneficial to the Arab masses. It would have therefore to be imposed provisionally, but would have a chance of ultimate acceptance by the masses.[139]

Niebuhr candidly characterized this position as "imperialistic realism,"[140] yet it flies in the face of his democratic convictions. On the one hand, he puts forward a paternalistic argument that sets aside "Arab rights," nullifies Arab "opinion" (owing to the lack of a middle class), and justifies provisional "imposition" of a settler people on indigenous inhabitants in the name of a "technical and dynamic civilization." On the other hand, Niebuhr eloquently states in his famous formulation: "Man's capacity for justice makes democracy possible; but man's inclination to injustice makes democracy necessary."[141] Are we to infer that "abject poverty" precludes a capacity for justice? Or that non-Europeans, i.e., those with a less "technical and dynamic civilization," require "imposed" arrangements?

Niebuhr's blindnesses here reaffirm the North Atlantic ethnocentrism that runs through much of the tradition of American pragmatism. In fact, his Zionist position can be seen as justifying a homeland not for Jews per se, but for North Atlantic Jews principally owing to their technical know-how and cultural refinement. Of course, the immeasurable evils of the Holocaust could be invoked, but such reasoning would justify homelands for Armenians, Cambodians, and other peoples who have been slaughtered by pernicious rulers.

Niebuhr's blindness abroad went hand-in-hand with a growing complacency toward injustice at home. Like Hook, Niebuhr moved toward the corporate liberals in the name of the cold war. In fact, he began to stress that the "oligarchy" was fluid, that inequalities of power were inevitable, that there was "rough justice" in America, and that the private ownership of property was a "relatively effective institution of social peace and justice."[142] Instead of critically examining the *hypocrisy* of American society and its *concrete* consequences for its victims, Niebuhr brilliantly probed into the *irony* of American history and its lesson for an aspiring (but wiser) new middle class.[143] With his picture on the cover of *Time* magazine's twenty-fifth anniversary issue (March 8, 1948), he was enshrined by senior editor Whittaker Chambers as "the official establishment theologian." And his membership on the exclusive Council on Foreign Relations—which facilitated his being seriously considered for the presidency of Yale University—made his liberal version of Christian pragmatism an official ideological weapon in the cold war.

After a debilitating stroke in 1952, Niebuhr was forced to slow down. Yet his slower pace amounted to a fast pace for others. Thereafter his religious piety became more private and his polemical writings less theological. He began to admire the organic gradualist approach to social problems best seen in Edmund Burke and analyzed the aftermath of the *Brown v. Board of Education* decision in light of it.[144] And, notwithstanding his support of King's civil rights movement and student antiwar activities, he was ready to vote Republican (for Nelson Rockefeller) in 1968, owing to his dislike of Richard Nixon, Hubert Humphrey, and Robert Kennedy.

Like Dewey—and in stark contrast to Mills and Du Bois—Niebuhr died (in 1971) a popular and prestigious figure. But, unlike Dewey, he had actually become for a brief period an organic intellectual of the corporate liberal establishment. Niebuhr responded to the crisis of American pragmatism with both prophetic defiance and priestly defense of mid-century America. His most profound and enduring yet ambiguous legacy was to link a Christian tragic perspective with a tempered Emersonian stress on human creative powers, a legacy best expressed in the famous prayer associated with him:

> O God, give us
> Serenity to accept what cannot be changed,
> Courage to change what should be changed,
> And Wisdom to distinguish the one from the other.

Throughout his career, Niebuhr appealed to "Christian pragmatism" to justify changes in the boundaries of what should be changed, but after him the Emersonian theodicy of American pragmatism would never be the same.

Lionel Trilling: The Pragmatist as Arnoldian Literary Critic

Lionel Trilling was one of the most renowned and revered literary critics of mid-century America. His unique response to the crisis of American pragmatism—the problem of the self and its circumstances, human will and impersonal fate—was to creatively sever pragmatist ideals of individuality and democracy from their Emersonian underpinnings; that is, he ultimately denounced and discarded Emersonian theodicy. By channeling his pragmatic sensibilities and intellectual energies into Arnoldian and Freudian channels, Trilling revealed what American pragmatism looked like without its aggressive and ameliorative features. In other words, in stark contrast to other contemporary pragmatic literary critics like Kenneth Burke, Trilling tried to salvage American pragmatism by purging it of its Emersonian elements.

An upwardly mobile son of a Jewish immigrant tailor and Anglophilic mother, Trilling had left sentiments as an adolescent and deep professional ambitions as a young adult. A rebel against his ethnic particularism, Trilling attempted to carve out new intellectual space on the American cultural terrain. Nurtured in the quest for Jewish cosmopolitanism of Horace Kallen (a student of William James) and Elliot Cohen (editor of the *Menorah Journal* and founder of *Commentary*), and educated at Columbia College and University, Trilling suffered from the normal bouts of identity crisis and insecurity that plague "outsiders." In later years he wrote this about his involvement in the *Menorah Journal*:

> To speak of the *Menorah Journal* as a response to "isolation" isn't merely enough—you must make the reader aware of the *shame* that young middle-class Jews felt; self-hatred was the word that later came into vogue but shame is simpler and better.[145]

And even after obtaining a full professorship at Columbia University in the English Department—the first Jew to achieve such stature—he noted in his private diary:

> And a sense of the absurdity of my having this rank at all—for no one could be more ignorant than I, without knowledge of any classical language, without any real command of any modern language, with no very wide reading and a great and growing laziness about reading and no wish for investigation. I have only a gift of dealing rather sensibly with literature, which surprises me for I always assume my intellectual feebleness. My being a professor and a much respected and even admired man

is a great hoax . . . Suppose I were to dare to believe that one could be a professor and a man! And a writer! — what arrogance and defiance of convention. Yet deeply I dare to believe it on the surface.[146]

Like Emerson, Trilling aspired to be not a mere academic or specialist but an intellectual who embodied what he enunciated.

It has been some time since we in America have had literary figures — that is, men who live their visions as well as write them, who *are* what they write, whom we think of as standing for something as men because of what they have written in their books. They preside, as it were, over certain ideas and attitudes. Mark Twain was in this sense a figure for us, and so was William James . . . There is something about the American character that does not take to the idea of the figure as the English character does.[147]

Trilling found such a figure who could help him become such a figure in Matthew Arnold. In his first and best book, *Matthew Arnold* (1939) — an extensive rewrite of his Columbia dissertation — Trilling meticulously dissected his model for his own instruction and inspiration. On the one hand, Arnold is attractive to Trilling because he unashamedly proclaims his allegiance to the middle class although a critic of and "alien" to that class. In a 1939 *Partisan Review* symposium Trilling echoed this allegiance:

My own literary interest . . . is in the tradition of humanistic thought and in the intellectual middle class which believes that it continues this tradition. Nowadays this perhaps [is] not properly pious; but however much I may acknowledge the historic role of the working class and the validity of Marxism, it would be only piety for me to say that my chief literary interest lay in this class and this tradition. What for me is so interesting in the intellectual middle class is the dramatic contradiction of its living with the greatest possibility (call it illusion) of conscious choice, its believing itself the inheritor of the great humanist and rationalist tradition, and the badness and stupidity of its action.
. . . it is for this intellectual class that I suppose I write.[148]

From Arnold, Trilling constructed his conception of culture, a conception of values and sensibilities, of ways of life and ways of struggle that put a premium on order and hierarchy, authority and respectability.[149] This Arnoldian view of culture promoted the norms of critical intelligence, refined civility, and intellectual modulation.[150] Trilling's project was to articulate and elaborate this conception of culture for the educated middle class in order to combat the encroachment of Stalinist politics and philistine culture. Just as Arnold opposed the complacent materialism of the aristocracy and the threatening "anarchism" of the working masses in nineteenth-century Britain, so Trilling exerted intellectual and moral leadership to offset the simplistic catechism of Marxism and the crude hedonism of the mass culture of consumption. He understood himself (quite early in his career) as a cosmopolitan intellectual emerging from a narrow ethnic parochialism and involved in a fierce struggle – at the "bloody crossroads where literature and politics met" – for Arnoldian hegemony over the educated middle class in mid-century America.

On the other hand, Trilling realized that the Arnoldian model could not be simply transplanted onto American soil. It had to be embellished by a distinct American tradition, that of American pragmatism. In his book, Trilling ingeniously depicted Arnold as an exemplary moral critic instinctively, though in the end inadequately, espousing and enacting a form of American pragmatism. First, Trilling pictured Arnold as involved in a crisis-ridden effort to create himself over against a burdensome European (especially French) tradition. Enamored with Senancour's *Obermann*, Arnold struggled with the relation between the creative powers of the self and the smothering circumstances of fate; the aim was to sidestep the "miserable frigidity and joyless malaise" of Senancour's conclusions. Trilling wrote:

> Yet when a man rummages among his various selves and creates a character for himself by selection, how does he know that he has made the right choice? Men feel, as they leave youth, that they have more or less consciously assumed a role by excluding some of the once-present elements from themselves. But ever after they are haunted by the fear that they might have selected another, better, role, that perhaps they have made the wrong choice. In his acquired *Tüchtigkeit*, Arnold always carried this doubt of fulfillment, this question of a life that he – or the world – has wrongly buried . . .
>
> No writer of his time – except perhaps Emerson – understood in terms as clear and straightforward as Arnold's this psychological phenomenon of the distortion of purpose and self and the assumption of a manner to meet the world.[151]

In this passage, Trilling not only depicts Arnold's struggle to become a self-chosen self and views his own sense of vocation through Arnold's struggle. He also posits Emerson as a possible master beyond Arnold – as one who better grasped the depths of the struggle and saw that "a commonality of joy"[152] was needed if a self-begotten self was to flourish. Trilling notes that it was Emerson who taught Arnold "the dangers of conformity and the need for preserving in oneself the glow of life."[153]

Trilling then linked Arnold to Dewey's efforts to overcome the gap between science and poetry, head and heart, intellect and feelings. Both Dewey and Arnold tried to overcome this chasm. Dewey chose philosophy, a worldly philosophy that disparaged epistemology; Arnold chose "poetry," a worldly literary criticism that discarded pedantry. The common denominator was a commitment to an engaged critical intelligence concerned with life.

If not exactly in the way Dewey suggests, if not quite "in the cold, reflective way of critical system," Arnold's criticism makes the instauration Dewey asks for. And only when we understand this synthesis can we understand the phrase which has bothered so many of Arnold's modern readers: "Poetry [or "literature": Arnold interchanges] is a criticism of life"; for Arnold, poetry is the highest expression of the imaginative reason.[154]

Moreover, Trilling attempted to show that Arnold arrived at a "joy whose grounds are true" by means of a Jamesian leap of faith; that is, by an appeal to the effects of positing a God for his own experience. Religion, for Arnold, is concerned neither with science nor with knowledge, but rather with "man insofar as he acts." In this sense, God is "real."

> "God is real since he produces real effects" was the doctrine of William James. It is also the doctrine of Arnold, and had not James read Arnold, we might have said that Arnold read James, for the earlier writer argued the pragmatic position with which the name of the later is more intimately associated . . .
>
> For Arnold poetry and science meet on the common ground they have of experience, and *experience* is the key-word to Arnold's religious discussion.[155]

Trilling's picture of Arnold as a protopragmatist is provocative and plausible but not persuasive. Among other things, James dismantled the very neoclassical notion of "right reason" that held Arnold captive and undergirded his central notion of "disinterestedness." In short, James's radical avowal of contingency was at odds with Arnold's search for security and stasis.

But what interests us here is not the validity of Trilling's interpretation, but rather the value of this misinterpretation for Trilling's own project. James may indeed be "perfectly at one with Arnold" on the matter of objectifying divine power and defending its "non-rationality."[156] Yet the bigger stakes, for Trilling, were that the Americanness of Arnold rests with his pragmatism.

Trilling's major criticism of Arnold is precisely what one might expect of a young Marxist-influenced critic of American pragmatism: the relative neglect of political and economic power when considering the impact of critical intelligence in society.

> The everlasting question of philosophical politics is how to place power and reason in the same agent, or how to make power reasonable; or how to endow reason with power. Clearly a state—which implies power—is required because some classes or individuals refuse to conform to reason and must be coerced for the good of the rest . . .
>
> Arnold's theory of the state does not hold up as a logical structure,

nor does it hold up as a practical structure. Its failure is the typical liberal failure, for it evades — it was intended to evade — the problems of what H. N. Brailsford calls "the crude issue of power . . . always the last of the realities that sensitive and reasonable men can bring themselves to face."[157]

Trilling did not entertain the possibility that Arnold, as inspector of schools and guardian of mass publishing ventures, indeed faced the issue of power by simply justifying the deployment of coercive power against "unreasonable" groups and classes. Instead Trilling highlighted Arnold's love of Rousseau and his support of the Paris Commune (1871), a love and support that justified "Arnold's claim that he was in the Revolutionary line."[158] More pointedly, Trilling accented the potential of Arnold's project for an American middle class sandwiched between a utopian left and a decrepit liberalism.

> We may best think of Arnold's effort as an *experimentum luciferum*, an experiment of light, rather than as an *experimentum fructiferum*, an experiment of fruit. It is that play of the mind over the subject, of which criticism consists: immediate practicality is not its point . . .
>
> Arnold, however, would not himself relish our leniency; he protested the practicability of his theory. His essentially mystic conception of the state reads almost like a Platonic myth . . . The value of any myth cannot depend on its demonstrability as a fact, but only on the value of the attitude it embodies, the further attitudes it engenders and actions it motivates. In these respects Arnold's myth is still fertile and valuable — and morally inescapable.[159]

The effective articulation of Trilling's version of Arnoldian ideology depended upon his ability to acquire intellectual authority. He achieved this in two ways. First, he worked diligently and cautiously within the anti-Semitic structures of the great Ivy League university which influenced public opinion (far more than Harvard and Yale at the time) — the Columbia University of John Dewey and President Nicholas Murray Butler. Trilling served as an instructor from 1932 to 1939 (with a brief stint at the University of Wisconsin, 1936–37), assistant professor until 1945, associate professor from 1945 to 1948, and professor from 1948 to 1965. He was made the George Edward Woodberry Professor of Literature in 1965, and he became a University Professor in 1970. Trilling retired from Columbia in 1974. As I noted earlier, he — along with Oscar Handlin at Harvard and John Blum at Yale — was one of the first Jews to enter the WASP-dominated faculties of the Ivy League.

Trilling's Arnoldian struggle to determine the worldview of an expanding intellectual class that was more and more pulled toward the academy for financial sustenance and personal status was won not simply because of his academic placement. His style of writing, his form of presentation, the tone, nuance, and attitude conveyed in his texts also played a role.

Trilling mastered a unique form of literary style that signified critical intelligence, a style that communicated "a faculty of generalship, an ability to marshall multitudes of ideas for combat."[160] This style reflected his overall approach that tried "to see literary situations as cultural situations, and cultural situations as great elaborate fights about moral issues, and moral issues as having something to do with gratuitously chosen images of personal being, and images of personal being as having something to do with literary style."[161]

Ironically, Trilling's preoccupation with his own style led him to downplay the role of form in the literary artists he examined. He shunned formalism as a mode of literary critical investigation. The indelible stamp on the reader's mind left by Trilling's writings has less to do with what he says than with how he says it. For example, his defense of moral realism in the great modern novels—like the similar defense of critical realism by his Marxist counterpart, Georg Lukács—was often unconvincing. And his loose readings of literary texts were usually irritating and frustrating. Yet his view of the novel "as an especially useful agent of the moral imagination" and his emphasis on the "variousness, complexity and difficulty" of acceptable political and literary discourse provided him with a huge canvas upon which to paint his portrait of the good life.

It is important to note that Trilling gave up on the book as a form of presentation after obtaining academic tenure. Thereafter he worked almost exclusively in the genre of the essay (and many short book reviews)—the occasional, nonacademic essay or the introductory essay to a canonical literary text. Through this genre, Trilling tried to create and cultivate an audience, a community of educated middle-class people like himself who acknowledged complexity, reveled in the felicities of the mind, and sidestepped the simplemindedness of Stalinism and the kitsch of popular culture.

This genre also reflected Trilling's own image of himself as a literary artist rather than an academic critic. Needless to say, his early short stories and his noteworthy novel, *The Middle of the Journey* (1947), bolstered this self-image. In some unusual autobiographical notes, he observed:

> I am always surprised when I hear myself referred to as a critic. After some thirty years of having been called by that name, the role and the function it designates seem odd to me . . .
>
> If I ask myself why this is so, the answer would seem to be that in some sense I did not ever undertake to be a critic—being a critic was not, in Wordsworth's phrase, part of the plan that pleased my boyish thought, or my adolescent thought, or even my thought as a young man. The plan that did please my thought was certainly literary, but what it envisaged was the career of a novelist. To this intention, criticism, when eventually I began to practice it, was always secondary, an afterthought: in short, not a vocation but an avocation . . .

I shall not attempt to be more specific about this than to say that my conception of what is interesting and problematical in life, of what reality consists in and what makes for illusion, of what must be held to and what let go, was derived primarily from novelists and not from antecedent critics or from such philosophers as speculate systematically about the nature and function of literature . . .

In remarking that my work in criticism took its direction from the novel, I have it in mind to point to its tendency to occupy itself not with aesthetic questions, except secondarily, but rather with moral questions, with the questions raised by the experience of quotidian life and by the experience of culture and history.[162]

Trilling's ingenious use of the essay as a literary form guided his audience through the cultural and political crisis of the times. This was so principally because of two basic rhetorical strategies. First, the conversational and elusive manner of his writings provided his world-weary audience an escape from the numerous clichés and shibboleths pervasive in mid-century American intellectual discourse. Trilling's relaxed prose simultaneously soothed his audience emotionally and stimulated them intellectually. His writings provided both a literary escape and a means to cultural sophistication; that is, they put him and them "above the fray" and reinforced the illusion of superiority.

Second, Trilling's interesting observations and intriguing formulations were put forward with little or no logical rigor or serious argumentation. His urbane style, a mix of Jewish oral eloquence and Jamesian patience, disarmed critical scrutiny and dispassionate objections. Instead, it prompted ideological readings and political responses—the very mode of discourse his style devalued and discredited.[163] In other words, Trilling's critics often fell into the traps he had set. Meaningful dialogue and substantive exchange deceptively appeared as an uncouth refusal to play by the rules of the refined parlance defined by Trilling's Arnoldian ideology and rhetorical strategies. In this way, Trilling's style shunned conflict in the name of "complexity, difficulty, variousness and modulation." As Jeffrey Cane Robinson has noted:

> The essay presupposes an ideal community of intimates who know and share without essential dispute and disagreement, being drawn together by a common belief in the ultimate pleasures of mind. This high state of civilization assumed and addressed by the essayists may be what Keats envisions as a grand democracy in which all whisper results to their neighbors. The essay-as-idyll, to the extent that it generates in its reader a special degree of pleasure in the activity of his own mind and that of the essayist and convincingly demonstrates that such shared activity is proof of health and attainment in a world which by and large does not encourage such activity, becomes the peculiar combative instrument of the self against society.[164]

This description of a certain form of essay writing—the essay-as-idyll—indeed holds for Trilling's style. His strategies endowed him and his audience with an unearned authority which sustained them through various crises. The peculiar and not-so-mysterious "we" Trilling often invoked reveals the cultural homogeneity he took for granted; it permitted him to parade prejudices as common sense. This authority was unearned because no rational case had been argued, no moral claim defended—only asserted and assumed. Just as Niebuhr's Augustinian interpretation of widely accepted Christian myths imposed constraints upon the aggressive self-righteous impulses of educated middle-class WASPs and resulted in "ironic" and "realistic" defenses of "the American way of life," so Trilling's version of agreed-upon Arnoldian values stressed the limits of Promethean aspirations among secular middle-class intellectuals and supported a tempered rapprochement with the American status quo.

Trilling's comments in the renowned "Our Country and Our Culture" *Partisan Review* symposium of 1952 gave a direct reply to his earlier Platonic question to Arnold of how power was to become reasonable. He applauds the fact that intellectuals and the corporate liberal economic elites are working cooperatively together.

> The needs of our society have brought close to the top of the social hierarchy a large class of people of considerable force and complexity of mind . . .
> Intellect has associated itself with power, perhaps as never before in history, and is now conceded to be in itself a kind of power.[165]

Trilling held that this association of intellect and power had profound consequences for intellectuals in modern society. In reply to a predictable critique from his colleague, C. Wright Mills, Trilling states:

> I am not a priori charmed by ideology taking the place of principle and honor, as it tends to do in our culture. But ideology carries with it some principle and some honor of its own. And a culture in which ideology is dominant offers an opportunity for the intellectual . . . A kind of cultural revolution has taken place, and like the Industrial Revolution, this cultural revolution creates a great deal of mess and vulgarity, but also brings with it many possibilities of revision and improvements.[166]

Trilling's apparently abstract formulations of the circumstantial and conditioned character of human will are intended as moral guidelines for the energies of this intellectual class. He wanted to guide them away from the simplicities of the left and infuse their cold war and corporate liberalism with a sense of the tragic. In short, Trilling was pointing out the reluctance of both literature and literary intellectuals to recognize the union of intellect and power; literature and literary criticism were political precisely because at their best they could disclose the blindnesses and rigidities of ideological orthodoxies, especially those of the left. This bid for both relevance and incorporation animates Trilling's classic work *The Liberal Imagination* (1950). Against the old humanists who cultivated marginality (preserving the classics) and the New Critics who fostered professionalism (new narrow techniques for close reading), Trilling posited the inescapability of politics and the unique way literary critics could with Arnoldian sensibilities revive a moribund liberal ideology for corporate and cold war ends.

> It has for some time seemed to me that a criticism which has at heart the interests of liberalism might find its most useful work not in confirming liberalism in its sense of general rightness but rather in putting under some degree of pressure the liberal ideas and assumptions of the present time. If liberalism is, as I believe it to be, a larger tendency rather than a concise body of doctrine, then as that large tendency makes itself explicit, certain of its particular expressions are bound to be relatively weaker than others, and some even useless and mistaken. If this is so, then for liberalism to be aware of the weak or wrong expressions of itself would seem to be an advantage to the tendency as a whole.[167]

For Trilling, literary criticism not only has a political role to play. It is simply shot through with political aims and interests. The function of a self-conscious criticism is to bring imagination to bear on how these aims and interests can be best achieved and satisfied. The intellectual arsenal for liberalism was in need of renovation, and Trilling was convinced that literary intellectuals could make a distinctive contribution to it.

> Our fate, for better or worse, is political. It is therefore not a happy fate, even if it has an heroic sound, but there is no escape from it, and the only possibility of enduring it is to force into our definition of politics every human activity and every subtlety of every human activity. There are manifest dangers in doing this, but greater dangers in not doing it. Unless we insist that politics is imagination and mind, we will learn that imagination and mind are politics, and of a kind that we will not like.[168]

Yet Trilling quickly backed off from even this assertion of liberal political will and imagination. In his masterpiece, "The Poet as Hero: Keats in His Letters" (1951)—his best essay and the pivotal point in his thinking—Trilling concluded that even the most attractive tragic vision can have neither redemptive nor ameliorative consequences acceptable to his kind of liberalism. Rather the very assertion of the will, even engendered by a tragic vision, could not but be utopian, antinomian, or anarchic in modern times. Therefore Trilling elevated circumstances over the self, life over imagination, world over the will, and wisdom over poetry. Ironically, Trilling the literary critic found himself pitted against most of modernist literature.

The early signs of this posture surfaced in the Keats essay. Trilling began by viewing Keats as not a mere poet but "as something even more interesting than a poet . . . as a man, and as a certain kind of man, a hero."[169] As with Hook, Trilling's reflections on heroism prompted a shift in the *use* to which the tragic vision is put. Yet Trilling's devaluation of the modern will—or willful self—goes far beyond that of Hook. For Trilling, Keats is unique in that his precociousness bred sagacity.

> And so we have the first of the vital contradictions which make the fascination of Keats' mind—we have the wisdom of maturity arising from the preoccupations of youth. This wisdom is the proud, bitter, and joyful acceptance of tragic life which we associate prominently with Shakespeare.[170]

This sagacity was linked to Keats's geniality, his "strong tendency of sociability and friendship" that nourished his creativity. Keats shunned solitude, thrived on company, and "could even compose in the same room with someone else." In a striking sentence, with important reverberations in his career, Trilling quipped: "He liked, we may say, to reconstitute the family situation."[171] Furthermore, Keats possessed great appetites—appetites he unashamedly expressed and enjoyed. Images of ingestion—of eating and drinking—are "pervasive and extreme." In short, Keats represented for Trilling the very ideal of European manhood.

> But the fact is that Keats's mature masculinity is . . . the essence of his being. One hesitates to say what one means by mature masculinity when the cultural anthropologists have been at such pains to disturb our old notions of it, and when in modern culture so much confusion exists about its nature and its value. Yet we may venture to say that in the traditional culture of Europe it has existed as an ideal that implies a direct relationship to the world of external reality, which, by activity, it seeks to understand, or to master, or to come to honorable terms with; and it implies fortitude, and responsibility for both one's duties and one's fate, and intention, and an insistence upon one's personal value and honor.[172]

Trilling's characterization of Keats's "personal ideal" sounds quite similar to the Arnoldian conception of the moral self—or an Emersonian self with an added sense of intractable limits. This is especially so given the very core of Keats's worldview: energy. "I must choose between despair and Energy," said Keats. For Trilling, Keats's tragic heroism was best exemplified in his notion of the world as "the vale of soul-making" (not a vale of tears). "Soul-making" is the protracted process whereby an "intelligence" acquires an "identity" and becomes a "soul" through strenuous effort and struggle in and against the world. To be a "soul" is simultaneously to see the utterly and ultimately tragic character of reality and to affirm the energy and reality of the self. This affirmation is possible only if one possesses negative capability, that is, if one is "capable of being in uncertainties, Mysteries, doubts, without any irritable reaching after fact and reason." In this way, Trilling argued, negative capability is not primarily a theory of art, but rather one component in a larger response to the problem of evil. On this view, only a mature self can see the beauty of the ugliness of tragedy—a beauty that permits the self to affirm itself and accept the fate that defines it. Such a self can "hold in balance the reality of self and the reality of circumstance."[173]

Trilling considered Keats's journal-letter to George and Georgiana Keats (February–May 3, 1819) as "one of the most remarkable documents of the culture of the century." The basic theme was a view "of the self confronting hostile or painful circumstances" yet showing "how it is that life may be called blessed when its circumstances are cursed."[174] This view was supported by a "simple affirmation of the self in its vital energy" and supplemented by a notion of the world as "the vale of soul-making."[175]

Trilling believed Keats to have written "the greatest exposition of the meaning of tragedy in our literature."[176] Yet it was un-Emersonian in its assumption that reality and truth were fundamentally hostile to human aspirations. And, as Trilling's favorite quote suggested, Keatsian theodicy elevated this reality and truth above literature, poetry, and politics.

> Though a quarrel in the streets is a thing to be hated, the energies displayed in it are fine; the commonest Man shows a grace in his quarrel—by a superior being our reasonings may take the same tone—though erroneous they may be fine—This is the very thing in which consists poetry; and if so it is not so fine a thing as philosophy—for the same reason that an eagle is not so fine a thing as truth.[177]

In his most startling statement, Trilling claimed that moderns no longer have access to Keats's heroic vision of the tragic life and the tragic situation; that is, Keats is not available because the modern impatience with or denial of the self precludes it. The modern obsession with the quest for an unconditioned self or with the surrender of the self to historical necessity reveals Keats to be "the last image of health at the very moment when the sickness of Europe began to be apparent."[178]

The Keats essay is pivotal in Trilling's thinking for three basic reasons. First, Trilling focuses no longer on the political task of criticism but rather on its psychocultural assumptions—assumptions that have to do with how one comes to terms with the problem of evil. His new focus will lead him into a deep and enduring preoccupation with Freud that moves him "beyond culture" toward biology. Therefore his concern is no longer modest social amelioration, an assertion of the will and imagination tempered by a sense of complexity, but rather impending social disintegration, a breakdown of selves into chaos and confusion. For Trilling, modernist literature portrays and at times promotes this.

Second, since Trilling can no longer view the political arena as a credible sphere for self-development, he moves toward the quotidian, the family, the domestic sphere. Keats's penchant for small-scale sociality will give way to the glories of William Dean Howells' "family piety" and Jane Austen's fixities of personal relations.

Third, Trilling severs any link between Emerson and Arnold—and associates Dewey more closely with Hegel. He severs the link because Arnold is on the side of those who attenuate the will and Emerson of those who accentuate it. Arnold is in the party of "sincerity," of duties, obligations, and authorities, whereas Emerson is in the party of "authenticity," of self-expansion, legislation, and rebellion. Similarly, Dewey's critical intelligence is no longer Arnold's imaginative reason but rather a version of Hegel's dynamic *Vernunft* valorizing self-realization.[179]

These shifts signify Trilling's retreat from politics into privacy. He becomes weary of the incessant ideological clashes and fatigued from the epicycles of ideas and characters that repeat the same blindnesses and rigidities—on the left and right. Therefore, Joseph Frank indeed is justified when he states in his well-known critique of Trilling's work at this juncture:

> For it is one thing to make the experience of art—the experience of pleasure and beauty, of harmony and reconciliation—the *ideal* form of moral life. It is quite another to attribute the virtues of this aesthetic ideal to concrete social behavior which, quite independently of any relationship with art, merely exhibits an abeyance or absence of the will. In other words, it is of the utmost importance not to confuse the boundaries of the ideal and the real, the aesthetic and the social; not to endow social passivity and quietism *as such* with the halo of aesthetic transcendence.[180]

By the mid-fifties, Trilling's preoccupation with the circumstantial and conditioned was deepened by his appropriation of the later Freud, the Freud of *Beyond the Pleasure Principle* (1920) and *Civilization and Its Discontents* (1930). Trilling had written poignantly about death in his early fiction and appreciatively of Freud in *The Liberal Imagination*. But his interpretation of the later Freud took him beyond the cultural constraints upon the will and beneath the recesses of the mind. And below the already fragile mind, that is, the middle-class world of refined manners, critical intelligence, and cultivated civility, there lurked a frightening smoldering of rebellious impulses, base instincts, and anarchic drives. For Trilling, the fateful circumstances that opposed the will consisted of not only the external world of "irrefrangible solidity" and "iron hardness,"[181] but also the internal dynamics of the self prone toward chaos and disorder. In short, his world of middle-class "sincere" values was easy prey for "authentic" desires of subversion.

In his last texts, *Beyond Culture* (1965), *Sincerity and Authenticity* (1972), "Mind in the Modern World" (1972), and "Why We Read Jane Austen" (1976), Trilling sensed that his project of consolidating the educated middle class under Arnoldian guidance would not last. His peak had been reached; his star was fading. With foreboding omens both literary (his former student Allen Ginsberg's "Beat" poetry and his bête noire Norman Mailer's "existential errands" and "white negroes") and, more important, political

(the civil rights movement, Black Power revolts in cities, and student dem-
onstrations in the streets and on college campuses, including Trilling's
own beloved Columbia), the liberal consensus he had helped create col-
lapsed. And like most liberal establishmentarians, Trilling was horrified.
In fact, this "modernism in the streets" led him to contemplate publicly
whether the teaching of modern (and modernist) literature had a salutary
effect on society.

> Nothing is more characteristic of modern literature than its discovery
> and canonization of the primal, non-ethical energies . . . for Nietzsche's
> Dionysian orgy and Blake's hell are much the same thing.[182]

> [We] may one day have to question whether in our culture the study
> of literature is any longer a suitable means for developing and refining
> the intelligence. The theory of literary education as it was first formulated
> supposed that literature carried the self beyond culture, that it induced
> or allowed the self to detach itself from its bondage to the idols of the
> Marketplace, the Tribe, the Theatre, and even of the Cave. Perhaps
> literature was once able to do this, or something near enough to it to
> satisfy the theory. But now we must ask whether this old intention has
> not been inverted, and whether literature does not, in fact, set up the
> old idols in new forms of its own contrivance.[183]

Trilling's famous conversational style became more shrill and frantic,
his message more apocalyptic and dystopian. And his brand of liberalism
blurred into a fatigue-ridden tempered conservatism, bereft of the crusading
energies of his neonationalist and neoconservative colleagues and former
students. In response to the turbulent sixties, Trilling, much like Arnold
in reaction to the Hyde Park riots of 1866, shunned complexity (the old
badge of refinement) and opted for Manichaean thinking. He denounced
dialectical dexterity and defended categorical pronouncement. In his
support of Jane Austen, Trilling wrote:

> Mansfield Park ruthlessly rejects the dialectical mode and seeks to impose
> the categorical constraints the more firmly upon us. It does not confirm
> our characteristic modern intuition that the enlightened and generous
> mind can discern right and wrong and good and bad only under the
> aspect of process and development, of futurity and the interplay and
> resolution of contradictions. It does not invite us to any of the pleasures
> which are to be derived from the transcendence of immediate and prag-
> matic judgement, such as grave, large-minded detachment, or irony, or
> confidence in the unfolding future . . . A work of art informed by so
> claustral a view might well distress our minds, might well give rise to
> anxiety . . . This is a dark thought, an archaic thought, one that detaches
> us from the predilections of our culture. But when its first unease has been
> accommodated, it can be seen to have in it a curious power of comfort.[184]

For Trilling, as for other mid-century pragmatist thinkers, the old frontiers have been closed. Unlike the others, he can foresee no new wilderness

to conquer, only a fortress to protect in which a pervasive claustrophobia awaits us. The question now becomes how to accommodate ourselves to and find comfort in this fortress—and fight off the new barbarians who threaten it.

In his last major effort, his Charles Eliot Norton Lectures at Harvard, *Sincerity and Authenticity*, Trilling's canvas became the *Bildung* of the self in North Atlantic civilization since Shakespeare. Much like Max Horkheimer and Theodor Adorno's *Dialectic of Enlightenment* (1947) and Georg Lukács's *The Destruction of Reason* (1954), this work traces the decline of reason and the rise of irrationality; that is, the slide of the Western self down the slippery slope from the "sincere" Horatio to the "authentic" Kurtz, from the heights of Shakespeare to the depths of Conrad, reaching rock bottom with the id-applauding polymorphous self in Herbert Marcuse, Norman O. Brown, Ronald Laing, and Michel Foucault. His nightmare had become a reality. The educated middle classes had become disaffected from their own bourgeois values. The fundamental themes of modern literature—"the disenchantment of our culture with culture itself" and "the bitter line of hostility to civilization"—had been incorporated in middle-class institutions and attitudes. American bourgeois life had socialized the antisocial, acculturated the anticultural, and legitimized the subversive.[185]

The major culprits were no longer Stalinism and philistinism but rather their latest forms and manifestations—the New Left and black revolt, rock 'n' roll, drugs, and free love. More pointedly, the new intellectual space Trilling had helped create—the space of liberal bourgeois humanist conversation and civil intercourse in which the cult of complexity reigned supreme, above political polemics and mass culture—had been eclipsed by an intensely polarized intellectual life in America, with Trilling clearly choosing sides yet too weary to take a strong stand in the fray. He preferred to lament while looking through his living room window in the privacy of his home with close friends and family.

Trilling's Arnoldian project had reached a dead end. The pessimism of the later Freud had replaced the ameliorative posture of the early "proto-pragmatist" Arnold and the impotent ideal of Keatsian tragic heroism. Unsurprisingly, only the Emerson of *English Traits* (1856) makes an appearance in *Sincerity and Authenticity*, and pragmatism is implicitly faulted for the enshrinement of the flux and futurity.

> About their being social rather than transcendent beings the English told the truth to themselves and the world. It is most engaging in Emerson that he should have taken so lively a pleasure in the moral style that followed from this avowal, for the characteristic tendency of his thought is to deny whatever the English affirm . . .
> Americans, we might say—D. H. Lawrence did in effect say it fifty years ago—had moved into that historical stage of Spirit which produces the "disintegrated" or "alienated" consciousness. What defines this

consciousness, according to Hegel, is its antagonism to "the external power of society" — the wish to be free of imposed social circumstances.[186]

The once liberal Trilling who valorized complexity and complication now echoed — in his own sophisticated style — the New Humanists of the twenties (e.g., Irving Babbit and Paul Elmer More) and the idiosyncratic conservative Yvor Winters: the Emersonian theodicy breeds unruly rebellion, anarchic chaos, and existential confusion. Only "inner checks," social duties, institutional power, and military might could preserve American civilization. So despite his self-proclaimed allegiance to critical intelligence, Trilling concluded not only that American pragmatism could not meet the crisis of mid-century America, but also that it fanned and fueled the crisis.

> For anyone concerned with contemporary education at whatever level, the assimilation that contemporary culture has made between social idealism, even political liberalism, and personal fluidity — a self without the old confinements — is as momentous as it is recalcitrant to correction. Among the factors in the contemporary world which militate against the formulation of an educational ideal related to the humanistic traditions of the past, this seems to me to be the most decisive.[187]

Despite the diversity of intellectual responses to the dilemma of mid-century pragmatists, there are three basic commonalities. All five figures reviewed here display varying degrees of suspicion of working- and lower-class people with limited education; deploy some notion of tragedy to describe their vision; and are themselves personally empowered by pragmatism to overcome marginality or inferiority complexes by means of their own acts of intellectual will, i.e., writing.

In his essay "The Development of American Pragmatism," John Dewey observed:

> If I were asked to give an historical parallel to this movement in American thought I would remind my reader of the French philosophy of the Enlightenment . . . As Hoffding writes, they were animated "by a fervent faith in intelligence, progress, and humanity." And certainly they are not accused today, just because of their educational and social significance, of having sought to subordinate intelligence and science to ordinary utilitarian aims. They merely sought to free intelligence from its impurities and to render it sovereign . . . It [pragmatism] is the formation of a faith in intelligence, as the one and indispensable belief necessary to moral and social life.[188]

Dewey's analogy between American pragmatists and the French philosophes is revealing in that both groups view the ordinary mass of uneducated people as a canaille, a mob in need of enlightenment, a rabble in need of refinement. Both groups indeed express the aspirations of specific sectors of distinct — and quite different — rising bourgeoisies at particular

moments in modern North Atlantic civilization. Yet American pragmatists, principally owing to their Emersonian heritage and their own personal
origins, possess egalitarian and democratic sensibilities alien to their earlier
French counterparts. Why then do they distrust working- and lower-class
Americans?

I suggest the explanation lies in the American pragmatists' obsession
with critical intelligence. This obsession assumes that bourgeois culture—its
professors, writers, and artists—has a monopoly on critical intelligence.
Furthermore, this obsession is motivated by a desire to get out from under
the smothering parochial anti-intellectualism of the various ethnic, racial,
class, and regional groups in American society. In this sense, pragmatism
is not simply a mere middle-class ideology blinded by the needs and
interests it serves. Rather it is articulated by those who themselves experience a kind of liberation from past constraints and circumstances, and
it is elaborated within institutional apparatuses which reinforce existential and cultural superiority over and distance from ordinary people. Even
Du Bois—himself organically linked with one of the most deprived and
despised people in America—did not fully overcome this superiority and
distance. Notwithstanding his own cultural marginality and political radicalism, C. Wright Mills views the ordinary masses in much the same terms
as his foe Talcott Parsons, that is, as personally empty and socially
manipulated objects with little agency or potential insurgency. Mills speaks
for much of the pragmatist tradition when he writes:

> The underdogs—those who get the least of what there is to get—are not
> the lowest stratum within U.S. society; they are largely outside of it.
> Those who are underprivileged economically are also underprivileged
> socially and psychologically. They have developed habits of submission;
> they do not now possess the means to see and hear what is going on,
> much less to have opinions about events beyond the narrow range of
> their daily routines. They lack the information that is required to under-
> stand a world where the determining causes in their lives lie beyond
> their direct vision.
>
> The underdogs lack the hardy self-confidence and capacity for indig-
> nation common to middle-class people. Their indignation is short-lived and
> often concerned with moral trivia. They have not been defeated; they
> have never tried. Defeat presupposes the impulse to dare, of which under-
> dogs know little. They do not participate in many of those areas of middle-
> class existence which form the main stream of American culture.[189]

It indeed is true that poor people have limited exposure, deferential attitudes, and, sometimes, fatalistic outlooks. But are they completely in the
dark regarding the reasons for their predicament? Do they lack self-confidence in every sphere of life or just in middle-class spheres? Are they bereft
of cultural agency and a "capacity for indignation"? Have they really never
tried or do they survive by trying, daring, risking? Mills's comments reveal

the degree to which he is ignorant of the life-worlds of common folk. Romanticization and denigration of the masses are both middle-class diseases—Mills, and much of the pragmatist tradition, suffer from the latter.

The preoccupation with tragedy on the part of mid-century American pragmatists principally results from a deep disillusionment with middle-class notions of perfection and progress. As Richard Hofstadter hyperbolically quipped, "The United States was the only country in the world that began with perfection and aspired to progress."[190] This disillusionment took the form of discourses on limits, constraints, circumstances, conditionedness, and fate. All of the figures felt some sense of "wandering between two worlds, one dead / the other powerless to be born."[191]

Yet, as I have noted earlier, tragedy is not a monolithic notion with universal meaning and homogeneous usage. Rather it is deployed in different ways by various people in specific circumstances so that it provides varying results. A tragic sense of life is indeed a defensible response to the battered hopes and dreams, the heart-tearing atrocities and brutalities of this century. But this response in no way *necessarily* entails privatistic quietism, cold war accommodationism,, academic professionalism, or individual martyrdom. As intimated in the early Hook and Niebuhr—and spelled out in Byron and Melville—the tragic sense of life can promote revolutionary action and attitudes.

> What makes an idea subversive is not so much what is intrinsic in it or the mere thinking of it, but the context of its articulation—to whom, and to how many and in what circumstances it is said or written.[192]

But none of the pragmatists—with the exception of Du Bois—could have possibly explored the depths of the connection between tragedy and subversion, principally because they avoided the contexts in which this connection would be best worked out: contexts of political struggles among ordinary people. A major blind spot in American pragmatism is precisely the relation between a tragic perspective and revolutionary and subversive agency. A good place to begin is with Raymond Williams' masterful yet overlooked book *Modern Tragedy* (1966) and the provocative response in Walter Stein's "Humanism and Tragic Redemption."[193] And a better place to end is in a context of struggle with subaltern groups.

Last, all five figures are strong-willed and ambitious men who started as outsiders, with a few remaining as outsiders. The fundamental difference that pragmatism made to them as persons was to support and strengthen their own volitions and aspirations. One reason why pragmatism has not attracted significant numbers of women—though Gertrude Stein comes to mind—is that its aggressive and self-confident stance toward the realities of the spheres of power has been virtually the possession of males in patriarchal America. Du Bois, notwithstanding his Victorian sensibilities, clumsily touches on this point in "The Damnation of Women," one of the few allusions in American pragmatism to the capacities and potentialities of women:

> The future woman must have a life work and economic independence. She must have knowledge. She must have the right of motherhood at her own discretion. The present mincing horror at free womanhood must pass if we are ever to be rid of the bestiality of free manhood . . .
>
> The world . . . forgets its darker sisters. They seem in a sense to typify that veiled melancholy . . .[194]

Does American pragmatism put too much of a premium on an aggressive will? Is it but another expression of patriarchal culture? Will the assertive agency of women from different classes and cultures shun this mode of intellectual expression in the future? These questions remain unanswered at present. Yet I suspect that American culture, with its Emersonian individualism and pragmatist experimentalism, cuts deeper than sexual identity. If so, the issue is how American women will reshape and revise pragmatism; that is, how their appeal to their own experiences can enrich and promote an Emersonian culture of creative democracy. For the difference pragmatism makes is always the difference people make with it.

The Decline and Resurgence of American Pragmatism: W. V. Quine and Richard Rorty

I believe that philosophy in America will be lost between chewing a historic cud long since reduced to woody fiber, or an apologetics for lost causes, or a scholastic, schematic formalism, unless it can somehow bring to consciousness America's own needs and its own implicit principle of successful action.

—John Dewey

Although American pragmatism is widely regarded as *the* distinctive American philosophy, it has never been hegemonic in the academic profession of philosophy. Even during the heyday of James and Dewey, old forms of idealism and new versions of naturalism and realism dominated the major philosophy departments in the country. Moreover, the major followers of James and Dewey tended not to be influential professional philosophers, but rather engaged public philosophers. There indeed were exceptions, most notably Ralph Barton Perry (a realist pupil of James) and C. I. Lewis (a self-styled conceptual pragmatist), both at Harvard. Yet in large measure American pragmatism did not gain a large following in the higher echelons of the academy.

This was so for three basic reasons. First, the antiprofessional implications of pragmatism discouraged its wholesale incorporation into the academy. Second, the revolution in and fascination with symbolic logic

182

initiated by Bertrand Russell and Alfred North Whitehead's *Principia Mathematica* (1913) — and reinforced by the breakthroughs of Leopold Lowenheim, Thoralf Skolem, Alonzo Church, and Kurt Gödel — turned professional philosophical attention to problems about which pragmatism had little to say. Third, and most important, Austrian and German émigrés, in flight from the Nazis, brought to the American philosophical scene a project of rigor, purity, precision, and seriousness — logical positivism. The impact of Rudolf Carnap, Hans Reichenbach, Alfred Tarski, Herbert Feigl, and Carl Hempel was immense. In fact, logical positivism seized the imagination of the most talented young philosophers in the country. Pragmatism appeared to them to be vague and muddleheaded.

The major effect of logical positivism was to turn attention away from historical consciousness and social reflection and toward logic and physics. Its chief aim was the analysis and clarification of meaning; its goal, to unify the sciences by providing an account of their operation while acknowledging the crucial role of logic and mathematics. Logical positivism was an extension of a nineteenth-century Viennese empirical tradition best seen in the antimetaphysical writings of Ernst Mach.

The famous "Vienna Circle," led principally by Moritz Schlick, Otto Neurath, Friedrich Waismann, Kurt Gödel, and Rudolf Carnap, was dominated by philosophers preoccupied with new developments in theoretical physics and symbolic logic. Notwithstanding its diversity and variety, logical positivism rested upon three basic assumptions. First, it assumed a form of sentential atomism which correlates isolated sentences with either possible empirical confirmation (those of science), logical necessity (those of logic and mathematics), or emotion (those of ethics, art, and religion). Second, it emerged with a kind of phenomenalist reductionism which translates sentences about physical objects into sentences about actual and possible sensations. Third, it presupposed a verification theory of meaning which holds observational evidence to be the criterion for cognitively meaningful sentences and hence the final court of appeal in determining valid theories of the way the world is. These independent yet interrelated doctrines held at various times by leading logical positivists were guided by fundamental distinctions between the analytic and the synthetic, the linguistic and the empirical, theory and observation.[1]

Logical positivism was buttressed by the formidable realist revolts enacted by Gottlob Frege, Alexius Meinong, Bertrand Russell, and G. E. Moore.[2] Frege revolted against John Stuart Mill's psychologism and John Venn's conventionalism in logic; Meinong, against Franz Brentano's psychologism in object theory; Russell and Moore against F. H. Bradley's Hegelian idealism in metaphysics and epistemology. To these realists of different stripes, pragmatism appeared to be but an American footnote to psychologism, conventionalism, and idealism.

In addition to these assaults and putdowns, pragmatism did not benefit from the other major developments in North Atlantic philosophy. Edmund Husserl's search for an alternative to naturalism and historicism (or skepticism and relativism) led to a conception of philosophy as rigorous science in which "essences" were grasped by presuppositionless phenomenological investigation.[3] Martin Heidegger, a student of Husserl, inaugurated an ontological inquiry into the conditions for the possibility of metaphysics, an inquiry that ignored pragmatism since American philosophy rested "outside the realm of metaphysics," i.e., was not serious philosophy.[4] Last, Jean-Paul Sartre, inspired by Heidegger, put forward an existentialism utterly alien to the upbeat temper of American pragmatism—yet it spoke to postwar Europe and, to some extent, America in a powerful way.[5] In short, pragmatism was on the wane in Euro-American philosophy; only in the notebooks of an imprisoned Marxist thinker, Antonio Gramsci, could one find a kind word said about pragmatism.[6] And these notebooks would not be published until decades later.

The genius of W. V. Quine, who had studied with Carnap in Prague, was to intervene in the most sophisticated discourses of symbolic logicians and logical positivists with pragmatic formulations and Emersonian, i.e., human-making, sensibilities. Though more a naturalist than a pragmatist, Quine made American pragmatism respectable in postwar academic philosophy. This wizard from Akron, Ohio, educated at Oberlin College, trained at Harvard, and now the world's most distinguished English-speaking philosopher and professor emeritus at Harvard, initiated the Americanization of analytic philosophy.[7]

In his numerous books and articles—most notably his classic essay "Two Dogmas of Empiricism" (1951)—Quine dismantled logical positivism by persuasively calling into question the fundamental distinctions upon which it rests.

Quine's breakthrough was threefold. First, he accented an epistemological holism which shifted the basic units of empirical significance from isolated sentences to systems of sentences or theories. The logical positivist notion of reducing each isolated sentence to a piece of evidence or set of actual or possible sensations was abandoned. After noting Carnap's move away from this notion, Quine states:

> But the dogma of reductionism has, in a subtler and more tenuous form, continued to influence the thought of empiricists. The notion lingers that to each statement or each synthetic statement, there is associated a unique range of possible sensory events such that the occurrence of any of them would add to the likelihood of truth of the statement, and that there is associated also another unique range of possible sensory events whose occurrence would detract from that likelihood. This notion is of course implicit in the verification theory of meaning.

The dogma of reductionism survives in the supposition that each statement, taken in isolation from its fellows, can admit of confirmation or infirmation at all. My countersuggestion, issuing essentially form Carnap's doctrine of the physical world in the *Aufbau*, is that our statements about the external world face the tribunal of sense experience not individually but only as a corporate body.[8]

Quine's critique of the atomism in logical positivism and of the empirical tradition in general echoes that of James and, especially, Dewey. He extends his critique to the most cherished notion of analytic philosophers—the notion of analyticity, the idea that a statement is true by virtue of meanings and independently of facts. Quine's methodological monism, motivated by an epistemological holism derived, in part, from Pierre Duhem, holds that the idea that an isolated statement can be true without empirical confirmation is as unacceptable as the idea of an isolated statement's being true with empirical confirmation. His main point is that competing theories, versions, or descriptions of the world, not isolated statements, are "the basic units of empirical significance," especially since the truth-value of such statements can change relative to one's theories, versions, or descriptions of the world. In this way, the "two dogmas of empiricism"—reductionism and the analytic-synthetic distinction—are not only inseparable but "at root identical."

The dogma of reductionism, even in its attenuated form, is intimately connected with the other dogma—that there is a cleavage between the analytic and the synthetic. We have found ourselves led, indeed, from the latter problem to the former through the verification theory of meaning. More directly, the one dogma clearly supports the other in this way: as long as it is taken to be significant in general to speak of the confirmation and infirmation of a statement, it seems significant to speak also of a limiting kind of statement which is vacuously confirmed *ipso facto*, come what may; and such a statement is analytic . . .

. . . if this view is right, it is misleading to speak of the empirical content of an individual statement—especially if it is a statement at all remote from the experiential periphery of the field. Furthermore it becomes folly to seek a boundary between synthetic statements, which hold contingently on experience, and analytic statements, which hold come what may. Any statement can be held true come what may, if we make drastic enough adjustments elsewhere in the system. Even a statement very close to the periphery can be held to be true in the face of recalcitrant experience by pleading hallucination or by amending certain statements of the kind called logical laws. Conversely, by the same token, no statement is immune to revision.[9]

Quine's abandonment of the analytic-synthetic distinction is done not only under the banner of Peirce's "first rule of reason"—do not block the way of inquiry[10]—but also in the spirit of the antidualism of James and Dewey and the stress on contingency in Emerson.

Last, Quine's naturalism rejects a first philosophy prior to science. Instead philosophy is viewed as continuous with science. More specifically, epistemology is not an autonomous discipline which grounds the claims of science, but rather a branch of psychology. Philosophical justification never stands alone; it is always part and parcel of some mode of theoretical explanation. Quine evades those Cartesian-inspired philosophers who "dreamed of a first philosophy, further than science and serving to justify our knowledge of the external world."[11] For him, epistemology is not so much abandoned as naturalized.

> Epistemology still goes on, though in a new setting and a clarified status. Epistemology, or something like it, simply falls into place as a chapter of psychology and hence of natural science. It studies a natural phenomenon, viz., a physical human subject. This human subject is accorded a certain experimentally controlled input—certain patterns of irradiation in assorted frequencies, for instance—and in the fullness of time the subject delivers as output a description of the three-dimensional external world and its history. The relation between the meager input and the torrential output is a relation that we are prompted to study for somewhat the same reason that always prompted epistemology; namely, in order to see how evidence relates to theory, and in what ways one's theory of nature transcends any available evidence.[12]

Yet Quine's evasion of modern epistemology is not as thorough as Dewey's. This is so owing to the residues of logical positivism in Quine's monumental breakthrough: namely, his ontological allegiance to physics and his need for minimally foundationalist (though radically underdetermined) "observation sentences" in his Skinnerian behavioristic psychology. For Quine, every significant difference is a physical difference determined by the best theories available in physics. He holds that metaphysics must go, epistemology virtually goes, but ontology remains. Ontology preserves his "robust realism"[13] and promotes the monopoly of physics on Truth and Reality. Quine's refusal to give up on ontology seems odd given statements like:

> As an empiricist I continue to think of the conceptual scheme of science as a tool, ultimately, for predicting future experience in light of past experience. Physical objects are conceptually imported into the situation as convenient intermediaries—not by definition in terms of experience, but simply as irreducible posits comparable, epistemologically, to the gods of Homer. For my part I do, *qua* lay physicist, believe in physical objects and not in Homer's gods; and I consider it a scientific error to believe otherwise. But in point of epistemological footing the physical objects and the gods differ only in degree and not in kind. Both sorts of entities enter our conception only as cultural posits. The myth of physical objects is epistemologically superior to most in that it has proved more efficacious than other myths as a device for working a manageable structure into the flux of experience.[14]

> The ontologies of physical objects and mathematical objects are myths. The quality of myth, however, is relative; relative, in this case, to the epistemological point of view. This point of view is one among various, corresponding to one among our various interests and purposes.[15]

In fact, Quine concludes his classic essay by affirming the spirit of American pragmatism.

> Carnap, Lewis and others take a pragmatic stand on the question of choosing between language forms, scientific frameworks; but their pragmatism leaves off at the imagined boundary between the analytic and the synthetic. In repudiating such a boundary I espouse a more thorough pragmatism. Each man is given a scientific heritage plus a continuing barrage of sensory stimulation; and the considerations which guide him in warping his scientific heritage to fit his continuing sensory promptings are, where rational, pragmatic.[16]

Given this gesture toward pragmatism, why then does Quine not support the pluralism of Dewey's *The Quest for Certainty?* Is not his defense of science as not only the best explanatory tool we have to cope with the world but also the Truth and Reality of the world a leap of faith on his part? Is it not a statement of his ontological loyalty to this authority in modern culture? Dewey's Emersonian refusal to defer to any authority on truth and reality pushes him toward epistemic pluralism though, as we saw earlier, not vulgar relativism; whereas Quine's positivistic heritage binds him to an ontological physicalism.

In his essay "The Pragmatists' Place in Empiricism," Quine explicitly attempts to distinguish his naturalism from Dewey's pragmatism by an appeal to their different ontologies.

> The pragmatists James, Schiller, and Dewey viewed science as a conceptual shorthand for organizing observations . . . and now I, for all my vaunted naturalism, seem drawn into the same position. Is there no difference?
>
> The difference is to be sought in ontology . . . Dewey's reality consisted of observable objects . . . For naturalistic philosophers such as I, on the other hand, physical objects are real, right down to the most hypothetical of particles, though this recognition of them is subject, like all science, to correction. I can hold this ontological line of naive and unregenerate realism, and at the same time I can hail man as largely the author rather than discoverer of truth. I can hold both lines because the scientific truth about physical objects is still the *truth*, for all man's authorship. In my naturalism, I recognize no higher truth than that which science provides or seeks.[17]

Quine's characterization of Dewey as both having *an* ontology at all and having an ontology of "observable objects" is problematic. Quine's view of Dewey rests—as he claims in his footnote—on Ernest Nagel's essay

"Dewey's Theory of Natural Science." Yet when one turns to this essay, there is no such characterization of Dewey. Instead, Nagel limits himself to Dewey's *epistemic* claims, claims that chime with Quine's concern to endorse fallibilism and reject relativism. Nagel does slip and use the term "naive realism" to distinguish Dewey's pluralism from "the dogmatic naiveté so frequently associated with philosophers of common sense,"[18] but he goes on to note that this "naive realism" is *not* an ontology of observable objects but rather a loosening of the common-sensical *and* scientific monopolies on what *really* is the case. Quine assigns to Dewey precisely the "dogmatic naive" position Dewey rejects—and Nagel highlights this rejection.

> Dewey's account of scientific objects is thus accompanied by a reaffirmation of the claims of gross experience . . . He emphatically includes the various qualities of ordinary experience among the ultimate furniture of the world. But he does not assume that the immediate apprehension of qualities constitutes knowledge of them. Knowledge for Dewey is always the terminus of *inquiry*, and involves the establishment of relations of dependence between what is thus directly experienced and what is not. What these relations are, however, is not to be settled by intuition or authority whether the problem under consideration involves issues of physics, private morality or public policy. It is pre-eminently a matter requiring reflective thought or experimental inquiry.[19]

Quine, like Dewey, rejects intuition but, unlike Dewey, invokes the *authority* of physics as that which tells us the way the world is, subject to revision. Dewey accepts the authority of physics (or of common sense or any other authority) only insofar as that authority works effectively. This means that physics, for example, predicts and explains well; that is, he gives it functional (or instrumental) allegiance but not ontological allegiance. As Nagel correctly notes regarding Dewey: "What is canonical for physics is not therefore a measure of objective existence; and only an arbitrary preference, rooted in an influential intellectual tradition, will assign exclusive reality to invariant relational orders."[20] And neither does Dewey assign exclusive reality to "observable objects," as Quine suggests. Dewey simply wants to defend those who posit "observable objects" in their version of the world as being on the same footing—relative to different aims and purposes—as those who posit "unobservable physical objects" in their version of the world. In short, Dewey affirms the pragmatism of Quine circa 1951. For Dewey, as we saw earlier, the very notion of assigning exclusive reality to the objects posited by any *one* version of the world is dogmatic, despite one's promotion of an "intradogmatic" notion of fallibilism. This is why he has no *one* ontology.

Does this make Dewey an idealist? Surely not, for an idealist indeed has an exclusive ontology of some sort, usually of the contents of consciousness. But he surely is no realist. What then is he? He rests outside the realist-idealist polarity, for he rejects the terrain on which this polarity is grounded. This is why he is a pragmatist—or, for lack of a better word, a pluralist whose only restraints are inquiry and interests.

The other positivist residue in Quine's project is his notion of observation sentences in his Skinnerian behaviorist psychology. One would have thought that Quine's devastating critique of the verification theory of meaning—especially its sentential atomism and reductionism and observational criterion—would have led him to talk only of core and periphery sentences or precious and less precious statements. Why the term "observation"? We discover that Quine prefers this term because he wants not an epistemological anchor (he's no foundationalist) but an epistemic hook for the intersubjective character of knowledge claims. He suggests that without observation sentences—those sentences "on which all speakers of the language give the same verdict when given the same concurrent stimulation"[21]—any causal connection between what people agree upon and what inputs they receive from the world is not possible. Without this hook, sociology and history of science rather than behavioristic psychology are the appropriate successors to epistemology. And, for Quine, this is "epistemological nihilism."[22] His evasion of epistemology remains confined to physics, biology, and psychology. He has a deep distrust of the social and historical dimensions of human existence. In this way, his breakthrough, though profound and enduring, remains confined by his positivist prejudices.

These confines come tumbling down in the innovative work of Nelson Goodman. Professor emeritus at Harvard, where he received his education and graduate training, Goodman is the "other" Harvard patriarch of postmodern American philosophy. Equipped with a unique amalgam of high-powered logical skills and finely honed artistic sensibilities, Goodman arrived independently at a Quinian critique of logical positivism in his own struggles with Carnap and with the problem of criteria of adequacy for constructional logical systems. Yet Goodman pushes this critique beyond the perimeters of the positivist heritage. Goodman opens Pandora's box and modern philosophy is fatally stricken.

His logical conventionalism replaces accurate pictorial depiction with acceptable verbal description as the end and aim of constructing a version of the world. Almost a decade after his painstaking study of Carnap's *Aufbau* (*The Logical Construction of the World*, 1928), Goodman concluded in his renowned essay "The Way the World Is,"

> What we must face is the fact that even the truest description comes nowhere near faithfully reproducing the way the world is . . . for it has explicit primitives, routes of construction, etc., none of them features of the world described. Some philosophers contend, therefore, that if systematic descriptions introduce an arbitrary artificial order, then we should make our descriptions unsystematic to bring them more into

accord with the world. Now the tacit assumption here is that the respects in which a description is unsatisfactory are *just those respects in which it falls short of being a faithful picture*; and the tacit *goal* is to achieve a description that as nearly as possible gives a living likeness. But the goal is a delusive one. For we have seen that even the most realistic way of picturing amounts merely to one kind of conventionalization. In painting, the selection, the emphasis, the conventions are different from but no less peculiar to the vehicle, and no less variable, than those of language. The idea of making verbal descriptions approximate pictorial depiction loses its point when we understand that to turn a description into the most faithful possible picture would amount to nothing more than exchanging some conventions for others.[23]

Goodman's postempiricist antireductionism highlights the theory-laden character of observation and the value-laden character of theory. After his search for a criterion of adequacy for constructional systems, such as Carnap's phenomenalistic one, or for scientific theories, such as Einstein's Special Theory of Relativity, Goodman held that the choice is based not primarily on mere agreement with the facts, e.g., observational data, but rather on, among other things, structural simplicity. In his influential essay "The Test of Simplicity," he wrote,

Thus selection of a theory must always be made in advance of the determination of some of the facts it covers; and, accordingly, some criterion other than conformity with such facts must be applied in making the selection. After as many points as we like have been plotted by experiment concerning the correlation of two factors (for example, of time and deterioration of radioactivity), we predict the remaining points by choosing one among all the infinitely many curves that cover the plotted points. Obviously, simplicity of some sort is a cardinal factor in making this choice (we pick the "smoothest" curve). The very validity of the choice depends upon whether the choice is properly made according to such criteria. Thus simplicity here is not a consideration applicable after truth is determined but is one of the standards of validity that are applied in the effort to discover truth.[24]

Last, Goodman's ontological pluralism relegates the notion of truth to that of fitness and encourages diverse, even conflicting, true versions of the world instead of a fixed world and unique truth. Quine's monocosmic naturalism now blossoms into a polycosmic pluralism which radically calls into question the ontological privileging of physics. Goodman posits an Emersonian version of the world in which radical contingency is the "norm" and human creative powers play the decisive role.

Briefly, then, truth of statements and rightness of descriptions, representations, exemplifications, expressions—of design, drawing, diction, rhythm—is primarily a matter of fit: fit to what is referred to in one way or another, or to other renderings, or to modes and manners of organization. The differences between fitting a version to a world, a world to a version, and a version together or to other versions fade when the role of versions in making the worlds they fit is recognized. And knowing or understanding is seen as ranging beyond the acquiring of true beliefs to the discovering and devising of fit of all sorts.[25]

Goodman does not abandon the notion of truth but multiplies it—within the regulations of reflective deliberation.

There are very many different equally true descriptions of the world, and their truth is the only standard of their faithfulness. And when we say of them that they all involve conventionalizations we are saying that no one of these different descriptions is *exclusively* true, since the others are also true. None of them tells us *the* way the world is, but each one of them tells us *a* way the world is.[26]

Like American pragmatists, Goodman holds a conception of knowledge that is elastic in character and creative in content.

Furthermore, if worlds are as much made as found, so also knowing is as much remaking as reporting. All the processes of worldmaking I have discussed enter into knowing. Perceiving motion . . . often consists in producing it. Discovering laws involves drafting them. Recognizing patterns is very much a matter of inventing and imposing them. Comprehension and creation go together.[27]

In stark contrast to Quine, Goodman by proliferating truth not only deprivileges—without devaluing—physics but also abandons any qualitative distinction in method between science and the arts.

Truth is not enough; it is at most a necessary condition. But even this concedes too much; the noblest scientific laws are seldom quite true. Minor discrepancies are overridden in the interest of breadth or power or simplicity. Science denies its data as the statesman denies his constituents—within the limits of prudence . . .
    Truth and its aesthetic counterpart amount to appropriateness under different name. If we speak of hypotheses but not works of art as true, that is because we reserve the terms "true" and "false" for symbols in sentential form: I do not say this difference is negligible, but it is specific rather than generic, a difference in field of application rather than in formula, and marks no schism between the scientific and the aesthetic.[28]

Goodman's conventionalism, antireductionism, and pluralism have elective affinities with American pragmatism. His own description of his position is "a radical relativism under rigorous restraints, that eventuates in something akin to irrealism."[29] His rhetoric about "worldmaking" indeed has idealist overtones, but his stress is on *versions* of the world. It is important not to confuse his *constructivist emphasis* with an *idealist position*. Like Dewey, Goodman doesn't fit on an ordinary philosophical spectrum. He is unique on the contemporary philosophical scene in that he has trod his own distinct path, making nuanced pragmatic moves in the process. Goodman is no pragmatist, for any label unduly simplifies his complex viewpoint, and yet no other label comes closer in characterizing it.

Wilfred Sellars is the last major figure in the postmodern American trio in philosophy. Unfortunately, his highly technical style of writing as well as his position at the University of Pittsburgh (slightly removed from the center of intellectual fashion) has rendered his writing less accessible and influential. I should add that after Harvard Pittsburgh has the finest philosophy department in the country, but it has *professional* eminence not *cultural* prowess.

Sellars, though far from being a pragmatist, has contributed to the resurgence of pragmatism in two ways. First, his antifoundationalism in epistemology has undermined attempts to invoke self-justifying, intrinsically credible, theory-neutral or noninferential elements in experience which provide foundations for other knowledge claims and serve as the terminating points for chains of epistemic justification. Second, his psychological nominalism defends the notion that knowledge begins with the ability to justify – the capacity to use words – and since language is public and intersubjective, all "given" elements in experience which purportedly ground knowledge are matters of social practice. In short, Sellars demythologizes the myth of the given (and any version thereof).

Sellars holds that the myth of the given primarily results from a confusion between the acquisition of knowledge and the justification of knowledge, between empirical causal accounts of how one comes to have a belief and philosophical investigations into how one justifies a belief one has. This confusion dissolves when one realizes that the traditional candidates for justifying beliefs – intuition, apprehension, acquaintance, and other forms of prelinguistic awareness – are not mental episodes but rather learned abilities. His psychological nominalism claims that

> *all* awareness of *sorts, resemblances, facts*, etc., in short all awareness of abstract entities – indeed, all awareness even of particulars – is a linguistic affair. According to it not even awareness of such sorts, resemblances, and facts as pertain to so-called immediate experience is presupposed by the process of acquiring the use of language.[30]

Of course, non-language-using persons, e.g., babies, have awareness, of for example hitting up against a hot stove. But this kind of minimal awareness is more akin to that of a record player responding to the stimulus of being turned on than to human awareness of justifying what one says. Sellars' point is that such a stimulus is a noncognitive causal antecedent that plays no role in grounding knowledge. There simply are no nonpropositional bases for knowledge, though there are nonpropositional events, e.g., pain, that are causal antecedents to knowledge. To confuse the justificatory with the causal—the ability to use language (public affair) with the occurrence of a mental event (incorrigible happening)—is to generate the myth of the given.

For instance, one of the forms of the myth of the given subscribed to by epistemology-centered philosophers

> is the idea that there is, indeed must be, a structure of particular matter of fact such that (a) each fact can not only be noninferentially known to be the case, but presupposes no other knowledge either of particular matter of fact, or of general truths; and (b) such that the noninferential knowledge of facts belonging to this structure constitutes the ultimate court of appeals for all factual claims—particular and general—about the world.[31]

This privileged stratum of fact is justified by appeals to prelinguistic awareness or self-authenticating, "phenomenal" qualities. Yet this attempt at epistemic justification fails because it conceals the "stage-setting" (Wittgenstein's term) requisite to make the purported "observation" of the noninferential "phenomenal" quality. As Sellars notes,

> One couldn't have observational knowledge of any fact unless one knew many other things as well . . . For the point is specifically that observational knowledge of any particular fact, e.g., that this is green, presupposes that one knows general facts of the form X is a *reliable symptom* of Y . . . The essential point is that in characterizing an episode or a state as that of *knowing*, we are not giving an empirical description of that episode or state; we are placing it in the logical space of reasons, of justifying and being able to justify what one says.[32]

Sellars concludes that the conception of knowledge based on the myth of the given, along with its concomitant picture of epistemology, generates false options of foundationalism or skepticism, certainty or nullity. This Cartesian-inspired view

> is misleading because of its static character. One seems forced to choose between the picture of an elephant which rests on a tortoise (what supports the tortoise?) and the picture of a great Hegelian serpent of knowledge with its tail in its mouth (where does it begin?). Neither will do. For empirical knowledge, like its sophisticated extension, science, is rational, not because it has a *foundation* but because it is a self-correcting enterprise which can put any claim in jeopardy, though not *all* at once.[33]

Needless to say, Sellars' critique of modern epistemology converges in a fundamental way with that of Peirce, James, and Dewey. Sellars goes on to adopt a neo-Tractarian notion of "picturing" that provides an Archimedean point from which to oversee and evaluate the progress of science, a notion that flies in the face of pragmatic rejections of any form of transcendentalism. Nonetheless, Sellars' antifoundationalism and psychological nominalism helped make pragmatism respectable again.

It is important to note the contributions of those lonely laborers in the vineyard who continued to keep alive the pragmatist tradition during the age of logical positivism: John McDermott, John Smith, Richard Bernstein, and Morton White. McDermott prefers a broadly engaged cultural critical style that relates a pragmatic temper to the present *Zeitgeist*.[34] Smith has provided the best overarching view of American pragmatism, making broad strokes on a canvas often ignored by analytic philosophers.[35] Bernstein has written the most illuminating comparative studies on pragmatism and continental philosophy, e.g., Marxism, existentialism, and phenomenology. In addition, he has teased out pragmatist aspects of many analytic philosophical viewpoints in incisive and insightful ways. He has brilliantly and persuasively insisted that pragmatism is a serious interlocutor in the professional philosophical conversation when it was not apparent to many.[36] Last, Morton White has sustained a distinguished tradition of intellectual history informed by and often focused on American pragmatism.[37]

Enter Richard Rorty. As far back as 1961, in his first published essays, Rorty proclaimed:

> Pragmatism is getting respectable again. Some philosophers are still content to think of it as a sort of muddle-headed first approximation to logical positivism — which they think of in turn as a prelude to our own enlightened epoch. But those who have taken a closer look have realized that the movement of thought involved here is more like a pendulum than like an arrow.[38]

For the next seventeen years, Rorty labored in the academic vineyard attempting to convince fellow philosophic analysts from within the predominant linguistic-centered paradigms that some form of pragmatism lay waiting after their rigorous efforts. In his early pragmatic period (1961–72), Rorty's major culprits were versions of reductionism and intuitionism. As a precocious humanist educated at the University of Chicago (influenced especially by Richard McKeon) and trained at Yale (under the guidance of Paul Weiss), Rorty was struck by the deeply ahistorical character of analytic philosophy. His first philosophical works tried to establish a conversation between contemporary philosophers and the Grand Tradition of Western Philosophy. For example, his lengthy dissertation on the concept of potentiality made Aristotle a contributing interlocutor to the dialogue, and his early papers contrasted Charles Peirce and Ludwig Wittgenstein; René Descartes, Alfred North Whitehead, and Gilbert Ryle; as well as Thomas Aquinas, Brand Blanshard, and J. L. Austin.[39]

Rorty's strategies in these early works were to promote notions of the indeterminacy of knowledge and the equivocality of terms like "true" and "real" in light of "the unavoidability of certain 'harmless' infinite regresses."[40] Principally preoccupied with understanding the nature of obeying rules and naming things, Rorty pleads for inescapable vagueness, yet he shuns the abstract alternatives of "absolute necessity" and "sheer arbitrariness."[41] Vagueness results simply from the fact that there always are a number of potential ways of interpreting a rule or naming a thing—a potential that need not (and cannot) be either fully actualized or eliminated in obeying a rule or naming a thing. Radical contingency of signs or language games is not the same as radical indeterminacy of interpretations owing to pragmatic appeals to practice.

> The fact [that] our understanding of how we follow a rule or give a name will be permanently vague does not interfere with our actually obeying rules and naming things . . .
>
> The permanent possibility of *practice* is what renders harmless the indefinite horizontal regress of interpretations, oscillating as they do between the purely determinate ("nothing accords with the rule") and the purely indeterminate ("everything accords with it").[42]

For Rorty at this stage in his development, the major alternatives to pragmatic appeals to practice are those that resort to some form of intuitionism to stop the infinite regress of interpretations. In stark contrast to pragmatic notions of contingent practices, intuitionists invoke types of prelinguistic awareness, apprehension (e.g., mental privacy), and non-inferential knowledge as means of terminating epistemic chains of justification. Therefore intuitionists appeal to notions of logical necessity or transcendental grounding for knowledge claims. Following a Wittgensteinian-motivated pragmatism, Rorty held that this battle between intuitions and practices is resolved only by acknowledging that (and showing how) forms of intuitionism confuse a special kind of "knowledge" with a causal condition for knowledge.[43] Rorty's exposure of this confusion of epistemic justification for psychological explanation—a strategy inspired by Wilfred Sellars' attack on "the myth of the given"—fans and fuels Rorty's pragmatism. In this stage, Rorty viewed the philosophical concern with linguistic practices as not only "putting the entire philosophical tradition, from Parmenides through Descartes and Hume to Bradley and Whitehead, on the defensive,"[44] but also forcing philosophers to engage first and foremost in metaphilosophical reflection—that is, reflection on the status, role, and function of philosophy in contemporary culture. In his influential introduction to *The Linguistic Turn* (1967), he asked,

> Is the linguistic turn doomed to suffer the same fate as previous "revolutions in philosophy"? The relatively pessimistic conclusions reached in the preceding sections entail that linguistic philosophers' attempts to turn philosophy into a "strict science" must fail. How far does this pessimism carry? If linguistic philosophy cannot be a strict science, if it has a merely critical, essentially dialectical, function, then what of the future? Suppose that all the traditional problems are in the fullness of time, dissolved—in the sense that no one is able to think of any formulations of these questions which are immune to the sort of criticisms made by linguistic

philosophers. Does that mean that philosophy will have come to an end—that philosophers will have worked themselves out of a job? Is a "post-philosophical" culture really conceivable?[45]

In response to these rhetorical questions in 1967, Rorty envisioned six possibilities for the future of philosophy. These were, roughly, Husserl's phenomenology that refused to reduce the nature of things either to empirical questions or to matters of language; the later Heidegger's poetic meditation on the problem of being, a view that rejects philosophy as an argumentative discipline; Waismann's return to the grand tradition of system building, a philosophy that shuns description of Reality and promotes proposals about what languages we use about Reality; Wittgenstein's call for a postphilosophical culture and a jettisoning of the bewitchments of philosophic languages; Austin's conception of philosophy as a form of lexicography pursued for its own sake; and Strawson's Kantianlike descriptive metaphysical project that seeks the necessary conditions for the possibility of language itself.

Rorty does not take a clear and unequivocal stand regarding these six possibilities in 1967. Yet he does make two crucial observations that provide clues to his preferences. First, he sees the linguistic turn in philosophy as heightening the self-consciousness of the tension between "the pull of the arts on one side and the pull of the sciences on the other."[46] Second, he suggests that a thorough rethinking of the fundamental epistemological issues and especially a critical scrutiny of the "spectatorial" account of knowledge will so revolutionize both philosophy and metaphilosophy that the basic distinctions, such as that between science and philosophy, used by contemporary philosophers will seem "artificial and pointless."[47] He concludes:

> If this happens, most of the essays in this volume will be obsolete, because the vocabulary in which they are written will be obsolete. This pattern of creeping obsolescence is illustrated by the fate of the notions of "meaninglessness" and "logical form" (and by my prediction that their successors, the notions of "misuse of language" and "conceptual analysis," will soon wither away). The notions which the metaphilosophers of the future will use in the struggle between philosophy-as-discovery and philosophy-as-proposal almost certainly will not be the notions used in the debates included in the present volume. But I do not know what they will be.[48]

As the thirty-six-year-old editor of *The Linguistic Turn* (1967), Rorty emerged as a noteworthy figure in American philosophy, yet he was far from being a major figure. From this time to 1972, Rorty grappled with metaphilosophical issues in the guise of highly technical discussions in the philosophy of mind and epistemology.[49] His aim was to lay the groundwork for the "rethinking of the fundamental epistemological issues which

have troubled philosophers since Plato and Aristotle." And the most revealing figure to surface in his writings is John Dewey.

I view the publication of Rorty's essay "The World Well Lost" (1972)
as marking the beginning of his later pragmatist period principally because
Dewey's influence is explicit and openly acknowledged in it. This influence
is manifest in both form and content, style and substance. The essay discloses the mature Rortian style that will become his trademark: broad
historical studies that paint a clear and lucid picture of what's at stake
philosophically and how it relates to the different currents of thought
in the past and present. This style, which rests upon both scholarly erudi-
tion and literary flair, ingeniously combines critical expository analysis
and illuminating historical narrative. It moves from technical argumentation to cultural commentary with ease and wit. Never deceptive, and
more than clever, Rorty's style leaves the reader always enlightened and
exhilarated, yet also with a quirky feeling that one has been seduced
rather than persuaded, talked into Rorty's perspective rather than talked
out of one's own position. I surmise—maybe wrongly—that his serious
encounter with Dewey's magisterial historical reconstructions of philosophy
significantly contributed to Rorty's style, a style that freed him from the
shackles of academic jargon and tapped the earlier humanist intellectual
style he first learned from Richard McKeon.

In regard to content and substance, Dewey's "naturalized version of
Hegelian historicism"[50] was broad enough to subsume and coalesce Quine's
holism, Goodman's pluralism, and Sellars' antifoundationalism in a creative (though tension-ridden) perspective. In short, Dewey enabled Rorty
to both better articulate his literary voice and elaborate his postphilosophical perspective.

The basic argument in "The World Well Lost" is that the theory-
laden character of observations relativizes talk about the world so that
realist appeals to "the world" as a final court of appeal to determine what
is true can only be viciously circular. We cannot isolate "the world" from
theories of the world, then compare these theories of the world with a
theory-free world. We cannot compare theories with anything that is not
a product of another theory. So any talk about "the world" is relative
to the theories available.

> I can now express the same point by saying that the notion of "the world"
> that is correlative with the notion of "conceptual framework" is simply
> the notion of a thing-in-itself, and that Dewey's dissolution of the Kantian
> distinctions between receptivity and spontaneity and between necessity
> and contingency thus leads naturally to the dissolution of the true
> realistic believer's notion of "the world" . . .
>
> Because the idealists kept this general picture and occupied them-
> selves with redefining the "object of knowledge," they gave idealism and the
> "coherence theory" a bad name—and realism and the "correspondence

theory" a good one. But if we can come to see both the coherence and correspondence theories as noncompeting trivialities, then we may finally move beyond realism and idealism and to the point at which, in Wittgenstein's words, we are capable of stopping doing philosophy when we want to.[51]

Like a good pragmatist, Rorty claims not that the world is not out there, only that the world does not speak our descriptive language of the world. The world indeed can cause us to hold certain beliefs, but these beliefs are elements of human languages, and human languages are our own creations—creations that change over time and space.

After 1972, Dewey moves to center stage in Rorty's writings. In his major essays prior to *Philosophy and the Mirror of Nature*, Rorty conducts a kind of crusade to resurrect the image and impact of Dewey in contemporary philosophy. In 1974, Rorty poses Dewey and Heidegger as the two great figures who point the way in "overcoming the tradition."

> What Dewey and Heidegger both wanted was a way of seeing things which would take us as far beyond the world of historicist philosophizing which succeeded Hegel, as Hegel had taken us beyond the epistemologically oriented philosophy of the eighteenth century. Dewey found what he wanted in turning away from philosophy as a distinctive activity altogether, and towards the ordinary world—the problems of men, freshly seen by discarding the distinctions which the philosophical tradition had developed.[52]

In 1975, Rorty confronts Dewey head-on in a critical reading of *Experience and Nature*, a provocative and problematic reading we examined in our chapter on Dewey. For Rorty, Dewey's work is a great achievement,

> not because it provides an accurate representation of the generic traits of nature or experience or culture or anything else. Its greatness lies in the sheer provocativeness of its suggestions about how to slough off our intellectual past, and about how to treat that past as material for playful experimentation rather than as imposing tasks and responsibilities upon us. Dewey's work helps us put aside that spirit of *seriousness* which artists traditionally lack and philosophers are supposed to traditionally maintain. For the spirit of seriousness can only exist in an intellectual world in which human life is an attempt to attain an end beyond life, an escape from freedom into the atemporal. The conception of such a world is still built into our education and our common speech, not to mention the attitudes of philosophers toward their work. But Dewey did his best to help us get rid of it, and he should not be blamed if he occasionally came down with the disease he was trying to cure.[53]

This interpretation of Dewey's intellectual style and sensibility reveals more about Rorty than about Dewey. The fact that it was published while Rorty was writing *Philosophy and the Mirror of Nature* seems to indicate that Rorty is invoking the authority of Dewey in order to encourage and empower himself in his emerging antiprofessionalism. Needless to say, Dewey was a professional par excellence, despite his criticisms of traditional philosophy. Furthermore, Dewey certainly saw himself as being closer to scientists than to artists, including those who would be surprised to discover that they lack "the spirit of seriousness" (e.g., Joyce? Kafka? Proust?) or reject the "escape from freedom into the atemporal" (e.g., Rilke? Eliot? Auden?). In short, Rorty's attempt to authorize his own style and perspective by appealing to Dewey constitutes an exemplary Emersonian instance of being provoked (not instructed) for purposes of personal empowerment.

Rorty's antiprofessionalism surfaced most clearly in his 1976 essay (read at the Bicentennial symposium of philosophy in New York) "Professionalized Philosophy and Transcendentalist Culture." Again, Rorty contrasts "the heroic period of Deweyan pragmatism"[54] with the professionalization of philosophy after World War II. There is some truth in this contrast, yet it tends to overlook the degree to which Dewey not only functioned as a professional philosopher (alongside his other roles) but also contributed to the professionalization of philosophy. For do we hear any protests from Dewey regarding the proliferation of narrow academic periodicals, the pecking order of the tenure system, or the *institutional* disciplinary division of specialized knowledges? Rorty rightly notes Dewey's wide-ranging intellectual interests and political concerns, but this does not in itself constitute an antiprofessional stance. Here James would be a better candidate. And, ironically, Rorty's own antiprofessionalism goes beyond that of Dewey, just as Dewey's political activism is far more extensive than that of Rorty.

Yet Rorty's promotion of Dewey is principally motivated by the ambitious project of resurrecting pragmatism in contemporary North Atlantic philosophy, and he has virtually single-handedly succeeded in doing so. The great contribution of Rorty to the present intellectual situation is that he constructs a powerful and penetrating narrative history of modern North Atlantic philosophy in light of the Quine-Goodman-Sellars breakthroughs and boldly draws the devastating conclusions for philosophy as a discipline. His *Philosophy and the Mirror of Nature* (1979) is a landmark text, the most important book in American metaphilosophy since Dewey's *The Quest for Certainty* (1929), primarily because it tells a relatively convincing story of how academic philosophy got into the deep crisis in which it now finds itself. Rorty's story constitutes the first major effort of analytic philosophers to engage critically in historical reflection and interpretations of themselves and their discipline. In a role parallel to that played in the philosophy of science by Thomas Kuhn's renowned *The Structure of Scientific Revolutions* (1962), Rorty's provocative and often profound interpretations of the present impasse in analytic philosophy impel philosophers to examine the problematic status of their subject matter—only to discover that modern North Atlantic philosophy has, in a significant sense, come to an end. In other words, between 1967 and 1979, Rorty arrived at a position regarding the future of philosophy in the form of a long and winding historical account of the present crisis and ways of overcoming it. And, under the selective influence of Dewey, he opts for the Wittgensteinian alternative of promoting a postphilosophical culture—of curing philosophers of the disease which they have contracted owing to their bewitchment by the academic discipline of philosophy.

Rorty credits Dewey, Wittgenstein, and Heidegger with having "brought us into a period of 'revolutionary' philosophy" by undermining (or setting aside) the prevailing refined versions of Cartesian and Kantian paradigms and advancing new roles and activities for philosophers.[55] And these monumental figures indeed inspire Rorty. Yet his philosophical debts—the actual sources of his particular anti-Cartesian and anti-Kantian arguments—are Quine's holism, Goodman's pluralism, and Sellars' antifoundationalism.

From the disparate figures of Wittgenstein, Heidegger, and above all Dewey, Rorty gets a historicist directive: to eschew the quest for certainty and the search for foundations.

> These writers have kept alive the suggestion that, even when we have justified true belief about everything we want to know, we may have no more than conformity to the norms of the day. They have kept alive the historicist sense that this century's "superstition" was the last century's triumph of reason, as well as the relativist sense that the latest vocabulary, borrowed from the latest scientific achievement, may not express privileged representations of essences, but be just another of the potential infinity of vocabularies in which the world can be described.[56]

For Rorty, the Western philosophical tradition can be overcome by adopting Dewey's strategy of holding at arm's length the ahistorical philosophical notions of necessity, universality, rationality, objectivity, and transcendentality. Instead, we should speak historically about contingent practices, transient descriptions, and revisable theories.

The basic lesson Rorty learns from Quine, Goodman, and Sellars is an antireductionist one: to refuse to privilege one language, language game, morality, or society over another by appealing *solely* to philosophical criteria. For Rorty, this temptation to look for such criteria is a species of the more traditional philosophical temptation to think of the world, society, self, or language as possessing an intrinsic nature or an essence. Since truth is a property of sentences, and languages are made rather than found, the results of appealing to philosophical criteria will be but viciously circular and apologetic arguments, rhetorical self-compliments regarding one's own perspective, "attempts to eternalize a certain contemporary language-game, social practice, or self-image."[57] In cases of conflict and disagreement, we should either support our prevailing practices, reform them, or put forward realizable alternatives to them, without appealing to ahistorical philosophical discourse as the privileged mode of resolving intellectual disagreements.

Rorty strikes a deathblow to modern North Atlantic philosophy by telling a story about the emergence, development, and decline of its primary props: the correspondence theory of truth, the notion of privileged representations, and the idea of a self-reflective transcendental subject. Rorty's detailed and fascinating tale—his-story—is regulated by three Quine-Goodman-Sellars shifts which he delineates and promotes: the move toward antirealism in ontology; the move toward antifoundationalism in epistemology; and the move toward dismissing the mind as a sphere of philosophical inquiry.

The move toward antirealism in ontology leaves no room for a correspondence theory of truth (of any philosophic significance) in that it undermines the very distinctions upon which such a theory rests: the distinctions between ideas and objects, words and things, language and the world, propositions and states of affairs, theories and facts, schemas and contents. The result is not a form of idealism because the claim of antirealism is not that ideas create objects, words create things, language creates the world, and so forth. Nor is the result a form of Kantianism because the antirealist claim is not that ideas constitute objects, words constitute things, language constitutes the world, and so on. Rather the result is a form of pragmatism because the claim is that evolving descriptions and ever-changing versions of objects, things, and the world issue forth from various communities as responses to certain problems, as attempts to overcome specific situations, and as means to satisfy particular needs and interests. To put it crudely, ideas, words, and language are not mirrors which copy the "real" or "objective" world but rather tools with which we cope with "our" world.

The second move, toward antifoundationalism in epistemology, extends Rorty's earlier attacks on various notions of intuition, especially prelinguistic awareness, as a candidate for stopping the "harmless" infinite regress of epistemic chains of justification. This antifoundationalism precludes the notion of privileged representations because it views knowledge as relations to propositions rather than as privileged relations to the objects certain propositions are about.

> If we think in the first way, we will see no need to end the potentially infinite regress of propositions-brought-forward-in-defense-of-other-propositions. It would be foolish to keep conversation on the subject going once everyone, or the majority, or the wise, are satisfied, but of course we *can*. If we think of knowledge in the second way, we will want to get behind reasons to causes, beyond argument to compulsion from the object known, to a situation in which argument would be not just silly

but impossible, for anyone gripped by the object in the required way will be *unable* to doubt or to see an alternative. To reach that point is to reach the foundations of knowledge.[58]

For Rorty, the search for such epistemic foundations expresses a need to be gripped, grasped, and compelled, a need that motivates predominant models of ocularity and specularity in epistemology. This holds for such proposed foundations as Plato's Eye of the Soul perceiving the realm of Being, Descartes's Eye of the Mind turned inward grasping clear and distinct mental representations, or Locke's Eye of the Mind turned outward seeing "singular presentations of sense." All such ocular models view ahistorical, terminal confrontation, rather than historical, fluid *conversation*, as the determinant of human belief. In short, the philosophical privileging of representations principally rests upon epistemological attempts to escape from history and put a closure upon human practices. Rorty concludes:

> When Sellars' and Quine's doctrines are purified they appear as complementary expressions of a single claim: that no "account of the nature of knowledge" can rely on a theory of representations which stand in privileged relations to reality. The work of these two philosophers enables us . . . to make clear why an "account of the nature of knowledge" can be, at most, a description of human behavior.[59]

The third move, toward dismissing the mind as a sphere of inquiry or detranscendentalizing the transcendental subject, relies, in part, on Gilbert Ryle's logical behaviorism in *The Concept of Mind* (1949) and Quine's radical behaviorism in *Word and Object* (1960). Rorty's own epistemological behaviorism links Ryle's attack on the Cartesian disembodied ego and Quine's assault on the Kantian transcendental subject (and Husserlian nonempirical ego) to a wholesale rejection of ocular metaphors in epistemology.

> A behavioral approach to episodes of "direct awareness" is not a matter of antimentalistic polemic, but a distrust of the Platonic quest for that special sort of certainty associated with visual perception. The image of the Mirror of Nature—a mirror more easily and certainly seen than that which it mirrors—suggests, and is suggested by, the image of philosophy as such a quest.[60]

Two noteworthy consequences flow from Rorty's historicist, antireductionist version of pragmatism. First, the widely held distinction between the "soft" human sciences and the "hard" natural sciences collapses. The basic difference between the *Geisteswissenschaften* and the *Naturwissenschaften* is neither the self-defining (or self-reflexive) character of the former nor the context-free (or repeatable) facts of the latter. Rather the difference is between the relative stability of normal vocabularies in the natural sciences and the relative instability of normal vocabularies in the human sciences (in some modern societies). And the irreducibility of one vocabulary to another implies not an ontological or methodological distinction but only a functional difference, i.e., different human aims of prediction and meaning endowment.

> As Kuhn says in connection with a smaller, though obviously related issue, we cannot differentiate scientific communities by "subject matter," but rather by "examining patterns of education and communication."[61]

Needless to say, this kind of demythologizing of the natural sciences is of immense importance for literary critics, artists, and religious thinkers who have been in retreat and on the defensive since the Enlightenment. And the sparks generated by such a novel viewpoint in our technocratic culture are only beginning to fly.

Second, the conception of philosophy is no longer that of a tribunal of pure reason which defends or debunks claims to knowledge made by science, morality, art, or religion. Rather the voice of the philosopher is but one voice—that of the informed dilettante or polypragmatic, Socratic thinker—among others in a grand Conversation. Rorty's demythologizing of philosophy as a subject, a *Fach*, a field of professional inquiry results in equalizing (or deprivileging) the voice of the philosopher in this grand conversation.

> In this conception, "philosophy" is not a name for a discipline which confronts permanent issues, and unfortunately keeps misstating them, or attacking them with clumsy dialectical instruments. Rather, it is a cultural genre, a "voice in the conversation of mankind" (to use Michael Oakeshott's phrase), which centers on one topic rather than another at some given time not by dialectical necessity but as a result of various things happening elsewhere in the conversation (the New Science, the French Revolution, the modern novel) or of individual men of genius who think of something new (Hegel, Marx, Frege, Freud, Wittgenstein, Heidegger), or perhaps of the resultant of several such forces. Interesting philosophical change (we might say "philosophical progress," but this would be question-begging) occurs not when a new way is found to deal with an old problem but when a new set of problems emerges and the old ones begin to fade away.[62]

Rorty's historicist, antireductionist perspective amounts to a distinctive neopragmatism. His plausible yet objectionable readings of Wittgenstein, Heidegger, and Dewey and his creative uses of Quine, Goodman, and Sellars yield the most adversarial position in American philosophy since the fervent antiprofessionalism of William James. His controversial viewpoint is a move back not simply to American pragmatism but, more fundamentally, to Ralph Waldo Emerson, in that we are left with no philosophically authoritative traditions with which to recreate and redescribe ourselves and the world.

Rorty's neopragmatism is implicitly of an Emersonian sort in that poetic activity tends to regulate his conception of human redescription and constitute the most noble of human practices.[63] Rorty's Emersonian rendering of Dewey, mediated by Heidegger's poetic displacement of philosophy, leads him to claim:

> To be authentic is to realize that the relation between Dasein and Being, between man and what he is trying to refer to when he creates such words ["the truth"], is not that of the particular to the general, or the temporal to the eternal archetype, but a relation to *himself. There is nothing more to him than his language, and nothing more to his language than what he puts into it.* There is nothing more for man to be, in short, *except a poet.*
> . . . Dewey can, I think, reasonably be described as a poet of technology — a thinker who attempted to develop a language to celebrate the modern age, and in particular to celebrate the sense of community which the liberation of mankind from toil — the universalization of leisure — would make possible. Alternatively, he can be described as the poet of human solidarity, the thinker who tried to make us see that our sense of community is all we have, and that bourgeois liberal democracy was the best example of community which we had yet envisaged.[64]

Needless to say, Rorty's Dewey is much more intellectually playful and politically tame than the Dewey we examined. But the important point here is that Rorty harks back to Emerson's stress on the human powers of creation and self-creation and the use of the past and present to provoke (not instruct) in his interpretation of Dewey. And though he does not explicitly invoke Emerson, he sounds like the sage of Concord when he states that his view posits

> the poet rather than the priest, the philosopher or the scientist as the paradigmatic human being.
> . . . the poet, in the general sense of the maker of new words, the shaper of new languages, as the vanguard of the species.[65]

Rorty's Emersonian sensibilities lead him to relegate even Dewey's historically derived authority of science to but one tradition among others, a tradition demythologized by "church historians" such as Thomas Kuhn and Paul Feyerabend.

> Pragmatism . . . does not erect Science as an idol to fill the place once held by God. It views science as one genre of literature — or, put the other way around, literature and the arts as inquiries, on the same footing as scientific inquiries. Thus it sees ethics as neither more "relative" or "subjective" than scientific theory, nor as needing to be made "scientific." Physics is a way of trying to cope with various bits of the universe; ethics is a matter of trying to cope with other bits. Mathematics helps physics do its job; literature and the arts help ethics do its. Some of these inquiries

come up with propositions, some with narratives, some with paintings. The question of what propositions to assert, which pictures to look at, what narratives to listen to and comment on and retell, are all questions about what will help us get what we want (or about what we *should* want).[66]

For Rorty, we are Emersonian sailors, self-rebegetting creatures, adrift in Neurath's boat, forever inventing and creating new self-images, vocabularies, techniques, and instruments in light of a useful backdrop of mortal beliefs and values which have no philosophical foundation or transhistorical justification. To put it bluntly, we are North Atlantic ethnocentrists in solidarity with a civilization (or a set of contemporary tribal practices) — and possibly a decaying and declining one — which has no philosophical defense. In this sense, Rorty's neopragmatism is a form of ethnocentric posthumanism. He is unashamedly ethnocentric in that he holds that no other way of life presently is worth choosing over "postmodernist bourgeois liberalism."[67]

> On my view, we should be more willing than we are to celebrate bourgeois capitalist society as the best polity actualized so far, while regretting that it is irrelevant to most of the problems of most of the population of the planet.[68]

Yet Rorty's viewpoint differs from Matthew Arnold's bourgeois humanism and John Dewey's plebeian humanism because he believes no philosophical base can be made for this civilization. In his presidential address delivered before the seventy-sixth annual Eastern Meeting of the American Philosophical Association in New York City on December 29, 1979, Rorty explicitly stated:

> The pragmatists tell us that the conversation which it is our moral duty to continue is merely our project, the European intellectual's form of life. It has no metaphysical nor epistemological guarantee of success. Further, and this is the crucial point, *we do not know what "success" would mean except simply "continuance."*
> . . . the pragmatist must avoid saying, with Peirce, that truth is *fated* to win. He must even avoid saying that truth will win. He can only say, with Hegel, that truth and justice lie in the direction marked by the successive stages of European thought. This is not because he knows some "necessary truths" and cites these examples as a result of the knowledge. It is simply that the pragmatist knows no better way to explain his convictions than to remind his interlocutor of the position they both are in, the contingent starting point they both share, the floating, ungrounded, conversations of which they are both members. This means that the pragmatist cannot answer the question "What is so special about Europe?" save by saying "Do you have anything non-European to suggest which meets *our* European purposes better?"[69]

Rorty's neopragmatism ingeniously echoes the strident antihumanist critiques—such as those of Martin Heidegger, Jacques Derrida, and Michel Foucault—of a moribund humanism. Yet his brand of neopragmatism domesticates these critiques in a smooth, seductive, and witty Attic prose and, more important, dilutes them by refusing to push his own project toward cultural and political criticisms of the civilization he cherishes (as, in varying ways and degrees, do we). In this way, Rorty circumscribes his ethnocentric posthumanism within a practical arena of bourgeois humanism.

Yet, from an ethical point of view—the central point of view for pragmatists—what is the difference that makes a difference here? Rorty's neopragmatism only kicks the philosophic props from under liberal bourgeois capitalist societies; it requires no change in our cultural and political practices. What then are the ethical and political consequences of his neopragmatism? On the macrosocietal level, there simply are none. As Rorty notes,

> But there is nothing wrong with liberal democracy, nor with the philosophers who have tried to enlarge its scope. There is only something wrong with the attempt to see their efforts as failures to achieve something which they were not trying to achieve—a demonstration of the "objective" superiority of our way of life over all other alternatives. There is, in short, nothing wrong with the hopes of the Enlightenment, the hopes which created the Western democracies. The value of the ideals of the Enlightenment is, for us pragmatists, just the value of some of the institutions and practices which they have created.[70]

In this way, Rorty's neopragmatic project for a postphilosophical culture is an ideological endeavor to promote the *basic* practices of liberal bourgeois capitalist societies, but he makes this project seem innocuous by discouraging philosophical defenses of such societies. Rorty's insouciance toward philosophy is coupled with a fervent vigilance to preserve the prevailing bourgeois way of life in North Atlantic societies, especially American society.

But, on the microinstitutional level, Rorty's neopragmatism makes a difference. The difference is that his viewpoint has immense antiprofessional implications for the academy. For Rorty, academic philosophers can neither justify their specialized activities nor legitimate their narrow results without the very philosophical defenses he undermines. He suggests that we view

> the problems about which philosophers are now offering "objective, verifiable, and clearly communicable" solutions as historical relics, left over from the Enlightenment's misguided search for the hidden essences of knowledge and morality. This is the point of view adopted by many of our fellow-intellectuals, who see us philosophy professors as caught in a time-warp, trying to live the Enlightenment over again.[71]

Rorty's neopragmatism does not put forward an earthshaking perspective for the modern West but rather is a symptom of the crisis in a highly specialized professional stratum of educational workers: those in the philosophy departments of universities and colleges. This crisis has produced a pervasive sense of demoralization in present-day academic philosophy, especially among its graduate students and younger faculty. Rorty's anti-epistemological radicalism and belletristic anti-academicism are refreshing and welcome in a discipline deeply entrenched in a debased and debilitating isolation. Yet, ironically, his project, though pregnant with rich possibilities, remains polemical (principally against other professional academics) and hence barren. It refuses to give birth to the offspring it conceives. Rorty leads philosophy to the complex world of politics and culture, but confines his engagement to transformation in the academy and to apologetics for the modern West.

This political narrowness is exemplified in Rorty's interpretation of the Western philosophical tradition in general and the Anglo-American philosophical tradition in particular. This interpretation is itself symptomatic of the ahistorical character of Anglo-American philosophy. Rorty's historicist sense remains too broad, too thin, devoid of the realities of power. His ethnocentric posthumanism is too vague, too nonchalant, and unmindful of the decline of liberalism. Furthermore, Rorty's demythologizing of modern philosophy retreats into the philosophical arena as soon as pertinent sociopolitical issues are raised.

For instance, is there a link between the emerging antirealism in ontology and the crisis of intellectual authority within our learned professional academies and educational institutions? Are the antirealist and antifoundationalist views propounded by neopragmatism, poststructuralism, and other avant-gardist professional ideologies shaped by and shaping the "stylistic and discursive heterogeneity without a norm"[72] (or without the old bourgeois consensus) that permeates academic culture in advanced capitalist countries today? Is the detranscendentalizing of the transcendental subject—a subject often associated with the North Atlantic bourgeoisies—related to the deep sense of impotence among the middle classes in contemporary capitalist societies, the sense of there being no liberating projects in the near North Atlantic future, and hence to the prevailing cynicism that feeds much of secular neoconservatism, apocalyptic forecasts, narcissistic living, and self-indulgent, ironic forms of thinking? And if science is, as Rorty notes, a "value-laden enterprise,"[73] is there an ideological character to the very methods of the natural sciences owing to an agreed-upon conception of and disposition toward nature which may promote the domination of not only our environment but also those people (the majority of the planet!) subsumed under the rubric "nature" such as women, non-Europeans, and even "earthy" workers?

The central concern underlying these provocative questions is that it is impossible to historicize philosophy without partly politicizing (in contrast to vulgarly ideologizing) it. Surely the relation of philosophy to culture and politics is complex, and it would be easiest to ignore it. Yet one cannot embark on a historicist project which demythologizes philosophy without dragging in the complexities of politics and culture. To tell a tale about the historical character of philosophy while eschewing the political content, role, and function of philosophies in various historical periods is to promote an ahistorical approach in the name of history. To undermine the privileged philosophic notions of necessity, universality, rationality, objectivity, and transcendentality without acknowledging and accenting the oppressive deeds done under the ideological aegis of these notions is to write an intellectual and homogeneous history, a history which fervently attacks epistemological privilege but remains relatively silent about forms of political, economic, racial, and sexual privilege. Such a history, which surreptitiously suppresses certain oppressed peoples' histories, hides the operations of power—both domination and resistance—in the past and present, even when this history undergirds sophisticated anti-epistemological and antimetaphysical tastes of postmodern avant-gardists.

Indeed, the relativist, even nihilist, implications of neopragmatism upset mainstream realists and old-style humanists. So the narrow though noteworthy battle within the academy between the professional avant-gardists and professional establishmentarians will continue to be intense. Yet after the philosophical smoke clears, the crucial task is to pursue social and heterogeneous genealogies, that is, detailed accounts of the emergence, development, sustenance, and decline of vocabularies, discourses, and (non-discursive) practices in the natural and human sciences against the background of dynamic changes in specific (and often coexisting) modes of production, political conflicts, cultural configurations, and personal turmoil.

Rorty is highly suspicious of genealogical accounts. For example, when a provisional explanation—even a speculative one—seems appropriate for the centrality of ocular metaphors in Western thought, he asserts that "there was, we moderns may say with the ingratitude of hindsight, no particular reason why this ocular metaphor seized the imagination of the founders of Western thought."[74] And when he contemplates questions about the acceptance and performance of modern science and moral consciousness in the West, Rorty concludes that "in no case does anyone know what might count as a good answer."[75]

In light of such pessimism regarding historical or genealogical accounts, one wonders whether Rorty takes his own neopragmatic viewpoint seriously on these matters. Is a "good answer" something more than a particular insightful and useful interpretation that is based on an emerging, prevailing, or declining social consensus and put to a specific purpose? Is not Rorty's narrative itself a "good answer" to Cartesians, Kantians, and analytic philosophers? In short, Rorty's neopragmatism has no place—and rightly so—for ahistorical philosophical justifications, yet his truncated historicism rests content with intellectual and homogeneous historical narratives and distrusts social and heterogeneous genealogical accounts. This truncated historicism, linked to the narrow ethical and tame political consequences of his narrative, is clearly illustrated in his frequent use of an all-encompassing and undifferentiated conception of society.

> Explaining rationality and epistemic authority by reference to what society lets us say, rather than the latter by the former, is the essence of what I shall call "epistemological behaviorism."[76]

It should be clear that Rorty's limited historicism needs Marx, Durkheim, Weber, Beauvoir, and Du Bois; that is, his narrative needs a more subtle historical and sociological perspective.

His relative lack of such a perspective results from the two major short-comings of Rorty's neopragmatism — *its distrust of theory* and *its preoccupation with transient vocabularies*. We first must distinguish between the pragmatic accentuation of consequences and a historicist concern with specific practices. A common vulgar pragmatic fallacy is to elevate the former at the expense of understanding the latter. This fallacy promotes a crude anti-theoreticism. In fact, the garden-variety critique of pragmatism focuses on its aversion to theory — a critique justified by the common vulgar pragmatic fallacy. Yet a more refined pragmatism, one that preserves its historicist sense and genealogical aims, accents both consequences and specific practices in light of a set of provisional and revisable theoretical frameworks while it resists grand theories. This resistance to and suspicion of grand theories is not to be confused with an aversion to theory per se. In fact, vulgar antitheoreticism is a knee-jerk reaction to vulgar grand theories that elide heterogeneity and complexity. *The goal of a sophisticated neopragmatism is to think genealogically about specific practices in light of the best available social theories, cultural critiques, and historiographical insights and to act politically to achieve certain moral consequences in light of effective strategies and tactics.*

This form of neopragmatism explodes the preoccupation with transient vocabularies and discourses. Instead it shuns any linguistic, dialogical, communicative, or conversational models and replaces them with a focus on the multileveled operations of power. This focus indeed takes seriously the power-laden character of language — the ideological weight of certain rhetorics and the political gravity of various discourses. Yet it refuses to posit language and its distinct features as the model for understanding other, nondiscursive operations of power such as modes of production, state apparatuses, and bureaucratic institutions. Of course, such operations presuppose language and discourse, yet this presupposition in no way entails that the dynamics of power in language and discourses dictate or even emulate the dynamics of power in social structures and institutions. Structuralists and poststructuralists have rightly alerted us to the materiality of sign systems, a materiality that was often overlooked by the classical social theorists. And neopragmatists have rightly reached limited historicist conceptions of antirealism and antifoundationalism. Now the task is that of building on these insights by conjoining them to the best of recent refinements in social theory, cultural criticism, and historiography *and* rooting them in possible social movements or social motion, those with efficacious strategies and tactics for fundamental social change. The time is now past for empty academic theoreticism, professional antitheoreticism, and complacent "radical" antiprofessionalism. The examples of intellectuals like John Dewey, W. E. B. Du Bois, Sheldon Wolin, Stuart Hall, Elizabeth Fox-Genovese, and Edward Said must be followed. Truncated neopragmatism with historicist positions must give way to genealogical accounts deployed as moral and political weapons in social and ideological contestations with those who rule and dominate the lives of most of us. In this way, neopragmatism learns from, builds upon, and goes beyond its own tradition from Emerson to Rorty—still concerned with human powers, provocation, and personality, it is now inextricably linked to oppositional analyses of class, race, and gender and oppositional movements for creative democracy and social freedom.

Prophetic Pragmatism: Cultural Criticism and Political Engagement

At the level of theory the philosophy of praxis cannot be confounded with or reduced to any other philosophy. Its originality lies not only in its transcending of previous philosophies but also and above all in that it opens up a completely new road, renewing from head to toe the whole way of conceiving philosophy itself . . . the whole way of conceiving philosophy has been "historicised," that is to say a new way of philosophising which is more concrete and historical than what went before it has begun to come into existence.

—*Antonio Gramsci*

The move from Rorty's model of fluid conversation to that of the multi-leveled operations of power leads us back to Ralph Waldo Emerson. Like Friedrich Nietzsche, Emerson is first and foremost a cultural critic obsessed with ways to generate forms of power. For Rorty, these forms are understood as activities of conversation for the primary purpose of producing new human self-descriptions. But for Emerson, conversation is but one minor instance of the myriad of possible transactions for the enhancement of human powers and personalities. Ironically, Rorty's adoption of Michael Oakeshott's metaphor of "conversation" reflects the dominant ideal of the very professionalism he criticizes. This ideal indeed is more a public affair than are Emerson's preferred ideal transactions, e.g., gardening, walking, reading, and yet it also is more genteel and bourgeois.

The tradition of pragmatism—the most influential stream in American thought—is in need of an explicit political mode of cultural criticism that refines and revises Emerson's concerns with power, provocation, and personality in light of Dewey's stress on historical consciousness and Du Bois' focus on the plight of the wretched of the earth. This political mode of cultural criticism must recapture Emerson's sense of vision—his utopian impulse—yet rechannel it through Dewey's conception of creative democracy and Du Bois' social structural analysis of the limits of capitalist democracy. Furthermore, this new kind of cultural criticism—we can call it prophetic pragmatism—must confront candidly the tragic sense found in Hook and Trilling, the religious version of the Jamesian strenuous mood in Niebuhr, and the tortuous grappling with the vocation of the intellectual in Mills. Prophetic pragmatism, with its roots in the American heritage and its hopes for the wretched of the earth, constitutes the best chance of promoting an Emersonian culture of creative democracy by means of critical intelligence and social action.

The first step is to define what an Emersonian culture of creative democracy would look like, or at least give some sense of the process by which it can be created. In retrospect, it is important to note that Emerson's swerve from philosophy was not simply a rejection of the Cartesian and Kantian models of epistemology; it also was an assertion of the primacy of power-laden people's opinion (doxa) over value-free philosophers' knowledge (episteme). Emerson's swerve was a democratic leveling of the subordination of common sense to Reason. Emerson realized that when philosophers "substitute Reason for common sense, they tend to view the sense of commoners to be nonsense."[1] Emerson's suspicion of philosophy was not simply that it bewitched thinkers by means of language but, more important, that it had deep antidemocratic consequences. For Emerson, reason, formal thought, foundations, certainty were not only far removed from the dynamism of human experience; they also were human creations that appear as detached abstractions which command their creators and thereby constrain their creators' freedom. This consequence is both antilibertarian and antidemocratic in that human potential and participation are suppressed in the name of philosophic truth and knowledge. Emerson's sensibilities are echoed in our own time by Benjamin Barber:

> In conquering the muddled uncertainties of politics and suborning reasonableness to rationality, they [philosophers] have served the ideal of enlightenment better than they have informed our political judgment . . . Rights get philosophically vindicated but only as abstractions that undermine the democratic communities that breathe life into rights; justice is given an unimpeachable credential in epistemology without giving it a firm hold on action or the deliberative processes from which

political action stems; talk is revivified as the heart of a political process and then recommended to citizens, but in a form that answers to the constraints not of citizenship but of philosophy; civility is celebrated, but construed as incompatible with the sorts of collective human choice and communal purposes that give civility its political meaning.[2]

To speak then of an Emersonian culture of creative democracy is to speak of a society and culture where politically adjudicated forms of knowledge are produced in which human participation is encouraged and for which human personalities are enhanced. Social experimentation is the basic norm, yet it is operative only when those who must suffer the consequences have effective control over the institutions that yield the consequences, i.e., access to decision-making processes. In this sense, the Emersonian swerve from epistemology is inseparable from an Emersonian culture of creative democracy; that is, there is political motivation and political substance to the American evasion of philosophy.

> Politics is what men do when metaphysics fails . . . It is the forging of common actuality in the absence of abstract independent standards. It entails dynamic, ongoing, common deliberation and action and it is feasible only when individuals are transformed by social interaction into citizens.[3]

The political motivation of the American evasion of philosophy is not ideological in the vulgar sense; that is, the claim here is not that philosophy is a mere cloak that conceals the material interests of a class or group. Rather, the claim is that once one gives up on the search for foundations and the quest for certainty, human inquiry into truth and knowledge shifts to the social and communal circumstances under which persons can communicate and cooperate in the process of acquiring knowledge. What was once purely epistemological now highlights the values and operations of power requisite for the human production of truth and knowledge.

The political substance of the American evasion of philosophy is that what was the prerogative of philosophers, i.e., rational deliberation, is now that of the people – and the populace deliberating is creative democracy in the making. Needless to say, this view is not a license for eliminating or opposing all professional elites, but it does hold them to account. Similarly, the populace deliberating is neither mob rule nor mass prejudice. Rather, it is the citizenry in action, with its civil consciousness molded by participation in public-interest-centered and individual-rights-regarding democracy.

Prophetic pragmatism makes this political motivation and political substance of the American evasion of philosophy explicit. Like Dewey, it understands pragmatism as a political form of cultural criticism and locates politics in the everyday experiences of ordinary people. Unlike Dewey, prophetic pragmatism promotes a more direct encounter with the

Marxist tradition of social analysis. The emancipatory social experimentalism that sits at the center of prophetic pragmatic politics closely resembles the radical democratic elements of Marxist theory, yet its flexibility shuns any dogmatic, a priori, or monistic pronouncements.

The encounter of prophetic pragmatism with Marxist theory can be best illustrated by an examination of the most significant and elaborate effort to put forward a Marxist-informed (though not Marxist) democratic social vision: namely, that found in Roberto Unger's multivolume work *Politics*. Unger is not a prophetic pragmatist – yet there are deep elective affinities between Unger's work and prophetic pragmatism. To put it crudely, both are noteworthy exemplars of third-wave left romanticism.

Roberto Unger and Third-Wave Left Romanticism

Roberto Unger's distinctive contribution to contemporary social thought is to deepen and sharpen in a radical manner John Dewey's notion of social experimentation in light of the crisis of Marxist theory and praxis. Unger's fundamental aim is to free Marxist conceptions of human society-making from evolutionary, deterministic, and economistic encumbrances by means of Deweyan concerns with the plethora of historically specific social arrangements and the often overlooked politics of personal relations between unique and purposeful individuals. The basic result of Unger's fascinating efforts is to stake out new discursive space on the contemporary political and ideological spectrum. Prophetic pragmatism occupies this same space. This space is neither simply left nor liberal, Marxist nor Lockean, anarchist nor Kantian. Rather, Unger's perspective is both post-Marxist and postliberal; that is, it consists of an emancipatory experimentalism that promotes permanent social transformation and perennial self-development for the purposes of ever-increasing democracy and individual freedom. Yet, in contrast to most significant social thinkers, Unger is motivated by explicit religious concerns, such as a kinship with nature as seen in romantic love, or transcendence of nature as manifest in the hope for eternal life. In this way, Unger highlights the radical existential insufficiency of his emancipatory experimentalism, which speaks best to human penultimate matters. For Unger, human ultimate concerns are inseparable from yet not reducible to the never-ending quest for social transformation and self-development.

I shall argue three claims regarding Unger's project. First, I shall suggest that his viewpoint can be best characterized as the most elaborate articulation of a *third-wave left romanticism* now sweeping across significant segments of principally the first-world progressive intelligentsia (or what is left of this progressive intelligentsia!). Second, I will show that this third-wave left romanticism – like prophetic pragmatism – is discursively situated between John Dewey's radical liberal version of socialism and Antonio

Gramsci's absolute historicist conception of Marxism. Third, I shall high-light the ways in which this provocative project, though an advance beyond much of contemporary social thought, remains inscribed within a Euro-centric and patriarchal discourse that not simply fails to theoretically con-sider racial and gender forms of subjugation, but also remains silent on the antiracist and feminist dimensions of concrete progressive politi-cal struggles.

The most striking impression one gets from reading Unger's work is his unabashedly pronounced romanticism. By romanticism here, I mean quite simply the preoccupation with Promethean human powers, the recog-nition of the contingency of the self and society, and the audacious pro-jection of desires and hopes in the form of regulative emancipatory ideals for which one lives and dies. In these postmodern times of cynicism and negativism—after the unimaginable atrocities of Hitler, Stalin, Tito, Musso-lini, and Franco, and the often forgotten barbarities committed in Asia, Africa, and Latin America under European and American imperialist auspices; and during the present period of Khomeini, Pinochet, Moi, and Mengistu in the third world, bureaucratic henchmen ruling the second world, and Reagan, Thatcher, Kohl, and Chirac setting the pace in the first world—Unger's romanticism is both refreshing and disturbing.

The ameliorative energies and utopian impulses that inform Unger's work are refreshing in that so many of us now "lack any ready way to imagine transformation."[4] We feel trapped in a world with no realizable oppositional options, no actualizable credible alternatives. This sense of political impotence—"this experience of acquiescence without commit-ment"[5]—yields three basic forms of politics: sporadic terrorism for impatient, angry, and nihilistic radicals; professional reformism for comfortable, culti-vated, and concerned liberals; and evangelical nationalism for frightened, paranoid, and accusatory conservatives. Unger's romantic sense that the future can and should be fundamentally different from and better than the present not only leads him to reject these three predominant kinds of politics, but also impels him to answer in the negative to "the great political question of our day: Is social democracy the best that we can reasonably hope for?"[6] Unger believes we can and must do better.

Yet Unger's third-wave left romanticism is disturbing in that we have witnessed—and are often reminded of—the deleterious consequences and dehumanizing effects of the first two waves of left romanticism in the modern world. The first wave—best seen in the American and French Revolutions—unleashed unprecedented human energies and powers, sig-nificantly transformed selves and societies, and directed immense human desires and hopes toward the grand moral and credible political ideals of democracy and freedom, equality and fraternity. Two exemplary figures of this first wave—Thomas Jefferson and Jean-Jacques Rousseau—would undoubtedly affirm the three basic elements of Unger's conception of human activity: the contextual or conditional quality of all human activity; the possibility of breaking through all contexts of practical or conceptual activity; and the need to distinguish between context-preserving, i.e., routinized, and context-breaking, i.e., transgressive, activities.[7]

Furthermore, both Jefferson and Rousseau would agree with Unger's romantic conception of imagination as a human power that conceives of social reality from the vantage point of change and for the purposes of transformation.[8] In this regard, Unger is deeply within the North Atlantic romantic grain. Why, then, ought we to be disturbed? Despite the great human advances initiated and promoted by first-wave left romanticism, its historical and social embodiments reinforced and reproduced barbaric practices: white supremacist practices associated with African slavery and imperial conquest over indigenous and Mexican peoples; male supremacist practices inscribed in familial relations, cultural mores, and societal restrictions; and excessive business control and influence over the public interest as seen in low wages, laws against unions, and government support of select business endeavors, e.g., railroads. These noteworthy instances of the underside of first-wave left romanticism should be disturbing not because all efforts to change the status quo in a progressive direction are undesirable, but rather because any attempt to valorize historically specific forms of human powers must be cognizant of and cautious concerning who will be subjected to those human powers.

The second wave of left romanticism, following upon the heels of profound disillusionment and dissatisfaction with the American and French Revolutions, is manifest in the two great prophetic and prefigurative North Atlantic figures: Ralph Waldo Emerson and Karl Marx. Both were obsessed with the problem of revolution, that is, the specifying and creating of conditions for the transformation of context-preserving activities into context-breaking ones. Both had a profound faith in the capacity of human beings to remake themselves and society in more free and democratic ways. And both looked toward science—the new cultural authority on knowledge, reality, and truth—as an indispensable instrument for this remaking and betterment.

Emersonian themes of the centrality of the self's morally laden transformative vocation; the necessity of experimentation to achieve the self's aims of self-mastery and kinship with nature; and the importance of self-creation and self-authorization loom large in Unger's work. In fact, the penultimate paragraph of volume 1 of *Politics* reads as if it comes right out of Emerson's *Nature*.

> In their better and saner moments men and women have always wanted to live as the originals that they all feel themselves to be and to cement practical and passionate attachments that respect this truth rather than submerge it. As soon as they have understood their social worlds to be made up and pasted together, they have also wanted to become the

co-makers of these worlds. Some modern doctrines tell us that we already live in societies in which we can fully satisfy these desires while others urge us to give them up as unrealistic. But the first piece of advice is hard to believe, and the second is hard to practice.[9]

Similarly, Marxist motifs of the centrality of value-laden political struggle; the necessity for transformation of present-day societies and for control over nature; and, most pointedly, the ability of human powers to reshape human societies against constraints always already in place play fundamental roles in Unger's project. Indeed, the last paragraph of volume 1 of *Politics* invokes the same metaphors, passions, and aims as Marx's *1844 Manuscripts* and *1848 Manifesto*.

> The constraints of society, echoed, reinforced, and amplified by the illusions of social thought, have often led people to bear the stigma of longing under the mask of worldliness and resignation. An anti-naturalistic social theory does not strike down the constraints but it dispels the illusions that prevent us from attacking them. Theoretical insight and prophetic vision have joined ravenous self-interest and heartless conflict to set the fire that is burning in the world, and melting apart the amalgam of faith and superstition, and consuming the power of false necessity.[10]

The second wave of left romanticism is dominated by Emersonian ideas of America and Marxist conceptions of socialism. From roughly the 1860s to the 1940s, human hopes for democracy and freedom, equality, and fraternity around the globe rested on the legacy of either Emerson or Marx. Needless to say, European efforts at nation building and empire consolidating—the major sources of second-wave right romanticism—violently opposed both the Emersonian and the Marxist legacies. Yet by the end of the Second World War, with the defeat of Germany's bid for European and world domination at the hands of the Allied forces led by the United States and Russia, the second wave of left romanticism began to wane. The dominant version of the Marxist legacy—Marxist-Leninist (and at the time led by Stalin)—was believed by more and more left romantics to be repressive, repulsive, and retrograde. And the major mode of the Emersonian legacy—Americanism (led then by Truman and Eisenhower)—was viewed by many left romantics as racist, penurious, and hollow.

The third wave of left romanticism proceeded from a sense of deep disappointment with Marxist-Leninism and Americanism. Exemplary activistic stirrings can be found in the third world or among people of color in the first world—Gandhi in India, Mariatequi in Peru, Nasser in Egypt, and Martin Luther King, Jr., in the United States. Yet principally owing to the tragic facts of survival, myopic leadership, and limited options, most third-world romanticism was diverted from the third wave of left romanticism into the traps of a regimenting Marxist-Leninism or a rapacious Americanism. The major exceptions—Chile under Salvador Allende,

Jamaica under Michael Manley, Nicaragua under the Sandinistas—encounter formidable, usually insurmountable, obstacles. Needless to say, similar projects in second-world countries—Hungary in 1956, Czechoslovakia in 1968, Poland in 1970—are tragically and brutally crushed.

The two great figures of the third wave of left romanticism are John Dewey and Antonio Gramsci. Dewey applies the Jeffersonian and Emersonian viewpoints to the concrete historical and social realities of our century. Similarly, Gramsci sharpens and revises the Rousseauistic and Marxist perspectives on these realities. As we observed earlier, in numerous essays, articles, and reviews, and, most important, in his texts *The Public and Its Problems* (1927), *Individualism: Old and New* (1929), *Liberalism and Social Action* (1935), and *Freedom and Culture* (1939), Dewey put forward a powerful interpretation of socialism that builds upon yet goes beyond liberalism. This interpretation highlights a conception of social experimentation which "goes all the way down"; that is, it embraces the idea of fundamental economic, political, cultural, and individual transformation in light of Jeffersonian and Emersonian ideals of accountable power, small-scale associations, and individual liberties. In various fragments, incomplete studies, and political interventions, and in works such as *The Prison Notebooks* (1929–35) and *The Modern Prince*, Gramsci sets forth a penetrating version of Marxism that rests upon yet spills over beyond Leninism. This version focuses on a notion of historical specificity and a conception of hegemony which preclude any deterministic, economistic, or reductionist readings of social phenomena. In this way, Dewey and Gramsci partly set the agenda for any acceptable and viable third wave of left romanticism in our time.

Unger's provocative project occupies the discursive space between Dewey and Gramsci; it is the most detailed delineation of third-wave left romanticism we have. Like prophetic pragmatism, he stands at the intersection of the Jefferson-Emerson-Dewey insights and the Rousseau-Marx-Gramsci formulations. Ironically, as an intellectual with third-world origins and sensibilities (Brazilian) and first-world academic status and orientations (Harvard law professor for almost twenty years), Unger is much more conscious of and concerned with his Rousseau-Marx-Gramsci heritage than with his Jefferson-Emerson-Dewey sentiments. In fact, his major aim is to provide an alternative radicalism—at the levels of method and political and personal praxis—to Marxism in light of his third-world experiences and first-world training.

> *Politics* is also the product of two very different experiences. One of these experiences is exposure to the rich, polished, critical and self-critical but also downbeat and Alexandrian culture of social and historical thought that now flourishes in the North-Atlantic democracies. This social-thought culture suffers from the influence of a climate of opinion in which the most generous citizens hope at best to avert military disasters and

to achieve marginal redistributive goals while resigning themselves to established institutional arrangements. The other shaping experience is practical and imaginative engagement in the murky but hopeful politics of Brazil, a country at the forward edge of the Third World. There, at the time of writing, at least some people took seriously the idea that basic institutions, practices, and preconceptions might be reconstructed in ways that did not conform to any established model of social organization.

Much in this work can be understood as the consequence of an attempt to enlist the intellectual resources of the North-Atlantic world in the service of concerns and commitments more keenly felt elsewhere. In this way I hope to contribute toward the development of an alternative to the vague, unconvinced, and unconvincing Marxism that now serves the advocates of the radical project as their *Lingua Franca*. If the arguments of this book stand up, the transformative focus of this theoretical effort has a cognitive value that transcends its immediate origins and motives.[11]

In this sense, Unger privileges Marxist discourse. On the one hand, Marxism's "structure and institutional fetishism"—its tendency to impose historical and social scripts in the name of deep-structure logics of inevitability—stand as the major impediment to Unger's radical project.[12] On the other hand, Marxism more than any other social theory contains the resources and analytical tools to resist this tendency and thereby aid and abet Unger's work.

Much of this book represents a polemic against what the text labels deep-structure social analysis. The writings of Marx and of his followers provide the most powerful and detailed illustrations of the deep-structure moves. Yet Marx's own writings contain many elements that assist the effort to free ambitious theorizing from deep-structure assumptions. People working in the Marxist tradition have developed the deep-structure approach. Yet they have also forged some of the most powerful tools with which to build a view of social life more faithful to the anti-naturalistic intentions of Marx and other classic social theorists than Marx's original science of history.[13]

Unger even more closely associates his project with a particular group of Marxists (whom he dubs "political Marxists"), though he by no means affirms their efforts to stay within the Marxist explanatory framework. The major figure in this group is Antonio Gramsci. Indeed, it can be said with assurance that Gramsci's flexible Marxism which emphasizes and explores "the relative autonomy of class situations and class consciousness from the defining features of a mode of production like capitalism" serves as the principal springboard for Unger's work.[14] His explicit acknowledgment of his debts to political Marxists such as Gramsci—a rare moment in Unger's self-authorizing texts—bears this out.

At times the political Marxists have sacrificed the development of their insights to the desire to retain a connection with the central theses of historical materialism. To them these tenets have seemed the only available basis for theoretical generalization and for critical distance from the arrangements and circumstances of the societies in which they lived. At other times, the political Marxists have simply given up on theory . . . They have then paid the price in the loss of an ability to convey a sense of sharp institutional alternatives for past, present, and future society. The constructive theory of *Politics* just keeps going from where the political Marxists leave off. It does so, however, without either renouncing theoretical ambitions or accepting any of the distinctive doctrines of Marx's social theory.[15]

Unger believes it is necessary to go beyond Gramsci not because Gramsci is a paradigmatic Marxist "super-theorist" who generates theoretical generalizations and schemas that fail to grasp the complexity of social realities, but rather because Gramsci despite his Marxism is an exemplary "ultra-theorist" who attempts to avoid broad explanations and theoretical systems in order to keep track of the multifarious features and aspects of fluid social realities.[16] As an unequivocal supertheorist (who tries to avoid the traps of positivism, naive historicism, and deep-structure logics), Unger criticizes ultratheorists like Gramsci and Foucault for rejecting explanatory or prescriptive theories and thereby ultimately disenabling effective emancipatory thought and practice. For Unger, the ultratheorist sees a deep-structure logic inside *every* theoretical system, confuses explanatory generalizations with epistemic foundationalism, and runs the risk of his work's degenerating into a nominalistic form of conventional social science. In short, the major lesson Unger learns from Gramsci is to be a more subtle, nuanced, and sensitive supertheorist than Marx by building on elements in Marx and others.

Despite the prominence of certain Deweyan themes in his project, Dewey is virtually absent in Unger's text. Furthermore, the one reference to Dewey is a rather cryptic and misleading statement. After alluding to Foucault and Gramsci as major ultratheorists, Unger adds:

Moreover, it would be wrong to associate ultra-theory solely with Leftist or modernist intellectuals. Why not, for example, John Dewey (despite the gap between the commitment to institutional experimentalism and the slide into institutional conservatism).[17]

This passage is perplexing for three reasons. First, is Unger implying that Dewey was neither a leftist nor a modernist intellectual? Second, is Unger drawing a distinction between his own social experimentalism and Dewey's institutional experimentalism? Third, in what sense and when did Dewey slide into institutional conservatism? If Unger answers the first question in the affirmative, he falls prey to the misinformed stereotypical view of Dewey as a vulgar Americanist. For as we saw earlier, Dewey's sixty-five-year political record as a democratic socialist speaks for itself. And no argument is needed for Dewey's being a modernist intellectual, when he stands as the major secular intellectual of twentieth-century America. If Unger is making a distinction between his form of experimentalism and that of Dewey, its validity remains unclear unless one remains fixated on Dewey's educational reform movement and neglects the broader calls for fundamental social change put forward during the years Dewey concentrated on progressive education as well as afterward, in the late twenties, thirties, and forties. And the implausible notion that Dewey slid into institutional conservatism holds only if one wrongly views his brand of anti-Stalinism in the forties as conservatism, for his critique of American society remained relentless to the end.

I do believe Unger has simply slipped in his brief mention of Dewey. Yet this slip is significant in that Dewey could provide Unger with some enabling insights and tools for his project. These insights and tools will not be comparable to those of Marx, for Dewey was not a social theorist. Yet Dewey's own brand of ultratheory could like Gramsci's chasten and temper Unger's supertheory ambitions.

For example, Unger's attempt to work out an analogical relation between scientific notions of objectivity and social conceptions of personality is prefigured—and more persuasive—in Dewey's linkage of scientific attitude (as opposed to scientific method) to democracy as a way of life. The key notions become not so much objectivity—not even Rorty's ingenious reformulation of objectivity as self-critical solidarity—as, more fundamentally, respect for the other and accountability as a condition for fallibility.[18] Similarly, Dewey's brand of ultratheory does not exclude, downplay, or discourage explanatory generalizations. In fact, Dewey holds that we cannot get by without some form of supertheory, for the same reasons Unger invokes (i.e., for explaining and regulating our practices). Yet Dewey admonishes us to view supertheories as we do any other instruments or weapons we have and to use them when they serve our purposes and satisfy our interests, and criticize or discard them when they utterly fail us. The significant difference between Gramsci and Dewey is not that the former accepts Marxist theory and the latter rejects it, but rather that Gramsci tenaciously holds onto Marxist theory in those areas where it fails, e.g., politics and culture. Dewey accepted much of the validity of Marxist theory and simply limited its explanatory scope and rejected its imperial, monistic, and dogmatic versions. These Deweyan correctives to Unger's project point toward prophetic pragmatism.

Dewey's radical liberal version of socialism might dampen Unger's fires of utopian quest in that Dewey recognized that authoritarian communisms and liberal capitalist democracies were and are the major *credible* options in the first world and second world at the moment. And social experimentation in the third world remains hampered by these limits. This is not to say we ought not to dream, hope, live, fight, and die for betterment, yet such romantic longings, even when dressed up in sophisticated social thought, do not alter the severe constraints of the international coordination of capital in the West and the bureaucratic stranglehold in the East. In this sense, Dewey's petit bourgeois radicalism, which is no tradition to trash despite its vast shortcomings, could not but be an incessant effort at radical reform in the West and a beacon light on repression in the East. In the same way, Gramsci's Communist party leadership, whose legacy now resides principally in Italy and Sweden, could not but comprise audacious attempts at democratization in the East and a beacon light on socially induced misery (e.g., poverty, racism) in the West. The fundamental challenge to Unger is to find space for historical maneuvering—for his emancipatory experimentalism—between Dewey and Gramsci, between petit bourgeois radicalism and Marxian socialism.

This challenge should be approached on two levels—that of highbrow academic production and consumption, and that of popular political organization and mobilization. Both levels have their own kinds of significance. Universities, colleges, and some professional schools, though increasingly given over to hi-tech and computers, still provide one of the few institutional arenas in which serious conversation about new ideological space can take place in liberal capitalist democracies. It indeed is no accident that much of the legacy of the New Left in the sixties now resides in such places. Most of the consumers of Unger's project consist of these progressive professional managers who exercise some degree of cultural authority in and from these educational institutions. Their importance, especially as transmitters of elite cultural values and sensibilities, should not be overlooked. But neither should their influence be exaggerated. In fact, for the most part, what they produce and consume of a left political orientation remains within the academy. Despite Unger's admirable efforts to write in a relatively jargon-free language, this holds for his own texts. So his attempt to put forward a left project between Dewey and Gramsci will more than likely remain the property of the same disillusioned progressives he chastises. The importance of influencing the left sectors of the "downbeat and Alexandrian" intellectual culture of our time ought not to be minimized; nevertheless, Unger wants to do more than this— he wants to make a significant programmatic intervention in the real world of politics.

This brings us to the level of political organization and mobilization. Unlike Dewey and Gramsci, Unger pays little attention to the burning cultural and political issues in the everyday lives of ordinary people— issues such as religious and nationalist (usually xenophobic) revivals, the declining power of trade unions, escalating racial and sexual violence, pervasive drug addiction and alcoholism, breakdowns in the nuclear family, the cultural and political impact of mass media (TV, radio, and videos), and the exponential increase of suicides and homicides. Unger invokes a politics of personal relations and everyday life, yet he remains rather vague regarding its content.

When I claim that Unger's discourse remains inscribed within a Eurocentric and patriarchal framework, I mean that his texts remain relatively silent—on the conceptual and practical levels—on precisely those issues that promote social motion and politicization among the majority of people in the country. I am not suggesting that Unger write simple pamphlets for the masses, but rather that his fascinating works give more attention to those issues that may serve as the motivating forces for his new brand of left politics. To write a masterful text of social theory and politics that does not so much as mention—God forbid, grapple with—forms of racial and gender subjugation in our time is inexcusable on political and theoretical grounds.[19] To do so is to remain captive to a grand though flawed Eurocentric and patriarchal heritage. More pointedly, it is to miss much of the new possibilities for a realizable left politics. Needless to say, to take seriously issues such as race and gender is far from a guarantee for a credible progressive politics, but to bypass them is to commit the fatal sin of supertheory: to elide the concrete at the expense of systemic coherence and consistency.

In conclusion, Unger's ambitious project warrants our close attention and scrutiny. It articulates many of the motives and ideals of the political project of prophetic pragmatism. It is, by far, the most significant attempt to articulate a third-wave left romanticism that builds on the best of the Jefferson-Emerson-Dewey and Rousseau-Marx-Gramsci legacies. Unfortunately, he remains slightly blinded by some of the theoretical and practical shortsightedness of these grand North Atlantic legacies. Yet Unger would be the first to admit that all prophets are imperfect and that all emancipatory visions and programs are subject to revision and transformation.

The Challenge of Michel Foucault

To praise Unger's project and that of prophetic pragmatism for their third-wave left romanticism is to go against the grain in some progressive circles owing to the influence of Michel Foucault. Foucault is the exemplary antiromantic, suspicious of any talk about wholeness, totality, telos, purpose, or even future.[20] Prophetic pragmatism shares with Foucault a preoccupation with the operation of powers. It also incorporates the genealogical mode of inquiry initiated by the later phase of Foucault's work. In fact, prophetic pragmatism promotes genealogical materialist modes of analysis similar in many respects to those of Foucault.[21] Yet prophetic pragmatism rejects Foucault's antiromanticism for three basic reasons.

First, despite the profound insights and rich illuminations of Foucault's renowned archeologies and genealogies, he remains preoccupied by one particular kind of operation of power, namely, the various modes by which human beings are constituted into subjects.[22] His powerful investigations into modes of inquiry that take the form of disciplinary powers of subjection and objectivization of human beings remain within a general Kantian framework. Foucault still asks questions such as "What are the conditions for the possibility of the constitution of the subject?" Instead of providing a transcendental response or even a historically anthropocentric answer, he gives us a genealogical account of anonymous and autonomous discourses that constitute subjects. In short, Foucault gives a Nietzschean reply to the Kantian question of the constitution of subjects.

> I wanted to see how these problems of constitution could be resolved within a historical framework, instead of referring them back to a constituent object (madness, criminality or whatever). But this historical contextualization needed to be something more than the simple relativisation of the phenomenological subject. I don't believe the problem can be solved by historicizing the subject as posited by the phenomenologists, fabricating a subject that evolves through the course of history. One has to dispense with the constituent subject, to get rid of the subject itself, that's to say, to arrive at an analysis which can account for the constitution of the subject within a historical framework. And this is what I would call genealogy, that is, a form of history which can account for the constitution of knowledges, discourses, domains of objects, etc., without having to make reference to a subject which is either transcendental in relation to the field of events or runs in its empty sameness throughout the course of history.[23]

The irony of this self-description is that while Foucault's work swerves from Kantian, Hegelian, and Marxist ways of accounting for the constitution of subjects, he remains obsessed with providing such an account *by asking the Kantian question*. In fact, he is interested in the operations of power only to the degree to which he can answer this subject-centered question. In his most detailed reflections on his own work, Foucault candidly states,

> I would like to say, first of all, what has been the goal of my work during the last twenty years. It has not been to analyze the phenomena of power, nor to elaborate the foundations of such an analysis.
>
> My objective, instead, has been to create a history of the different modes by which, in our culture, human beings have been made subjects . . .
>
> Thus, it is not power but the subject which is the general theme of my research.[24]

Prophetic pragmatism objects to Foucault's project not because he has no historical sense but rather because it remains truncated by the unhelpful Kantian question he starts with. Dewey and Rorty—as well as Wittgenstein and Heidegger—have shown that a question that begins, "What are the conditions for the possibility of . . ." is misleading in that the question itself is inextricably tied to a conception of validity that stands above and outside the social practices of human beings. In this regard, Foucault's answer—anonymous and autonomous discourses, disciplines, and techniques—is but the latest addition to the older ones: the dialectical development of modes of production (vulgar Marxisms); workings of the *Weltgeist* (crude Hegelians); or activities of transcendental subjects (academic Kantians).[25] All such answers shun the centrality of dynamic social practices structured and unstructured over time and space.

The second prophetic pragmatist objection is, unsurprisingly, to his reification of discourses, disciplines, and techniques. By downplaying human agency—both individual and collective human actions—Foucault surreptitiously ascribes agency to discourses, disciplines, and techniques. There indeed are multiple unintended consequences and unacknowledged antecedent conditions of human actions that both produce and are produced by institutions and structures. Methodological individualism in social theory, according to which isolated and atomistic individual actions fully account for humans' societies and histories, will not suffice. But the alternative is not the exclusive ascription of agency to impersonal forces, transcendental entities, or anonymous and autonomous discourses. For prophetic pragmatists, human agency remains central—all we have in human societies and histories are structured and unstructured human social practices over time and space. Edward Said perceptively states regarding Foucault:

> Yet despite the extraordinary worldliness of this work, Foucault takes a curiously passive and sterile view not so much of the uses of power, but of how and why power is gained, used, and held onto. This is the most dangerous consequence of his disagreement with Marxism, and its result is the least convincing aspect of his work . . . However else power may be a kind of indirect bureaucratic discipline and control, there are ascertainable changes stemming from who holds power and who dominates whom.
>
> . . . what one misses in Foucault is something resembling Gramsci's analyses of hegemony, historical blocks, ensembles of relationship done from the perspective of an engaged political worker for whom the fascinated description of exercised power is never a substitute for trying to change power relationships within society.[26]

Foucault is a political intellectual—a "specific" intellectual geared to and affiliated with local struggles rather than a "universal" intellectual representing and speaking for the interests of a class, nation, or group—yet his Kantian questions lead him to downplay human agency, to limit the revisability of discourses and disciplines, and thereby to confine his attention to a specific set of operations of power, i.e., those linked to constituting subjects. For instance, he pays little attention to operations of power in economic modes of production and nation-states.

The last prophetic pragmatist criticism of Foucault's project is that he devalues moral discourse. His fervent anti-utopianism—again in reaction to Hegelian and Marxist teleological utopianisms—rejects all forms of ends and aims for political struggle. Therefore, he replaces reform or revolution with revolt and rebellion. In this way, Foucault tends to reduce left ethics to a bold and defiant Great Refusal addressed to the dominant powers that be. Yet by failing to articulate and elaborate ideals of democracy, equality, and freedom, Foucault provides solely negative conceptions of critique and resistance. He rightly suspects the self-authorizing and self-privileging aims of "universal" intellectuals who put forward such ideals, yet he mistakenly holds that *any attempt* to posit these ideals as guides to political action and social reconstruction must fall prey to new modes of subjection and disciplinary control. Foucault rightly wants to safeguard relentless criticism and healthy skepticism, yet his rejection of even tentative aims and provisional ends results in existential rebellion or micropolitical revolt rather than concerted political praxis informed by moral vision and systemic (though flexible) analyses. In stark contrast, prophetic pragmatists take seriously moral discourse—revisable means and ends of political action, the integrity and character of those engaged, and the precious ideals of participatory democracy and the flowering of the uniqueness of different human individualities.

Therefore, prophetic pragmatists reject Foucault's Kantian question, viewing it as a wheel that turns yet plays no part in the mechanism. Instead, they move directly to strategic and tactical modes of thinking and acting.[27] These modes highlight the operations of powers and the uses of provocation for the development of human personalities. Like Foucault, prophetic pragmatists criticize and resist forms of subjection, as well as types of economic exploitation, state repression, and bureaucratic domination. But these critiques and resistances, unlike his, are unashamedly guided by moral ideals of creative democracy and individuality.

Tragedy, Tradition, and Political Praxis

A major shortcoming of Emersonian pragmatism is its optimistic theodicy. The point here is not so much that Emerson himself had no sense of the tragic but rather that the way he formulated the relation of human powers and fate, human agency and circumstances, human will and constraints made it difficult for him and for subsequent pragmatists to maintain a delicate balance between excessive optimism and exorbitant pessimism regarding human capacities. The early Emerson stands at one pole and the later Trilling at another pole. For prophetic pragmatism only the early Hook and Niebuhr—their work in the early thirties—maintain the desirable balance.

This issue of balance raises a fundamental and long-ignored issue for the progressive tradition: the issue of the complex relations between tragedy and revolution, tradition and progress. Prophetic pragmatism refuses to sidestep this issue. The brutalities and atrocities in human history, the genocidal attempts in this century, and the present-day barbarities require that those who accept the progressive and prophetic designations put forth some conception of the tragic. To pose the issue in this way is, in a sense, question begging since the very term "tragic" presupposes a variety of religious and secular background notions. Yet prophetic pragmatism is a child of Protestant Christianity wedded to left romanticism. So this question begging is warranted in that prophetic pragmatism stands in a tradition in which the notion of the "tragic" requires attention.

It is crucial to acknowledge from the start that the "tragic" is a polyvalent notion; it has different meanings depending on its context. For example, the context of Greek tragedy—in which the action of ruling families generates pity and terror in the audience—is a society that shares a collective experience of common metaphysical and social meanings. The context of modern tragedy, on the other hand—in which ordinary individuals struggle against meaninglessness and nothingness—is a fragmented society with collapsing metaphysical meanings. More pointedly, the notion of the "tragic" is bound to the idea of human agency, be the agent a person of rank or a retainer, a prince or a pauper.

> The real key, to the modern separation of tragedy from "mere suffering," is the separation of ethical control and, more critically, human agency, from our understanding of social and political life.
> . . . The events which are not seen as tragic are deep in the pattern of our own culture: war, famine, work, traffic, politics. To see no ethical content or human agency in such events, or to say that we cannot connect them with general meanings, and especially with permanent and universal meanings, is to admit a strange and particular bankruptcy, which no rhetoric of tragedy can finally hide.[28]

It is no accident that James, Hook, Niebuhr, and Trilling focused on the content and character of heroism when they initially grappled with theodicy and the "tragic." Although they had little or no interest in revolution, their preoccupation with human agency, will, and power resembles that of the Promethean romantics, e.g., Blake, Byron, Shelley. Yet the ideological sources of their conceptions of the "tragic" loom large in their deployment of the term.

James's focus on the individual and his distrust of big institutions and groups led him to envision a moral heroism in which each ameliorative step forward is a kind of victory, each minute battle won a sign that the war is not over, hence still winnable. Hook's early Marxism provided him with a historical sense in which the "tragic" requires a choice between a proven evil, i.e., capitalism, and a possible good, i.e., socialism. As the possible good proved to be more and more evil, the old "proven evil" appeared more and more good. The notion of the "tragic" in Hook underwent a metamorphosis such that all utopian quests were trashed in the name of limits, constraints, and circumstances. The later Trilling is even more extreme, for the mere exertion of will was often seen as symptomatic of the self's utopian quest for the unconditioned.

Niebuhr held the most complex view of the "tragic" in the pragmatist tradition. Even more than the middle Trilling's intriguing ruminations on Keatsian theodicy, Niebuhr's struggle with liberal Protestantism — especially with Richard Rorty's grandfather, Walter Rauschenbusch — forced him to remain on the tightrope between Promethean romanticism and Augustinian pessimism. In fact, Niebuhr never succumbs to either, nor does he ever cease to promote incessant human agency and will against limits and circumstances. In his leftist years, mindful of the novel forms of evil in the new envisioned social order yet fed up with those in the present, he supported the insurgency of exploited workers. In his liberal years, obsessed with the evil structures in the communist world and more and more (though never fully) forgetful of the institutional evil in American society, Niebuhr encourages state actions against the Soviet Union and piecemeal reformist practice within America.

Prophetic pragmatism affirms the Niebuhrian strenuous mood, never giving up on new possibilities for human agency — both individual and collective — in the present, yet situating them in light of Du Bois' social structural analyses that focus on working-class, black, and female insurgency. Following the pioneering work of Hans-Georg Gadamer and Edward Shils, prophetic pragmatism acknowledges the inescapable and inexpungible character of tradition, the burden and buoyancy of that which is transmitted from the past to the present.[29] This process of transmittance is one of socialization and appropriation, of acculturation and construction. Tradition, in this sense, can be both a smothering and a liberating affair, depending on which traditions are being invoked, internalized, and invented.

In this way, the relation of tragedy to revolution (or resistance) is intertwined with that of tradition to progress (or betterment). Prophetic pragmatism, as a form of third-wave left romanticism, tempers its utopian impulse with a profound sense of the tragic character of life and history. This sense of the tragic highlights the irreducible predicament of unique individuals who undergo dread, despair, disillusionment, disease, and death *and* the institutional forms of oppression that dehumanize people. Tragic thought is not confined solely to the plight of the individual; it also applies to social experiences of resistance, revolution, and societal reconstruction. Prophetic pragmatism is a form of tragic thought in that it confronts candidly individual and collective experiences of evil in individuals and institutions — with little expectation of ridding the world of *all* evil. Yet it is a kind of romanticism in that it holds many experiences of evil to be neither inevitable nor necessary but rather the results of human agency, i.e., choices and actions.

This interplay between tragic thought and romantic impulse, inescapable evils and transformable evils makes prophetic pragmatism seem schizophrenic. On the one hand, it appears to affirm a Sisyphean outlook in which human resistance to evil makes no progress. On the other hand, it looks as if it approves a utopian quest for paradise. In fact, prophetic pragmatism denies Sisyphean pessimism and utopian perfectionism. Rather, it promotes the possibility of human progress and the human impossibility of paradise. This progress results from principled and protracted Promethean efforts, yet even such efforts are no guarantee. And all human struggles—including successful ones—against specific forms of evil produce new, though possibly lesser, forms of evil. Human struggle sits at the center of prophetic pragmatism, a struggle guided by a democratic and libertarian vision, sustained by moral courage and existential integrity, and tempered by the recognition of human finitude and frailty. It calls for utopian energies and tragic actions, energies and actions that yield permanent and perennial revolutionary, rebellious, and reformist strategies that oppose the status quos of our day. These strategies are never to become ends-in-themselves, but rather to remain means through which are channeled moral outrage and human desperation in the face of prevailing forms of evil in human societies and in human lives. Such outrage must never cease, and such desperation will never disappear, yet without revolutionary, rebellious, and reformist strategies, credible and effective opposition wanes. Prophetic pragmatism attempts to keep alive the sense of alternative ways of life and of struggle based on the best of the past. In this sense, the praxis of prophetic pragmatism is tragic action with revolutionary intent, usually reformist consequences, and always visionary outlook. It concurs with Raymond Williams' tragic revolutionary perspective:

> The tragic action, in its deepest sense, is not the confirmation of disorder, but its experience, its comprehension and its resolution. In our own time, this action is general, and its common name is revolution. We have to see the evil and the suffering, in the factual disorder that makes revolution necessary, and in the disordered struggle against the disorder. We have to recognize this suffering in a close and immediate experience, and not cover it with names. But we follow the whole action: not only the evil, but the men who have fought against evil; not only the crisis, but the energy released by it, the spirit learned in it. We make the connections, because that is the action of tragedy, and what we learn in suffering is again revolution, because we acknowledge others as men and any such acknowledgement is the beginning of struggle, as the continuing reality of our lives. Then to see revolution in this tragic perspective is the only way to maintain it.[30]

This oppositional consciousness draws its sustenance principally from a tradition of resistance. To keep alive a sense of alternative ways of life and of struggle requires memory of those who prefigured such life and struggle in the past. In this sense, tradition is to be associated not solely with ignorance and intolerance, prejudice and parochialism, dogmatism and docility. Rather, tradition is also to be identified with insight and intelligence, rationality and resistance, critique and contestation. Tradition per se is never a problem, but rather those traditions that have been and are hegemonic over other traditions. All that human beings basically have are traditions—those institutions and practices, values and sensibilities, stories and symbols, ideas and metaphors that shape human identities, attitudes, outlooks, and dispositions. These traditions are dynamic, malleable, and revisable, yet all changes in a tradition are done in light of some old or newly emerging tradition. Innovation presupposes some tradition and inaugurates another tradition. The profound historical consciousness of prophetic pragmatism shuns the Emersonian devaluing of the past. Yet it also highlights those elements of old and new traditions that promote innovation and resistance for the aims of enhancing individuality and expanding democracy. This enhancement and expansion constitute human progress. And all such progress takes place within the contours of clashing traditions. In this way, just as tragic action constitutes resistance to prevailing status quos, the critical treatment and nurturing of a tradition yield human progress. Tragedy can be an impetus rather than an impediment to oppositional activity; tradition may serve as a stimulus rather than a stumbling block to human progress.

Prophetic pragmatism understands the Emersonian swerve from epistemology—and the American evasion of philosophy—not as a wholesale rejection of philosophy but rather as a reconception of philosophy as a form of cultural criticism that attempts to transform linguistic, social, cultural, and political traditions for the purposes of increasing the scope of individual development and democratic operations. Prophetic pragmatism conceives of philosophy as a historically circumscribed quest for wisdom that puts forward new interpretations of the world based on past traditions in order to promote existential sustenance and political relevance. Like Emerson and earlier pragmatists, it views truth as a species of the good, as that which enhances the flourishing of human progress. This does not mean that philosophy ignores the ugly facts and unpleasant realities of life and history. Rather, it highlights these facts and realities precisely because they provoke doubt, curiosity, outrage, or desperation that motivates efforts to overcome them. These efforts take the forms of critique and praxis, forms that attempt to change what is into a better what can be.

Prophetic pragmatism closely resembles and, in some ways, converges with the metaphilosophical perspectives of Antonio Gramsci. Both conceive of philosophical activity as "a cultural battle to transform the popular 'mentality.' "[31] It is not surprising that Gramsci writes:

What the pragmatists wrote about this question merits re-examination
. . . they felt real needs and "described" them with an exactness that
was not far off the mark, even if they did not succeed in posing the problems fully or in providing a solution.[32]

Prophetic pragmatism is inspired by the example of Antonio Gramsci principally because he is the major twentieth-century philosopher of praxis,
power, and provocation without devaluing theory, adopting unidimen-
sional conceptions of power, or reducing provocation to Clausewitzian
calculations of warfare. Gramsci's work is historically specific, theoretically engaging, and politically activistic in an exemplary manner. His concrete and detailed investigations are grounded in and reflections upon
local struggles, yet theoretically sensitive to structural dynamics and international phenomena. He is attuned to the complex linkage of socially
constructed identities to human agency while still convinced of the crucial
role of the ever-changing forms in class-ridden economic modes of production. Despite his fluid Leninist conception of political organization and
mobilization (which downplays the democratic and libertarian values of
prophetic pragmatists) and his unswerving allegiance to sophisticated
Marxist social theory (which is an indispensable yet ultimately inadequate
weapon for prophetic pragmatists), Gramsci exemplifies the critical spirit
and oppositional sentiments of prophetic pragmatism.

This is seen most clearly in Gramsci's view of the relation of philosophy
to "common sense." For him, the aim of philosophy is not only to become
worldly by imposing its elite intellectual views upon people, but to become
part of a social movement by nourishing and being nourished by the philosophical views of oppressed people themselves for the aims of social change
and personal meaning. Gramsci viewed this mutually critical process in
world-historical terms.

> From the disintegration of Hegelianism derives the beginning of a new
> cultural process, different in character from its predecessors, a process
> in which practical movement and theoretical thought are united (or are
> trying to unite through a struggle that is both theoretical and practical).
>
> It is not important that this movement had its origins in mediocre
> philosophical works or, at best, in works that were not philosophical
> masterpieces. What matters is that a new way of conceiving the world
> and man is born and that this conception is no longer reserved to the
> great intellectuals, to professional philosophers, but tends rather to
> become a popular, mass phenomenon, with a concretely world-wide
> character, capable of modifying (even if the result includes hybrid com-
> binations) popular thought and mummified popular culture.
>
> One should not be surprised if this beginning arises from the con-
> vergence of various elements, apparently heterogeneous . . . Indeed, it is
> worth noting that such an overthrow could not but have connections
> with religion.[33]

Gramsci's bold suggestion here relates elite philosophical activity to the cultures of the oppressed in the name of a common effort for social change. Prophetic pragmatist sensibilities permit (or even encourage) this rejection of the arrogant scientistic self-privileging or haughty secular self-images of many modern philosophers and intellectuals. The point here is not that serious contemporary thinkers should surrender their critical intelligence, but rather that they should not demand that all peoples mimic their version of critical intelligence, especially if common efforts for social change can be strengthened. On this point, even the nuanced secularism of Edward Said—the most significant and salient Gramscian critic on the American intellectual scene today—can be questioned.[34] For Gramsci, ideologies of secularism or religions are less sets of beliefs and values, attitudes and sensibilities and more ways of life and ways of struggle manufactured and mobilized by certain sectors of the population in order to legitimate and preserve their social, political, and intellectual powers. Hence, the universities and churches, schools and synagogues, mass media and mosques become crucial terrain for ideological and political contestation. And philosophers are in no way exempt from this fierce battle— even within the "serene" walls and halls of the academy. Similar to the American pragmatist tradition, Gramsci simply suggests that philosophers more consciously posit these battles themselves as objects of investigation and thereby intervene in these battles with intellectual integrity and ideological honesty.

Prophetic pragmatism purports to be not only an oppositional cultural criticism but also a material force for individuality and democracy. By "material force" I simply mean a practice that has some potency and effect or makes a difference in the world. There is—and should be—no such thing as a prophetic pragmatist movement. The translation of philosophic outlook into social motion is not that simple. In fact, it is possible to be a prophetic pragmatist and belong to different political movements, e.g., feminist, Chicano, black, socialist, left-liberal ones. It also is possible to subscribe to prophetic pragmatism and belong to different religious and/or secular traditions. This is so because a prophetic pragmatist commitment to individuality and democracy, historical consciousness and systemic social analyses, and tragic action in an evil-ridden world can take place in— though usually on the margin of—a variety of traditions. The distinctive hallmarks of a prophetic pragmatist are a universal consciousness that promotes an all-embracing democratic and libertarian moral vision, a historical consciousness that acknowledges human finitude and conditionedness, and a critical consciousness which encourages relentless critique and self-criticism for the aims of social change and personal humility.

My own version of prophetic pragmatism is situated within the Christian tradition. Unlike Gramsci, I am religious not simply for political aims but also by personal commitment. To put it crudely, I find existential

sustenance in many of the narratives in the biblical scriptures as inter-
preted by streams in the Christian heritage; and I see political relevance
in the biblical focus on the plight of the wretched of the earth. Needless
to say, without the addition of modern intepretations of racial and gender
equality, tolerance, and democracy, much of the tradition warrants rejection. Yet the Christian epic, stripped of static dogmas and decrepit doctrines, remains a rich source of existential empowerment and political
engagement when viewed through modern lenses (indeed the only ones
we moderns have!).

Like James, Niebuhr, and to some extent Du Bois, I hold a religious
conception of pragmatism. I have dubbed it "prophetic" in that it harks
back to the Jewish and Christian tradition of prophets who brought urgent
and compassionate critique to bear on the evils of their day. The mark
of the prophet is to speak the truth in love with courage—come what
may. Prophetic pragmatism proceeds from this impulse. It neither requires
a religious foundation nor entails a religious perspective, yet prophetic
pragmatism is compatible with certain religious outlooks.

My kind of prophetic pragmatism is located in the Christian tradition
for two basic reasons. First, on the existential level, the self-understanding
and self-identity that flow from this tradition's insights into the crises and
traumas of life are indispensable *for me* to remain sane. It holds at bay
the sheer absurdity so evident in life, without erasing or eliding the tragedy
of life. Like Kierkegaard, whose reflections on Christian faith were so profound yet often so frustrating, I do not think it possible to put forward
rational defenses of one's faith that verify its veracity or even persuade
one's critics. Yet it is possible to convey to others the sense of deep empti-
ness and pervasive meaninglessness one feels if one is not critically aligned
with an enabling tradition. One risks not logical inconsistency but actual
insanity; the issue is not reason or irrationality but life or death. Of course,
the fundamental philosophical question remains whether the Christian
gospel is ultimately true.[35] And, as a Christian prophetic pragmatist whose
focus is on coping with transient and provisional penultimate matters yet
whose hope goes beyond them, I reply in the affirmative, bank my all
on it, yet am willing to entertain the possibility in low moments that I
may be deluded.

Second, on the political level, the culture of the wretched of the earth
is deeply religious. To be in solidarity with them requires not only an
acknowledgment of what they are up against but also an appreciation
of how they cope with their situation. This appreciation does not require
that one be religious; but if one is religious, one has wider access into
their life-worlds. This appreciation also does not entail an uncritical acceptance of religious narratives, their interpretations, or, most important, their
often oppressive consequences. Yet to be religious permits one to devote
one's life to accenting the prophetic and progressive potential within those

traditions that shape the everyday practices and deeply held perspectives of most oppressed peoples. What a wonderful privilege and vocation this is!

The prophetic religious person, much like C. Wright Mills's activist intellectual, puts a premium on educating and being educated by struggling peoples, organizing and being organized by resisting groups. This political dimension of prophetic pragmatism as practiced within the Christian tradition impels one to be an organic intellectual, that is, one who revels in the life of the mind yet relates ideas to collective praxis. An organic intellectual, in contrast to traditional intellectuals who often remain comfortably nested in the academy, attempts to be entrenched in and affiliated with organizations, associations, and, possibly, movements of grass-roots folk. Of course, he or she need be neither religious nor linked to religious institutions. Trade unions, community groups, and political formations also suffice. Yet, since the Enlightenment in eighteenth-century Europe, most of the progressive energies among the intelligentsia have shunned religious channels. And in these days of global religious revivals, progressive forces are reaping the whirlwind. Those of us who remain in these religious channels see clearly just how myopic such an antireligious strategy is. The severing of ties to churches, synagogues, temples, and mosques by the left intelligentsia is tantamount to political suicide; it turns the pessimism of many self-deprecating and self-pitying secular progressive intellectuals into a self-fulfilling prophecy. This point was never grasped by C. Wright Mills, though W. E. B. Du Bois understood it well.

Like Gramsci, Du Bois remained intimately linked with oppositional forces in an oppressed community. And in his case, these forces were (and are) often led by prophetic figures of the black Christian tradition. To be a part of the black freedom movement is to rub elbows with some prophetic black preachers and parishioners. And to be a part of the forces of progress in America is to rub up against some of these black freedom fighters.

If prophetic pragmatism is ever to become more than a conversational subject matter for cultural critics in and out of the academy, it must inspire progressive and prophetic social motion. One precondition of this kind of social movement is the emergence of potent prophetic religious practices in churches, synagogues, temples, and mosques. And given the historical weight of such practices in the American past, the probable catalyst for social motion will be the prophetic wing of the black church. Need we remind ourselves that the most significant and successful organic intellectual in twentieth-century America—maybe in American history—was a product of and leader in the prophetic wing of the black church? Rarely has a figure in modern history outside of elected public office linked the life of the mind to social change with such moral persuasiveness and political effectiveness.

The social movement led by Martin Luther King, Jr., represents the best of what the political dimension of prophetic pragmatism is all about.

Like Sojourner Truth, Walter Rauschenbusch, Elizabeth Cady Stanton, and Dorothy Day, King was not a prophetic pragmatist. Yet like them he was a prophet, in which role he contributed mightily to the political project of prophetic pragmatism. His all-embracing moral vision facilitated alliances and coalitions across racial, gender, class, and religious lines. His Gandhian method of nonviolent resistance highlighted forms of love, courage, and discipline worthy of a compassionate prophet. And his appropriation and interpretation of American civil religion extended the tradition of American jeremiads, a tradition of public exhortation that joins social criticisms of America to moral renewal and admonishes the country to be true to its founding ideals of freedom, equality, and democracy. King accented the antiracist and anti-imperialist consequences of taking seriously these ideals, thereby linking the struggle for freedom in America to those movements in South Africa, Poland, South Korea, Ethiopia, Chile, and the Soviet Union.

Prophetic pragmatism worships at no ideological altars. It condemns oppression anywhere and everywhere, be it the brutal butchery of third-world dictators, the regimentation and repression of peoples in the Soviet Union and Soviet-bloc countries, or the racism, patriarchy, homophobia, and economic injustice in the first-world capitalist nations. In this way, the precious ideals of individuality and democracy of prophetic pragmatism oppose all those power structures that lack public accountability, be they headed by military generals, bureaucratic party bosses, or corporate tycoons. Nor is prophetic pragmatism confined to any preordained historical agent, such as the working class, black people, or women. Rather, it invites all people of goodwill both here and abroad to fight for an Emersonian culture of creative democracy in which the plight of the wretched of the earth is alleviated.

Prophetic Pragmatism and Postmodernity

Prophetic pragmatism emerges at a particular moment in the history of North Atlantic civilization—the moment of postmodernity. A critical self-inventory of prophetic pragmatism—a historical situating of its emergence and possible development—requires an understanding of this postmodern moment.

Postmodernity can be understood in light of three fundamental historical processes. First, the end of the European Age (1492–1945) shattered European self-confidence and prompted intense self-criticism, even self-contempt. This monumental decentering of Europe produced exemplary intellectual reflections such as the demystifying of European cultural hegemony, the destruction of the Western metaphysical traditions, and the deconstruction of North Atlantic philosophical systems. Second, in the wake of European devastation and decline and upon the eclipse of

European domination, the United States of America emerged as the world power with respect to military might, economic prosperity, political direction, and cultural production. Third, the advent of national political independence in Asia and Africa signaled the first stage of the decolonization of the third world.

Much of the current "postmodernism" debate, be it in architecture, literature, painting, photography, criticism, or philosophy, highlights the themes of difference, marginality, otherness, transgression, disruption, and simulation. Unfortunately, most of the treatments of these issues remain narrowly focused on the European and Euro-American predicament. For example, Jean-François Lyotard's celebrated and influential book *The Postmodern Condition* defines postmodernism as a progressive loss of faith in master narratives, e.g., religion, Marxism, liberalism; a rejection of representation in epistemic outlook; and a demand for radical artistic experimentation. For Lyotard, postmodernism becomes a recurring moment within the modern that is performative in character and aesthetic in content. The major sources from which Lyotard borrows—Kant's notion of the sublime and Wittgenstein's idea of language games—are deployed to promote certain modernist practices, namely, nonrepresentational, experimental techniques and viewpoints that shun and shatter quests for wholeness and totality.

Although both Jacques Derrida and Michel Foucault reject the term "postmodernism," their philosophies are widely viewed as major examples of postmodern thought. As with their fellow Frenchman Lyotard, Eurocentric frameworks and modernist loyalties loom large in the work of Derrida and Foucault. Derrida's deconstructionist version of poststructuralism accents the transgressive and disruptive aspects of Nietzsche and Heidegger, Mallarmé and Artaud. As an Algerian Jew in a French Catholic (and anti-Semitic) society, Derrida attacks the major philosophic traditions of the West in the form of fascinating though ultimately monotonous deconstructions. This version of relentless skepticism toward logical consistency and theoretical coherence, which refuses to entertain or encourage novel reconstructions, may be symptomatic of the relative political impotence of marginal peoples, their inability to creatively transform and build on the ambiguous legacy of the Age of Europe.

Foucault provides rich social and historical substance to contemporary inquiries into the operations of otherness and marginality in his studies on the insane and the incarcerated. But even the "others" he investigates remain within European (usually French) boundaries. His heroes, like those of Derrida, are transgressive modernists such as Nietzsche and Bataille. Needless to say, the prominent opponents of "postmodernism"—Jürgen Habermas from the moderate left and Hilton Kramer from the far right—invoke past European projects, that is, the German Enlightenment and Anglo-American modernism, respectively.

Noteworthy attempts to broaden the "postmodernism" debate from its current focus on architecture and painting to post–World War II American cultural practices and artifacts in general can be seen in the work of William Spanos and the early Paul Bové.[36] In their illuminating neo-Heideggerian readings of American poets like Wallace Stevens, Robert Creeley, and Charles Olson, postmodern formulations of temporality, difference, and heterogeneity are put forward. Yet both Spanos and Bové remain at the level of philosophic outlooks and artistic strategies; that is, they understand postmodernism as a complex set of sensibilities, styles, or worldviews. This observation holds for the pioneering work of Rosalind Krauss.[37]

The significant breakthroughs of Fredric Jameson, Craig Owens, Hal Foster, and Andreas Huyssen are to push the "postmodernism" debate beyond narrow disciplinary boundaries, insulated artistic practices, and vague pronouncements of men and women of letters.[38] Instead of viewing "postmodernism" as a set of styles, sensibilities, or viewpoints, they posit "postmodernism" as a social category, a cultural dominant. They understand "postmodernism" as embracing certain exemplary social and cultural responses to new structural and institutional processes at work in the world.

For example, Jameson views such prevalent social and cultural features as depthlessness, ubiquitous images and simulacra, waning historical consciousness, escalating emotional intensities, schizophrenic subjects, and the breakdown of the distinction between high and low cultures as having been shaped by and as shaping advanced capitalist societies in which commodity production has a hold over all spheres of contemporary life. The important point here is not whether one fully agrees with Jameson's laundry list of postmodern constitutive characteristics or whether one approves of his treatments of individual cultural artifacts. Rather, what is salutary about Jameson's project is that he forces the debate to become more consciously historical, social, political, and ideological. Jameson helps situate the emergence of the "postmodernism" debate in relation to larger developments in society and history by providing a heuristic framework (in his case, a Marxist one) that discloses its broader significance.

Prophetic pragmatism arrives on the scene as a particular American intervention conscious and critical of its roots, and radically historical and political in its outlook. Furthermore, it gives prominence to the plight of those peoples who embody and enact the "postmodern" themes of degraded otherness, subjected alienness, and subaltern marginality, that is, the wretched of the earth (poor peoples of color, women, workers).

Prophetic pragmatism is a deeply American response to the end of the Age of Europe, the emergence of the United States as the world power, and the decolonization of the third world. The response is "American" not simply because it appropriates and promotes the major American tradition of cultural criticism, but also because it is shaped by the immediate

American intellectual situation. This situation is not a "closing of the American mind," as nostalgically and tendentiously understood by Allan Bloom's popular work. Rather, it is a complex configuration of the effects on American intellectual life of the decentering of Europe, the centering of the United States, and the decolonizing of Asia and Africa.

The first consequence of these three historical processes for American intellectual life was the emergence of the first major subcultures of non-WASP intellectuals as exemplified in the so-called New York intellectuals, the abstract expressionist group, or the bebop jazz artists. These subcultures constituted a major challenge to an American male WASP cultural elite loyal to an older and eroding European model of culture, that of a genteel tradition. Irving Babbitt's fervent defense of highbrow humanism in the academy and Royal Cortissoz's philistine trashing of modernism outside of the academy represent two distant poles of this declining genteel tradition.

The first significant and salutary blow consisted of the entrance of gifted assimilated Jewish Americans like Lionel Trilling into the higher echelons of the academy, especially the fervently anti-Semitic Ivy League institutions of the forties. This development signified the slow but sure undoing of male WASP cultural harmony and homogeneity. Furthermore, the postwar American economic boom laid the groundwork for expansion, professionalization, and specialization in institutions of higher education, forcing humanistic scholars to forge self-images of rigor and scientific seriousness. New methods that helped create such self-images included the close reading techniques of New Criticism in literature, the logical precision of reasoning in analytic philosophy, and the theoretical jargon of Parsonian structural functionalism in sociology. Only the new programs of American studies in the fifties provided academic space for broad cultural criticism, criticism that often remained rather muted owing to the repressive atmosphere of McCarthyism.

The sixties constitute the watershed period in contemporary American intellectual life. The inclusion of Afro-Americans, Spanish-speaking Americans, Asian Americans, Native Americans, American women, and working-class white men in significant numbers in the academy shattered male WASP cultural pretension and predominance. Accompanied by great fanfare and tremendous turbulence, often at the expense of intellectual seriousness on the part of both defenders and opponents of the status quo, this development revealed the pervasive political character of academic life in America. The sixties did not simply politicize American intellectual life; rather, they repoliticized in an explicit manner what had been political in an implicit manner. The consequent disorienting intellectual polemics and inescapable ideological polarization that tend to reduce complex formulations and traduce genuine conversations have been a lasting legacy of the sixties. It was initiated by the worst of the New Left and has been perfected by the best of the New Right.

Another intellectual legacy of the sixties is the American obsession with theories from continental Europe. These theories internationalized American humanistic discourses, yet also turned American intellectuals away from their own national traditions of thought. Only in historiography did American intellectuals dig deep to recover and revise the understanding of the U.S. past in light of those on its underside. A final legacy was the onslaught of forms of popular culture, such as TV and film, on highbrow literate culture. Academic humanists were rendered marginal to the intellectual life of the country, displaced by journalists usually ill equipped for the task yet eager to speak to an ever-growing middlebrow audience.

The academic inclusion on a grand scale of the students of color, working-class origins, and women produced ideologies of institutional pluralism to mediate between the clashing methods and perspectives in the structurally fragmented humanistic departments and programs. Dissensus reigned and reigns supreme. Pluralism served both to contain and often to conceal unsolvable ideological conflict; yet it also ensured a few slots for ambitious and upwardly mobile young left professors enchanted with their bold oppositional rhetoric even as they remained too anxious to retain their professional-managerial class status to be anything but politically innocuous in larger American society. The influential conservative strategy was to attack this academic inclusion of the "new barbarians" in the name of standards, tradition, and cultural literacy. Ironically, both the right and left critics posit academicism and commercialism as major culprits in American intellectual life.

Prophetic pragmatism is a form of American left thought and action in our postmodern moment. It is deeply indebted to the continental traveling theories such as Marxism, structuralism, and poststructuralism, yet it remains in the American grain. It is rooted in the best of American radicalism but refuses to be simply another polemical position on the ideological spectrum. Prophetic pragmatism calls for reinvigoration of a sane, sober, and sophisticated intellectual life in America and for regeneration of social forces empowering the disadvantaged, degraded, and dejected. It rejects the faddish cynicism and fashionable conservatism rampant in the intelligentsia and general populace. Prophetic pragmatism rests upon the conviction that the American evasion of philosophy is not an evasion of serious thought and moral action. Rather such evasion is a rich and revisable tradition that serves as the occasion for cultural criticism and political engagement in the service of an Emersonian culture of creative democracy.

Notes and Index

NOTES

Chapter 1. The Emersonian Prehistory of American Pragmatism

1. The two major recent attempts to reflect upon this "swerve" are Stanley Cavell's "Thinking of Emerson" and "An Emerson Mood" in *The Senses of Walden*, 2d ed. (San Francisco: North Point Press, 1981), pp. 123–38, 141–60; and Harold Bloom's *Agon: Towards a Theory of Revisionism* (New York: Oxford University Press, 1982), pp. 16–51, 145–78.

2. Emerson himself notes in his *Journals*, "My reasoning faculty is proportionately weak" and speaks of a "logical mode of thinking & speaking – which I do not possess, & may not reasonably hope to obtain." Instead, Emerson speaks of his "moral imagination" and of "a passionate love for the strains of eloquence." *Emerson in His Journals*, selected and edited by Joel Porte (Cambridge: Harvard University Press, 1982), pp. 45, 46. For evidence of this lack of rigor, see David Van Leer, *Emerson's Epistemology: The Argument of the Essays* (New York: Cambridge University Press, 1986).

3. "That idea which I approach & am magnetized by – is my country." *Emerson in His Journals*, p. 321.

4. If there is an overriding theme in Emerson's thought, it is encapsulated in the famous concluding words of his essay "Experience": "The true romance which the world exists to realize will be the transformation of genius into practical power." *Selected Writings of Ralph Waldo Emerson*, ed. William H. Gilman (New York: New American Library, 1965), pp. 347–48.

5. "Every man is not so much a workman in the world, as he is a suggestion of that he should be. Men walk as prophecies of the next age . . . Step by step we scale this mysterious ladder: the steps are actions; the new prospect is power . . . The only sin is limitation." "Circles," *Selected Writings of Ralph Waldo Emerson*, pp. 298, 299. "Society is fluid." "Politics," ibid., p. 349. "The plasticity of the tough old planet is wonderful." "Journals and Letters," ibid., p. 179.

6. The pertinent texts are John Jay Chapman, "Emerson," *Selected Writings of John Jay Chapman*, ed. Jacques Barzun (New York: Funk and Wagnalls, Minerva Press, 1968); Quentin Anderson, "The Failure of the Fathers," *The Imperial Self: An Essay in American Literary and Cultural History* (New York: Alfred A. Knopf, 1971), pp. 3–58; O. W. Firkins, *Ralph Waldo Emerson* (Boston: Houghton Mifflin, 1915); Stephen E. Whicher, *Freedom and Fate: An Inner Life of Ralph Waldo Emerson*

(Philadelphia: University of Pennsylvania Press, 1953); Joel Porte, *Representative Man: Emerson in His Time* (New York: Oxford University Press, 1979); Sherman Paul, *Emerson's Angle of Vision* (Cambridge: Harvard University Press, 1952); F. O. Matthiessen, *American Renaissance: Art and Expression in the Age of Emerson and Whitman* (New York: Oxford University Press, 1941); B. L. Packer, *Emerson's Fall: A New Interpretation of the Major Essays* (New York: Continuum, 1982).

7. Henry James makes this point when he notes the "thinness of the New England atmosphere" and the "terrible paucity of alternatives," and when he claims that Emerson's America was "not fertile in variations." "The Correspondence of Carlyle and Emerson" and "Emerson," *Henry James: The American Essays*, ed. Leon Edel (New York: Vintage, 1956), pp. 31–51, 51–76. The quotes are found on pp. 45, 56.

8. These four influential views of Emerson are put forward by George Santayana, Quentin Anderson, Harold Bloom, and Sacvan Bercovitch, respectively. See George Santayana, "The Genteel Tradition in American Philosophy," *Winds of Doctrine* (London: J. M. Dent and Sons, 1913), pp. 186–215; Anderson, *Imperial Self*, pp. 3–58; Harold Bloom, *Poetry and Repression: Revisionism from Blake to Stevens* (New Haven: Yale University Press, 1976), pp. 235–66; Sacvan Bercovitch, *The American Jeremiad* (Madison: University of Wisconsin Press, 1979), pp. 182–205.

9. Ralph Waldo Emerson, *The American Scholar*, *Selected Writings of Ralph Waldo Emerson*, pp. 238, 239–40.

10. For a powerful interpretation of this idea, see Sacvan Bercovitch, "Emerson the Prophet: Romanticism, Puritanism, and Auto-American–Biography," in *Ralph Waldo Emerson*, ed. Harold Bloom (New York: Chelsea House, 1985), pp. 29–40.

11. Emerson, *American Scholar*, p. 240.

12. Ibid., pp. 236, 240.

13. Quoted in Gay Wilson Allen, *Waldo Emerson* (New York: Penguin Books, 1982), p. 381.

14. Ibid., p. 495.

15. Ibid., p. 545.

16. Ibid., p. 554.

17. Ibid., p. 555. See also *Emerson in His Journals*, p. 426. Regarding the immorality of slavery, Emerson had written as early as February 2, 1835: "Let Christianity speak ever for the poor and the low. Though the voice of society should demand a defence of slavery from all its organs that service can never be expected from me. My opinion is of no worth, but I have not a syllable of all the language I have learned, to utter for the planter. If by opposing slavery I go to undermine institutions, I confess I do not wish to live in a nation where slavery exists." *Emerson in His Journals*, p. 136.

18. Ralph Waldo Emerson, "Politics," *Selected Writings of Ralph Waldo Emerson*, pp. 352–53.

19. *Emerson in His Journals*, p. 354. Note also his quip "America is the idea of emancipation" (p. 428).

20. Ralph Waldo Emerson, *Nature*, *Selected Writings of Ralph Waldo Emerson*, pp. 186–87.

21. Ralph Waldo Emerson, "Circles," *Selected Writings of Ralph Waldo Emerson*, pp. 296, 305.

22. Emerson, *Nature*, pp. 222, 223.

23. Ibid., pp. 221, 222–23.

24. Emerson, "Circles," p. 299.

25. This formulation is my Emersonian revision of Santayana's famous characterization of Calvinism: "Calvinism, essentially, asserts three things: that sin exists, that sin is punished, and that it is beautiful that sin should exist to be punished." "Genteel Tradition in American Philosophy," p. 189.

26. Sydney E. Ahlstrom, A Religious History of the American People (New Haven: Yale University Press, 1972), p. 605. Bloom, Agon, p. 145.

27. This quote comes from Santayana's description of the typical American idealist: "Idealism in the American accordingly goes hand in hand with present contentment and with foresight of what the future very likely will actually bring. He is not a revolutionist; he believes he is already on the right track and moving towards an excellent destiny. In revolutionists, on the contrary, idealism is founded on dissatisfaction and expresses it." "Materialism and Idealism in American Life," Character and Opinion in the United States (1920; New York: Norton Library, 1967), p. 176.

28. Emerson, "Politics," p. 354. This vague political position can be described as a thorough libertarian view with significant though limited left substance and strong anarchist leanings.

29. Emerson, Nature, p. 189.

30. Cavell, "Thinking of Emerson" and "Emerson Mood," pp. 126, 154. See also Emerson, "Experience," p. 341.

31. Emerson, "Experience," pp. 342, 344, 346.

32. Bloom, Agon, p. 19.

33. Michael Lopez, "Transcendental Failure: 'The Palace of Spiritual Power,'" in Emerson: Prospect and Retrospect, ed. Joel Porte (Cambridge: Harvard University Press, 1982), p. 140. A relevant passage from Emerson is: "I wish that war as peace shall bring out the genius of the men . . . War, I know, is not an unmitigated evil: It is a potent alternative, tonic, magnetizer, reinforces manly power a hundred and a thousand times. I see it come as a frosty October, which shall restore intellectual and moral power to these languid and dissipated populations." Emerson in His Journals, p. 512. Note also his quip "Sometimes gunpowder smells good," in Allen, Waldo Emerson, p. 608.

34. Emerson in His Journals, p. 426.

35. Richard Slotkin, The Fatal Environment: The Myth of the Frontier in the Age of Industrialization, 1800–1890 (New York: Atheneum, 1985), pp. 33–47. Earlier crude treatments of this myth that highlight its socio-economic basis are: Bernard Smith, Forces in American Criticism (New York: Harcourt, Brace, 1939), pp. 95–114; V. F. Calverton, The Liberation of American Literature (New York: Scribners, 1932), pp. 244–57; Ernest Marchand, "Emerson and the Frontier," American Literature, 3, no. 2 (May 1931), 149–74.

36. Ralph Waldo Emerson, "Self-Reliance," Selected Writings of Ralph Waldo Emerson, pp. 269–70.

37. Ibid., p. 278.

38. The phrase "omnivorous consciousness" comes from Anderson, Imperial Self, p. 58; "digestion of vacancy" is found in Santayana, "Genteel Tradition in American Philosophy," p. 192.

39. See Lopez, "Transcendental Failure," p. 152. Emerson wrote, "I dreamed that I floated at will in the great Ether, and I saw this world floating also not

far off, but diminished to the size of an apple. Then an angel took it in his hand and brought it to me and said, 'This must thou eat.' And I ate the world."

40. These important themes have been invoked in a suggestive though not thorough manner by major scholars in Emerson studies. See, for example, Stephen E. Whicher, "Emerson's Tragic Sense," in *Emerson: A Collection of Critical Essays*, ed. Milton R. Konvitz and Stephen E. Whicher (Englewood Cliffs, N.J.: Prentice-Hall, 1962), pp. 39-45; Newton Arvin, "The House of Pain: Emerson and the Tragic Sense," in ibid., pp. 46-59; George Santayana, "Emerson," in ibid., pp. 31-38.

41. Quoted in Lopez, "Transcendental Failure," pp. 130-31.

42. Quoted in Allen, *Waldo Emerson*, p. 365.

43. *Emerson in His Journals*, pp. 246, 247, 248.

44. Allen, *Waldo Emerson*, pp. 315, 363.

45. Henry Nash Smith, "Emerson's Problem of Vocation," in *Emerson: A Collection of Critical Essays*, pp. 63-64.

46. Even Emerson's active role in the abolitionist movement was radically inadequate in his own eyes. This sense surfaces in one of his notebooks: "I waked at night, and bemoaned myself, because I had not thrown myself into this deplorable question of slavery, which seems to want nothing so much as a few assured voices. But then, in hours of sanity, I recover myself, and say, God must govern His own world, and knows His way out of this pit, without my desertion of my post which has none to guard it but me. I have quite other slaves to free than those negroes — imprisoned spirits, imprisoned thoughts, far back in the brain of man . . ." *The Journals and Miscellaneous Notebooks of Ralph Waldo Emerson*, Vol. 13, ed. Ralph H. Orth and Alfred R. Ferguson (Cambridge: Harvard University Press, 1977), p. 80.

47. Allen, *Waldo Emerson*, p. 591.

48. *Emerson in His Journals*, pp. 129, 508, 509. *Selected Writings of Ralph Waldo Emerson*, p. 178.

49. Santayana, "Emerson," p. 36.

50. *Emerson in His Journals*, pp. 157, 439. Emerson, *Selected Writings of Ralph Waldo Emerson*, p. 141.

51. This dimension of Emerson's thought is captured by the renowned Belgium Catholic mystical dramatist Maurice Maeterlinck in *On Emerson and Other Essays* (New York, 1912), p. 50: "Emerson has come to affirm simply this equal and secret grandeur of our life. He has encompassed us with silence and with wonder."

52. Quoted in Arvin, "House of Pain," p. 59.

53. *Emerson in His Journals*, p. 283.

54. Emerson, "Experience," p. 341.

55. Lopez, "Transcendental Failure," p. 141.

56. Jean-Christophe Agnew, *Worlds Apart: The Market and the Theater in Anglo-American Thought, 1550-1750* (New York: Cambridge University Press, 1986), p. 4.

57. Ibid., pp. 97-98. The Emerson quip is from "Experience," p. 336. Note also the claim of Henry James, Sr. — good friend of Emerson and father of William James — that Emerson had "no private personality." Henry James, Sr., "Mr. Emerson," *Henry James, Sr.*, ed. Giles Gunn (Chicago: American Library Association, 1974), p. 249.

58. Quoted in Allen, *Waldo Emerson*, p. 293.

59. Quoted in Michael T. Gilmore, "Emerson and the Persistence of the Commodity," in *Emerson: Prospect and Retrospect*, p. 73.

60. Ibid., p. 67.

61. Ibid., p. 68.

62. Ibid., p. 70.

63. Ibid. *Emerson in His Journals*, p. 403. For Gilmore's most recent discussion on the impact of commodity exchange on Emerson's thought, see *American Romanticism and the Marketplace* (Chicago: University of Chicago Press, 1985), pp. 18–34.

64. Quoted in Lopez, "Transcendental Failure," p. 126.

65. *Emerson in His Journals*, p. 236.

66. Philip Nicoloff, *Emerson on Race and History* (New York: Columbia University Press, 1961), p. 124.

67. *Emerson in His Journals*, p. 194.

68. Ibid., p. 338.

69. Ibid., pp. 19, 20, 21.

70. Ibid., p. 44.

71. Ibid., p. 245.

72. Ibid., p. 329.

73. *The Journals and Miscellaneous Notebooks of Ralph Waldo Emerson*, Vol. 12, ed. Linda Allardt (Cambridge: Harvard University Press, 1976), p. 152. Note also his letter to Thomas Carlyle regarding the latter's *The Nigger Question* and *Latter-Day Pamphlets* in *The Correspondence of Thomas Carlyle and Ralph Waldo Emerson, 1834–1872*, Vol. 2 (Chatto, Windus, and Piccadilly, 1883), p. 192n.

74. *Selected Writings of Ralph Waldo Emerson*, pp. 158–59.

75. Two exemplary statements by Emerson regarding women are found in his essay "Woman" and his journals. "Man is the Will, and woman the sentiment. In this ship of humanity, Will is the rudder, and sentiment the sail: When woman affects to steer, the rudder is only a masked sail. When women engage in any art or trade, it is usually as a resource, not as a primary object. The life of the affections is primary to them, so that there is usually no employment or career which they will not with their own applause and that of society quit for suitable marriage. And they give entirely to their affections, set their whole fortune on the die, lose themselves eagerly in the glory of their husband and children." Quoted in Allen, *Waldo Emerson*, pp. 559–60. "Few women are sane. They emit a coloured atmosphere, one would say, floods upon floods of coloured light, in which they walk evermore, and see all objects through this warm tinted mist which envelopes them. Men are not, to the same degree, temperamented; for there are multitudes of men who live to objects quite out of them. As to politics, to trade, to letters, or an art, unhindered by any influence of constitution." *Emerson in His Journals*, pp. 431–32.

76. Quoted in Nicoloff, *Emerson on Race and History*, p. 234.

77. In an interesting preface to this text, Howard Mumford Jones states, "Emerson was an idealist, but he was also a hardheaded Yankee, and he was never more the Yankee than when writing *English Traits*, the tone of which is so radically different from that, say, of *Nature* that if, a thousand years from now, both books were dug up and the name of the author disappeared, a cautious scholar of the

thirty-first century would scarcely dare assign them to the same pen." Ralph Waldo Emerson, *English Traits*, ed. Howard Mumford Jones (Cambridge: Harvard University Press, 1966).

78. Nicoloff, *Emerson on Race and History*, pp. 236–37.

79. Emerson, *English Traits*, p. 30.

80. Ibid., pp. 30, 31.

81. Ralph Waldo Emerson, "Fate," *Selected Writings of Ralph Waldo Emerson*, pp. 384, 385, 386, 387, 388.

82. Ibid., p. 389.

83. Ibid., pp. 393–94, 395. These claims fly in the face of Howard Mumford Jones's apologetic statement that "in truth Emerson had no great faith in the racial theorists he read." *English Traits*, p. xx.

84. *Selected Writings of Ralph Waldo Emerson*, p. 119.

85. Nicoloff, *Emerson on Race and History*, pp. 245–46.

86. On his skepticism regarding a foundationalist epistemology, Emerson quips, "I know that the world I converse with in the city and in the farms is not the world I *think*. I observe that difference, and shall observe it. One day, I shall know the value and law of this discrepance. But I have not found that much was gained by manipular attempts to realize the world of thought. Many eager persons successively make an experiment in this way, and make themselves ridiculous." "Experience," p. 347. For a detailed treatment of Emerson's rejection of traditional epistemological perspectives, see Van Leer, *Emerson's Epistemology*, pp. 188–207. Van Leer concludes, "Emerson outlines a proto-pragmatic theory of truth that permits both general stability and local freedom, without flirting with the reifying tendency of his earlier epistemological formulations . . . In the late essays in general and 'Fate' in particular, Emerson seems to confess his disinterest in the epistemological project so prominent up through 'Experience' (pp. 206, 207).

87. Ralph Waldo Emerson, "The Poet," *Selected Writings of Ralph Waldo Emerson*, p. 322. For fascinating reflections on this matter, see Richard Poirier, "The Question of Genius," in *Ralph Waldo Emerson*, ed. Harold Bloom, pp. 163–86, and Poirier, *The Renewal of Literature: Emersonian Reflections* (New York: Random House, 1987), pp. 3–94, 182–223.

88. The first Emerson statement is quoted in Robert Frost's insightful "On Emerson," in *Emerson: A Collection of Critical Essays*, p. 13. The second is from *Emerson in His Journals*, p. 257.

89. This lovely formulation comes from Stanley Cavell's comparison of Emerson with the early Heidegger—both viewed as proponents of "a kind of epistemology of moods." See "Thinking of Emerson," p. 125.

90. *Emerson in His Journals*, p. 484.

91. Ibid., p. 536.

92. Ibid., pp. 65, 125, 131. For a classic essay on the relation of Emerson's thought to Jacksonian democracy, see Perry Miller, "Emersonian Genius and the American Democracy," in *Emerson: A Collection of Critical Essays*, pp. 72–84.

93. Slotkin, *Fatal Environment*, pp. 109–58. Michael Paul Rogin, *Fathers and Children: Andrew Jackson and the Subjugation of the American Indian* (New York: Knopf, 1975).

94. Regarding this social base of Emerson's project, see Daniel Aaron, "Emerson and the Progressive Tradition," in *Emerson: A Collection of Critical Essays*,

pp. 85–99; Anne C. Rose, *Transcendentalism as a Social Movement, 1830–1850* (New Haven: Yale University Press, 1981); Allen, *Waldo Emerson*, p. 630; Mary K. Cayton, "The Making of an American Prophet: Emerson, His Audiences, and the Rise of the Culture Industry in Nineteenth-Century America," *American Historical Review*, 92, no. 3 (June 1987), 597–620.

95. Allen, *Waldo Emerson*, pp. 231, 258, 293.

96. For a recent treatment of Thomas Skidmore's democratic ideal, see Sean Wilentz, *Chants Democratic* (Oxford: Oxford University Press, 1984), pp. 182–89, 198–206. In this sense, John Dewey's famous characterization of Emerson as a philosopher of democracy requires severe qualification.

97. Allen, *Waldo Emerson*, pp. 364–65.

Chapter 2. The Historic Emergence of American Pragmatism

1. Max H. Fisch, "Was There a Metaphysical Club in Cambridge?" in *Studies in the Philosophy of Charles Sanders Peirce*, 2d ser., ed. Edward C. Moore and Richard S. Robin (Amherst: University of Massachusetts Press, 1964), pp. 3–32. Chauncey Wright, a leading member of this club, had little interest in modernizing religion.

2. Relevant statements by Charles Peirce and William James are: "I was born and reared in the neighborhood of Concord–I mean Cambridge–at the time when Emerson, Hedge, and their friends were disseminating the ideas that they had caught from Schelling, and Schelling from Plotinus, from Boehm, or from God knows what minds stricken with the monstrous mysticism of the East. But the atmosphere of Cambridge held many an antiseptic against Concord transcendentalism; and I am not conscious of having contracted any of that virus. Nevertheless, it is probable that some cultured bacilli, some benignant form of the disease was implanted in my soul, unawares, and that now, after long incubation, it comes to the surface, modified by mathematical conceptions and by training in physical investigations." *Collected Papers of Charles Sanders Peirce*, ed. Charles Hartshorne, Paul Weiss, and Arthur Burks (Cambridge: Harvard University Press, 1933–58), 6: 86. "Reading the whole of him [Emerson] over again continuously has made me feel his real greatness as I never did before." "Divine Emerson." Letters to Miss Frances R. Morse and Henry James, Jr., in *The Letters of William James*, ed. Henry James (Boston: Atlantic Monthly Press, 1920), 2: 190. Note William James, "Address at the Emerson Centenary in Concord," *Memories and Studies* (London: Longmans, Green, 1911). See also two seminal and suggestive essays by Frederick I. Carpenter, "Charles Sanders Peirce: A Pragmatic Transcendentalist," *New England Quarterly*, 14 (1941), 34–48, and "William James and Emerson," *American Literature* (March 1939), pp. 39–57.

3. Exemplary efforts include James Feibleman, *An Introduction to Peirce's Philosophy* (New York: Harpers, 1946); Murray G. Murphey, *The Development of Peirce's Philosophy* (Cambridge: Harvard University Press, 1961); W. B. Gallie, *Peirce and Pragmatism* (New York: Dover, 1966); Karl-Otto Apel, *Charles S. Peirce: From Pragmatism to Pragmaticism*, trans. John Michael Krois (Amherst: University of Massachusetts Press, 1981); Christopher Hookway, *Peirce* (Boston: Routledge, Kegan Paul, 1985). For a text that highlights the role of transcendentalism in Peirce's

philosophy, see Thomas A. Goudge, *The Thought of C. S. Peirce* (Toronto: University of Toronto Press, 1950).

4. *Collected Papers of Charles Sanders Peirce*, 5: 376.

5. Ibid., p. 2 or 5: 3.

6. See especially "Questions concerning Certain Faculties Claimed for Man" and "Some Consequences of Four Incapacities" in *Collected Papers of Charles Sanders Peirce*, 5: 213-63, 264-317 (or pp. 135-55, 156-89).

7. Ibid., 5: 265 (p. 157).

8. Ibid., 5: 265 (p. 158).

9. Gallie, *Peirce and Pragmatism*, p. 78.

10. *Collected Papers of Charles Sanders Peirce*, 6: 290.

11. Ibid., p. 294.

12. Ibid., 1: 55.

13. Ibid., pp. 623, 637, 662.

14. For a fine treatment of this often neglected dimension of Peirce's thought, see R. Jackson Wilson, *In Quest of Community: Social Philosophy in the United States, 1860-1920* (New York: Oxford University Press, 1968), pp. 32-59.

15. *Collected Papers of Charles Sanders Peirce*, 6: 449 (p. 309); 6: 451 (p. 310). See also John Smith, "Religion and Theology in Peirce," *Studies in the Philosophy of Charles Sanders Peirce*, ed. Philip P. Weiner and Frederic H. Young (Cambridge: Harvard University Press, 1952).

16. *Collected Papers of Charles Sanders Peirce*, 1: 673, 677.

17. Ibid., 5: 585.

18. Ibid., 5: 394.

19. Ibid., 5: 401-2 (pp. 257-58).

20. Ibid., 5: 402 n. 2 (pp. 258-59).

21. For this second definition of pragmatism, see ibid., p. 9, and Feibleman, *Introduction to Peirce's Philosophy*, p. 295.

22. See Peirce's review of Friedrich Paulsen's *Kant* in the *Nation*, 75 (1902), 209f.

23. *Collected Papers of Charles Sanders Peirce*, 5: 384 (pp. 242-43).

24. Ibid., 6: 610 (p. 420).

25. Peirce tried to ground his agapism on his complicated doctrine of synechism – the idea that everything is continuous. This doctrine, based on highly technical mathematical notions of the continuum that avoid the paradoxes of set theory, tries to solve the problem of unactualized possibilities. For more on this matter, see Murphey, *Development of Peirce's Philosophy*, pp. 379-407.

26. *Collected Papers of Charles Sanders Peirce*, 6: 293 (p. 196).

27. Ibid., p. 295 (p. 197).

28. Ibid., 2: 655 (pp. 399-400).

29. Ibid., 1: 310 (pp. 153-54).

30. Ibid., 1: 354n (p. 181).

31. This metaphor is found in a letter from William James to F. C. S. Schiller noted in Gay Wilson Allen, *William James* (New York: Viking, 1967), p. 428.

32. Paul Conkin, *Puritans and Pragmatists: Eight Eminent American Thinkers* (Bloomington: Indiana University Press, 1968), p. 281.

33. *Collected Papers of Charles Sanders Peirce*, 5: 402 n. 2 (pp. 259-60).

34. Ibid., p. 414 (p. 276).

35. These phrases pertaining to James's life and thought are found in George Santayana's lovely essay "William James," *Character and Opinion in the United States* (1920; New York: Norton Library, 1967), pp. 65, 82.

36. William James, *Pragmatism* (Cambridge: Harvard University Press, 1975), p. 13.

37. Ibid., pp. 39, 43–44.

38. William James, *The Will to Believe* (Cambridge: Harvard University Press, 1979), p. 45.

39. William James, *Talks to Teachers on Psychology* (Cambridge: Harvard University Press, 1983), p. 164.

40. William James, *Essays in Religion and Morality* (Cambridge: Harvard University Press, 1982), pp. 170, 172.

41. James, *Talks to Teachers on Psychology*, p. 159.

42. James, *Pragmatism*, p. 31.

43. *The Letters of William James*, ed. Henry James (Boston: Atlantic Monthly Press, 1920), 2: 90.

44. James, *Talks to Teachers on Psychology*, pp. 165–66.

45. On the constraints on fundamental social change, James writes: "The next instinct I shall mention is that of ownership, also one of the radical endowments of the race . . . The depth and primitiveness of this instinct would seem to cast a sort of psychological discredit in advance upon all radical forms of communistic Utopia. Private proprietorship cannot be practically abolished until human nature is changed." *Talks to Teachers on Psychology*, p. 42.

46. One example of James's moral sensitivity is found in his poignant letter condemning the terrorism, including lynching, directed at Afro-Americans. Ralph Barton Perry, *The Thought and Character of William James* (Cambridge: Harvard University Press, 1948), brief version, pp. 249–50.

47. This description comes from Santayana, "William James," p. 64.

48. *Letters of William James*, 2: 284.

49. Quoted in Perry, *Thought and Character of William James*, p. 240.

50. Ibid.

51. William James, *Memories and Studies* (New York: Longmans, Green, 1911), p. 284. This view echoes James's characterization of the Chicago anarchists as foreigners since American natives, i.e., white Anglos, do not behave in such a manner.

52. Ibid., pp. 315, 319, 323. For a broad exploration of the historical and cultural role of James in his times, see Josiah Royce, "William James and the Philosophy of Life," *William James and Other Essays on the Philosophy of Life* (New York: Macmillan, 1911), pp. 3–45.

53. These phrases come from James's address to the Anti-Imperialist League in 1903. See excerpts from the report of the fifth annual meeting of the New England Anti-Imperialist League, November 28, 1903, in Perry, *Thought and Character of William James*, pp. 246–47. Note also the discussion in H. S. Thayer, *Meaning and Action: A Critical History of Pragmatism* (New York: Bobbs-Merrill, 1968), pp. 437–45.

54. In a revealing statement, James writes, "The highest ethical life . . . consists at all times in the breaking of rules which have grown too narrow for the actual case." "The Moral Philosopher and the Moral Life," *Will to Believe*, p. 158. This holds only for individuals, not groups.

55. Quoted in Perry, *Thought and Character of William James*, p. 245.

56. Ibid., p. 246.

57. James, *Talks to Teachers on Psychology*, pp. 132–49.

58. Letter to *Boston Evening Transcript*, March 4, 1899, quoted in C. Wright Mills, *Sociology and Pragmatism: The Higher Learning in America*, ed. Irving Louis Horowitz (New York: Oxford University Press, 1964), p. 266.

59. Quoted in Perry, *Thought and Character of William James*, p. 246.

60. Ibid., p. 299.

61. William James, "The Meaning of the Word Truth," *The Meaning of Truth* (Cambridge: Harvard University Press, 1975), p. 117.

62. James, *Pragmatism*, p. 35.

63. Ibid.

64. Ibid., p. 97.

65. Ibid., p. 37.

66. Ibid., p. 98.

67. Ibid., pp. 36, 98.

68. William James, "The Energies of Men," *Essays on Religion and Morality* (Cambridge: Harvard University Press, 1982), p. 145.

69. James, *Will to Believe*, p. 159. James puts it well when he writes, "What is this but saying that our opinions about the nature of things belong to our moral life?" "Lewes' Problems of Life and Mind," *Collected Essays and Reviews* (New York: Russell and Russell, 1969), p. 11.

70. James, *Will to Believe*, p. 161.

71. Santayana, "William James," p. 77.

72. William James, "The Pragmatist Account of Truth and Its Misunderstandings," *Meaning of Truth*, pp. 99–116. See also Marcus Peter Ford, *William James's Philosophy* (Amherst: University of Massachusetts Press, 1982), pp. 59–74; Henry Samuel Levinson, *The Religious Investigations of William James* (Chapel Hill: University of North Carolina Press, 1981), pp. 209–39.

73. Gay Wilson Allen notes that James's desire to be known as a philosopher bordered on the neurotic. For example, James worried for weeks before his Harvard honorary degree was granted that President Eliot would say "William James, Psychologist" rather than "William James, Philosopher." The latter occurred, to James's delight. Allen, *William James*, p. 437.

74. Santayana, "William James," p. 92.

Chapter 3. The Coming-of-Age of American Pragmatism

1. Dewey's deep historical consciousness sets him apart from William James. James is preoccupied with the solitudinal individual in time; Dewey, with the social and historical forces that shape the creative individual. Dewey had profound respect for James, yet he was well aware that his emphasis differed from James's. In his essay "The Philosophy of William James," Dewey explicitly states regarding James's thought, "There are no signs of concern with the spectacle of history." John Dewey, *Problems of Men* (New York: Philosophical Library, 1946), p. 379. In reaction to James's famous essay "The Moral Equivalent of War," Dewey

wrote, in a letter to Scudder Klyce on May 29, 1915, that James's understanding of war "seemed to me to show that even his sympathies were limited by his experience; the idea that most people need any substitute for fighting for life, or that they have to have life made artificially hard for them in order to keep up their battling nerve, could come only from a man who was brought up an aristocrat and who had lived a sheltered existence. I think he had no real intimation that the 'labor question' has always been for the great mass of people a much harder fight than any war; in fact one reason people are so ready to fight is the fact that that is so much easier than their ordinary existence." Quoted in Gerald E. Myers, *William James: His Life and Thought* (New Haven: Yale University Press, 1986), p. 602 n. 151. For James's combination of genuine moral compassion and relative political naiveté, see Myers' treatment, pp. 435–45.

2. As late as 1930, Dewey admitted that he did not know enough about Marx to discuss his philosophy. Max Eastman wrote that Dewey told him that he had never read Marx—which I find hard to believe. See Gary Bullert, *The Politics of John Dewey* (Buffalo: Prometheus Books, 1983), p. 142 n. 26; Max Eastman, *Einstein, Trotsky, Hemingway, Freud, and Other Great Companions* (New York: Collier Books, 1959), p. 280.

3. John Dewey, *Characters and Events* (New York: Holt, Rinehart, and Winston, 1929), 1: 378–431. Note also John Dewey, *Freedom and Culture* (New York: Capricorn Books, 1939), pp. 74–102.

4. Horace Kallen, "Freedom and Education," in *The Philosophy of the Common Man: Essays in Honor of John Dewey to Celebrate His Eightieth Birthday* (New York: G. P. Putnam's Sons, 1940), pp. 31–32.

5. John Dewey, "Ralph Waldo Emerson," *Characters and Events*, 1: 69–77. This essay was first read as a paper at the Emerson Memorial Meeting, University of Chicago, May 25, 1903. It was initially published under the title "Emerson—The Philosopher of Democracy," in the *International Journal of Ethics*, July 1903. Note also John Dewey, "Maurice Maeterlinck," *Characters and Events*, 1: 41. In a revealing sentence, Dewey states, "Emerson, Walt Whitman, and Maeterlinck are thus far, perhaps, the only men who have been habitually, and, as it were, instinctively, aware that democracy is neither a form of government nor a social expediency, but a metaphysic of the relation of man and his experience to nature: Among these Maeterlinck has at least the advantage of greater illumination by the progress of natural science" (p. 43).

6. Dewey, "Ralph Waldo Emerson," 1: 69.

7. Ibid.

8. Ibid., p. 70.

9. Ibid., pp. 72, 73.

10. John Dewey, "Experience, Knowledge, and Value: A Rejoinder," in *The Philosophy of John Dewey*, ed. Paul Arthur Schilpp, Library of Living Philosophers (New York: Tudor, 1939, 1951), p. 538 n. 22. See also John Dewey, *The Quest for Certainty* (1929; New York: Capricorn, 1960), pp. 212–13.

11. Dewey, "Ralph Waldo Emerson," 1: 73, 74.

12. Ibid., pp. 74, 75.

13. Ibid., p. 76.

14. For a fine reading of Dewey on this issue by his most famous student and disciple, see Sidney Hook, "The Philosopher of American Democracy," *John*

Dewey: An Intellectual Portrait (New York: John Day, 1939), pp. 226–39. See also Richard J. Bernstein, "Dewey, Democracy: The Task ahead of Us," in *Post-Analytic Philosophy*, ed. John Rajchman and Cornel West (New York: Columbia University Press, 1985), pp. 48–58.

15. Dewey, "Ralph Waldo Emerson," 1: 75–76.

16. For useful biographical material on Dewey, see George Dykhuizen, *The Life and Mind of John Dewey* (Carbondale: Southern Illinois University Press, 1973); "Biography of John Dewey," ed. Jane M. Dewey, in *The Philosophy of John Dewey*, ed. Paul Arthur Schilpp, pp. 3–45; Neil Coughlan, *Young John Dewey: An Essay in American Intellectual History* (Chicago: University of Chicago Press, 1973); and drafts of Robert Westbrook's long-awaited biography of Dewey. I have benefited immensely from the work of and conversations with Robert Westbrook.

17. The impact of Dewey's early Congregational Christian faith on his later philosophy is explored in Bruce Kuklick, *Churchmen and Philosophers: From Jonathan Edwards to John Dewey* (New Haven: Yale University Press, 1985), pp. 230–53.

18. Coughlan, *Young John Dewey*, pp. 43–53.

19. In a letter to Croom Robertson, editor of *Mind*, William James wrote: "Dewey is out with a psychology which I have just received and but one-half read. I felt quite 'enthused' at the first glance, hoping for something really fresh; but am sorely disappointed when I come to read. It's no use trying to mediate between the bare miraculous self and the concrete particulars of individual mental lives; and all that Dewey effects by so doing is to take all the edge and definiteness away from the particulars when it falls to their turn to be treated." Quoted in Dykhuizen, *Life and Mind of John Dewey*, p. 55.

20. "Biography of John Dewey," ed. Jane M. Dewey, p. 20.

21. Ibid., p. 21.

22. Dykhuizen, *Life and Mind of John Dewey*, p. 50.

23. Richard N. Current, T. Harry Williams, and Frank Freidel, *American History: A Survey* (New York: Knopf, 1961), pp. 488–516.

24. C. Vann Woodward, *Origins of the New South, 1877–1913* (Chapel Hill: University of North Carolina Press, 1951).

25. Robert H. Wiebe, *The Search for Order, 1877–1920* (New York: Hill and Wang, 1967), pp. 11–43, 78, 95.

26. Coughlan, *Young John Dewey*, p. 91.

27. John Dewey, "Ernest Renan," *Characters and Events*, 1: 18–30.

28. Dykhuizen, *Life and Mind of John Dewey*, p. 72.

29. John Dewey, *Outlines of a Critical Theory of Ethics* (Ann Arbor: Registrar, 1891); Dewey, *The Study of Ethics: A Syllabus* (Ann Arbor: Registrar, 1894).

30. Coughlan, *Young John Dewey*, p. 83.

31. Ibid., p. 101.

32. John Dewey, "Matthew Arnold and Robert Browning," *Characters and Events*, 1: 16, 17. This essay originally was published under the title "Poetry and Philosophy," in the *Andover Review*, August 1891.

33. Coughlan, *Young John Dewey*, p. 101.

34. Ibid.

35. Ibid., pp. 103, 104.

36. Ibid., p. 107.

37. Dykhuizen, *Life and Mind of John Dewey*, p. 104. The dismissal of

economics professor Edward Bemis from the University of Chicago, principally for his support of labor during the Pullman strike, not simply alerted Dewey to the risks of radical political activism but also forced him to channel his reformist zeal into *respectable* forms of cultural and social change. This combination of pessimism regarding the possibility of significant attenuation of the dominance of capital in American society and a professionalism that puts a premium on acceptance by one's peers continued to circumscribe Dewey's activism.

38. Wiebe, *Search for Order*, p. 119. See also C. Wright Mills, *Sociology and Pragmatism: The Higher Learning in America* (New York: Oxford University Press, 1964), pp. 325–37, 338–46.

39. Henry F. May, *The End of American Innocence: A Study of the First Years of Our Own Time, 1912–1917* (New York: Alfred A. Knopf, 1957); Morton White, *Social Thought in America: The Revolt against Formalism* (Boston: Beacon Press, 1957). The phrase "revolt against formalistic positions" also occurs in Mills, *Sociology and Pragmatism*, p. 364. The book—Mills's dissertation—was written in the early 1940s. Morton White had made this same point in his first book—his dissertation—*The Origins of Dewey's Instrumentalism* (New York: Columbia University Press, 1943), p. 151.

40. John Dewey, "Philosophy and Democracy," *Characters and Events*, 2: 843.

41. John Dewey, "The Need for a Recovery of Philosophy," *On Experience, Nature, and Freedom: Representative Selections*, ed. Richard J. Bernstein, Library of Liberal Arts (New York: Bobbs-Merrill, 1960), pp. 19–69. This classic essay first appeared in *Creative Intelligence: Essays in the Pragmatic Attitude* (New York: Henry Holt, 1917), pp. 3–69.

42. Ibid., p. 21.

43. Ibid.

44. Ibid.

45. Ibid., p. 43.

46. Ibid., pp. 25, 26, 45.

47. Ibid., p. 45.

48. Ibid., p. 28. Note Emerson's attack on "a paltry empiricism" in his essay "Experience," *Selected Writings of Ralph Waldo Emerson*, ed. William H. Gilman (New York: New American Library, 1965), p. 347f.

49. John Dewey, "Context and Thought," *On Experience, Nature, and Freedom*, pp. 88–110.

50. Dewey, *Quest for Certainty*, pp. 193–94.

51. Dewey, "Need for a Recovery of Philosophy," p. 27.

52. Dewey, *Quest for Certainty*, p. 81.

53. Dewey, "Need for a Recovery of Philosophy," p. 23.

54. Wilfred Sellars, "Empiricism and the Philosophy of Mind," in *Minnesota Studies in the Philosophy of Science*, Vol. 1, ed. Herbert Feigl and Michael Scriven (Minneapolis: University of Minnesota Press, 1956), pp. 253–329.

55. Dewey, *Quest for Certainty*, p. 178.

56. John Dewey, "The Development of American Pragmatism," *Philosophy and Civilization* (1931; New York: Peter Smith Edition, 1968), pp. 24–25.

57. Dewey, "Need for a Recovery of Philosophy," p. 28.

58. John Dewey, "The Subject Matter of Metaphysical Inquiry," *John Dewey: The Essential Writings*, ed. David Sidorsky (New York: Harper and Row, 1977),

p. 102f. Dewey adds freely to this list—such items as qualitative individuality, need, and arrest—in his 1925 Carus Lectures *Experience and Nature* (New York: Dover, 1958), p. 413.

59. Dewey, "Need for a Recovery of Philosophy," pp. 40, 41.

60. Dewey, *Quest for Certainty*, p. 17.

61. Ibid.

62. Dewey, "From Absolutism to Experimentalism," *On Experience, Nature, and Freedom*, p. 18.

63. Dewey, "Need for a Recovery of Philosophy," pp. 43–44.

64. John Dewey, *Reconstruction in Philosophy* (Boston: Beacon Press, 1957), pp. 123–24.

65. Dewey, "Need for a Recovery of Philosophy," p. 58.

66. Ibid., p. 59.

67. Joseph Ratner, "Dewey's Conception of Philosophy," in *The Philosophy of John Dewey*, ed. Paul Arthur Schilpp, p. 66f.

68. "Biography of John Dewey," ed. Jane M. Dewey, pp. 35–36; Dykhuizen, *Life and Mind of John Dewey*, pp. 173, 209. For a discussion of the nature and role of philosophy, see John Dewey, *Experience and Nature*, 2d ed. (New York: Dover, 1929), pp. 398–437; R. W. Sleeper, "Dewey's Aristotelian Turn," *The Necessity of Pragmatism: John Dewey's Conception of Philosophy* (New Haven: Yale University Press, 1986), pp. 78–105. Note also the pertinent reflections in Jürgen Habermas, *The Philosophical Discourse of Modernity* (Cambridge: MIT Press, 1987), pp. 316–26.

69. Richard Rorty, "Dewey's Metaphysics," *Consequences of Pragmatism* (Minneapolis: University of Minnesota Press, 1982), pp. 72–89.

70. Ibid., p. 72.

71. Stephen C. Pepper, "Some Questions on Dewey's Esthetics," in *The Philosophy of John Dewey*, ed. Paul Arthur Schilpp, pp. 371–89.

72. Rorty, "Dewey's Metaphysics," p. 73.

73. Ibid., p. 85.

74. John Dewey, "Philosophy and Civilization," *Philosophy and Civilization*, p. 9.

75. Dewey, "Philosophy and Democracy," *Characters and Events*, 2: 846.

76. Dewey, *Quest for Certainty*, p. 228.

77. Dewey, "Need for a Recovery of Philosophy," p. 66.

78. Dewey, *Quest for Certainty*, pp. 135–36, 220.

79. John Dewey, *Human Nature and Conduct: An Introduction to Social Psychology* (1922; New York: Modern Library, 1957), pp. 178–206.

80. John Dewey, *Logic: The Theory of Inquiry* (New York: Henry Holt, 1938), pp. 3–4.

81. Quoted in ibid., p. 345n.

82. Bertrand Russell, "Dewey's New *Logic*," in *The Philosophy of John Dewey*, ed. Paul Arthur Schilpp, p. 144. For Dewey's reply, see pp. 571–74.

83. Hilary Putnam, *Reason, Truth, and History* (New York: Cambridge University Press, 1981), pp. 49–74.

84. Dewey, "From Absolutism to Experimentalism," p. 18.

85. Dewey, "Need for a Recovery of Philosophy," p. 61.

86. Ibid., pp. 66–67.

87. Ibid., p. 69.

88. Dewey, *Experience and Nature*, p. 420.

89. Mills, *Sociology and Pragmatism*, p. 405.

90. Ibid., p. 394.

91. See n. 2, above.

92. Milton R. Konvitz, "Dewey's Revision of Jefferson," in *John Dewey: Philosopher of Science and Freedom*, ed. Sidney Hook (New York: Dial Press, 1950), pp. 164–76.

93. Jim Cork, "John Dewey and Karl Marx," in *John Dewey: Philosopher of Science and Freedom*, p. 349.

94. Ibid., pp. 348–49.

95. John Dewey, *Individualism: Old and New* (New York: Capricorn, 1929), pp. 74–100; Dewey, *Liberalism and Social Action* (New York: Capricorn, 1935), pp. 56–93; Dewey, *The Public and Its Problems* (1927; Athens, Ohio: Swallow Press, 1954), pp. 143–84.

96. Dewey, *Individualism: Old and New*, p. 171.

97. Dewey, *Liberalism and Social Action*, pp. 90, 91.

98. Hook, *John Dewey: An Intellectual Portrait*, p. 158.

99. Dewey, *Liberalism and Social Action*, p. 91.

100. Dewey, *Public and Its Problems*, p. 137.

101. John Dewey, "The American Intellectual Frontier," *Characters and Events*, 2: 451.

102. Ibid., pp. 451–52.

103. Dewey, *Public and Its Problems*, p. 203; Dewey, *Liberalism and Social Action*, p. 85.

104. Dewey, *Public and Its Problems*, p. 208.

105. Ibid., p. 142. For a somewhat Deweyan critique of Habermas' regulative ideal, see Rüdiger Bubner, *Modern German Philosophy* (New York: Cambridge University Press, 1981), pp. 183–202.

106. Dewey, *Public and Its Problems*, p. 213.

107. Ibid., p. 184.

108. John Dewey, "No Half Way House for America," *People's Lobby Bulletin* (November 1934), p. 1.

109. For a poignant portrait of Dewey's trip to Mexico for the Trotsky hearings, see James T. Farrell's "Dewey in Mexico," in *John Dewey: Philosopher of Science and Freedom*, pp. 351–77.

110. John Dewey, "Introduction," in Henry George, *Poverty and Progress*, ed. Harry Brown (New York: Doubleday, 1928), p. 3.

111. Dewey, *Characters and Events*, 1: 149–431. Note also Ou Tsuin-Chen, "Dewey's Lectures and Influence in China," in *Guide to the Works of John Dewey*, ed. Jo Ann Boydston (Carbondale: Southern Illinois University Press, 1970), pp. 339–62.

112. Dewey, *Characters and Events*, 1: 383.

113. Ibid., p. 401.

114. Ibid., pp. 392–93.

115. Ibid., p. 272.

116. John Dewey, *Freedom and Culture* (1939; New York: Capricorn, 1963), p. 148.

117. Ibid., p. 16. See Ernesto Laclau and Chantal Mouffe, *Hegemony and*

Socialist Strategy: Towards a Radical Democratic Politics (London: Verso, 1985); Stanley Aronowitz, *The Crisis in Historical Materialism: Class, Politics, and Culture in Marxist Theory* (New York: Praeger, 1981); and Frank Cunningham, *Democratic Theory and Socialism* (New York: Cambridge University Press, 1987).

118. Dewey, *Freedom and Culture*, pp. 23, 84.

119. Ibid., p. 98.

120. Ibid., p. 99.

121. Mills, *Sociology and Pragmatism*, pp. 434 n. 24, 446.

122. Dewey, *Freedom and Culture*, p. 77.

123. John Dewey, "What I Believe," in *I Believe*, ed. Clifton Fadiman (New York: Simon and Schuster, 1939), pp. 347–48.

Chapter 4. The Dilemma of the Mid-Century Pragmatic Intellectual

1. Milton R. Konvitz, "Sidney Hook: Philosopher of Freedom," in *Sidney Hook and the Contemporary World: Essays on the Pragmatic Intelligence*, ed. Paul Kurtz (New York: John Day, 1968), p. 18. Sidney Hook, *Out of Step: An Unquiet Life in the Twentieth Century* (New York: Harper and Row, 1987), pp. 7–16.

2. Charles Peirce, *Chance, Love, and Logic*, ed. Morris R. Cohen (New York: Peter Smith, 1949).

3. Sidney Hook, *The Metaphysics of Pragmatism* (Chicago: Open Court, 1927), p. 6.

4. Ibid., p. 9.

5. Ibid., p. 17.

6. Ibid., p. 14.

7. *Collected Works of Vladimir Ilyich Lenin* (New York: International Publishers, 1927). Hook collaborated with David Kvitko in this translation, the only authorized version permitted by the Lenin Institute at the time. Hook confirms this in his autobiography *Out of Step*, p. 122.

8. Sidney Hook, *Towards the Understanding of Karl Marx: A Revolutionary Interpretation* (New York: John Day, 1933), pp. 289, 290.

9. Ibid., pp. 296–97.

10. Sidney Hook, *John Dewey: An Intellectual Portrait* (New York: John Day, 1939), p. 170.

11. Sidney Hook, *The Hero in History: A Study in Limitation and Possibility* (New York: Humanities Press, 1943), p. xiii.

12. Hook had already condemned the Russian Revolution in *Reason, Social Myths, and Democracy* (New York: Harpers, 1940), pp. 142–80.

13. Sidney Hook, "The Future of Socialism," *Partisan Review*, 14 (January–February 1947), 25.

14. Sidney Hook, "Intelligence and Evil in Human History," *Pragmatism and the Tragic Sense of Life* (New York: Basic Books, 1974), p. 43. This essay first appeared in *Commentary* in 1947.

15. Sidney Hook, "On the Battlefield of Philosophy," *Partisan Review*, 16 (March 1949), quoted in Richard H. Pells, *The Liberal Mind in a Conservative Age* (New York: Harper and Row, 1985), pp. 124–25. This cold war division of the

world into two opposing camps of U.S. freedom and U.S.S.R. despotism remains the central theme in Hook's autobiography, *Out of Step*, pp. 199, 353, 403, 580, 600–601.

16. Sidney Hook, *Democracy and Desegregation* (New York: Taiment Institute, 1952).

17. Sidney Hook, "Pragmatism an the Tragic Sense of Life," *Pragmatism and the Tragic Sense of Life*, pp. 4, 5.

18. Ibid., p. 5.

19. Ibid., p. 7.

20. Ibid., pp. 9–10.

21. Ibid., p. 17.

22. Ibid., p. 18.

23. Ibid.

24. Ibid., p. 19.

25. Ibid.

26. Ibid., p. 23.

27. Ibid., pp. 22, 25.

28. Sidney Hook, "The Quest for Certainty – Existentialism without Tears," *Pragmatism and the Tragic Sense of Life*, p. 48.

29. C. Wright Mills, *Sociology and Pragmatism: The Higher Learning in America* (New York: Oxford University Press, 1964), p. 35.

30. Ibid., p. 417.

31. Randolph Bourne, "Twilight of Idols," *The Radical Will: Selected Writings, 1911–1918* (New York: Urizen, 1977), pp. 336–47.

32. Mills, *Sociology and Pragmatism*, p. 382.

33. John Dewey, *The Quest for Certainty* (1929; New York: Capricorn, 1960), pp. 195–222.

34. C. Wright Mills, "Liberal Values in the Modern World," *Power, Politics, and People: The Collected Essays of C. Wright Mills*, ed. Irving Louis Horowitz (New York: Oxford University Press, 1963), pp. 189, 191.

35. Ibid., p. 191.

36. C. Wright Mills, "The Social Role of the Intellectual," *Power, Politics, and People*, p. 292.

37. C. Wright Mills, *The New Men of Power: America's Labor Leaders* (New York: Harcourt, Brace, 1948), p. 281.

38. C. Wright Mills, *The Sociological Imagination* (New York: Grove Press, 1959), pp. 25–75.

39. C. Wright Mills, *The Power Elite* (New York: Oxford University Press, 1956), p. 277. See also Mills, *The Marxists* (New York: Delta, 1963), pp. 105–31. For a noteworthy Marxist reply, see Paul Sweezey, "Power Elite or Ruling Class?" *Monthly Review* (September 1956), reprinted in *C. Wright Mills and the Power Elite*, compiled by G. William Domhoff and Hoyt B. Ballard (Boston: Beacon Press, 1968), pp. 115–32, esp. p. 129 n. 4.

40. C. Wright Mills, "Comment on Criticism," in *C. Wright Mills and the Power Elite*, p. 243.

41. This essay was retitled and reprinted as "The Social Role of the Intellectual," *Power, Politics, and People*, pp. 294, 295.

42. Ibid., p. 296.

43. Ibid., p. 297.

44. Ibid., pp. 297, 298.

45. Mills, *Sociological Imagination*, pp. 8–13.

46. C. Wright Mills, "Social Role of the Intellectual," p. 299.

47. C. Wright Mills, "Introduction to the Mentor Edition," in Thorstein Veblen, *The Theory of the Leisure Class: An Economic Study of Institutions* (New York: Mentor, New American Library, 1953), pp. viii, ix.

48. Ibid., p. vi.

49. Ibid., p. xi.

50. Irving Louis Horowitz, *C. Wright Mills: An American Utopian* (New York: Free Press, 1983), pp. 84–87.

51. Mills, "Introduction to the Mentor Edition," pp. x, xi.

52. Ibid., pp. vii, xi.

53. Ibid., p. vii.

54. Mills, *New Men of Power*, p. 251.

55. Ibid., p. 252.

56. Ibid., p. 260.

57. Ibid., p. 265.

58. C. Wright Mills, *White Collar: The American Middle Classes* (New York: Oxford University Press, 1951), p. xii.

59. Ibid., p. 9.

60. Ibid., p. 326.

61. Ibid.

62. Ibid., pp. 350, 354.

63. Mills, *Power Elite*, p. 347.

64. Ibid., p. 349.

65. Ibid., pp. 360–61.

66. C. Wright Mills, "Culture and Politics," *Power, Politics, and People*, pp. 244, 245; C. Wright Mills, "On Knowledge and Power," ibid., p. 610; C. Wright Mills, *The Causes of World War Three* (New York: Simon and Schuster, 1958).

67. Mills, "On Knowledge and Power," p. 610.

68. Ibid., pp. 611, 612–13.

69. Mills, "Culture and Politics," p. 243.

70. Mills, *White Collar*, p. 131.

71. Ibid., p. 130.

72. C. Wright Mills, *Listen, Yankee: The Revolution in Cuba* (New York: McGraw-Hill, 1960), p. 189.

73. C. Wright Mills, "The Decline of the Left," *Power, Politics, and People*, p. 235.

74. W. E. B. Du Bois, *The Autobiography of W. E. B. Du Bois: A Soliloquy on Viewing My Life from the Last Decade of Its First Century* (New York: International Publishers, 1968), p. 126.

75. Ibid.

76. Ibid., p. 133.

77. Ibid., pp. 133, 148.

78. Ibid., p. 149.

79. Francis L. Broderick, *W. E. B. Du Bois: Negro Leader in Time of Crisis* (Palo Alto: Stanford University Press, 1959), pp. 27–28; Manning Marable, *W. E. B. Du Bois: Black Radical Democrat* (Boston: Twayne, 1986), pp. 19–20.

80. Du Bois, *Autobiography of W. E. B. Du Bois*, p. 159.

81. Ibid., p. 157.

82. Ibid., p. 183.

83. Ibid., p. 182.

84. Ibid., p. 186.

85. Arnold Rampersad, *The Art and Imagination of W. E. B. Du Bois* (Cambridge: Harvard University Press, 1976), p. 50.

86. W. E. B. Du Bois, *Dusk of Dawn: An Essay toward an Autobiography of a Race Concept* (New York: Harcourt, Brace, 1940), p. 58.

87. Du Bois, *Autobiography of W. E. B. Du Bois*, p. 222.

88. W. E. B. Du Bois, *The Souls of Black Folk: Essays and Sketches* (1903; New York: Fawcett, 1961), p. 81.

89. Ibid., p. 15.

90. Ibid., p. 17.

91. Ibid.

92. Ibid., p. 190.

93. Ibid., pp. 48, 50, 75, 76, 83, 87, 101, 107, 109, 125, 126, 132, 139, 150, 170, 171, 182, 189.

94. Ibid., p. 132.

95. Du Bois, *Dusk of Dawn*, p. 261.

96. W. E. B. Du Bois, "My Mission," *Crisis*, 18, no. 1 (April 1919), 9, in *The Seventh Son: The Thought and Writings of W. E. B. Du Bois*, ed. Julius Lester, Vol. 2 (New York: Vintage Books, 1971), p. 199.

97. W. E. B. Du Bois, "The Negro and Radical Thought," *Crisis*, 22, no. 3 (July 1921), 103, in *Seventh Son*, 2: 264.

98. W. E. B. Du Bois, "The Class Struggle," *Crisis*, 22, no. 4 (August 1921), 151, in *Seventh Son*, 2: 265.

99. Du Bois, *Dusk of Dawn*, p. 284.

100. Ibid., p. 290.

101. Ibid., p. 291.

102. W. E. Burghardt Du Bois, *Black Reconstruction: An Essay toward a History of the Part Which Black Folk Played in the Attempt to Reconstruct Democracy in America, 1860–1880* (New York: Russell and Russell, 1935), pp. 29–30. For the most sophisticated treatment of Reconstruction that builds on and goes beyond Du Bois' classic, see Eric Foner's magisterial *Reconstruction: America's Unfinished Revolution, 1863–1877* (New York: Harper and Row, 1988).

103. Du Bois, *Dusk of Dawn*, p. 295.

104. Du Bois, *Autobiography of W. E. B. Du Bois*, p. 379. For more details on this matter, see Marable, *W. E. B. Du Bois*, pp. 182–89.

105. Du Bois, *Autobiography of W. E. B. Du Bois*, p. 395.

106. Quoted from Gerald Horne, *Black and Red: W. E. B. Du Bois and the Afro-American Response to the Cold War, 1944–1963* (Albany: State University of New York Press, 1986), p. 345.

107. W. E. B. Du Bois, *Against Racism: Unpublished Essays, Papers, Addresses, 1887-1961*, ed. Herbert Aptheker (Amherst: University of Massachusetts Press, 1985), p. 320.

108. This term is used to describe Niebuhr's thought in Arthur Schlesinger, Jr., "Reinhold Niebuhr's Role in American Political Thought and Life," in *Reinhold Niebuhr: His Religious, Social, and Political Thought*, ed. Charles W. Kegley (1956; New York: Pilgrim Press, 1984), p. 196.

109. Quoted from a letter to his former Eden professor Samuel Press in June Bingham, *Courage to Change: An Introduction to the Life and Thought of Reinhold Niebuhr* (New York: Charles Scribner's Sons, 1961, 1972), p. 84. See also Richard Wightman Fox, *Reinhold Niebuhr: A Biography* (New York: Pantheon Books, 1985), p. 28.

110. Fox, *Reinhold Niebuhr*, p. 32.

111. Bingham, *Courage to Change*, p. 224. See also Richard Fox's claim that "Niebuhr was a thoroughgoing Jamesian pragmatist," *Reinhold Niebuhr*, pp. 84, 110.

112. Schlesinger, "Reinhold Niebuhr's Role in American Political Thought and Life," pp. 195-96.

113. Bingham, *Courage to Change*, p. 83; Fox, *Reinhold Niebuhr*, p. 34.

114. Paul Tillich, "Reinhold Niebuhr's Doctrine of Knowledge," in *Reinhold Niebuhr: His Religious, Social, and Political Thought*, p. 90.

115. Fox, *Reinhold Niebuhr*, pp. 36, 37.

116. Ibid., pp. 28, 43.

117. Ibid., p. 49.

118. Ibid., p. 55.

119. Reinhold Niebuhr, *Moral Man and Immoral Society: A Study in Ethics and Politics* (New York: Charles Scribner's Sons, 1932, 1960), p. xxv.

120. Ibid., p. xx.

121. Reinhold Niebuhr, *Leaves from the Notebook of a Tamed Cynic* (Chicago: Willett, Clark, and Colby, 1929), p. 43. Similar liberal motifs are apparent in his first book, *Does Civilization Need Religion? A Study in the Social Resources and Limitations of Religion in Modern Life* (New York: Macmillan, 1927). For a fine exposition of this liberal moment in Niebuhr's career, see Ernest F. Dibble, *Young Prophet Niebuhr: Reinhold Niebuhr's Early Search for Social Justice* (Washington, D.C.: University Press of America, 1977), pp. 26-95.

122. Fox, *Reinhold Niebuhr*, p. 145.

123. Niebuhr, *Moral Man and Immoral Society*, p. 155.

124. Ibid., pp. 21-22.

125. Reinhold Niebuhr, "The Truth in Myths," *Faith and Politics*, ed. Ronald H. Stone (New York: Braziller, 1968), pp. 15-32; Reinhold Niebuhr, *An Interpretation of Christian Ethics* (1935; New York: Seabury, 1979), p. 15f.

126. Emil Brunner, "Some Remarks on Reinhold Niebuhr's Work as a Christian Thinker," in *Reinhold Niebuhr: His Religious, Social, and Political Thought*, p. 86.

127. Reinhold Niebuhr, "Reply to Interpretation and Criticism," in *Reinhold Niebuhr: His Religious, Social, and Political Thought*, p. 522.

128. *Commonweal*, 45, no. 11 (December 16, 1966), reprinted as "Reinhold Niebuhr," in *Theologians at Work*, ed. Patrick Granfield (New York: Macmillan, 1967), p. 63.

129. Reinhold Niebuhr, *Reflections on the End of an Era* (New York: Charles Scribner's Sons, 1934), p. ix.

130. Ibid., p. 83.

131. Ibid., pp. 93–94.

132. Ibid., p. 229.

133. Reinhold Niebuhr, *The Nature and Destiny of Man: A Christian Interpretation*, Vol. 1: *Human Nature* (New York: Charles Scribner's Sons, 1941, 1964), pp. 182, 183.

134. Ibid., pp. 185–86.

135. Reinhold Niebuhr, *The Nature and Destiny of Man: A Christian Interpretation*, Vol. 2: *Human Destiny* (New York: Charles Scribner's Sons, 1943, 1964), pp. 125–26.

136. Robert Calhoun, *Journal of Religion*, 21 (October 1941), 477–78, quoted in Fox, *Reinhold Niebuhr*, pp. 203, 204.

137. Reinhold Niebuhr, "Jews after the War," *Nation*, February 21 and 28, 1942, pp. 214–16, 253–55.

138. Quoted in Fox, *Reinhold Niebuhr*, p. 209. See also p. 288.

139. Reinhold Niebuhr, "New View of Palestine," *Spectator*, August 16, 1946, p. 162. For a serious critique of this article, see Edward W. Said, *The Question of Palestine* (New York: Times Books, 1979), pp. 31–34.

140. Fox, *Reinhold Niebuhr*, p. 210.

141. Reinhold Niebuhr, *The Children of Light and the Children of Darkness: A Vindication of Democracy and a Critique of Its Traditional Defense* (New York: Charles Scribner's Sons, 1944), p. xiii.

142. *Reinhold Niebuhr on Politics*, ed. Harry R. Davis and Robert C. Good (New York: Charles Scribner's Sons, 1960), p. 220.

143. Reinhold Niebuhr, *The Irony of American History* (New York: Charles Scribner's Sons, 1952).

144. Reinhold Niebuhr, "We Need an Edmund Burke," unsigned editorial, *Christianity and Society* (Summer 1951); Niebuhr, "The Supreme Court on Segregation in the Schools," *Christianity and Crisis*, June 14, 1954, pp. 75–77; Niebuhr, "School, Church, and the Ordeals of Integration," *Christianity and Crisis*, 16, no. 16 (October 1, 1956), 121–22; Niebuhr, "The Mounting Racial Crisis," *Christianity and Crisis*, 23, no. 12 (July 8, 1963), 121–22.

145. Lionel Trilling to Alan M. Wald, June 10, 1974, quoted in Alan M. Wald, "From Cultural Pluralism to Revolutionary Internationalism: Jewish Identity and the New York Intellectuals in the Early 1930s," *Jewish Socialist Critique*, no. 3 (Spring–Summer 1980), p. 36. See also, Alan M. Wald, *The New York Intellectuals* (Chapel Hill: University of North Carolina Press, 1987), p. 36.

146. Lionel Trilling, "From the Notebooks of Lionel Trilling," *Partisan Review*, 51 (1984), 511.

147. Lionel Trilling, "George Orwell and the Politics of Truth," *The Opposing Self: Nine Essays in Criticism* (1955; New York: Harcourt Brace Jovanovich, 1979), pp. 136–37.

148. Lionel Trilling, "The Situation in American Writing: A Symposium," *Partisan Review*, 6, no. 5 (Fall 1939), 111.

149. A leading humanist critic, Denis Donoghue, agrees when he states, "It is well established that Trilling associated mind with the idea of order and even

with the idea of hierarchy." "Trilling, Mind, and Society," *Sewanee Review*, 86, no. 2 (Spring 1978), 169.

150. "Modulation" is a distinctively Trillingian term, dating back to his conception of the liberal protagonist John Laskell in his novel *The Middle of the Journey* (New York: Viking Press, 1947) as "an idea in modulation" (p. 302).

151. Lionel Trilling, *Matthew Arnold* (1939; New York: Harcourt Brace Jovanovich, 1977), p. 136.

152. Ibid., p. 302.

153. Ibid., p. 19.

154. Ibid., p. 194.

155. Ibid., p. 319.

156. Ibid., p. 348.

157. Ibid., pp. 253, 255.

158. Ibid., p. 280.

159. Ibid., p. 255.

160. Lionel Trilling, *E. M. Forster* (1943; New York: New Directions, 1964), p. 57.

161. Lionel Trilling, *Beyond Culture: Essays on Literature and Learning* (1965; New York: Harcourt Brace Jovanovich, 1979), p. 12.

162. Lionel Trilling, "Some Notes for an Autobiographical Lecture," *The Last Decade: Essays and Reviews, 1965–1975*, ed. Diana Trilling (New York: Harcourt Brace Jovanovich, 1981), pp. 227–28.

163. The two major examples of such responses are Delmore Schwartz, "The Duchess' Red Shoes," *Selected Essays of Delmore Schwartz*, ed. Donald A. Dike and David H. Zucker (Chicago: University of Chicago Press, 1970), pp. 203–22, and Joseph Frank, "Lionel Trilling and the Conservative Imagination," *The Widening Gyre: Crisis and Mastery in Modern Literature* (New Brunswick: Rutgers University Press, 1963), pp. 253–74.

164. Jeffrey Cane Robinson, "Lionel Trilling and the Romantic Tradition," *Massachusetts Review*, 20, no. 2 (Summer 1979), 217.

165. Lionel Trilling, "The Situation of the American Intellectual at the Present Time," *A Gathering of Fugitives* (Boston: Beacon Press, 1956), p. 65. This piece was Trilling's contribution to the renowned symposium "Our Country and Our Culture," *Partisan Review*, 19, no. 3 (May 1952).

166. Irving Louis Horowitz, *C. Wright Mills: An American Utopian* (New York: Free Press, 1983), p. 86.

167. Lionel Trilling, *The Liberal Imagination: Essays on Literature and Society* (New York: Charles Scribner's Sons, 1950, 1976), pp. x–xi.

168. Ibid., p. 100.

169. Lionel Trilling, "The Poet as Hero: Keats in His Letters," *Opposing Self*, p. 3.

170. Ibid., p. 5.

171. Ibid., pp. 8, 12.

172. Ibid., pp. 21–22.

173. Ibid., p. 37.

174. Ibid.

175. Ibid., p. 39.

176. Lionel Trilling, "William Dean Howells and the Roots of Modern Taste," *Opposing Self*, p. 89.

177. Trilling, "Poet as Hero," pp. 38–39. Trilling quotes this same passage in "On the Teaching of Modern Literature" and "The Two Environments: Reflections on the Study of English," *Beyond Culture*, pp. 26, 202, respectively.

178. Trilling, "Poet as Hero," p. 43.

179. Lionel Trilling, "Mansfield Park," *Opposing Self*, p. 202.

180. Frank, "Lionel Trilling and the Conservative Imagination," p. 259.

181. Lionel Trilling, "Hawthorne in Our Time," *Beyond Culture*, pp. 172, 179.

182. Trilling, "On the Teaching of Modern Literature," p. 17.

183. Trilling, "Two Environments," pp. 201–2.

184. Lionel Trilling, *Sincerity and Authenticity* (Cambridge: Harvard University Press, 1972), pp. 79–80.

185. Trilling, "On the Teaching of Modern Literature," pp. 3, 23.

186. Trilling, *Sincerity and Authenticity*, p. 114.

187. Lionel Trilling, "The Uncertain Future of the Humanistic Educational Ideal," *Last Decade*, pp. 175–76. For further elaboration on the later Trilling, see William M. Chace, *Lionel Trilling: Criticism and Politics* (Stanford: Stanford University Press, 1980), pp. 117–89; and Mark Krupnick, *Lionel Trilling and the Fate of Cultural Criticism* (Evanston: Northwestern University Press, 1986), pp. 135–90.

188. John Dewey, "The Development of American Pragmatism," *Philosophy and Civilization* (1931; New York: Peter Smith Edition, 1968), pp. 34, 35.

189. Mills, *New Men of Power*, p. 267.

190. Richard Hofstadter, *The Age of Reform: From Bryan to F. D. R.* (1955; New York: Vintage, 1960), p. 36.

191. Matthew Arnold, "Stanzas from the Grand Chartreuse" (11.85–86). *The Poetical Works of Matthew Arnold*, ed. C. B. Tinker and H. F. Lowry (London: Oxford University Press, 1950).

192. Jonathan Dollimore, *Radical Tragedy: Religion, Ideology, and Power in the Drama of Shakespeare and His Contemporaries* (Chicago: University of Chicago Press, 1984), p. 22. See also John P. Farrell, *Revolution as Tragedy: The Dilemma of the Moderate from Scott to Arnold* (Ithaca: Cornell University Press, 1980), pp. 17–68, 281–90.

193. Raymond Williams, *Modern Tragedy* (Stanford: Stanford University Press, 1966), pp. 13–84; Walter Stein, "Humanism and Tragic Redemption," *Criticism as Dialogue* (Cambridge: Cambridge University Press, 1969), pp. 183–246.

194. W. E. B. Du Bois, *Darkwater: Voices from within the Veil* (New York: Schocken, 1920, 1969), p. 165.

Chapter 5. The Decline and Resurgence of American Pragmatism

1. The major essays on the philosophical refinement and rejection of these distinctions are Carl G. Hempel, "Empiricist Criteria of Cognitive Significance: Problems and Changes" and "The Theoretician's Dilemma: A Study in the Logic of Theory Construction" in his *Aspects of Scientific Explanation and Other Essays in the Philosophy of Science* (New York: Free Press, 1965), pp. 101–22, 173–226, respectively.

2. The pertinent works of Frege, Meinong, Russell, and Moore I have in mind are Frege's classic essay "On Sense and Reference," in *Translations from the*

Philosophical Writings of Gottlob Frege, ed. Peter Geach and Max Black (Oxford: Oxford University Press, 1952); Meinong's "The Theory of Objects," in *Realism and the Background of Phenomenology*, ed. Roderick Chisholm (Glencoe, Calif.: Glencoe, 1960); Russell's "Meinong's Theory of Complexes and Assumptions," *Mind*, 13 (1904), 204–19, 336–54, 509–24; and Moore's "The Refutation of Idealism," *Philosophical Studies* (London, 1922).

3. Edmund Husserl, "Philosophy as Rigorous Science," *Phenomenology and the Crisis of Philosophy*, ed. and trans. Quentin Laver (New York: Harper and Row, 1965). This essay was first published in 1910.

4. Martin Heidegger, *Being and Time*, trans. John Macquarrie and Edward Robinson (New York: Harper and Row, 1962). It appeared in 1927.

5. Jean-Paul Sartre, *Being and Nothingness*, trans. Hazel E. Barnes (New York: Pocket Books, 1956). It was first published in 1943.

6. Antonio Gramsci, *Selections from the Prison Notebooks*, ed. and trans. Quintin Hoare and Geoffrey Nowell Smith (New York: International Publishers, 1971), pp. 348–49, 372–73, 391.

7. For the life history of Quine, see W. V. Quine, "Autobiography of W. V. Quine," *The Philosophy of W. V. Quine*, ed. Lewis Edwin Hahn and Paul Arthur Schilpp, Library of Living Philosophers (La Salle, Ill.: Open Court, 1986), pp. 3–46; W. V. Quine, *The Time of My Life* (Cambridge: MIT Press, 1985).

8. Willard Van Orman Quine, "Two Dogmas of Empiricism," *From a Logical Point of View* (New York: Harper, 1963), pp. 40–41.

9. Ibid., pp. 41, 43. For a slightly earlier attempt to reject the analytic-synthetic distinction, see Morton White, "The Analytic and the Synthetic: An Untenable Dualism," in *John Dewey: Philosopher of Science and Freedom*, ed. Sidney Hook (New York: Dial, 1950), pp. 316–30.

10. *Collected Papers of Charles Sanders Peirce*, ed. Charles Hartshone, Paul Weiss, and Arthur Burks (Cambridge: Harvard University Press, 1933–58), 1: 135.

11. W. V. Quine, "Grades of Theoreticity," in *Experience and Theory*, ed. L. Foster and J. W. Swanson (Amherst: University of Massachusetts Press, 1970), p. 2.

12. W. V. Quine, "Epistemology Naturalized," *Ontological Relativity and Other Essays* (New York: Columbia University Press, 1969), pp. 82–83.

13. For Quine's full-scale defense of what he calls his "ontological line of naive and unregenerate realism" and "robust realism," see *The Roots of Reference* (La Salle, IL: Open Court, 1971); and *Theories and Things* (Cambridge: Harvard University Press, 1981), especially pp. 38–42, 96–99, 173–78, 182–84, his responses to Donald Davidson, Nelson Goodman, Saul Kripke, Grover Maxwell, and David Armstrong.

14. Quine, "Two Dogmas of Empiricism," p. 44.

15. W. V. Quine, "On What There Is," *From a Logical Point of View*, p. 19.

16. Quine, "Two Dogmas of Empiricism," p. 46.

17. W. V. Quine, "The Pragmatists' Place in Empiricism," in *Pragmatism: Its Sources and Prospects*, ed. Robert J. Mulvaney and Philip M. Zeltner (Columbia: University of South Carolina Press, 1981), pp. 33–34.

18. Ernest Nagel, "Dewey's Theory of Natural Science," in *John Dewey: Philosopher of Science and Freedom*, p. 237.

19. Ibid.

20. Ibid.

21. Quine, "Epistemology Naturalized," p. 86.

22. For Quine's claim that Norman Hanson, Michael Polanyi, and Thomas Kuhn reject this "hook" and thereby open the door to "epistemological nihilism," see ibid., pp. 86–90.

23. Nelson Goodman, "The Way the World Is," *Problems and Projects* (New York: Bobbs-Merrill, 1972), pp. 29–30.

24. Nelson Goodman, "The Test of Simplicity," *Problems and Projects*, pp. 279–80.

25. Nelson Goodman, *Ways of Worldmaking* (Indianapolis: Hackett, 1978), p. 138.

26. Goodman, "Way the World Is," pp. 30–31.

27. Goodman, *Ways of Worldmaking*, p. 22.

28. Nelson Goodman, "Art and Inquiry," *Problems and Projects*, pp. 117, 118.

29. Goodman, *Ways of Worldmaking*, p. x.

30. Wilfred Sellars, "Empiricism and the Philosophy of Mind," in *Minnesota Studies in the Philosophy of Science*, Vol. 1, ed. Herbert Feigl and Michael Scriven (Minneapolis: University of Minnesota Press, 1956), p. 289.

31. Ibid., p. 293.

32. Ibid., pp. 298–99.

33. Ibid., p. 300.

34. John I. McDermott, *The Culture of Experience: Philosophical Essays in the American Grain* (New York: New York University Press, 1976); McDermott, *Streams of Experience: Reflections on the History and Philosophy of American Culture* (Amherst: University of Massachusetts Press, 1986).

35. John Smith, *The Spirit of American Philosophy* (New York: Oxford University Press, 1963); Smith, *Themes in American Philosophy* (New York: Harper and Row, 1970); Smith, *Purpose and Thought: The Meaning of Pragmatism* (New Haven: Yale University Press, 1978).

36. Richard J. Bernstein, *John Dewey* (Atascadero, Calif.: Ridgeview, 1965); Bernstein, *Praxis and Action* (Philadelphia: University of Pennsylvania Press, 1971); Bernstein, *Beyond Objectivism and Relativism* (Philadelphia: University of Pennsylvania Press, 1983); Bernstein, *Philosophical Profiles* (Philadelphia: University of Pennsylvania Press, 1986).

37. Morton White, *Social Thought in America* (Boston: Beacon Press, 1957); White, *Science and Sentiment in America* (New York: Oxford University Press, 1972); White, *Pragmatism and the American Mind* (New York: Oxford University Press, 1973); White, *The Philosophy of the American Revolution* (New York: Oxford University Press, 1978).

38. Richard Rorty, "Pragmatism, Categories, and Language," *Philosophical Review*, 70 (1961), 197.

39. The exemplary essays—among over two dozen significant ones—in Rorty's early period are "The Limits of Reductionism," in *Experience, Existence, and the Good: Essays in Honor of Paul Weiss*, ed. Irwin C. Lied (Carbondale: University of Illinois Press, 1961), pp. 100–116; "Intuition," in *Encyclopedia of Philosophy*, ed. Paul Edwards (New York: Macmillan and Free Press, 1967), 4: 204–12; "Wittgenstein, Privileged Access, and Incommunicability," *American Philosophical Quarterly*, 7 (1970), 192–205.

40. Rorty, "Pragmatism, Categories, and Language," p. 219.

41. Ibid., p. 207.

42. Ibid., p. 221.

43. Rorty, "Intuition," p. 210.

44. Richard Rorty, "Introduction: Metaphilosophical Difficulties of Linguistic Philosophy," in *The Linguistic Turn: Recent Essays in Philosophical Method,* ed. Richard Rorty (Chicago, 1967), p. 33.

45. Ibid., pp. 33–34.

46. Ibid., p. 38.

47. Ibid., p. 39.

48. Ibid.

49. The pertinent essays I have in mind are "Cartesian Epistemology and Changes in Ontology," *Contemporary American Philosophy,* 2d ser., ed. John E. Smith (New York, 1970), pp. 273–92; "Incorrigibility as the Mark of the Mental," *Journal of Philosophy,* 67, no. 12 (June 25, 1970), 399–424; "Strawson's Objectivity Argument," *Review of Metaphysics,* 24 (1970), 207–44; "Verificationism and Transcendental Arguments," *Nous,* 5, no. 1 (February 1971), 3–14.

50. Richard Rorty, "The World Well Lost," *Journal of Philosophy,* 69, no. 19 (October 26, 1972), 665.

51. Ibid., pp. 664, 665.

52. Richard Rorty, "Overcoming the Tradition: Heidegger and Dewey," *Consequences of Pragmatism: Essays, 1972–1980* (Minneapolis: University of Minnesota Press, 1982), p. 53. This essay first appeared in *Review of Metaphysics,* 30 (1976), 280–305, though written in 1974.

53. Richard Rorty, "Dewey's Metaphysics," *Consequences of Pragmatism,* pp. 87–88. This essay was originally published in *New Studies in the Philosophy of John Dewey,* ed. Steven M. Cahn (Hanover, N.H.: University Press of New England, 1977), pp. 45–74.

54. Richard Rorty, "Professionalized Philosophy and Transcendentalist Culture," *Consequences of Pragmatism,* p. 61.

55. Richard Rorty, *Philosophy and the Mirror of Nature* (Princeton: Princeton University Press, 1979), p. 6.

56. Ibid., p. 367.

57. Ibid., p. 10.

58. Ibid., p. 159.

59. Ibid., p. 182.

60. Ibid., p. 181.

61. Ibid., p. 331. Rorty's quote is from Thomas S. Kuhn's *The Essential Tension* (Chicago: University of Chicago Press, 1977), p. xvi.

62. Ibid., p. 264.

63. Ibid., pp. 267, 278, 358–59, 362.

64. Richard Rorty, "Heidegger against the Pragmatists," unpublished essay, pp. 20, 22–23. This essay was to serve as the point of departure for Rorty's book on Heidegger in the Cambridge University Press Modern European Philosophy Series. Rorty has abandoned this project—and so it seems this intriguing essay may never see the light of day.

65. Richard Rorty, "The Contingency of Language," *London Review of Books,* April 17, 1986, pp. 4, 6. See also Rorty's important yet often overlooked essay

"Mind as Ineffable," in *Mind in Nature*, ed. Richard Q. Elvee (New York: Harper and Row, 1982), pp. 60–95, in which he writes, "What is really distinctive about us is that we can rise above questions of truth or falsity. We are the poetic species, the one which can change itself. . ." (p. 88).

66. Richard Rorty, "Introduction: Pragmatism and Philosophy," *Consequences of Pragmatism*, p. xliii.

67. Richard Rorty, "Post-Modernist Bourgeois Liberalism," *Journal of Philosophy*, 80 (1983), 583–89. Rorty's distinctive brand of cold war liberalism is not to be associated with the fashionable neoconservatism. Rather, it is closer to an old-style American social democratic view, e.g., that of George McGovern or Henry Jackson, that calls for greater equality for the disadvantaged on the domestic front and hemming in the "Red menace" on the international front. For further elaboration of Rorty's politics, see his essay "Thugs and Theorists: A Reply to Bernstein," *Political Theory* (October 1987).

68. Richard Rorty, "Method, Social Science, and Social Hope," *Consequences of Pragmatism*, p. 210 n. 16.

69. Richard Rorty, "Pragmatism, Relativism, and Irrationalism," *Consequences of Pragmatism*, pp. 172, 173–74.

70. Richard Rorty, "Solidarity or Objectivity?" in *Post-Analytic Philosophy*, ed. John Rajchman and Cornel West (New York: Columbia University Press, 1985), p. 16.

71. Rorty, "Pragmatism, Relativism, and Irrationalism," p. 170.

72. Fredric Jameson, "Postmodernism, or the Cultural Logic of Late Capitalism," *New Left Review*, no. 146 (July–August 1984), p. 65.

73. Rorty, *Philosophy and the Mirror of Nature*, p. 341.

74. Ibid., p. 38.

75. Ibid., p. 341.

76. Ibid., p. 174.

Chapter 6. Prophetic Pragmatism

1. Benjamin Barber, *The Conquest of Politics: Liberal Philosophy in Democratic Times* (forthcoming), chap. 8.

2. Ibid.

3. Ibid. The best practical outline of the desirable economy I know is in Alec Nove's *The Economics of Feasible Socialism* (London: George Allen and Unwin, 1983), pp. 197–230.

4. Roberto Unger, *Social Theory, Its Situation and Its Task: A Critical Introduction to Politics – A Work in Constructive Social Theory* (Cambridge: Cambridge University Press, 1987), p. 41.

5. Ibid.

6. Ibid., p. 14.

7. Ibid., pp. 18–22.

8. Ibid., p. 43.

9. Ibid., p. 214.

10. Ibid., pp. 214–15.

11. Ibid., pp. 223–24.

12. Ibid., p. 200.

13. Ibid., p. 216.

14. Ibid., p. 233.

15. Ibid., p. 219.

16. Ibid., pp. 165–69.

17. Ibid., p. 237.

18. Richard Rorty, "Solidarity or Objectivity?" *Post-Analytic Philosophy*, ed. John Rajchman and Cornel West (New York: Columbia University Press, 1985), pp. 3–19.

19. For a preliminary effort in this regard pertaining to race, see Cornel West, "Race and Social Theory: Towards a Genealogical Materialist Analysis," in *American Left Yearbook 2*, ed. Michael Davis et al. (London: Verso, 1987), pp. 74–90.

20. See Foucault's influential essay "Nietzsche, Genealogy, History," *Language, Counter-Memory, Practice*, trans. Donald F. Bouchard and Sherry Simon (Ithaca: Cornell University Press, 1977), pp. 139–64.

21. The best example of Foucault's powerful genealogical investigations is his work *Discipline and Punish: The Birth of the Prison*, trans. Alan Sheridan (New York: Vintage Books, 1979).

22. For a reading of Foucault that highlights this aspect of his work, see John Rajchman, *Michel Foucault: The Freedom of Philosophy* (New York: Columbia University Press, 1985), pp. 103–8.

23. Michel Foucault, "Truth and Power," *Power/Knowledge: Selected Interviews and Other Writings, 1972–1977*, trans. Colin Gordon et al. (New York: Pantheon Books, 1980), p. 117.

24. Michel Foucault, "The Subject and Power," *Critical Inquiry*, 8, no. 1 (Summer 1982), 777, 778.

25. Rajchman, *Michel Foucault*, p. 103.

26. Edward W. Said, *The World, the Text, and the Critic* (Cambridge: Harvard University Press, 1983), pp. 221, 222.

27. In discussions with Professor Daniel Defert in Paris during the spring of 1987, he informed me that Foucault's letters contain evidence of deep familiarity with American pragmatism (Foucault's neighbor in Tunisia for two years was France's leading interpreter of American philosophy, Gérard Deledalle). Furthermore, Foucault's reading of materials produced by the Black Panther party was instrumental in his turn toward the centrality of the strategic and tactical in genealogical work. My basic claim here is that certain Kantian residues still haunt Foucault's later work.

28. Raymond Williams, *Modern Tragedy* (Stanford: Stanford University Press, 1966), pp. 48–49.

29. Hans-Georg Gadamer, *Truth and Method* (New York: Seabury Press, 1975), pp. 245–341. Edward Shils, *Tradition* (Chicago: University of Chicago Press, 1981).

30. Williams, *Modern Tragedy*, pp. 83–84.

31. Antonio Gramsci, *Selections from the Prison Notebooks*, ed. and trans. Quintin Hoare and Geoffrey Nowell Smith (New York: International Publishers, 1971), p. 348.

32. Ibid., pp. 348, 349.

33. Ibid., p. 417. For an elaboration of this Gramscian viewpoint, see Cornel West, "Religion and the Left," *Prophetic Fragments* (Grand Rapids, Mich.: Eerdmans, 1988), pp. 13–21.

34. Said, *The World, the Text, and the Critic*, pp. 1–30.

35. For a prophetic pragmatist treatment of this matter, see Cornel West, "The Historicist Turn in Philosophy of Religion," in *Knowing Religiously*, ed. Leroy S. Rouner (Notre Dame: University of Notre Dame Press, 1985), pp. 36–51. See also, Cornel West, "On Leszek Kolakowski's *Religion*," in *Prophetic Fragments*, pp. 216–21.

36. William Spanos, *Repetitions: Essays on the Postmodern Occasion* (Bloomington: Indiana University Press, 1987); Paul Bové, *Destructive Poetics: Heidegger and Modern American Poetry* (New York: Columbia University Press, 1980). Bové has since become one of the few sophisticated Foucaultian critics in America as seen in *Intellectuals in Power: A Genealogy of Critical Humanism* (New York: Columbia University Press, 1986). See also the essays by Jonathan Arac, Donald Pease, and Joseph Buttigieg in *Criticism without Boundaries: Directions and Cross-currents in Postmodern Critical Theory*, ed. Joseph Buttigieg (Notre Dame: Notre Dame University Press, 1987).

37. Rosalind E. Krauss, *The Originality of the Avant-Garde and Other Modernist Myths* (Cambridge: MIT Press, 1985).

38. *The Anti-Aesthetic: Essays on Postmodern Culture*, ed. Hal Foster (Port Townsend: Bay Press, 1983); Hal Foster, *Recodings: Art, Spectacle, Cultural Politics*; Andreas Huyssen, *After the Great Divide: Modernism, Mass Culture, Postmodernism* (Bloomington: Indiana University Press, 1986); Fredric Jameson, "Postmodernism, or the Cultural Logic of Late Capitalism," *New Left Review* (July–August 1984), 53–92.

INDEX

273